Agency in Transnational Memory Politics

Worlds of Memory

Editors:
Jeffrey Olick, University of Virginia
Aline Sierp, Maastricht University
Jenny Wüstenberg, Nottingham Trent University

M
S A
MEMORY

Published in collaboration with the Memory Studies Association

This book series publishes innovative and rigorous scholarship in the interdisciplinary and global field of memory studies. Memory studies includes all inquiries into the ways we—both individually and collectively—are shaped by the past. How do we represent the past to ourselves and to others? How do those representations shape our actions and understandings, whether explicitly or unconsciously? The "memory" we study encompasses the near-infinitude of practices and processes humans use to engage with the past, the incredible variety of representations they produce, and the range of individuals and institutions involved in doing so.

Guided by the mandate of the Memory Studies Association to provide a forum for conversations among subfields, regions, and research traditions, Worlds of Memory focuses on cutting-edge research that pushes the boundaries of the field and can provide insights for memory scholars outside of a particular specialization. In the process, it seeks to make memory studies more accessible, diverse, and open to novel approaches.

AGENCY IN TRANSNATIONAL MEMORY POLITICS

Edited by
Jenny Wüstenberg and Aline Sierp

berghahn
NEW YORK · OXFORD
www.berghahnbooks.com

First published in 2020 by
Berghahn Books
www.berghahnbooks.com

Library of Congress Cataloging-in-Publication Data

A C.I.P. cataloging record is available from the Library of Congress
Library of Congress Cataloging in Publication Control Number: 2020936850

British Library Cataloguing in Publication Data

A catalogue record for this book is available from the British Library

ISBN 978-1-78920-694-4 hardback
ISBN 978-1-80539-133-3 paperback
ISBN 978-1-80539-402-0 epub
ISBN 978-1-78920-695-1 web pdf

https://doi.org/10.3167/9781789206944

CONTENTS

ILLUSTRATIONS

Figures

Tables

ACKNOWLEDGMENTS

Our foremost thanks go to the contributors of this volume for their willingness to engage in this process and for providing not only their own chapters but also continuous input for the project as a whole—never denying our requests to "please provide comments" in that Google document one more time! We would also like to thank three especially astute commentators who helped us refine our approach in the early stages of the volume: Professors Jonathan Bach (New School), Jennifer Dixon (Villanova University), and Jan Kubik (Rutgers University). Michael Bernhard and Jan Kubik's edited book *Twenty Years after Communism: The Politics of Memory and Commemoration* (Oxford University Press, 2014) served as a model of how to think about agency in memory politics systematically and comparatively. The Council for European Studies and Villanova University generously provided funding for our 2016 workshop, while Maastricht University and the Department of Politics at York University (Toronto) did so for our 2017 workshop at Copenhagen University. We are grateful for the productive feedback received from three anonymous reviewers on the manuscript, as well as to Chris Chappell, Mykelin Higham, and Lizzie Martinez of Berghahn Books for the excellent editorial accompaniment. Finally we thank Jeff Olick, our coeditor of the Worlds of Memory series for his encouragement.

Part I

FOUNDATIONS

INTRODUCTION

Agency and Practice in the Making of Transnational Memory Spaces

Jenny Wüstenberg

The field of memory studies is experiencing an impressive growth spurt. Scholars from across diverse disciplines are joining the field, convening regularly, building institutions, and making concerted efforts to push toward more theoretical and methodological sophistication (Dutceac-Segesten and Wüstenberg 2017). In the "third phase" of memory studies, greater attention is now devoted to understanding the complex, multiple, and mobile character of remembrance (Erll 2011). New research is taking into account global dynamics without discounting the continued salience of local and national categories. This volume seeks to build on and expand this scholarship by focusing on the role of agency in transnational memory politics. It assembles a diverse set of innovative studies that follow a common framework for analyzing transnational agency in memory politics. Collectively, we make the case that memory studies in the third wave is becoming and needs to be *relational and processual* in approach, rather than "merely" stressing its interdisciplinary and dynamic character. The authors highlight the agents and practices that make transnational remembrance happen, as well as the ways in which these reproduce or transform the multilevel structures that confine and enable them in turn. Thus, we seek to contribute to the difficult task of understanding and rethinking what memory means under conditions of globalization and technological change.

Our focus on agency as a guiding theme is particularly productive. Curiously, despite the fact that memory research talks a great deal about *actors*—human rights activists, politicians, historians, supranational organizations, nonprofits, and more—very little has been done to systematically consider the role of *agency* in the making, reproduction, and transformation of memory. Agency, in contrast to the concept of actors, implies the power (either latent or exercised) to create or prevent change. This definition enables us to shift attention from merely identifying actions of commemoration that cross borders in some manner to inquiring about their social and political drivers and outcomes. In other words, the contributions here think explicitly about how the interplay of local, national, regional, international, and global dynamics—and the agents that shape them—result in the emergence of transnational memory spaces. In this sense, the book offers something truly new—an empirical exploration of transnational spaces through the lens of memory studies. As I will show below, our collective focus on agency not only builds on recent existing (albeit unsystematic) work in the field but also examines how different types of agency create and maintain transnational mnemonic spaces. I want to stress that by "transnational remembering," I mean more than references to global connectedness in any given realm of memory. Transnational memory spaces are certainly grounded in concrete locations, but they are made meaningful through cross-border linkage and through the practices of transnational agents. Through this linkage a new space is created that straddles various kinds of borders and that is highly significant in terms of the political stakes of the memory action at hand—with real effects on outcomes of recognition, justice, democratization, and more. Drawing on social theorists such as Norbert Elias, Anthony Giddens, and William Sewell, we seek to contribute to the third wave of memory studies by underpinning the relationality of transnational remembering.

My starting point in this introduction is to situate this book project in recent developments in memory studies. While various concepts have been employed in productive ways to "capture flows and interactions at a level that is not contained within the nation or the national" (Kennedy and Nugent 2016: 63), this book adopts the term "transnational" to problematize "container-thinking" (de Cesari and Rigney 2014: 1). That is, we add to the project of questioning the explicit and implicit epistemological organization of the field around *national* remembrance. I also discuss our understanding of the transnational in relation to the importance of notions of place and space in memory studies. I then consider the problem of structure and agency as it pertains to transnational memory politics, suggesting the need for a relational approach. I argue that our interest in agency necessitates a careful examination of the practices that mediate between agents and structures and that shape, maintain, or create transnational memory spaces. This approach is grounded in the "practice-centered" perspective in cultural studies, as well as in insights from relational sociology.

The final portion of this introduction explains the organizational logic and provides an overview of the volume. Based on the recognition that memory agency is shaped by inequalities in resources and power, I argue that mnemonic agency tends to exhibit a dominant logic. By this I mean that agents often operate (and identify) explicitly in terms of bottom-up, top-down, or horizontal activities. The chapters are consequently organized according to these dominant organizational logics, despite the fact that many cases actually contain multiple, even countervailing kinds of agency. As is the case with most, if not all, edited volumes, not all chapters fit equally well into this matrix. But although the contributions vary widely in terms of the kinds of remembrance processes, geographies, and contexts they study and the methodologies they employ, each of them examines agents, practices, and structures, as well as the—highly variable—outcomes. This overarching framework, which was developed in the collaborative process that made this book possible, enables us to make comparisons and conclusions about the politics of transnational memory spaces without disregarding the cultural and historical distinctiveness of each case.

Transnational Memory Spaces

During the first two phases of memory studies, remembrance had been understood primarily as contained in and shaped by local and national settings (Feindt et al. 2014). One of Halbwachs's most important contributions was to state that even though individuals do the remembering, this happens necessarily within a *social* framework and that collective memories change based on their immersion in groups "delimited in space and time" (2011: 145). The space Halbwachs discussed was inhabited by relatively distinct social categories situated within national borders. Memory studies is still very much in Halbwachs's debt, as it follows logically that when our social reality changes through technological upheaval and globalization, so must the foundation for collective memory—which is essentially what more recent memory scholars have sought to achieve. Building on Halbwachs's work, more recent theorists such as Jan Assmann and Pierre Nora have sought to understand the practice and transformation of collective memory over time. Assmann clarified Halbwachs's notion of "collective memory" by arguing that it was "communicative": "non-institutional; . . . it is not formalized and stabilized by any forms of material symbolization; it lives in everyday interaction and communication and, for this very reason, has only a limited time depth which normally reaches no farther back than eighty years, the time span of three interacting generations" (Assmann 2008: 111). By contrast, "cultural memory" is institutionalized and no longer depends on the direct communication and passing down of traditions of community members. It relies on "external objects" as material symbols of the past (Assmann 2008: 110). All of the contributions in this book examine instances of "cultural" memory. Pierre Nora (1996) also considers the ways in which memory changes over time, arguing that the proliferation of "lieux de mémoire"—symbolic representations of the past, both material and nonmaterial—can be explained by the decline of more directly transmitted and cultivated "milieux de mémoire." Thus, for Nora, the emergence of such sites is inextricably bound up with the development of the modern nation-state and has helped us understand the centrality of memory to national identity formation.

As Erll points out, the approach of examining *lieux de mémoire* has already spawned a rich array of studies and could keep memory researchers busy indefinitely (2011: 4)—it has even produced work on bi- and multilateral *lieux* (den Boer et al. 2011; Hahn and Traba 2013). But it has not been equally successful when it comes to moving beyond epistemological blinders that, among other things, make it difficult to grasp the role of agency—whether it operates within or beyond national borders. The first prominent recognition of this limitation was the research program pursued by Daniel Levy and Nathan Sznaider, who argue that through processes of globalization, the Holocaust has become a global "memory imperative" and cosmopolitan moral reference point (Levy and Sznaider 2001; Levy 2010). In contrast to this idea of a universalized discourse of remembrance, more recent work on transnational memory emphasizes the diverse and sometimes conflictual ways in which memory moves beyond borders. From traveling (Erll 2011), to multidirectional (Rothberg 2009), to multivocal (de Cesari and Rigney 2014), and entangled (Feindt et al. 2014) memory, scholars have done much to begin to elucidate the complex processes by which transnational commemoration takes place. As Bond et al. contend, "Memory . . . does not stay put but circulates, migrates, travels; it is more and more perceived as a process, as work that is continually in progress, rather than as a reified object" (2016: 1). A key contribution of this discussion has been to problematize the ordering concepts in memory theory and to think carefully about how to avoid reproducing similar boundaries at higher (or lower) levels of analysis. Perhaps unsurprisingly, there has also been a significant amount of research on the politics of memory as they operate in supranational settings and on "regions of memory" (Sierp 2014; Sierp 2017; Kübler 2012; Sierp and Wüstenberg 2015b; Kroh 2008; Schwelling 2012; Mink and Neumeyer 2013; Troebst 2014). These works tap into a broader debate about European and transnational identity that responds to rapid empirical development and policy demands on the ground.

The different terms and concepts used to capture the new theories of border-crossing memory often depend on which challenge their progenitors regard as most pressing—and I will not attempt to review them all here. To note just one example, Erll uses the concept of the "transcultural" in order to move away from the idea of "tying culture—and by extension cultural memory—to clear-cut territories and social formations" (2011: 6). Barbara Törnquist-Plewa distinguishes between transnational memories as those shared across borders, while transcultural memories are those hybrid memories that not only cross borders but also enable "the imagining of new communities and new types of belonging" (2018: 302). In this volume, we define "transnational memory" as practices or narratives of remembrance that extend across or beyond borders, are shaped by agents located at various levels of analysis, or are produced in global or supranational forums. We use the term "transnational," not to discount the national or other levels of analysis but to stress the tensions and potentials for productivity between them. Thus, consistent with Törnquist-Plewa's usage, the term "transnational memory" does not necessitate a particular result in terms of identity-building. Transnational memory should also not be misconceived as having an automatically "progressive" effect on reconciliation, democratization, or the possibility of confronting the past "honestly," though much empirical research does demonstrate such an effect. However, there is also evidence that transnational remembrance can have detrimental impacts on local memory politics, for example by superimposing narratives that resonate with touristic demand but not with local processes of reckoning (Björkdahl and Kappler 2019; see also Glucksam in this volume). What we do claim in this volume is that transnational processes of remembering have recognizable outcomes in the sense of "transnational spaces of memory." The concept of transnational memory addresses head on the most serious limitation of earlier work in memory studies: its confinement to the nation-state as the most important structure determining memory politics (Feindt et al. 2014: 34). This kind of approach addresses the shortcomings of theories of memory in which commemoration is often studied in static terms, revolving around manifestations of material culture and narratives abstracted from an explanation of the origins of remembrance and potential challenges to its dominant forms. In sum, recent moves to "transnationalize" memory studies have not only opened up the field to novel research agendas but also called into question existing conceptual limitations. As Aline Sierp and I have argued elsewhere, it is important not to let our habit of studying the *national* "structure our interpretation of *transnational* memory politics" (Sierp and Wüstenberg 2015a: 322, emphasis in original).

In addition to rethinking central ordering concepts in the field and challenging the primacy of the nation in many explanations of remembrance, the transnational turn in memory studies is also about recognizing that we are living in an era increasingly shaped by globalization. While transnational politics are not completely new or unprecedented, more and different kinds of transnational memory-making are happening today than a few decades ago. The revolution in communication, digitalization, the easing of global travel, and increased mobility of people, narratives, norms, and cultural products have changed the quality and quantity of transnational remembrance. Consequently, there is no singular or straightforward way of conceptualizing the transnational in relation to memory. In fact, David Inglis lists seven different ways in which recent scholarship has addressed this link (2016: 144). Rather than privileging one of these approaches, I argue that a focus on agency can provide a useful handle on how memory is made transnational, how transnational remembrance processes are transformed (or reproduced), and how transnational memory spaces are created (or not).

Notions of place, sites, and space all play an important role in memory studies—and they remain so with the transnational turn. Remembrance is inextricably linked to concrete locations—whether real or imagined. As Julia Creet writes,

> The link between memory and place has historically attended the study of memory in every sense: in its contents (our attachment to memories of home); in its practices (place as an aid to rote memorization); in its externalizations (monuments and museums); in its linguistic expressions ("I can't quite place you"); and in its psychological and physiological theorizations (the conscious and unconscious brain as the loci of memory, firing across well- or little-used synaptic gaps). (2011: 3)

Certainly, work in the tradition of *lieux de mémoire* reinforced this link between memory and place, despite the fact that Pierre Nora's original concept did not focus only on physical memorial sites. Even more recent scholarship emphasizing mobility, migration, and the transnational has stressed that movement across borders does not undo this connection between memory and place (Radstone 2011). It is clear, however, that when we study transnational processes, the notion of place or space becomes more difficult to pin down. What does it mean to speak about the creation of transnational spaces of commemoration? I argue elsewhere that, whether a site of memory is understood (and by whom it is understood) to be "locally authentic" or "transnational" in character (or note), either understanding must be evoked through agency—memory work—that stabilizes this particular reading (Wüstenberg 2019). In other words, a site's meaning and its linkage to different scales of organization must be actively created or maintained (and it can be subject to challenge).

Sarah Mahler and Patricia Pessar define transnational social spaces as "spaces that are anchored in but extend beyond the borders of any one nation-state"

(2001: 441). In this book, we similarly conceive of transnational memory spaces as instances or processes of remembrance that are anchored—through agency—in concrete locations (though sometimes these exist in an imaginary rather than material sense), but that extend beyond national borders. Such places link to locations on the other side of or transcending borders, so that the memory of/at these places does not make sense without that linkage. *Together, the practices and relevant places form transnational mnemonic spaces* that are inherently *relational in nature*. Such spaces may evoke memories or experiences of transnational action or meaning, of transnational norms, of mobility and movement, of longing for places "elsewhere," and more. In other cases, transnational memory spaces may be outcomes of the impossibility or inadequacy of (safely) remembering locally, as in the case in numerous examples discussed in this book. These spaces are created through concrete practices and action and in the context of dynamic structures. In other words, transnational mnemonic spaces are the outcome of mnemonic agency, operating within structural constraints. Each of the contributions to this volume thus examines *agents, structures, practices,* and *outcomes* in terms of transnational memory spaces. Importantly, the memory-making that is analyzed here through this framework is potentially highly political and consequential. The agents invest labor, expertise, strategy, and emotions in the construction of these spaces because it allows them to pursue concrete goals. While of course there are instances of transnational remembering that are not the result of strategic action, all the cases in this volume follow this pattern.

In sum, moving beyond the first two phases of memory studies has allowed for an epistemological shift—away from a kind of "container thinking" that privileges structures as a basis for explaining social and political processes. However, as I discuss in the next section, when we think through the notion of agency in memory politics, the concept of structure inevitably moves back into the equation. To understand the character and influence of agency in memory requires examining its relationship to a variety of structures—from narrative "blueprints" to media systems, normative regimes, standards of the global memorialization and tourism sectors, fields of organized struggle, and broader political opportunity structures—to name just a few. The question, then, is not one of getting rid of structure altogether but how to understand it in a *relational sense*, as shaped by agency and as shaping agency in turn.

Agency in Transnational Memory Politics

Memory studies until recently have not developed a comprehensive account of the role of agents in commemorative processes. This cannot be attributed to a lack of empirical evidence concerning memory actors. There have been countless studies in which the role of a variety of actors—historians, politicians, artists, educators, civic activists, entrepreneurs, state bureaucrats and so forth—are analyzed in specific cases. However, most of these studies concentrate on the case(s) at hand without drawing out implications for agency in memory politics writ large. More theoretical writings on memory have likewise mostly confined themselves to stating the centrality of actors, without theorizing agency as such: their power and efficacy to bring about change and their position in a constellation of other actors and within structural contexts. For example, Jan-Werner Müller points out that remembrance is always a product of ongoing intellectual and political negotiations between the social "carriers of memory" (Müller 2002). Michael Kohlstruck similarly argues that in order to become "memory," history must be interpreted and represented by concrete actors (2004: 176). The term "carrier" is somewhat of a misnomer as these actors are not merely passive transmitters of history; rather, they reshape images of the past in the course of struggling for their acceptance. "Remembering . . . *is* a form of action," as Müller puts it (2002: 30). Alon Confino has similarly proposed "writing the history of memory's construction as commingling with that of memory's contestation" (1997: 1398). But how do we actually go about systematically studying the construction and contestation of memory by a variety of agents, across various times, geographic spaces, and levels of analysis? How can we compare different instances of transnational memory-making and its outcomes?

The most sophisticated effort at developing a comparative, actor-centered account of memory politics is Michael Bernhard and Jan Kubik's *Twenty Years after Communism*, which presents a typology of memory actors in postcommunist states, as well as concomitant memory regimes (i.e., structures of commemoration). To my knowledge, the volume was the first attempt to provide generalizations about mnemonic actors' motivations, goals, and outcomes, and it served as an important model for our own volume as we debated a joint analytical framework to study mnemonic agency in a comparative manner. As it pertains to the study of *transnational mnemonic agency*, however, Kubik and Bernhard's framework requires further development. First, because the volume is focused on the comparison of national case studies, the concepts put forward (understandably) rely heavily on their "national container." But how do competitors in memory politics determine their claims to legitimacy, their audiences and rivals, and, for that matter, the pasts that they reference when their practices are not bounded by the nation-state? What are the structures that shape how actors operate in transnational realms? Second, Kubik and Bernhard advocate an unapologetically instrumentalist approach. However, in this book, we contend that politics is not always about manipulation and that memory agency is not exclusively aimed at strategies "to make others remember in certain, specific ways" (Kubik and Bernhard 2014: 7). How do we conceive of the building of transnational memory networks, for example? This is an activity that is political in the sense of having implications for the exercise of power but is not narrowly focused on the manipulation of narratives about the past. Third, Kubik and Bernhard's account is mostly unidirectional. The authors argue that the cultural choices of mnemonic actors, as well as the cultural and structural constraints within which they must operate, determine the type of memory regime that develops in a given country. However, how do mnemonic regimes in turn influence the actions of memory actors? Furthermore, what are the mnemonic structures at the transnational level? These theoretical concerns are not new, of course: they amount to the sticky "problem of structure and agency," which political and social theorists have long debated.

The Structure-Agency Dilemma in Memory Politics

To put it simply, the dilemma of structure and agency is that of how to relate different units of analysis to each other and what to regard as having primary explanatory power. In the field of international relations, the problem was raised in connection with disagreements about whether individual actors (usually states) or the inter-state system best explain outcomes in international affairs. Applying these concepts to memory studies requires significant adaptation because it is not clear how to define the different types of structures in which memory agents operate. Though the framework for this volume focuses on agency, it is necessary to consider the relevant—but highly variegated—structures in order to examine the relationship between them and agents. The way forward, following Norbert Elias's process-sociological approach, is not to begin either with individual agents or with structures but with "figurations" that are just as real as individual actors (Morrow 2009). Following Elias's groundwork, theorists such as Bourdieu and Giddens have argued that the goal is not to identify whether agents or structures are more influential but rather to understand "recurrent social practices and their transformations . . . , how actors are at the same time the creators of social systems yet created by them" (Scholte 1993: 127; see also Bourdieu 1977; Giddens 1984). Without delving deeper into this debate, it is crucial to identify ways of understanding the mutual constitution of the agency of individuals, groups, and organizations engaged in making, (re)producing, and dismantling narratives about the past and the mnemonic regimes and structures that both result from and shape these actions. This book shows that the tension between structure and agency is productive of new memory spaces which result from dynamic practices that deserve to be studied as such. The authors of this volume closely examine the evolution of and power dynamics underpinning *the practice of interaction, or the relationships, between agents and structures.*

I therefore advocate beginning our inquiry into transnational memory politics with a focus on agency and practice. A focus on agency does not mean reverting to the methodological individualism of the behavioral era (when the study of "political culture" first became popular). In many ways, memory studies of the modern era can be seen as a reaction to attitudinal and individual studies of culture. Students of memory often endorsed a basically structural approach that was akin to Clifford Geertz's notion of culture as a system of meaning within which political action must be understood. Geertz argued that "man is an animal suspended in the webs of significance he himself has spun. I take culture to be those webs" (1973: 5; see also Geertz 1999). The implication of this view of culture as structure is that different social groups have unique cultures (and memories) that are distinct and comparatively stable (and possibly not very interactive). This understanding of culture insists on coherence—on a system of meanings in which individuals maneuver (Wedeen 2002). A similar approach has long been dominant in social scientific research on memory. Both Maurice Halbwachs and Pierre Nora argued that there are as many memories as groups in society, that the individual can understand her past only as a group member, and that memory only makes sense in the larger system of group meaning (Halbwachs 1992; Nora and Kritzman 1996b; Nora 1996; see also the preface to the English-language edition in Nora and Kritzman 1996a and Winter and Sivan's critique of structural approaches to memory in sociology in Winter and Sivan 1999). Eviatar Zerubavel adopts an even more explicitly structural model. He writes, "I believe that the social meaning of past events is essentially a function of the way they are structurally positioned in our minds vis-à-vis other events. I am therefore ultimately interested in examining the *structure* of social memory" (Zerubavel 2003: 7, emphasis in original). Consequently, it makes sense that during the first phases of memory studies, the structures that framed remembrance activity were unproblematically assumed to be the state, the local community, and the national culture—Erll's "clear-cut territories and social formations."

While it is important to understand the social context through which individuals comprehend their world and which helps them make sense of their past, a focus on coherence would entail serious limitations for this volume: we are interested in highly dynamic and contested memory processes and thus need an approach that can help us understand this dynamism. Moreover, an assumption of coherence ignores the possibility of resistance to or alternative forms of practice. Such an approach has trouble explaining how and why memory changes (or not).

The "practice" perspective on culture offers a way to deal with the structure-agency dilemma in the realm of memory politics, without privileging one explanatory variable. This approach insists that "culture is a sphere of practical activity shot through by willful action, power relations, struggle, contradictions, and change" (Sewell 1999: 44). William Sewell argues that while human action is always structured by social and institutional context and power relations, culture does not exist apart from a succession of practices that reproduce or transform that structure. In other words, culture does indeed display a certain coherence, but it is constantly subject to resistance, and its boundaries do not neatly correspond with those of social groups. Sewell (1999) contends further that, though no single actor alone controls culture, cultural practice clusters around powerful institutional "nodes," especially those with large resource endowments. This is especially relevant for our purposes because the actors seeking to influence (transnational) memory must take into account existing "cultural maps" and directly address existing institutions (at multiple scales) if they want to be successful. Memory officials, activists, entrepreneurs, and others interact with the position of their interlocutors in mind, as well as prevailing cultural norms and historical contexts. Sewell writes that "even when they attempt to overcome or undermine each other, they are mutually shaped by their dialectical dance. Struggle and resistance, far from demonstrating that cultures lack coherence, may paradoxically have the effect of simplifying and clarifying the cultural field" (1999: 57). Thus, Noga Glucksam's critical account in this volume of the operation of human rights norms in the Liberian context suggests that it is precisely the interaction between local and transnational memory agents and the powerful structure of the human rights regime that produces a coherence of commemorative testimonies that are not "natural" but the result of transnational agency.

Social movement scholars have recently taken up this understanding of the interplay between actors and institutions and their roles of mutually shaping one another. Indeed, Ann Swidler argues that many movements are explicitly focused on effecting "cultural recodings" in the absence of more conventional tools of power (2000: 277). As we can see in multiple examples in this book, particularly agents that are conventionally thought of as "powerless" have been highly effective in tapping into transnational narratives and networks to push for changes in local or national memory politics. This is a dynamic identified by international relations scholars Margaret Keck and Katherine Sikkink (1998) in what they term the "boomerang effect," through which local activists ally with transnational networks in order to exert pressure on domestic politics because they cannot achieve their objectives through domestic action alone. This dynamic is most clearly demonstrated by Mary McCarthy's chapter on transnational memory activism on sexual slavery in Asia and Andrea Hepworth's on Spanish and Argentinian efforts to address the impunity after the end of dictatorships.

Drawing on Sewell's conceptualization, Sharon Hays provides a helpful distinction for our purposes: one notion of agency relies strongly on the idea of everyday practice and amounts to what Hays calls "structurally reproductive agency" (1994: 63). It is an approach that assumes the durability and coherence of structure while acknowledging the role played by humans in the process of reproduction. When thinking about the notions of agency implicitly present in the literature on memory, one might cite as examples scholarship that foregrounds tradition and heritage as relatively immutable cultural regimes that are lived and reworked through everyday practices of commemoration.

By contrast, a second understanding of agency hones in on agents' power to alter cultural systems. Hays calls this "structurally transformative agency" and argues that it is crucial to examine under which historical circumstances such agency becomes possible (1994: 64). Given that many of us are interested precisely in those moments when previously underrepresented versions of the past achieve prominence, this concept of agency is just as important. Whether memory is regarded primarily as exhibiting longevity or being subject to challenge, what is crucial is to develop systematic avenues for investigating memory's structural aspects, the agents that maintain or challenge them, and the practices by which they are linked. Relational sociology holds much promise in this respect. Founded on the writings of Elias, Bourdieu, and others, this approach does not privilege either agents or structures but rather argues that it is the relationships, or the networks, between actors that make up social life. Unlike more classical social network analysis, relational sociology since the "cultural turn" has explicitly sought to think through culture in terms of practice (Breiger 2010; Bourdieu 1977).

For Ann Mische, "relational thinking is a way to overcome stale antinomies between structure and agency through a focus on the dynamics of social interactions in different kinds of social settings" (2011: 80). She argues that networks can be regarded as "cultural forms" where "the meaning of one concept can be deciphered only in terms of its 'place' in relation to the other concepts in its web. . . . Network techniques help to show the robust and interlocking nature of cultural structures, as well as the social locations and historical periods in which these can be challenged and reformulated." This approach seems to be compatible with the notion of "structurally reproductive agency," as it lays emphasis on relatively durable networks of meaning within which (memory) cultures must make sense to agents. In an alternative conceptualization, Mische sees networks themselves as composed of cultural processes of communicative interaction. This approach allows us to examine "how actors actively construct relations of solidarity or alliance through the communicative activation (or deactivation) of network ties (Mische 2011: 88). This approach, then, appears especially fruitful when we seek to understand types and practices of "structurally transformative agency." More generally, relational sociology, according to Sophie Mützel, operates at the "meso-level," trying to maintain a clear link between theory and empirical research (Mützel and Fuhse 2010; see also Tilly 2001). An approach that highlights agency and practice—and that can also account for the maintenance and transformation of structure—is therefore best suited for this volume. We hope to contribute to a better understanding of the dynamics of memory politics at various scales and the resultant transnational memorial spaces.

The chapters in this book, while following the distinct logics of their research questions and empirical findings, were all guided by common questions that emerge from this theoretical foundation and were developed in a collaborative process. They were:

- Who are the agents that participate in transnational memory processes?
- What kinds of practices do these agents use?
- What were the structures that shaped, delimited, or enabled agency in these cases?
- What were the outcomes in terms of the creation of transnational memory spaces and otherwise?

Organization of the Volume

Central to the existing work on transnational memory is the ordering concept of scale. As Chiara de Cesari and Ann Rigney argue, "transnationalism allows us to grasp the multi-scalarity of socio-cultural processes and the fundamental 'mutual construction of the local, national and global' (Glick and Schiller 2012, 23)" (de Cesari and Rigney 2014, 3). In other words, the assumption that mnemonic action is potentially constituted simultaneously at various levels of analysis in the global system allows us to investigate how and where memory "happens" rather than taking for granted that memory is located in or shifted from one place to another without being altered in the process. However, the idea of the mutual construction of memory at various scales can, as Rosanne Kennedy and Maria Nugent have noted, also suggest "a kind of equality—a certain give and take, or influence, that runs in both directions" (2016: 64)—and thus lead to a neglect of power imbalances in transnational memory politics. What becomes abundantly clear with the chapters in this volume, however, is that those agents who come to shape transnational memory spaces are characterized by differential resources, media access, institutional clout, reputational power, and more. As a result, transnational memory practice is not often one of equal give-and-take, and the relevant fault lines are not only those of scale. While many of the cases in this book show multiple simultaneous dynamics and relevant scales, more often than not the practices under scrutiny exhibit a dominant power dynamic. For this reason, we have organized the case studies according to their *dominant logics*, that is, we distinguish between top-down, bottom-up, and horizontal practices of mnemonic space-making in order to emphasize the power dynamics involved and to stress the stakes invested in transnational memory politics. We, as editors, settled on this organizational logic, knowing full well that in every contribution there may also be dynamics that push in other, sometimes countervailing directions.

The next chapter in this foundational section, Zoltan Dujisin's "A Field-Theoretical Approach to Collective Memory," provides an in-depth consideration of transnational memory spaces and practices exemplified in this book through a relational and sociological lens. Building on Pierre Bourdieu's field theory, Dujisin argues that transnational memory politics are best understood as a regime made up of overlapping and intertwined fields of struggle. He highlights the critical process of transforming fluid modes of remembering into seemingly "hard" identities that suggest homogeneity and sameness over time. Especially powerful identity and memory makers, according to Dujisin, are those actors that inhabit hybrid spaces in which they are able to connect a variety of relational fields.

The contributions in part II of this volume are case studies of bottom-up agency. The chapters discuss agents and practices that link local memory action or conventionally weaker actors to transnational norms or institutions, or build transnational linkages in order to circumvent barriers to remembrance locally or nationally. In her contribution "Transnational Memories and the Practices of Global Justice in the Ayotzinapa Case," Silvana Mandolessi investigates the case of the highly publicized disappearance in 2014 of forty-three students in Mexico. At the outset, she makes the argument that transnational memory politics should be analyzed as part of the larger project of global justice. Mandolessi then discusses three concrete initiatives through which a variety of agents—international organizations, research centers, activists, and artists—seek to dismantle the system of impunity in Mexico. Thus, local activists connect "from the bottom up" with transnational actors and networks and tap into the global discourse of human rights and justice in order to influence national memory politics in turn. Orli Fridman and Katarina Ristić's chapter "Online Transnational Memory Activism and Commemoration: The Case of the White Armband Day" also examines a case in which those who wanted to remember atrocities committed during the war in Bosnia-Herzegovina were barred from doing so locally. Specifically, they discuss the use of social media to commemorate online and transnationally what could not be remembered onsite. They contend that the online memory activism surrounding #whitearmbandday not only enabled memory but also allowed a de-ethnicized form of remembrance that challenged the fault lines that were reinforced by the dominant state-sponsored memory politics. In this case, online activism began as a bottom-up dynamic but ended up transforming memory on the ground as well. While the mechanism of local activists teaming up with transnational ones in order to effect change "on the ground" is clearly operative in the Mexican and Bosnian cases, the next two contributions highlight it even more explicitly by drawing on social movement scholarship, especially Keck and Sikkink's "boomerang effect." Andrea Hepworth, in "Memory Activism across Borders: The Transformative Influence of the Argentinean Franco Court Case and Activist Protest Movements on Spain's Recovery of Historical Memory," offers a comparative analysis of the ways in which memory activists in Argentina and Spain effectively constructed a transnational memory space, particularly through the diffusion of the notion of "desaparecidos." She focuses in particular on the activities of the Argentinean Mothers of the Plaza de Mayo, the Spanish Association for the Recovery of Historical Memory, and activist lawyers, as well as their interlinkage in order to explain how these "memory entrepreneurs" worked—with mixed results—to create transnational remembering as well as to transform national memory politics. Mary M. McCarthy examines the creation of transnational spaces for the remembrance of sexual violence during World War II in Asia. In "The Creation and Utilization of Opportunity Structures for Transnational Activism on World War II Sexual Slavery in Asia," the author argues that these spaces are the outcome of transnational activism that emerged due to domestic barriers to critical commemoration and—from the 1990s onward—transnational opportunities. She argues that this bottom-up memory activism has been able to disrupt the power of states to determine the character of public memory about the "comfort women."

Devin Finn's chapter, "The Political Agency of Victims through Transnational Processes of Forensic Anthropology and Memory Construction in Latin America," discusses the agency of activists in cooperation with forensic anthropology organizations to understand how the process of searching for and identifying victims of violence impacts the formation of transnational memory spaces. Forensic anthropology organizations collaborate with one another on technical analysis and in efforts to facilitate memory construction and activism in conflict-affected communities, cultivating a transnational network of practice and a space for political demand-making—therefore, Finn's work showcases both a bottom-up agency of challenging states' narratives and a horizontal one through networks of expertise and cooperation. Gruia Bădescu, in "Transnational Place-Making after Political Violence: Agencies and Practices of Site Memorialization in the Latin American Southern Cone," in a sense straddles the bottom-up and top-down categories. He explores sites of memory in the Southern Cone of Latin America, specifically in Argentina and Chile, distinguishing between processes of transnational space-making and those of transnational place-making. While the former corresponds to dynamics that we see repeated throughout this volume, the latter denotes sites that engage notions of transnationalism as a mnemonic outcome. The reason Bădescu's contribution inhabits a hybrid position is that he studies both agents that challenge dominant memory politics and norms that shape memorial sites from above.

Due to the fact that scholars of memory are often interested precisely in those contentious moments when dominant mnemonic narratives are shaken up, there may be a tendency to assume that transnational memory tends to benefit progressive or "countermnemonic" actors. Indeed, state actors and elites usually do seek to defend the status quo, and that often means counteracting transnational norms based on human rights and the global "politics of regret" (Olick 2007). However, even when they pursue reproductive rather than transformative strategies, states are powerful transnational memory agents, as are various international organizations and agencies, and elites. Top-down agency, in part III, does not necessarily refer to a directionality across scales but rather to a power differential: a dynamic of imposition of particular mnemonic norms or resources from a dominant position. Noga Glucksam's chapter "My Grief, Our Grievance: Universal Human Rights and Memory Standardization in Liberia's Truth Commission" analyzes the hearings of the Liberia Truth and Reconciliation Commission, showing how individual witnesses were gradually led to adapt their testimony to universal human rights discourses. A forum that might have functioned as a place to empower the agency of victims instead became a venue of top-down mnemonic standardization. A similar dynamic is at play in "Transitional Justice in Public: Communicating Transnational Memories of Mass Violence" by Courtney E. Cole, who studies the discourse and documentation of postconflict transitional justice processes in post–World War II Germany, in Liberia, and in Sierra Leone. She argues that transitional justice institutions function as instruments to create both local and transnational public memory. Their engagement with everyday and "grassroots" recollections helps transform these from individual stories into official memory narratives that are shaped— as Glucksam also notes—by a globalized memory culture and the universal human rights regime. Taking a different vantage point, Amy Sodaro assesses the process of creating the 9/11 Memorial and Museum in New York City. In "Transnational Memory Movements in the 9/11 Museum," she provides a discussion of the museum's mission in the broader context of the "memorial museum" as a cosmopolitan framework for the work of memory. Despite the availability of this persuasive—and arguably more critical—transnational approach to commemoration, Sodaro argues that, ultimately, the national narrative has been powerfully imposed through a top-down mechanism.

Part IV collects case studies in which agency operates horizontally, that is, where no dominant power dynamic is evident (though of course power is not absent by any means). Till Hilmar's chapter "Links to the Past, Bridges for the Present? Recognition among Memory Organizations in a European Network" most squarely fits into this category, as he employs social network analysis to study connections among memory organizations in Europe. He argues that while this network is genuinely transnational, it also exhibits notable gaps in recognition, with groups devoted to the commemoration of Nazism less connected to those remembering Communism. Hilmar draws on analysis of hyperlinks between the organizations, as well as a survey. Thus, here we cannot point to a dynamic of imposition or challenge of memory narratives, but the power dynamics are present in Hilmar's identification of powerful nodes and structural "holes" within the transnational network. Mihaela Precup and Dragoş Manea in "'Life Was a Precarious Dance': Graphic Narration and the Construction of a Transcultural Memory Space in the PositiveNegatives Project," present another case of horizontal memory agency: that of the nonprofit project PositiveNegatives, which is supported by a variety of human rights and media organizations and which, the authors argue, constructs a transcultural forum for commemoration and testimony. The project transmits the testimonies of refugees into graphic narration and makes them accessible online and through educational material. Here, the objective is not to challenge a national discourse (as in bottom-up initiatives) or to adapt individual commemoration to universal discourses (as in top-down dynamics) but to create a shared mnemonic space. Taking an altogether different approach, Balázs Majtényi and György Majtényi argue that local places of memory link dispersed Roma communities and that they together form the foundation of "A Transnational Nation: Roma National Identity in the Making." The authors provide a historical account of the process of nation-building and show the role of commemoration in creating a common political language for the purpose of expressing joint demands. Again, despite the absence of top-down/bottom-up dynamics, Majtényi and Majtényi demonstrate the high political stakes of transnational memory politics. Ricardo A. Velasco Trujillo's study "Border-Crossing Cultural Initiatives of Memory and Reconciliation across the Colombia-Panama Border" presents three memory projects in the border region between Panama and Columbia that are entangled in the complex assemblage of initiatives that have emerged as a result of Colombia's national reconciliation process. He argues that this horizontal memory agency has created a transnational memory space that straddles a range of sociocultural spheres, including forcibly displaced communities in rural areas at the limits of national sovereignty. Velasco Trujillo highlights the relevance of cross-border commemoration for communities that have migrated under different conditions as a result of the dynamics of the conflict.

Aline Sierp concludes the volume by distilling the types of agents, structures, practices, and mechanisms that we the contributions to this volume have brought together into one analytical framework. Cutting across our organizational logic of bottom-up, top-down, and horizontal memory agency, she highlights not only the theoretical innovations made by the authors but also the empirical contributions to understanding the creation of transnational memory space. Sierp also offers a summary table of common agents, structures, and practices that should serve as a useful tool for future research in the field of transnational memory politics.

Jenny Wüstenberg is Professor of History & Memory Studies at Nottingham Trent University. She is the founder and past Co-President of the Memory Studies Association (2016-2023), as well as Chair of the COST Action on "Slow Memory: Transformative Practices in Times of Uneven and Accelerating Change" (2021-2025). She is the author of *Civil Society and Memory in Postwar Germany* (Cambridge University Press, 2017) and the co-editor of *De-Commemoration: Removing Statues and Renaming Places* (with Sarah Gensburger, Berghahn, 2023), *Agency in Transnational Memory Politics* (with Aline Sierp, Berghahn, 2020), and the *Routledge Handbook of Memory Activism* (with Yifat Gutman, 2023).

References

Assmann, Jan. 2008. "Communicative and Cultural Memory." In *A Companion to Cultural Memory Studies: An International and Interdisciplinary Handbook*, edited by Astrid Erll and Ansgar Nünning, 109–18. Berlin: De Gruyter.

Björkdahl, Annika, and Stefanie Kappler. 2019. "The Creation of Transnational Memory Spaces: Professionalization and Commercialization." Special issue, *International Journal of Politics, Culture and Society* 32(4) (December): 383–401.

Bond, Lucy, Stef Craps, and Pieter Vermeulen. 2016. "Introduction: Memory on the Move." In *Memory Unbound: Tracing the Dynamics of Memory Studies*, edited by Lucy Bond, Stef Craps, and Pieter Vermeulen, 1–26. New York: Berghahn Books.

Bourdieu, Pierre. 1977. *Outline of a Theory of Practice*. Translated by Richard Nice. Cambridge: Cambridge University Press.

Breiger, Ronald L. 2010. "Dualities of Culture and Structure: Seeing through Cultural Holes." In *Relationale Soziologie: Zur kulturellen Wende der Netzwerkforschung*, edited by Jan Fuhse and Sophie Mützel, 37–47. Wiesbaden: VS Verlag für Sozialwissenschaften.

Confino, Alon. 1997. "Collective Memory and Cultural History: Problems of Method." *American Historical Review* 102(5): 1386–403.

Creet, Julia. 2011. "Introduction: The Migration of Memory and Memories of Migration." In *Memory and Migration: Multidisciplinary Approaches to Memory Studies*, edited by Julia Creet and Andreas Kitzmann, 3–26. Toronto: University of Toronto Press.

de Cesari, Chiara, and Ann Rigney. 2014. "Introduction." In *Transnational Memory: Circulation, Articulation, Scales*, edited by Chiara de Cesari and Ann Rigney, 1–25. Berlin: De Gruyter.

den Boer, Pim, Heinz Duchhardt, Georg Kreis, and Wolfgang Schmale, eds. 2011. *Europäische Erinnerungsorte*. Vols. 1–3. Munich: De Gruyter Oldenbourg.

Dutceac-Segesten, Anamaria, and Jenny Wüstenberg. 2017. "Memory Studies—the State of the Field." *Memory Studies* 10(4) (October): 474–89.

Erll, Astrid. 2011. "Travelling Memory." *Parallax* 17(4): 4–18.

Feindt, Gregor, Félix Krawatzek, Daniela Mehler, Friedemann Pestel, and Rieke Trimcev. 2014. "Entangled Memory: Toward a Third Wave in Memory Studies." *History and Theory* 53: 24–44.

Geertz, Clifford. 1973. "Thick Description: Toward an Interpretive Theory of Culture." In *The Interpretation of Cultures*, edited by Clifford Geertz, 3–30. New York: Basic Books.

———. 1999. "Deep Play: Notes on the Balinese Cockfight." In *Culture and Politics—A Reader*, edited by Lane Crothers and Charles Lockhart, 175–201. New York: St. Martin's Press. Original edition, 1972.

Giddens, Anthony. 1984. *The Constitution of Society: Outline of the Theory of Structuration*. Cambridge: Polity Press.

Hahn, Hans Henning, and Robert Traba, eds. 2013. *Deutsch-Polnische Erinnerungsorte*. Vols. 1–5. Paderborn: Ferdinand Schöningh Verlag.

Halbwachs, Maurice. 2011. "The Collective Memory," in *The Collective Memory Reader*, edited by Jeffrey K. Olick, Vered Vinitzky-Seroussi, and Daniel Levy, 139–49. Oxford: Oxford University Press.

Hays, Sharon. 1994. "Structure and Agency and the Sticky Problem of Culture." *Sociological Theory* 12(1): 57–72.

Inglis, David. 2016. "Globalization and/of Memory: On the Complexification and Contestation of Memory Cultures and Practices." In *Routledge International Handbook of Memory Studies*, edited by Anna Lisa Tota and Trever Hagen, 143–57. Oxon: Routledge.

Keck, Margaret E., and Kathryn Sikkink. 1998. *Activists beyond Borders: Transnational Advocacy Networks in International Politics*. Ithaca, NY: Cornell University Press.

Kennedy, Rosanne, and Maria Nugent. 2016. "Scales of Memory: Reflections on an Emerging Concept." *Australian Humanities Review* 59 (April/May): 61–76.

Kohlstruck, Michael. 2004. "Erinnerungspolitik: Kollektive Identität, Neue Ordnung, Diskurshegemonie." In *Politikwissenschaft als Kulturwissenschaft: Theorien, Methoden, Problemstellungen*, edited by Birgit Schwelling, 173–94. Wiesbaden: Verlag für Sozialwissenschaften.

Kroh, Jens. 2008. *Transnationale Erinnerung: Der Holocaust im Fokus geschichtspolitischer Initiativen*. Frankfurt: Campus Verlag.

Kubik, Jan, and Michael Bernhard. 2014. "A Theory of the Politics of Memory." In *Twenty Years after Communism: The Politics of Memory and Commemoration*, edited by Michael Bernhard and Jan Kubik, 7–34. Oxford: Oxford University Press.

Kübler, Elisabeth. 2012. *Europäische Erinnerungspolitik: Der Europarat und die Erinnerung an den Holocaust*. Bielefeld: transcript Verlag.

Levy, Daniel. 2010. "Changing Temporalities and the Internationalization of Memory Cultures." In *Memory and the Future: Transnational Politics, Ethics and Society*, edited by Yifat Gutman, Adam D. Brown, and Amy Sodaro, 15–30. Basingstoke: Palgrave Macmillan.

Levy, Daniel, and Natan Sznaider. 2001. *Erinnerung im globalen Zeitalter: Der Holocaust*. Edited by Ulrich Beck, *Edition Zweite Moderne*. Frankfurt: Suhrkamp Verlag.

Mahler, Sarah J., and Patricia R. Pessar. 2001. "Gendered Geographies of Power: Analyzing Gender across Transnational Spaces." *Identities* 7(4): 441–59.

Mink, Georges, and Laure Neumeyer, eds. 2013. *History, Memory and Politics in Central and Eastern Europe. Memory Games*. London: Palgrave Macmillan.

Mische, Ann. 2011. "Relational Sociology, Culture and Agency." In *The Sage Handbook of Social Network Analysis*, edited by John Scott and Peter J. Carrington, 80–97. London: Sage Publications.

Morrow, Raymond A. 2009. "Review: Norbert Elias and Figurational Sociology; The Comeback of the Century." *Contemporary Sociology* 38(3): 215–19.

Müller, Jan-Werner. 2002. "Introduction: The Power of Memory, the Memory of Power and the Power over Memory." In *Memory and Power in Post-War Europe: Studies in the Presence of the Past*, edited by Jan-Werner Müller, 1–35. Cambridge: Cambridge University Press.

Mützel, Sophie, and Jan Fuhse. 2010. "Einleitung: Zur relationalen Soziologie; Grundgedanken, Entwicklungslinien und transatlantische Brückenschläge." In *Relationale Soziologie: Zur kulturellen Wende der Netzwerkforschung*, edited by Jan Fuhse and Sophie Mützel, 7–35. Wiesbaden: VS Verlag für Sozialwissenschaften.

Nora, Pierre. 1996. "General Introduction: Between Memory and History." In *Realms of Memory*, edited by Pierre Nora and Lawrence D. Kritzman, 1–20. New York: Columbia University Press. Original edition, 1992, in French in 7 vols.

Nora, Pierre, and Lawrence D. Kritzman. 1996a. "Preface." In *Realms of Memory*, edited by Pierre Nora and Lawrence D. Kritzman, xv–xxiv. New York: Columbia University Press. Original edition, 1992, in French in 7 vols.

———, eds. 1996b. *Realms of Memory*. Vol. 1. New York: Columbia University Press. Original edition, 1992, in French in 7 vols.

Olick, Jeffrey K. 2007. *The Politics of Regret: On Collective Memory and Historical Responsibility*. London: Routledge Press.

Radstone, Susannah. 2011. "What Place Is This? Transcultural Memory and the Locations of Memory Studies." *Parallax* 17(4): 109–23.

Rothberg, Michael. 2009. *Multidirectional Memory: Remembering the Holocaust in the Age of Decolonization*. Stanford, CA: Stanford University Press.

Scholte, Jan Aart. 1993. *International Relations of Social Change*. Buckingham: Open University Press.

Schwelling, Birgit, ed. 2012. *Reconciliation, Civil Society, and the Politics of Memory: Transnational Initiatives in the 20th and 21st Century*. Bielefeld: transcript Verlag.

Sewell, William M., Jr. 1999. "The Concept(s) of Culture." In *Beyond the Cultural Turn: New Directions in the Study of Society and Culture*, edited by Victoria E Bonnell and Lynn Hunt, 35–61. Berkeley: University of California Press.

Sierp, Aline. 2014. *History, Memory and Trans-European Identity*. London: Routledge.

———. 2017. "1939 versus 1989: A Missed Opportunity to Create a European Lieu de Mémoire?" *East European Politics & Societies* 31(3): 439–55.

Sierp, Aline, and Jenny Wüstenberg. 2015a. "Linking the Local and the Transnational: Rethinking Memory Politics in Europe." *Journal of Contemporary European Studies* 23(3): 321–29.

———. 2015b. "Transnational Memory Politics in Europe: Interdisciplinary Approaches." Special issue, *Journal of Contemporary European Studies* 23(3).

Swidler, Ann. 2000. "Cultural Power and Social Movements." In *Culture and Politics: A Reader*, edited by Lane Crothers and Charles Lockhart, 269–83. New York: St. Martin's Press.

Tilly, Charles. 2001. "Mechanisms in Political Processes." *Annual Review of Political Science* 4: 21–41.

Törnquist-Plewa, Barbara. 2018. "The Transnational Dynamics of Local Remembrance: The Jewish Past in a Former Shtetl in Poland." *Memory Studies* 11(3): 301–14.

Troebst, Stefan. 2014. "Gemeinschaftsbildung durch Geschichtspolitik? Anläufe der Europäischen Union zur Stiftung einer erinnerungsbasierten Bürgeridentität." *Jahrbuch für Politik und Geschichte* 5: 43–65.

Wedeen, Lisa. 2002. "Conceptualizing Culture: Possibilities for Political Science." *American Political Science Review* 96(4): 713–28.

Winter, Jay, and Emmanuel Sivan. 1999. "Setting the Framework." In *War and Remembrance in the Twentieth Century*, edited by Jay Winter and Emmanuel Sivan, 6–39. Cambridge: Cambridge University Press.

Wüstenberg, Jenny. 2017. *Civil Society and Memory in Postwar Germany*. Cambridge: Cambridge University Press.

———. 2019. "Locating Transnational Memory." Special issue, *International Journal of Politics, Culture and Society* 32(4) (December): 371–82.

Zerubavel, Eviatar. 2003. *Time Maps: Collective Memory and the Social Shape of the Past*. Chicago: University of Chicago Press.

Chapter 1

A FIELD-THEORETICAL APPROACH TO MEMORY POLITICS

Zoltan Dujisin

Collective memory has been studied from a variety of perspectives, namely psychological, cultural, literary, political, and social, inviting interdisciplinary endeavors that have however struggled to advance a theoretically generative dialogue. I do not argue that this ambition should be altogether abandoned but that instead we begin treating memory studies as a discipline in its own right, one that unfolds in a number of subdisciplines whose theoretical development begs for segmented elaboration. In the introduction, Wüstenberg identifies two fundamental limitations in much of the memory studies literature: an overreliance on structures to explain outcomes and an enclosure within an overdeployed national framework. As a corrective, she suggests focusing on agency as a "useful handle on how memory is made transnational," calling on contributors to "closely examine the evolution of and power dynamics underpinning *the practice of interaction . . . between agents and structures*" (emphasis in original). My own chapter interprets the above as a call for a relational and sociological approach to memory politics and puts forth four distinct propositions.

Firstly, this chapter positions itself within the subdiscipline of memory politics and does so by exploring how collective memory is coherently and consistently articulated in separate fields to produce a regime of remembrance. As I argue further ahead, this examination reveals an important distinction: if collective memory is an unending process of societal negotiation, of struggles for hegemony, recognition, institutionalization, or forgetting, then a regime of remembrance represents the synchronic capture of this process by a political constellation bent on legitimating specific identities, interests, and agendas. A critical engagement with the distinctive dynamics of memory politics thus requires us to ask how memory moves from struggle, contestation, and instability to a hard identity that projects sameness, permanence, and homogeneity.

Secondly, I approach this task by envisioning collective memory as a process articulated within fields of organized struggle, one that only assumes the semblance of a memory regime through consistent efforts to coordinate these struggles across said fields. I provide a brief theoretical introduction to Bourdieuan field theory and, in the spirit of Wüstenberg's introduction, ponder its insights for a theory of action that grapples with the entanglements between individual agency and social structure.

Thirdly, and building from Bernhard and Kubik's (2014) assertion that each politically salient issue of the past gives rise to its own regime of remembrance—an assertion motivated by the thematic constraint of their book—I suggest we treat regimes of remembrance as a single constellation that potentially incorporates various salient issues. The resulting mnemonic identity incorporates said issues with varying degrees of salience and explicitness, and manifest narratives will be as revealing of the overall power configuration behind it as conspicuous silences. Hence, I suggest it is more accurate to view so-called discreet historical-mnemonic issues as interrelated elements that together constitute a larger symbolic repertoire on which mnemonic identities rest. These identities follow a relational logic not only from the conceptual and ideational point of view; they are also sown together by the interpretative efforts of actors operating in several fields of struggle. Once again, my purpose will be to highlight precisely how exercises in interpretation, translation, and negotiation across fields result in a legitimating semblance of coherent collective memories.

Fourthly, and to pay heed to the editors' call to transnationalize memory studies, I suggest ways in which social scientists can encompass multiple fields in their surveys of memory politics, including by scaling up to the transnational arena. As I will show, several contributions in this volume provide important cues as to the kind of cross-field and transnationalization dynamics that are behind much successful memory work, inviting my own attempt to systematize and theorize these processes.

Collective Memory: Process or Identity?

Our concern with memory is very much grounded in a deeply ingrained disquiet with our contemporary predicament, a historical self-awareness that is inseparable from collective insecurities precipitated by globalization. The term "memory boom" conveys the severity of this condition (Huyssen 1993), manifested by all kinds of public practices of memorialization, including in the young but burgeoning academic subfield of memory studies. Memory seems to respond to a need to ground a shifting present by connecting it with a reassuring, immutable past, "a form of neoconservative 'comfort' and 'cultural compensation' for the social and psychological dislocations caused by an 'accelerated' or even 'second' modernity" (Müller 2002:16). Yet most social theorists have eschewed memory, and most studies of memory remain profoundly bounded to the idiosyncratic methods and concepts developed for specific cases (Olick 2006: 8). Among scholars of memory politics, Müller has noted that while there is broad agreement that memory matters politically, we know very little about how this importance is manifested (2002: 2).

By drawing on field theory (Bourdieu 1984; 1996), this section proposes a common theoretical thread for understanding memory politics, one that accommodates the theoretical insights required for grasping collective memory's move from unpredictable struggle to stable identity. I begin by taking a position in the conceptual debate around collective memory and its implications for delimiting memory politics as a subdiscipline of memory studies.

Precisely what collective memories are and how they are formed has been the subject of extensive scholarly debate. Accounts of collective memory that derive their analytical frameworks from psychology may have been discredited, but the latter's conceptual toolkit is still unconsciously applied, as scholars attribute to collectivities the mechanisms and properties of individual psyches. Collective memory is thus variously caught recollecting, forgetting, or dealing with trauma. This remains particularly the case with most regional overviews of postcommunist collective memory (Leggewie 2010; Mälksoo 2009), whereby Eastern European political elites are merely delegated with the task of conveying the previously subdued collective memory of a society that demands hearing out.

Still, no contemporary scholar would deny that there is a dialectic relation at play between individual and collective memory. Disagreement is usually centered on which particular direction of causality is emphasized. Individual memories provide essential building blocks to the cultural and social construct that is collective memory, and this aspect of the relationship is stressed particularly in political discourse, where political entrepreneurs foreground certain individual memories while backgrounding others. At the same time, Halbwachs's (1992: 37–40) observation that collectively meaningful historical interpretations structure the cognitive and neurological configuration of individual memories has been not only internalized by memory scholars but also corroborated by current psychological research (Schacter 1995). This current was largely responsible for the development of a presentist, or instrumentalist, approach, one almost indistinguishable from the study of memory politics, and whose most prominent representative was the late Eric Hobsbawm. The British historian famously introduced the term "invented traditions" to emphasize the ability of political actors to invent or manipulate symbols and notions of the past in the pursuit of partisan or state interest (Ranger and Hobsbawm 1983).

While some of his critics have accused Hobsbawm of placing excessive weight on political elites' ability to shape perceptions of the past, the British historian sowed the seeds for a growing awareness that "past-oriented meaning frameworks are prominent modes of legitimation and explanation" (Olick and Robbins 1998: 108). My own work is also inserted in the instrumentalist tradition initiated by Hobsbawm, but one that, rather than positing memory as invariably manipulated by political elites, suggests that memory *politics* ought to concern itself with how memory comes to be deployed at the service of instilling political identities. This deployment is the result both of individual agency and of structural constraints that direct and incite particular uses of the past—uses that respond to iterative, rather than top-down social dynamics. Hence memory can be political *regardless* of the more or less relevant intentions and motivations of a narrative's proponents, which are of little use when taken in isolation from the structures in which they operate and moreover difficult to measure unless taken at face value. If memory is political, it is acting as a resource in political struggles. This does not entail that memories are necessarily false, fabricated, or necessarily propagated with a deceitful intent. It simply invites a healthy awareness of the complex political entanglements of narratives about the past that are potentially constitutive of our fundamental political identities, in both conscious and unconscious ways.

This definition of memory politics is, in my view, fully compatible with Olick's critique of the concept of collective memory, all too often deployed either as an independent or a dependent variable, or both, taking for granted the very phenomenon it supposedly explains (2006: 8). Recently, other scholars have expressed similar concerns. Bell (2008: 155) has argued that the concept of collective memory is often bestowed with a static immanence that conceals its fundamentally processual nature. Sturken (2008: 74) implicitly makes the same critique by suggesting that we think of memory in terms of practices that convey the cultural negotiation of memory in the praxis of individuals, groups, and institutions rather than its inert apprehension in objects or sites of memory. In other words, collective memory "refers to a wide variety of mnemonic products and practices" that represent different "moments in a dynamic process" (Olick 2006: 12). Collective memory would thus be better grasped in terms of the dialectic, iterative oscillations between individual memory and cognition, the shared meanings we attach to memories, and their material and institutional inscription in an extensive array of realms.

While an enormous breakthrough, Olick's critique did not solve all the tensions inherent in the discipline, particularly its profound relation to the concept of identity. Olick and Robbins have called memory the "central medium through which identity is constituted" (1998: 133), whereas Nora goes as far as asserting that they "have become all but synonymous" (2002: 9). For most of the twentieth century, memory was mostly deployed by nation-states seeking to exploit the past to forge a cohesive identity, although the last decades have seen "a self-reflexive turning point attributing legitimacy to nation transforming forms of memory" (Levy 2011: 489), one whereby grass-roots movements or transnational activism challenge state monopolies and invite critical introspection. Nevertheless, few would dispute that national forms of identity have overwhelmingly remained "hard," connoting sameness, permanence across time and space, group boundedness, and homogeneity (Brubaker and Cooper 2000: 10–11).

Distinguishing Collective Memory from . . . Collective Memory

As this short overview illustrates, memory seems to be doing too many things. And as with any concept that is overstretched, it risks becoming meaningless and analytically impractical. But the literature on collective memory has done more than assign an unreasonably wide scope of activity to collective memory; it has also left it with a seemingly unresolvable contradiction. Collective memory is supposedly dynamic and processual; it is expressed and reformulated through and in individual and collective practices, practices that have various social moments and cannot be encapsulated in a single social domain. At the same time, collective memory is deemed an essential component of, or even synonymous with, identity. An identity that, more often than not, is studied in its "hard," national, or ethnic manifestations rather than in the fluid, interchangeable variants of postmodernity. In these accounts, collective memory is an antidote to the insecurities conjured by a fast-changing world, allowing subjects to relate to a comforting and ageless past.

I will not venture another definition of collective memory in what is a relatively saturated debate, nor do I suggest the concept was misinterpreted as overly dynamic or static. Instead, *I propose we shift our attention from the question of what is collective memory to the question of how political communities interiorize a collective memory as natural, representative, and encompassing.* This concern is hardly new: Halbwachs had noted that mnemonic agents bent on conveying stable meanings will seek to capture the fluctuations of collective memory through formal storage and interpretation (1992: 24). More recently, Assmann underlined precisely why this capture is ultimately a political question:

As we pass the shadow line from short-term to long-term durability, an embodied, implicit, heterogenous, and fuzzy bottom-up memory is transformed into
an explicit, homogeneous, and institutionalized top-down memory. . . . Hence
a political memory is necessarily a mediated memory. It resides in material
media, symbols and practices which have to be engrafted into the hearts and
minds of individuals. (2006: 215–16)

Unfortunately, Halbwachs's and Assmann's vital contributions on this
topic offer no systematic account of the social mechanisms that lead from the
first—collective memory as a process—to the second—collective memory
as an identity. It is with this criticism in mind that I favor a research agenda
that explores *how* unofficial, spontaneous memories become entangled with
institutionalized memories in the exercise of power or, put differently, *what is
the work* that goes into extracting a socially resonant *mnemonic identity* out of
a complex web of social and power relations. This agency-focused approach is
meant not so much as a general ontological statement, but as a heuristic device
that illuminates *the mechanisms by which memory regimes are held together*.
Any attempt at providing an account of such *memory work* must begin by
distinguishing the fluid process of collective memory from one of its essential
components, a *regime of remembrance*. A memory regime is fundamentally a
sociopolitical configuration entrusted with disciplining collective memory's
oscillations by safeguarding a given identity. It responds to an injunction to
remember by which memory is problematized, citizens reminded of their duty
to remember, and political cultures reaffirmed (Eyal 2004: 9).

More mundanely, regime of remembrance refers to the set of institutionalized, at times officially endorsed practices that embody how a power coalition
or polity promotes opportunities for citizens to relate to their past. It can
be distilled into two, partly overlapping analytical components that copro-
duce it: (1) a mnemonic substance, which is the content invoked as a polity's collective memory, its founding myths and historical interpretations; (2)
the regime's mode of remembrance, which answers the question of why we
should remember and how we engage with a particular mnemonic substance.
This point is most directly pertinent for examining memory's political implications and overcoming a tendency for descriptive and reificatory scholarship.
The distinction between these two components can be eloquently illustrated
via the Holocaust-centered memory regime embraced by the EU, particularly
throughout the 1990s and 2000s—albeit one that has been challenged with
the EU accession of eight postcommunist countries in 2004 (Mälksoo 2009).
The EU has placed the Holocaust at the core of its mnemonic substance—a
negative founding formula that symbolizes Europe's descent into barbarity.
Simultaneously, this mode of remembrance has encouraged European states
to admit guilt for past mistakes, most notably, but not exclusively, Holocaust
collaboration, in what Olick (2007) has called the *politics of regret*.

Transitional justice efforts offer a privileged opportunity to observe the formation of such regimes of remembrance as, through the set-up of an institutional apparatus, these regimes attempt to capture and organize an uncontrolled flux of traumatic and conflictive recollections. Deconstructing this process can moreover help highlight the class, race, gender, or religious inequalities that memory regimes may variously reflect. Cole's chapter conceptualizes transitional justice as a discursive, symbolic, material, and spatio-temporal space where public memory is organized, often with the aim to create, articulate, and circulate "an official narrative of the past in order to create a shared history" and construct a specific idea of community—what I would call a mode of remembrance. Her work highlights the tensions inherent in processes of memory regime construction: vernacular accounts, which may be abundant and difficult to reconcile, may clash with elite accounts or become subject to elite political imperatives. What comes to feature in the regime's resulting mnemonic identity will thus be affected not just by the substance of the traumatic memories at stake but crucially by the location and political interests of participants in memory-making. This is all too obvious in the work of truth commissions, as noted in Glucksam's chapter. She shows how in Liberia, the Truth and Reconciliation Commission was entrusted with repackaging "performative narrations of experiences" into a novel regime of remembrance. This exercise invariably reproduced existing power structures, reflected in a controversial list of recommendations as to who should be banned from political office or prosecuted for crimes against humanity. Such recommendations were not backed by a systematic methodology, raising concern over backroom dealings affecting inclusion and exclusion from the list and underlining just how vulnerable personal testimonies were to political instrumentalization. In a more general sense, the case of the Liberian Truth Commission also brings to our attention the contingency of memory agency and the ability of specific actors to mold collective memory to their purposes.

What makes these and other studies of memory politics both challenging and fascinating is precisely that regimes of remembrance are built to naturalize their attendant identities in ways that may obscure the actors and interests constituting them, meaning the processes leading up to their enshrinement will not always leave obvious traces. How then to unpack regimes of remembrance in ways that reveal their constitutive elements and interests, allowing us to discern why certain memories succeed whereas others fail? The diffusion of collective memory suggests that this complex process engages a variety of actors operating from within diverse domains: collective memory resides in domains as diverse as museums, art galleries, record offices, the educational system, the public media, and newspapers (Johnson and Dawson 1982: 208–9). Yet as a shifting and socially mediated entity, constantly invoked and reinterpreted across realms, collective memory never quite sojourns in merely one domain. Selecting one of these domains and treating it as a bounded, isolated reality risks overlooking precisely those constant invocations and contingencies that endow the concept with its processual, dynamic properties. The challenge thus lies in treating memory relationally, not just within the scope of any given local order but across them as well. In what follows, I propose a systematic approach that can accommodate the indisputably diffuse nature of collective memory and help us make sense of how an array of structures, discourses, and agencies eventually coalesce into a regime of remembrance.

The Field-Theory Solution

While much work on collective memory reflects and elaborates on its relational nature, few scholars in the discipline have expressly produced a theoretical framework that treats memory accordingly—one exception can be found in Hilmar's contribution to this volume. In what follows, I argue that concepts from field theory, most significantly developed in the social sciences by Pierre Bourdieu, provide a suitable starting point for approaching memory politics relationally. This proposition has, of course, important precedents. Field theory has been applied to several areas relevant to memory studies, such as academia (Bourdieu 1984), colonialism (Steinmetz 2008), art and literature (Bourdieu 1996; Sapiro 2003), politics (Singh 2016), or regional integration (Georgakakis and Rowell 2013; Mudge and Vauchez 2012). Claus Leggewie and Erik Meyer (2005) have also mobilized the concept of field to specify the judicial, cultural, pedagogical, administrative, and instrumental arenas where the memory politics of the Berlin Holocaust memorial unfolded. What all these applications of field theory share is an epistemological preference for seeing the social world as driven by complex webs of relations rather than direct causal lines linking independent and dependent variables. While field analysis points to a promising avenue of research for transnational memory politics, much work needs to be done in terms of adapting the concept to transnational settings. A great deal of work in this sense has been done by Bernhard and Kubik (2014), who besides operationalizing the concepts of *mnemonic field* and *memory regime* offer a seemingly universally applicable toolkit to categorize the most prominent mnemonic actors operating within fields of memory—mnemonic warriors, abnegators, pluralists, and prospectives.

Fields represent attempts to carve out a *relatively autonomous* space of action from the encompassing dynamics imposed by a larger societal structure. Autonomy is invariably relative, as the field has to grapple with external causal chains (Steinmetz 2008: 595), most visibly in the form of momentous historical transformations. Yet such external influences are just as invariably mediated by the structure of the field, which molds, interprets, and translates them into an amenable logic. Structurally, a field is to be considered as a "a network, or configuration, of objective relations between positions" (Bourdieu and Wacquant 1992: 97), positions that are variously occupied by individual actors, collective agencies, and formal institutions who strive for the specific profits and prizes at stake in the field, as well as over the rules that define this "game" (Martin 2003: 31). These prizes can be products, recognition, status, services, goods or knowledge, and agents' success in reaping these rewards is conditional on their capacity to accumulate relevant forms of capital.

Capital denotes a particular species of power or domination recognized as legitimate in attaining the abovementioned prizes—status, goods—by all actors operating in the field. Actors' possession of capital, as well as the principles of its distribution—which are also the subject of struggles—determine the overall configuration of positions in the field. By way of example, in a political field actors fight—and cooperate—for certain rewards, such as holding office, but also to redefine the rules of political competition, with a view on facilitating future access to those rewards, as is the case with gerrymandering. Their ability for success will be conditional on the forms of capital that prevail in a given political field—in some polities, economic capital will be sufficient for ensuring necessary alliances and control of knowledge production institutions such as media outlets; in others, some form of cultural capital may prove just as, if not more, pivotal, as Zarycki (2009) argues for postcommunist Poland. Attempts to claim the symbolic capital of anticommunism, for instance, were pivotal to the first free elections in Romania, where any revision of nationhood warranted an outright rejection of communism (Verdery 1996). Everywhere in Central and Eastern Europe, collective memory became a central object of dispute by actors populating the political field via denunciations of the communist past and a competition to identify oneself with resistance to the previous regime. Memory will not always play such a blatantly dominant role in field struggles, but that should not lead us to underestimating the subdued power of memory when linked to other, more prominent political identities.

Within a field, agency is ultimately determined by how actors resolve the often contradictory pulls occasioned by the specific role-demands of the field position they occupy, and the individual habitus each of them brings into the game. A central concept in Bourdieu's social theory, the habitus of individuals refers to the set of embodied cultural dispositions that filter an actor's perception of, and reaction to, his or her surroundings. Operating below the level of explicit ideology, the habitus reflects a unique social trajectory, shaped by political, institutional, and informal mechanisms of socialization. As Wacquant put it, "habitus is never the replica of a single social structure but a dynamic, multiscalar, and multilayered set of schemata subject to 'permanent revision' in practice" (Wacquant 2016: 64). The habitus thus induces motions within the field, albeit always in interaction with the interests prescribed by the field position they occupy. The way in which agency occasionally needs to resolve the tensions between field position and habitus can be illustrated by the figure of Vaclav Havel, a former dissident turned president. Bound not only by his position of president of the Czechoslovak Republic but also by his possession of an anticommunist symbolic capital gained during decades of resistance to communist power, Havel often struggled to reconcile his presidential field role with a dissident habitus. This was clear in his somewhat hesitant handling of the question of lustration of former communist officials, where his institutional recognition of criticism against the lustration law often ran contrary to many of the expectations arising from his own past as a dissident (See Kopeček 2011).

Critics of Bourdieu dismiss the concept of habitus as overly static and thus incapable of accommodating the more emancipated definitions of agency they favor. This is misleading for two reasons. Firstly, while it is true that fields are constantly and unconsciously reproduced by the social structures that actors assimilate into their habitus, suggesting unconscious automatisms, the regeneration of field structures also encompasses elements of unpredictability and spontaneity. Agents' habituses bring to bear *unique* intersections of social structures into the field—everyone embodies a specific combination of family and informal socialization, schooling or media exposure, political culture, and so on, notwithstanding the substantial cultural overlaps occasioned by the ubiquity of these socializing structures. Secondly, an additional degree of ambiguity is introduced by the constant interplay between individual habituses and the role demands of individuals' respective field positions (Martin 2003: 22–23, 27–28), as Havel's example suggests. Field actors are thus constantly called upon to reconcile the potentially conflicting pulls occasioned by field-prescribed interests and habitus-induced reactions, a conflict whose outcome cannot be considered as given. A far cry from structural determinism—albeit possibly unsatisfactory for supporters of unbridled agency—this understanding of field theory merely posits that it is the interaction between the inherited and embodied dispositions of the habitus and the structure of the field that induces motions within it. Hence, field theory and habitus provide frameworks for understanding agency as essentially in interaction with a variety of structures that are both enabling and constraining to it.

Application to Memory Studies

There are several advantages to this approach that correct some of the epistemological shortcomings of memory studies. By encouraging us to think about power relationally, field theory heeds Halbwachs's call to treat memory not simply as a subjective matter but as a socially mediated phenomenon. Field theory upgrades our ability to analyze collective memory as conflictive, as the concept itself suggests: terms such as "milieu," "context," or "social background" are too "positive" to bring to bear conflictive social dynamics (Swartz 2012: 119). Instead, the concept of field underscores precisely this conflictual dimension of social life, as suggested by instrumentalist approaches (Bodnar 1992; Ranger and Hobsbawm 1983; Müller 2002). It envisions various potential mediating realms where struggles over memory can be resolved, also through forms of cooperation. Returning to the distinction between collective memory as a societal negotiation and a regime of remembrance as an attempt to systematically intervene on this process for purposes of identity production, field analysis offers an opportunity to highlight the power dynamics responsible for enshrining certain identities over others.

Field theory allows for this by moving us beyond the formalistic perils of institutionalist approaches. Field effects operate independently from their inscription in well-recognized institutional practices, bringing informal dimensions of power to the fore that are essential to how memory exerts its influence in social life. Moreover, these realms are treated as abstract spaces where formal and informal mechanisms exert and distribute power, encouraging the transgression of national frameworks that tends to limit our musings on collective memory. The centrality of collective memory in field struggles will vary according to the field, but this is not something that can be determined through hasty, superficial, or overly formalistic assessments of power dynamics in the fields under examination.

In sum, fields—whether political, journalistic, or academic—provide a framework within which the abstract flux of individual memories, collective meanings, disparate motivations and institutionalized identities converge into an intelligible narrative. Field analysis offers the tools to contemplate mnemonic interventions as contingent and meaningful, as embedded in institutional and spatial arrangements that are consequential to the range of memory's oscillations. It also allows us to trace those oscillations back to the strategies, positions, and capital holdings of individual and collective agents.

But how does collective memory assume the semblance of an identity, and how does a regime of remembrance enshrine this same identity? If we assume, like Connerton, that "participants in any social order must presuppose a shared memory" (1989: 3), how are the multiple, field-bound rearticulations of collective memory amalgamated, negotiated, and re-adapted across realms to produce the sort of coherence an identity demands? In other words, and to put it in Latourian (1987) language, how is collective memory rearticulated and black-boxed into a memory regime? Once again, the key is in the actors, the linkages they facilitate, and the constraints and possibilities warranted by their field positions.

The Spaces between Fields

The above questions redirect us to the issue of the relations between fields. Field theory has only recently witnessed a growth in interest in this issue, hitherto dominated by Bourdieuan visions of fields as nested into each other in hierarchical fashion. As Bourdieu himself conceded, relations between fields do not seem to follow trans-historic laws (Bourdieu and Wacquant 1992: 109), since each field is relatively autonomous and directed by its "own internal temporality, pace, and rhythm" (Steinmetz 2011: 55). The absence of an overarching set of rules governing cross-field interactions presupposes that various ad hoc orders emerge to oversee them, orders that are contingent on the unique dialectic created by their encounter. These encounters should develop in an area of friction or overlap between fields where these different temporalities, paces, and rhythms are somehow reconciled through sustained interaction. In the case of collective memory, this wealth of orders poses a serious challenge: how do we envision the coalescing of multiple, field-bound mnemonic practices into a coherent regime of remembrance?

Before answering this question, we need to take a step back and consider the social topographies where such local orders may emerge. In an attempt to reconcile Bourdieu with the ideas of Latour, Eyal (2013: 162) suggests we reconsider the role of boundaries as lines that mark the end of one field and the beginning of another and start treating them as the indispensable social entity they are: areas with enough volume to accommodate the struggles, flows, and exchanges between fields. In this view, these spaces generate mechanisms indispensable to the existence of fields as relatively bounded and coherent entities, but they also allow the mobilization of resources and alliances across them. Such encounters do not, however, occur spontaneously or by simple inertia but by the willful actions of actors who promote profitable and legitimating exchanges and alliances across fields.

Interstitial spaces—the intersections of fields—are of obvious interest to the development of a research agenda in memory politics. To reiterate my previous point, such memory work consists in ensuring that mnemonic identities, which rely on a common symbolic repertoire, are consistently and successfully deployed in struggles that traverse various fields, with mutually legitimating effects. It is only through efforts to maintain a coherent "message" across crucial arenas of struggle, such as the political, judicial, scholarly, or media fields, that collective memories can become embedded in larger, politically entangled identities. While not wholly ineffective or inconsequential, uncoordinated struggles, or those limited to a single field, are less likely to enlist crucial allies and attain wider resonance and legitimacy. This realization is, for instance, palpable among the activists described in McCarthy's chapter: seeking justice for Korean comfort women, these actors and their organizations became internationally prominent throughout the 1990s thanks to their accumulation of various forms of capital across multiple fields. For instance, the Korean Council for the Women Drafted for Sexual Slavery by Japan, a nongovernmental organization, pushed its agenda all the way up to the United Nations, legitimated by a combination of fundraising, information-gathering, public education, and support for victim groups. The Washington Coalition for Comfort Women Issues, a similar organization created by Korean Americans, similarly engaged with adjacent fields, collaborating with universities to provide lectures, seminars, conferences, and exhibits.

The point of this and other ventures into various mnemonically relevant fields is not—necessarily—to make memory central to its struggles or to ensure a particular narrative emerges unconditionally hegemonic. Rather, it is to distribute these struggles, to make them more manageable, to sustain the resonance of a specific historical interpretation so that those who subscribe to its attendant identity can find an additional source of validation. If properly institutionalized—a thorny process, as each field imposes specific constraints—these mnemonic coalitions may become part and parcel of a proper regime of remembrance. The diffusion of mnemonic struggles across fields for legitimation purposes can be observed in the case of Nazi-Communist equalization narratives promoted by postcommunist politicians at the European level (Littoz-Monnet 2012). This "anti-totalitarian" identity (Clarke 2014), understood as national, pro-democratic resistance to a totalitarian threat that may be embodied by both Nazism and Communism, is sustained through linkages to adjacent fields, such as the scholarly one. Legitimation for the anti-totalitarian identity does not result from a hegemonic position of its scholarly counterpart, the totalitarian framework famously developed by Hannah Arendt in the 1950s, in national historiographies of communism. In fact, throughout the 1970s, the theory of totalitarianism was largely superseded by a generation of social historians who traveled to the Soviet Union and encountered a very different reality (Engerman 2009). However, a minority of public historians who still defend the model, such as Anne Applebaum or Timothy Snyder, have been crucially conjured by political actors promoting Nazi-Communist equalization in Pan-European settings,[1] with legitimating effects for an anti-totalitarian identity that resonates across the region. The European Parliament's 2008 decision to implement a European Day of Remembrance for Victims of Stalinism and Nazism on August 23 was a crucial step in institutionalizing this mnemonic coalition into a proper memory regime operating at the regional level.

This politically contingent exercise of backgrounding certain linkages between fields while foregrounding others (in this case, the choice to link a political identity to "totalitarian" rather than mainstream historiography) is not an exception but rather the rule when it comes to how regimes of remembrance are erected. Assmann (2006: 213) claims that the selectivity of collective memory is indebted to its ability to form larger ensembles that absorb individual memories, variously highlighting or suppressing them. Individual memories, according to Assmann, exhibit connective and adaptive properties that encourage linkages with wider networks of memories, facilitating their social re-adaptation. Similarly, Schacter (1995) has demonstrated how our psychological vulnerability to distortion makes memory highly malleable. Regimes of remembrance will naturally rely on this malleability to enlarge the scope of available alliances and linkages across fields, not just between actors but also with objects, ideas, and institutions. In other words, with anything we may consider a mnemonic device. The lesson here is that the power of a mnemonic identity does not lie in the immanent characteristics of a single component in the coalition or regime of remembrance that sustains it. Instead, the power we often observe in a single component derives from its entanglement in a larger ensemble through which said power circulates.

The mechanisms facilitating such linkages will be as variable as the number of possible intersections among fields. Given that this is frequently no simple task—requiring a great deal of negotiation and translation of interests and narratives across them—we are likely to encounter uniquely qualified actors implementing those same mechanisms, whether we speak of Korean activists denouncing sexual slavery at the UN or postcommunist actors denouncing communist crimes in the EU. I venture that these actors will most likely be interstitial actors, individuals, or institutions with a familiarity in more than one field, possessing what we may call a *hybrid habitus*. This unique habitus habilitates them to negotiate compromises, invest in and interact with various fields, circulate capital across them, and ultimately legitimate a coherent, mnemonic identity. For instance, Cole's chapter illustrates how truth commissions and international criminal tribunals—institutions that generally provide the backbone of memory regimes—fit neatly into such interstitial categories. These hybrid bodies of transitional justice, argues Cole, frequently cross into religious, aesthetic, legal, scientific, media, and state bureaucratic fields without "fitting neatly into any one of them." Similarly, Finn provides an account of such actors in the form of forensic anthropologists lobbying Latin American states to take responsibility for searching for the bodies of the disappeared. Engaging in trans-sectoral and transnational cooperation via sharing of training experiences, investigation, and interactions with victim groups, forensic anthropologists amass cultural and social capital in ways that allow them to successfully shake the foundations of the memory regimes they oppose. Through such mnemonic practices, these hybrid actors successfully build cross-field coalitions that embed human rights work in scientific practice, ultimately legitimating their political pressure on Latin American states.

Transnationalization

Field theory in general and hybrid actors in particular can also help us make sense of a crucial question that increasingly puzzles observers of memory politics. What is the significance, purpose, and reach of efforts at transnationalizing mnemonic coalitions and regimes of remembrance? The Latin American example above provides important cues: in a globalized world, forensic anthropologists used all transnationally available means to recruit the expertise (cultural capital), resources (economic capital), and alliances (social capital) that would legitimate their pressure on nation-states. Still in Latin America, Bădescu shows how the memorialization of sites of violence followed a similar pattern, through the emergence of a transnational network bringing together actors operating in different fields. Groups of victims of repression and their relatives; human rights activists; local, national, and transnational civil society and memory organizations; state institution at local, regional, or national level; and aesthetic professionals such as artists, curators, or architects came together in challenging existing memory regimes. Regional networks such as the Latin American Sites of Conscience network, for instance, grew out of international meetings of memory professionals working at Latin American museums and memory sites, generating a circulation of knowledge and practices that led to the establishment of common professional canons and trends. These extended networks, as Bădescu shows, help project what would otherwise be purely domestic discussions on memorialization onto transnational arenas, with multiple implications in terms of visibility, connections, material, and technical support and other tangible or intangible forms of capital.

Crucially, memory entrepreneurs' transnationalization strategies imperil the nation-state's monopoly on memory-making, first sidestepping it only to force it to react later. Scaling up from the national to the supranational level usually occurs when memory entrepreneurs encounter obstacles to pursue their causes in domestic arenas and prop up their capacity to confront uncooperative governments via transnational legitimacy and visibility. This they attempt by accumulating forms of capital (whether social, economic, or symbolic) embedded in resources and expertise that are often scarce or unavailable domestically but widely available in transnational fields. Hepworth illustrates this point compellingly in her chapter on the emergence of the term *desaparecidos*: by scaling up to a transnational level, Argentinean and Spanish activists mingled in consequential ways, generating social and cultural capital and legitimating their calls to apply the concept of universal jurisdiction in both Spain and Argentina. Noteworthy also are efforts at side-stepping state actors via the rise of new media and technologies, a particularly promising avenue of research. As Fridman and Ristić show in their chapter on the #whitearmbandday online commemoration in Bosnia, new media technologies offer enormous mobilization potential for nonstate actors and various countermovements. The authors show how a small number of activists mobilized a transnational network, including local, regional, and international NGOs and civil society activists, reaching wider audiences beyond Bosnia and the post-Yugoslav region, and thus challenging state monopolies on mnemonic production.

While transnationalization is an increasingly attractive option for actors seeking justice and recognition, this strategy is also available to states, which may deploy it for altogether different purposes. As I have shown elsewhere (Dujisin 2015), political forces have used state mechanisms to transnationalize and thus strengthen what are domestically contested narratives of the past. I illustrate this point by showing how attempts by postcommunist leaders to have the EU recognize an "anti-totalitarian" memory are embedded in conservative strategies of domestic political competition. Far from representing the natural rise of a hitherto repressed collective memory, or merely the agency of dedicated activists, the transnationalization of anti-totalitarianism reflects the interests prescribed by postcommunist political fields while concealing deep societal divisions over how to commemorate communism.

Conclusions and Suggestions for Future Research

I have attempted to make five essential contributions in this chapter: (1) To reformulate memory politics in ways that allow us to distinguish between the hitherto confusing usages of the term "collective memory." I did this by distinguishing collective memory as a process from the mnemonic identity that is sustained by a mnemonic coalition or memory regime. (2) To posit that studies of memory politics should focus on the question of *how* a specific mnemonic identity prevails at the expense of others, that is, how memory regimes are extracted and created from the complex flux of collective memory. This renewed focus should replace the prevailing emphasis on the mnemonic substances that typify memory regimes, often leading to overly descriptive accounts. (3) To redefine collective memory and memory regimes as occurring between and across fields, in a coordinated fashion, for purposes of legitimation. (4) To suggest that such processes merit a focus not just on the actors that dominate the political field but also on those that populate field intersections and organize from there the networks that may give rise to memory regimes. (5) To conceptualize agency in memory politics as both enabled and constrained by the interests prescribed by fields and the unique habitus each actor embodies.

Together, I take these contributions as an invitation to think of memory regimes as networks drawing mnemonic resources from across disparate fields, as tasked with maintaining and reifying a mnemonic identity. These identities are generally more resilient than the elements and processes that sustain them. Regimes of remembrance may project rigidity, but they are actually quite fluid in their composition, as no single network constituent—actor, institution, symbol, i.e., a mnemonic device—is indispensable to the regime. However, components must be replaced carefully and gradually to maintain a semblance of consensus and continuity. Mnemonic identities and their proponents may therefore shift, but they will nevertheless "posture as if the past is incontestably unitary, as unitary as the social group they claim to represent and whose divisions they cannot admit without losing a sense of identity and the right to act in its name" (Olick 2006: 8). A regime's effectiveness will be ultimately predicated on an ability to black-box the necessary choices, negotiations, and exclusions that sustain its attendant identity while maintaining the illusion of a stable, representative, and consensual collective memory.

Here lies the key to my understanding of agency in memory politics. Memory makers will always be entangled in mnemonic coalitions that cannot be arbitrarily changed. Their ability to alter the composition of these networks will be conditional on the fields they inhabit and the habitus they embody, which is why future research on memory politics would do well to focus on the actors engaged in memory-making, the biographies they bring to bear, and what they tell us about their field positions and strategies. As areas where transactions, exchanges, and compromises between fields are negotiated, field intersections provide the greatest realm of possibilities in memory-making. Those actors qualified to inhabit these interstitial spaces—usually as a result of a hybrid professional trajectory/habitus—find themselves in a privileged position. This is a logical consequence of their networks extending into spaces rarely accessible to actors operating within a single field: their interstitial position allows them to overlook and mold the mnemonic networks that traverse various fields. Agency is thus not simply a matter of free, unbridled choice but consists of an awareness of the choices and possibilities at hand, and of an ability to subsequently negotiate the exchanges and coalitions that make memory work successful.

Acknowledgments

This chapter has received funding from the European Union's Horizon 2020 research and innovation program under the Marie Skłodowska-Curie grant agreement No. 707404. The opinions expressed in this document reflect only the author's view. The European Commission is not responsible for any use that may be made of the information it contains.

Zoltan Dujisin is a Marie Curie Leading Fellow at Erasmus University Rotterdam. He obtained his PhD in sociology at Columbia University in New York. He also received an MPhil in political science and an MA in nationalism studies from Central European University in Budapest. He graduated in political science from the Technical University of Lisbon, Portugal. Outside academia, Zoltan worked for almost a decade as a foreign correspondent for Portuguese weekly *Expresso* and Inter Press Service news agency in Kiev, Budapest, and Prague.

Note

1. A most telling example comes from the Baltic states, prominent European promoters of the notion that Nazi and Communist crimes are equivalent. These states have consistently honored renowned historians whose perception of World War II coincides with state narratives. Namely, Estonian presidents have awarded the Estonian Cross of Terra Mariana, a state award given to foreigners who have rendered special services to the country, to Anne Applebaum, Robert Conquest, Stephane Courtois, and Timothy Snyder, all of them endorsers of the totalitarian framework. Lithuania has proceeded similarly.

References

Assmann, Aleida. 2006. "Memory, Individual and Collective." In *The Oxford Handbook of Contextual Political Analysis*, vol. 9, edited by Robert E. Goodin and Charles Tilly, 210–26. Oxford: Oxford University Press.

Bell, Duncan. 2008. "Agonistic Democracy and the Politics of Memory." *Constellations* 15(1): 148–66.

Bernhard, Michael H., and Jan Kubik. 2014. "A Theory of the Politics of Memory." In *Twenty Years after Communism: The Politics of Memory and Commemoration*, edited by Michael H. Bernhard and Jan Kubik, 7–34. Oxford: Oxford University Press.

Bodnar, John E. 1992. *Remaking America: Public Memory, Commemoration, and Patriotism in the Twentieth Century*. Princeton, NJ: Princeton University Press.

Bourdieu, Pierre. 1984. *Homo Academicus*. Stanford, CA: Stanford University Press.

———. 1996. *The Rules of Art: Genesis and Structure of the Literary Field*. Stanford, CA: Stanford University Press.

Bourdieu, Pierre, and Loïc J. D. Wacquant. 1992. *An Invitation to Reflexive Sociology*. Chicago: University of Chicago Press.

Brubaker, Rogers, and Frederick Cooper. 2000. "Beyond 'Identity.'" *Theory and Society* 29(1): 1–47.

Clarke, David. 2014. "Communism and Memory Politics in the European Union." *Central Europe* 12(1): 99–114.

Connerton, Paul. 1989. *How Societies Remember*. Cambridge: Cambridge University Press.

Dujisin, Zoltan. 2015. "Post-Communist Europe: On the Path to a Regional Regime of Remembrance?" In *Thinking through Transition*, edited by M. Kopeček and P. Wciślik, 553–86. New York: Central European University Press.

Engerman, David C. 2009. *Know Your Enemy: The Rise and Fall of America's Soviet Experts*. New York: Oxford University Press.

Eyal, Gil. 2004. "Identity and Trauma: Two Forms of the Will to Memory." *History & Memory* 16(1): 5–36.

———. 2013. "Spaces between Fields." In *Bourdieu and Historical Analysis*, edited by P. S. Gorski, 158–82. Durham, NC: Duke University Press.

Georgakakis, Didier, and Jay Rowell. 2013. *The Field of Eurocracy: Mapping EU Actors and Professionals*. New York: Springer.

Halbwachs, Maurice. 1992. *On Collective Memory*. Chicago: University of Chicago Press.

Holy, Ladislav. 1996. *The Little Czech and the Great Czech Nation: National Identity and the Post-Communist Social Transformation*. Vol. 103. Cambridge: Cambridge University Press.

Huyssen, Andreas. 1993. "Monument and Memory in a Postmodern Age." *Yale Journal of Criticism* 6(2): 249.

Johnson, Richard, and Graham Dawson. 1982. "Popular Memory: Theory, Politics, Method." In *Making Histories: Studies in History-Writing and Politics*, edited by R. Johnson, G. McLennan, B. Schwarz, and D. Sutton, 205–52. Minneapolis: U of Minnesota Press.

Kopeček, Michal. 2011. "The Rise and Fall of Czech Post-Dissident Liberalism after 1989." *East European Politics and Societies* 25(2): 244–71.

Latour, Bruno. 1987. *Science in Action: How to Follow Scientists and Engineers through Society*. Cambridge, MA: Harvard University Press.

Leggewie, Claus. 2010. "Seven Circles of European Memory." *Cultural Memories* 4: 1–29.

Leggewie, Claus, and Erik Meyer. 2005. *Ein Ort, an Den Man Gerne Geht*. Munich: Hanser.

Levy, Daniel. 2011. "Memory Practices and Theory in a Global Age." In *Routledge International Handbook of Contemporary Social and Political Theory*, edited by G. Delanty and S. P. Turner, 482–92. London: Routledge.

Littoz-Monnet, Annabelle. 2012. "The EU Politics of Remembrance: Can Europeans Remember Together?" *West European Politics* 35(5): 1182–202.

Mälksoo, Maria. 2009. "The Memory Politics of Becoming European: The East European Subalterns and the Collective Memory of Europe." *European Journal of International Relations* 15(4): 653–80.

Martin, John Levi. 2003. "What Is Field Theory?" *American Journal of Sociology* 109(1): 1–49.

Mudge, Stephanie Lee, and Antoine Vauchez. 2012. "Building Europe on a Weak Field: Law, Economics, and Scholarly Avatars in Transnational Politics." *American Journal of Sociology* 118(2): 449–92.

Müller, Jan-Werner. 2002. *Memory and Power in Post-War Europe: Studies in the Presence of the Past*. New York: Cambridge University Press.

Nora, Pierre. 2002. "Reasons for the Current Upsurge in Memory." *Transit* 22(1): 4–8.

Olick, Jeffrey K. 2006. "Products, Processes, and Practices: A Non-Reificatory Approach to Collective Memory." *Biblical Theology Bulletin* 36(1): 5–14.

———. 2007. *The Politics of Regret: On Collective Memory and Historical Responsibility*. London: Routledge.

Olick, Jeffrey K., and Joyce Robbins. 1998. "Social Memory Studies: From 'Collective Memory' to the Historical Sociology of Mnemonic Practices." *Annual Review of Sociology* 24(1): 105–40.

Ranger, Terence O., and Eric J. Hobsbawm. 1983. *The Invention of Tradition*. Cambridge: Cambridge University Press.

Sapiro, Gisèle. 2003. "Forms of Politicization in the French Literary Field." *Theory and Society* 32(5–6): 633–52.

Schacter, Daniel L. 1995. "Memory Distortion: History and Current Status." In *Memory Distortion: How Minds, Brains, and Societies Reconstruct the Past*, 1–43. Cambridge: Harvard University Press.

Singh, Sourabh. 2016. "Political Field Dynamics and the Elite's Interest in Democracy: Insights from the Political Elite's Role in Consolidating Indian Democracy." *International Journal of Politics, Culture, and Society* 29(2): 183–208.

Steinmetz, George. 2008. "The Colonial State as a Social Field: Ethnographic Capital and Native Policy in the German Overseas Empire before 1914." *American Sociological Review* 73(4): 589–612.

Steinmetz, George. 2011. "Bourdieu, Historicity, and Historical Sociology." *Cultural Sociology* 5(1): 45–66.

Sturken, Marita. 2008. "Memory, Consumerism and Media: Reflections on the Emergence of the Field." *Memory Studies* 1(1): 73–78.

Swartz, David. 2012. *Culture and Power: The Sociology of Pierre Bourdieu*. Chicago: University of Chicago Press.

Verdery, Katherine. 1996. *What Was Socialism, and What Comes Next?* Princeton, NJ: Princeton University Press.

Wacquant, Loïc. 2016. "A Concise Genealogy and Anatomy of Habitus." *Sociological Review* 64(1): 64–72.

Zarycki, Tomasz. 2009. "The Power of the Intelligentsia: The Rywin Affair and the Challenge of Applying the Concept of Cultural Capital to Analyze Poland's Elites." *Theory and Society* 38(6): 613–48.

Part II

BOTTOM-UP AGENCY

Chapter 2

TRANSNATIONAL MEMORIES AND THE PRACTICES OF GLOBAL JUSTICE IN THE AYOTZINAPA CASE

Silvana Mandolessi

The question of transnational memory is indissolubly linked with the emergence and consolidation of globalization, a process that has undermined and reconfigured the importance of the nation as a locus of meaning. Although a variety of competing—and sometimes contradictory—ways in which to define "globalization" exist, there is agreement on the increase and influence of transnational phenomena in the last four decades. Transnationalism "refers variously to forces, processes, institutions and structures which, by going across, above, below and through hitherto relatively stable national borders, render the latter ever more porous and flexible in complex ways" (Inglis 2016: 143). This proliferation of transnational phenomena as a defining feature of globalization had a profound impact on memory studies. If hitherto the research on the formation of collective memory had been centered on the nation as the privileged territory of inquiry and the realm in which collective memory was defined and contested, the necessity to transcend theses boundaries in order to interrogate memory as a "transnational formation" soon became evident (Erll 2011; De Cesari and Rigney 2014; Assmann and Conrad 2010; Assmann 2014; Bond and Rapson 2014; Sierp and Wüstenberg 2015).

Nevertheless, in spite of the multifarious studies on transnational memory, the role of agency and the social and political effects of transnational memory work have remained undertheorized. Much attention has been devoted to how memory travels and is appropriated in different contexts far from the original one, and how memory becomes hybrid, "multidirectional" (Rothberg), "globital" (Reading), "travelling" (Erll), "cosmopolitan" (Levy and Sznaider), or "unbound" (Bond et al.), but the effects or the outcomes of these movements has aroused less interest in the literature.

As Sierp and Wüstenberg point out in the introduction, "despite the fact that memory research talks a great deal about *actors*, . . . very little has been done to systematically consider the role of *agency* in the making, reproduction, and transformation of memory" (emphasis in original). Since agency implies the power to create change, focusing on agency is essential to understand the extent to which transnational memory work contributes to fight against structural and situational forms of violence, advocating for the respect of human rights in places where these are violated.

In this chapter, I analyze transnational memory following the four elements outlined in the introduction—actors, structures, practices, and outcomes—in the case of the disappearances of forty-three students from Ayotzinapa, Mexico, in 2014. First, I discuss why the issue of agency and the outcomes of transnational memory represents a "hard" aspect for theorization. Then, drawing on the work of Kurasawa (2007), I propose to approach transnational memory as a crucial component of the project of global justice. Kurasawa stresses the importance of conceiving of human rights not as ontological attributes that we enjoy as members of humankind but as a set of *practices*, "capacities that groups and persons produce, activate and must exercise by pursuing ethico-political labor." After sketching the sociopolitical context of the Mexican "War on Drugs," I analyze the transnational memory work in this case in three different initiatives: the work of the Interdisciplinary Group of Independent Experts (GIEI for its Spanish initials), the Forensic Architecture online platform "The Ayotzinapa Case: A Cartography of Violence," and the initiative Ayotzinapa: Visual Action. Read together, these actions cover a spectrum of actors—intergovernmental organizations, research centers, activists, and artists, as well as different dimensions: legal, forensic, aesthetic. Finally, I discuss the potential of "structurally transformative agency" (Hays 1994: 64) to disrupt the structure of impunity that has prevailed in Mexico.

The lack of attention devoted to agency in the study of transnational memory may due to the convergence of different factors. The issue of *agency* and the *outcomes* of transnational memory can be seen as representing either a "hard" aspect for theorization or a shortcoming of certain perspectives adopted to approach this discursive formation.

First and at the most profound level, the temporality of memory is discontinuous. A traumatic event that was not perceived as significant at the time when it happened can remain latent and gain relevance many years or decades after it took place. In this sense, the work of memory carried out by organizations or individuals around this event might appear as having no impact and, thus, no outcomes in the public sphere. When, in a different political or historical situation the event becomes an object of collective memory, it is revealed that the previously unnoticed work followed a kind of subterranean trajectory, producing effects at a time distant from the original one in which it was performed. In order to assess the effects, therefore, it is necessary to pay attention to long-term developments, which involves *expanding the temporal horizons* of memory studies, something that Erll and Rigney in a recent special issue on "Cultural Memory Studies after the Transnational Turn" identify as a necessary step to take discussions forward (Erll and Rigney 2018: 272).

Second, many of the studies on transnational memory have focused on "cultural memory," the flagship concept for scholars approaching the study of memory from various disciplines in the humanities (literary studies, media studies, cultural studies, cultural history), for whom the primary focus of research is culture rather than the actors and institutions involved in its formation (who take center stage in social science research, whose main concept is "collective memory") (Rigney 2016). Here the interest lies in media, forms, symbols, and contents more than in the carriers of memory, which is reflected in how the circulation of memory is often described—movement appears as incessant, continuous, unintentional, restless, without beginning and without end. Erll, for example, defines "travelling memory" as the "*incessant* wandering of carriers, media, contents, forms, and practices of memory, their *continual* 'travels' and *ongoing* transformations through time and space, across social, linguistic and political borders" (2011: 11, emphasis added).

Third, digital media play a crucial role in the transnationalization of memory (Garde-Hansen et al. 2009; Assmann and Conrad 2010; Neiger et al. 2011; Hoskins 2018; Groes 2016). Digital media has a pervasive capacity to connect, distribute, and put objects in motion, giving room to an unprecedented volume of flows. The hyperconnectivity that characterizes digital culture posits a constituting agency that is both technological and human, that is, a different type of agency that, according to Hoskins, is so pervasive that it implies the end of "collective memory" and the emergence of the "memory of the multitude" (Hoskins 2018: 92).

Fourth, even if we focus on the literature from the perspective of social sciences, where authors are more interested in the work performed by concrete actors, the agency and the possibility of assessing the outcomes of these actions still seems difficult. In their pioneering work *Activists beyond Borders* (1998), Keck and Sikkink posit the "boomerang pattern" as a model to explain how transnational advocacy networks influence domestic scenarios. If, for whatever reason, individuals (or organizations) in a country are unable to effectively persuade their government to initiate change, they may nonetheless be able to activate a transnational network focused on the issue. This network can in turn influence other states and international organizations that can then exert pressure on the original state at the global level. As the boomerang pattern model demonstrates, agency is not linear or the property of a single actor but rather results from a combination of diverse "agencies" that interact in complex and recursive ways. Understood in this way, the "boomerang pattern," which has proved to be essential to describe the way in which transnational advocacy networks work, highlights the inherent complexity and the multiplicity of agents and dimensions involved in the analysis. Hence, I argue that the scholarship on transnational advocacy networks and the constitution of a global civil society is the most fruitful framework to analyze agency and outcomes of transnational memory.

Global Civil Society and the Work of Global Justice

In the book *The Work of Global Justice* (2007), Fuyuki Kurasawa proposes a critical theory of global justice. According to Kurasawa, the project of global justice stands as shorthand for numerous and diverse struggles around the planet aiming to fully and universally realize socioeconomic and civil-political rights via an alternative globalization (2007: 2). These struggles are enacted "from below" by what has been called the "global civil society," a constellation of nonstate actors including multiple forms of associations such as nongovernmental organizations, international networks, social movements, campaigns, and activists. Relying on the discourse of human rights, agents in global civil society fight against structural and situational forms of violence, advocating for the respect of human rights in places where these are violated. It is important to highlight that human rights are here conceived of not as—or not only as—ontological attributes that we enjoy as members of humankind or entitlements that are legislated on our behalf by states or international organizations but as a set of *practices*, or, as Kurasawa puts it, "capacities that groups and persons produce, activate and must exercise by pursuing ethico-political labor" (2007: 14). The argument made by Kurasawa relies entirely on the notion of *work*, that is, on the concrete actions performed by groups and individuals in order to transform the "abstract" discourse of human rights into a set of emancipatory possibilities. As Kurasawa puts it,

> Whether or not these possibilities become actualized depends less on formal normative principles and institutional arrangements than on the work of global justice, that is, how and to what extent civic associations enact the social labour required to counter the sources of structural and situational violence around the planet. (2007: 2)

Without this ethico-political labor, human rights are at risk of remaining merely as a well-meaning but ineffective discourse.

What then is the relationship between transnational activism and memory? Memory is the first terrain in which this labor is performed. Based on the human rights discourse, activist groups "push for greater public debate about the past (how do we remember crimes against humanity, and how do we deal with their contemporary effects?), the present (how should we halt collective suffering in our midst, and how do we achieve a just world order?) and the future (how do we avert eventual humanitarian disasters, and how do we promote the capacities of all?), including challenging systemic sources of inequality and domination" (Kurasawa 2007: 3). In this sense, we can affirm that in pursuing the work of global justice, transnational groups and individuals simultaneously perform memory work. Memory originates here because human rights violations that are not recognized as such do not give rise to collective memory. Moreover, in human rights activism, memories from other latitudes are mobilized to make sense of a case, memories not only in terms of content or forms but also of practices and procedures, memories of "knowledge." Paraphrasing Michael Edwards (2011), seen in this way, memory is simultaneously a goal to aim for, a means of achieving it, and a framework for engaging with each other about ends and means. The practices of global justice become (transnational) memory practices that give way to hybrid, local, and cosmopolitan formations of memory. In fact, the five modes of practice of global justice posited by Kurasawa—bearing witness, forgiveness, foresight, aid, and solidarity—are also memory practices. Each of them, although perhaps "aid" to a lesser extent, are regular components of what we conceive of as the work of memory, a work that relates past human rights violations, present suffering, and the possibility of a better future in an inextricable way.

What place does the issue of agency and the assessment of outcomes occupy in this view? Kurasawa states at a general level that the importance attached to *work* and *practice* in his theory counteracts a deterministic view of globalization, a view that presupposes that forces and fluxes work independently from human agents. "Practice" is understood as both "structuring and structured," which means that actors engaging in a mode of practice have the capacity to contribute to the creation, reproduction, and transformation of established relations and institutional fields of power within which it is located (2007: 11–12). Acting together, groups and individuals can obtain results, even if these results are "rather modest" (2007: 15) when we consider the state of the world today. The word "struggle," in fact, points to the "Sisyphean character" of the work of global justice, which essentially consists of perpetually difficult, even flawed and aporetic labor.

The question about the "success" of human rights has provoked vigorous debate among scholars in recent years (De Greiff and Cronin 2002; Bleiker

2004; Chandler 2004; Jordan 2011). The recent book *Evidence for Hope* (2017) by Kathryn Sikkink opens with this question: "Do human rights work? That is, have human rights law, institutions and activism produced positive change in the world?" (Sikkink 2017: 3). Sikkink makes the case that yes, human rights work. In the same vein as Kurasawa, who stresses that there is "no moment of transcendence, finality of perfection" but rather a contingent and constant struggle (Kurasawa 2007: 15), Sikkink contends that change comes slowly, but in the long term, human rights movements have been largely effective. The relevance of this question for memory is rather obvious: given the intrinsic link between human rights and memory—memory has been understood since the inception as *a memory of atrocious past*—to predict the failure of human rights would imply to decree the failure of memory, its incapacity to function as prevention of future atrocities. What is at stake when we formulate questions about the outcomes of memory is no less than one of the premises underpinning the belief in the function of memory work, that is, the "never again" mandate, according to which remembering the atrocities of the past is a crucial condition for preventing their repetition.

In what follows, I draw upon this literature to analyze a recent case of a human rights violation in Mexico, the September 2014 disappearance of forty-three students from Ayotzinapa, which had global resonance. After briefly sketching the context—of Latin America as a region, and Mexico in particular—I examine three transnational initiatives created around the case of Ayotzinapa. I conclude by suggesting how to conceive of the outcomes of transnational memory in this case, when observed against the background of the "undeniable atrocities" that have taken—and are taking—place in the context of the War on Drugs.

The Context

Although Latin America has a long history of structural and situational violence, it is the period of the 1970s and 1980s that has become the privileged object of the construction of memory in the continent. During these decades, many countries underwent serious human rights violations in the context of dictatorships or authoritarian regimes. In the Southern Cone, a series of diverse military coups overthrew elected governments: military forces took power in Chile and Uruguay in 1973 and in Argentina in 1976, while Brazil and Paraguay had begun their long dictatorial experiences several years before, in 1954 and 1964 respectively. The repression was coordinated at the regional level, under what was called "Plan Condor," resulting in thousands of deaths, political prisoners, exiles, and disappeared persons.

It was the human rights movement that became the pivotal force behind inscribing dictatorial repression as a "violation of human rights." This required a change of paradigm: before, domination and social and political struggles were interpreted in terms of class struggles or national revolutions. With the advent of the human rights movement, memory policies were framed in human rights terms.

Interesting to note is that it was not political parties who led this paradigmatic change but a wide network that included relatives of victims, members of religious communities, activists, and intellectuals—new social movements that until then had not had leadership or a visible presence in the public sphere. Women, for example, became key players, particularly in Argentina with groups that would become emblematic, such as the Mothers and Grandmothers of Plaza de Mayo (Jelin 2017: 49–50).

Together with domestic human rights networks, supporting their struggles and amplifying their demands, transnational actors played a crucial role during the period. Focusing on Argentina, which can be considered the paradigmatic case of the Southern Cone, Keck and Sikkink attribute this success to the working together of domestic and transnational networks. In *Activists beyond Borders* (1998), they show how the human rights movement in Argentina was supported by a transnational advocacy network:

> The value of the network perspective in the Argentine case is in highlighting the fact that international pressures did not work independently, but rather in coordination with national actors. Rapid change occurred because strong domestic human rights organizations documented abuses and protested against repression, and international pressures helped protect domestic monitors and open spaces for their protest. International groups amplified both information and symbolic politics of domestic groups and projected them onto an international stage, from which they echoed back into Argentina. This classic boomerang process was executed nowhere more skilfully than in Argentina. (Keck and Sikkink 1998: 118)

While Argentina appears as "the" example of effective work of transnational advocacy networks, Keck and Sikkink consider Mexico as the "counterexample" of these struggles. In the same period, Mexico failed to attract the attention of the international community to the massacre of the students in Tlatelolco Square in 1968.

In fact, Mexico is frequently considered an atypical case within Latin America. While the Southern Cone countries endured very repressive military dictatorships during the 1970s and 1980s, Mexico maintained a long-established civil government, the political structure of which did not change substantially until the 1990s. While the South American dictatorships adopted a language on the extreme right that radicalized the anticommunist discourse of the Cold War, the Mexican government adopted slogans emanating from the Revolution at the beginning of the century and attacked the human-rights-violating practices of dictatorships in human rights forums, while also providing asylum to many politically persecuted individuals from South America (Dutrénit Bielous and Varela Petito 2010: 11–12). However, during the same period, the Mexican state carried out a policy of repression against political activists and social leaders during the so-called "Dirty War." As a result of this policy, there are currently more than six hundred cases of persons who disappeared at the hands of the Mexican government during that period and which have been registered by state agencies such as the National Human Rights Commission (CNDH). Unofficial figures estimate the number of disappeared persons between six and twelve hundred, yet official responsibility has not been recognized in all of these cases.

Although relatives have requested clarification regarding the whereabouts of the disappeared and demanded justice since the 1970s, their struggle against impunity remains largely invisible. As Sylvia Karl states,

> The Mexican Dirty War is a somewhat forgotten event, both in Mexican and international conflict recollection . . . In thinking of political violence and Dirty Wars in Latin America, Mexico is not often the first country to come to mind. (Karl 2014: 2)

The disappearances that took place in the framework of the Dirty War of the 1970s and 1980s belong to a first wave of disappearances. Since 2006, with the beginning of the War on Drugs, a new and complex scenario emerged in Mexico, characterized by an essential ambivalence: while, on the one hand, violence has increased in the last decade in an inconceivable way, the framework in which violence is exercised poses a problem to frame it as violations of human rights. Since the beginning of the "war," nearly two hundred thousand people have been killed and more than sixty thousand have disappeared. But the violations of human rights—particularly of physical integrity rights, such as arbitrary detentions, torture, executions, and disappearances—were not seen as "real" violations of human rights norms capable of stirring international attention. According to Anaya Muñoz (2013) Mexico represents a "hard case" for the globalization of human rights law, for two main reasons: first, a large proportion of victims of violence were presumed to be actively involved in criminal activities, and thus they could not easily be presented as innocent or vulnerable individuals worthy of solidarity and protection from international actors. Second, the human rights regime is based on the enduring principle of state responsibility. In this case the direct perpetrators are presumed to be nonstate actors, namely, criminal organizations. Alleged involvement of the victims in criminal activities and lack of evidence for direct involvement of the state as perpetrator were the main causes preventing the effective framing of deaths in Mexico as violations of human rights.

The Ayotzinapa Case: Global Civil Society and the Work of Global Justice

On the night of 26 September 2014 and into the early hours of 27 September, students from the Escuela Normal Rural de Ayotzinapa were attacked by local police acting in collusion with criminal organizations in the town of Iguala, Guerrero. Numerous other branches of the Mexican security apparatus were also involved in the assault, including state and federal police forces and the military. Six people were murdered—including three students—forty wounded, and forty-three students forcibly disappeared. In an attempt to close the case, the Mexican state constructed a fraudulent narrative—*verdad histórica* (historical truth)—according to which the students were assassinated by the cartel Guerreros Unidos and then incinerated in the Cocula landfill. The whereabouts of the students remain unknown, and their status as disappeared continues to this day.

The mass disappearance brought about the biggest political crisis in Mexico in the last decade. In contrast to other cases that have taken place during the War on Drugs, this case also resonated particularly strongly in the global arena. During the months following the disappearance of the forty-three students, transnational actors became actively involved in different practices of denouncing the crime and demanding justice.

Global civil society became involved in the Ayotzinapa case in three ways that can be described as follows: *forms* of association life, such as international nongovernmental associations (INGOs), social movements, and human rights organizations, organized campaigns to denounce the violation and demand justice; these agents based their collective work on the *norms* of a good society, defined by values such as cooperation, nonviolence, and respect for human rights; finally, these struggles, taken together, formed *a global arena for public deliberation* (Jordan 2011: 94).

Among the many actions performed as modes of practice of the work of global justice in the Ayotzinapa case, I will explore three: the work of the Interdisciplinary Group of Independent Experts (GIEI), the Forensic Architecture online platform "The Ayotzinapa Case: A Cartography of Violence," and the initiative Ayotzinapa: Visual Action. Read together, these actions cover a spectrum of actors—intergovernmental organizations, research centers, activists and artists, as well as different dimensions: legal, forensic, aesthetic. All of them enact the work of global justice through the practice of bearing witness and solidarity (Kurasawa 2007).

The Inter-American Commission on Human Rights and the Work of the GIEI

The Mexican government initiated an investigation of the case shortly after the disappearance of the students. However, this investigation was questioned from the beginning, marked by inconsistencies, irregularities, and the suspicion that the government wanted to quickly "close" the case by shifting blame to local forces and organized crime and thus obliterating the federal government's responsibility in what happened. Faced with this situation, the Inter-American Commission on Human Rights, an intergovernmental body that plays a central role in Latin America, in agreement with representatives of the victims and the Mexican state, intervened and formed an independent expert group to investigate the case.

The GIEI (Grupo Interdisciplinario de Expertos Independientes) was made up of five specialists from different Latin American and European countries who carried out an independent investigation in two stages between 2015 and 2016 on the forced disappearance of the students. Drawing on the sources and data provided by the government and their own research, the GIEI produced two reports. Although this investigation could not discover the ultimate truth of the facts since the whereabouts of the students remain unknown to this day, the work of the GIEI was fundamental to deny the version that was—and continues to be—sustained by the Mexican government. According to the *verdad histórica*, the police handed the students over to members of Guerreros Unidos, who took them to a rubbish dump outside of the town of Cocula where they killed them and burned the bodies on a pyre. Their remains were then collected in plastic bags and dumped into a river. On the contrary, the GIEI showed that the alleged incineration of the students was scientifically impossible. Moreover, in its reports, the GIEI contextualizes the violence historically, highlights the necessary measures that have to be taken to assist the relatives of the victims—who are victims themselves because the crime of enforced disappearance implies psychological wounds sustained from the uncertainty and the impossibility to mourn—and makes recommendations to the Mexican government regarding the investigation of human rights violations in the country. By contesting the "historical truth," the name that the government itself uses for its version of what happened, the GIEI shows that Ayotzinapa was not an isolated case. On the contrary, the reports describe how the government tried to cover up information and evidence, thereby placing the case into a wider context of state-sponsored violence. Far from being a singular case or an exception that can be reduced to the local level, the reports show the extent of corruption and involvement of all levels of the state.

"This report provides an utterly damning indictment of Mexico's handling of the worst human rights atrocity in recent memory," said José Miguel Vivanco, director of the Americas division at Human Rights Watch (Human Rights Watch 2015). Following the report of the GIEI, the Inter-American Commission on Human Rights created "The Special Follow-Up Mechanism for the Ayotzinapa Case" (MESA, for its Spanish initials), which monitors compliance with Precautionary Measure 409/14 and with the recommendations that the GIEI formulated in its two reports. MESA grants the families of the forty-three missing students a central role in its efforts.

The Inter-American Commission on Human Rights (IACHR), along with the Inter-American Court of Human Rights, is one of the bodies that comprise the Inter-American system for the promotion and protection of human rights in the continent. As an independent legal organ, the commission's intervention in domestic scenarios, such as this case, always has a strong impact. Even if the results of this intervention in terms of achieving justice can be considered partial or incomplete, the authority of the commission as an independent body that imposes limits on the power of a national government challenges the prevailing structural impunity. As is clear in the case of Ayotzinapa, the transnational legal framework allows domestic actors to seek justice when the channels in their country are blocked. Even if achieving justice ultimately depends on the political will of the national government, without the intervention of transnational legal mechanisms and bodies, such as the IACHR, the demand for justice becomes even more precarious.

In terms of memory, the GIEI was the product of legal mechanisms in which a regional memory of past human rights violations is inscribed—and not only a memory of the violations but also a memory of activism, of the struggles that led to the very existence of these norms and frameworks. At the same time, and considering the involvement of the Argentine Forensic Anthropology Team (EAAF) in this case, it is also possible to identify the existence of a memory of *knowledge*, of *procedures* that were learned and then transmitted in the context of struggles against human rights violations and are then recuperated and transnationalized. Thus, beyond the strict legal framework, the intervention of the IACHR represents the circulation of transnational memories on disappearances across and beyond boundaries. The regional character of the body, far from limiting this circulation, reinforces its meaning.

"The Ayotzinapa Case: A Cartography of Violence"

A very different initiative, although connected with the previous one, is the platform "The Ayotzinapa Case: A Cartography of Violence," designed by Forensic Architecture in 2017. Forensic Architecture is an independent research agency based at Goldsmiths, University of London, composed of an interdisciplinary team of investigators, including architects, scholars, artists, filmmakers, software developers, investigative journalists, archaeologists, lawyers, and scientists. They often undertake collaborative investigations with partners, such as Amnesty International, Human Rights Watch, and Centro para la Acción Legal en Derechos Humanos, and work with international offices such as the UN Special Rapporteur for Counter-Terrorism and Human Rights. Forensic Architecture combines a set of innovative tools—architectural analysis, models, and animations—to investigate human rights violations and uncover facts denied by governments. This evidence is presented in political and legal contexts, including international courts, truth commissions, and human rights and environmental forums. The work of Forensic Architecture involves not only a redefinition of the terms "forensic" and "architecture," which shift each other's meaning when brought together, but also an innovative way of conceiving the relationship between "aesthetic" and "research" in the context of human rights activism.

In 2017, Forensic Architecture was commissioned by—and worked in collaboration with—the EAAF and Centro de Derechos Humanos Miguel Agustín Pro Juárez (Centro Prodh, one of the leading Mexican nongovernmental organizations) to create an interactive cartographic platform to map out the different narratives of the attack on the students from Ayotzinapa. The collaboration itself conveys the entanglement of national and transnational actors and the mobilization of resources from European as well as American sources. As they describe it,

> The project aims to reconstruct, for the first time, the entirety of the known events that took place that night in and around Iguala, and to provide a forensic tool for researchers to further the investigation. The data on which the platform is based draws from publicly available investigations, videos, media histories, photographs and phone logs. The first and more important of our sources are two reports by a group of five experts referred to as the International Group of Independent Experts (GIEI) . . .
>
> Thousands of pages of reports have thereafter been broken down into almost five thousand data-points, each recording a single reported incident, such as an instance of two-way communication, movements or the mishandling of evidence. These data-points have been located, timed and tagged according to the actors involved, and the type of incident they describe. Each data-point is also assigned a narrative description.
>
> This demonstrates, in a clear graphic and cartographic form, the level of collusion and coordination between state agencies and organised crime, throughout the night . . .

The project thus reveals a cartography of violence spanning from the street corner level to the entire state of Guerrero. It describes an act of violence that is no longer a singular event but a prolonged act, which persists to this day in the continued absence of the 43 students.

It also seeks to demonstrate the way in which collective civil society initiatives, undertaking independent investigations using innovative analytical tools, could help investigate complex crimes and confront criminal impunity and the failures of Mexican law enforcement.

In particular, it reaffirms our commitment to heal the open wound of the Ayotzinapa case and to work until the truth of the night is clarified, and the students' whereabouts are known. (https://www.forensic-architecture.org)

Unlike other investigations that Forensic Architecture conducted, the Ayotzinapa project did not present new evidence. Among the main sources used were the two reports published by the GIEI and the book *Una historia oral de la infamia: Los ataques a los normalistas de Ayotzinapa* (2016) by John Gibler, a book composed entirely of interviews conducted with survivors in the months following the disappearance. Rather than uncovering new evidence, Forensic Architecture instead honed in this project the practice of collating and presenting data in an accessible manner.

In addition to the platform, the project was exhibited as part of Forensic Architecture: Towards an Investigative Aesthetic from 9 September 2017 until 7 January 2018 at the Museo Universitario de Arte Contemporáneo (MUAC) in Mexico City.

Taking into account that this platform utilizes the reports published by the GIEI as one of its main sources, it is possible to establish both a continuation as well as significant differences. Both are investigations whose main goal is to uncover the truth. Forensic Architecture developed this platform not as a new investigation to add more or better evidence to a trial but as a way to communicate what happened that night to a global audience. Instead of using the established format of a "report," a principal way in which NGOs perform the task of "information politics" (Keck and Sikkink 1998), they developed an aesthetic object—the platform—that was exhibited in museums. Unlike the report, the interactive character of the platform engages the visitor, who also becomes a detective in a certain sense who has to discover the facts while navigating the website. The exhibition at the MUAC also encompassed immersive experiences, such as entering a dark room that reproduces the acoustic experience of a prison in Saydnaya.

"We share our work with the public via leading research and cultural institutes. Our main beneficiaries are always the victims of human rights violations, and communities in conflict zones or otherwise subject to state failure or violence," they affirm. Here, "public" appeals to a global civil society capable of being interpellated by the event and multiplying the efforts to achieve justice.

Ayotzinapa: Visual Action

Ayotzinapa: Visual Action was an initiative launched by the Argentine photographer Marcelo Brodsky, together with the Centro de Derechos Humanos de la Montaña Tlachinollan in November 2014. For this action, Brodsky invited people from all over the world to photograph themselves in groups with the slogan that has become a symbol for the search of the disappeared: "Vivos se los llevaron, vivos los queremos" (They took them alive, we want them alive). The initiative was aimed to create a transnational campaign that could help provide legitimacy to the cause through the expression of solidarity with the local activists. The relevance of Ayotzinapa: Visual Action is that, beyond constituting an enactment of two modes of practices of the work of global justice—bearing witness and solidarity—it draws upon transnational memories on disappearance, particularly from Argentina, to reframe the meaning of the event.

Due to a strong response to the initiative, Visual Action became an exhibition composed of hundreds of photos from all over the world. While the primary space of exhibition was the web, I analyze here a book publication that gathers a selection of the pictures from the action, as well as a compilation of other photos, short texts, and essays related to the case. The first part of the book—the Action—is composed of fifty-two photos. All of them follow a similar pattern with slight variations. The pictures depict an assemblage of people standing or sitting in rows, facing the camera directly.

The participants are holding up banners. These are either letters placed together to show the complete message or single banners in which the manifestation chant is fully included. Along with the most important slogan, "They took them alive, we want them alive," one can find "Justice for Ayotzinapa," "We are all Ayotzinapa," "No podemos ni queremos olvidar," "We can't and don't want to forget," mostly in Spanish. The settings also vary: some are taken outdoors, in scenarios that can be easily recognizable, such as Nueva Delhi in India or La Boca in Buenos Aires, while others are framed in spaces such as the European Center for Constitutional Rights in Berlin or the University of New Brunswick in Canada.

The photos perform a transnational community of belonging composed by anonymous individuals that can nevertheless unite in a new transnational space created by the photos themselves. The more remote the place depicted, the stronger the idea that Ayotzinapa is a cause with such an importance that it received the attention of communities far away, for example from Bangladesh.

Despite their differences, the photos are identical in the message that each and all of the people convey and the solidarity with the cause of Ayotzinapa, which is inscribed in the slogans, the photos of the disappeared students, or in the use of the term "Ayotzinapa" itself. But *solidarity*—even if it is the most conventional meaning and therefore the most explicit—is neither the exclusive nor the main meaning that these carefully staged photos aim to transmit. Read as a whole, the initiative aims to contest the Mexican structures of impunity by framing the disappearances of the students of Ayotzinapa as an "enforced disappearance," and thus as a human rights violation perpetrated by the state.

To do so, the initiative operates by reframing the issue. Keck and Sikkink stress that building cognitive frames is an essential component of networks' political strategies. If the new framework succeeds, it will influence broader public understanding, which is called *frame resonance* (Keck and Sikkink 2011: 28–29).

For reframing the issue, the exhibition removes the disappearance of the forty-three students from the frame of the War on Drugs—where the boundaries between victims and perpetrators are blurred and the responsibility of the state as perpetrator is not clear—and inscribes it in the long history of enforced disappearances experienced by Latin America in the 1970s and 1980s, linking it particularly with Argentina. It does so by mobilizing the repertoire of the Argentine visual legacy and applying it in order to give meaning to the event in Mexico. Visual Action thus closely links both contexts—Argentina and Mexico—so that they become, in certain sense, identical.

The first photo we see in Visual Action is not one of the group pictures showing transnational solidarity with Ayotzinapa but the picture *Buena Memoria* (Good Memory), a well-known work of Marcelo Brodsky. Brodsky, who launched the initiative, is an Argentine visual artist known for his exhibitions and essays on memory. These include works such as *Nexus, Tree Time, Visual Correspondences*, or *1968: The Fire of Ideas*.

Buena Memoria is a visual essay that deals with the collective memory of the years under the Argentine dictatorship. It consists of a class picture of 1967 of the Colegio Nacional de Buenos Aires, the artist's own class picture. In their essay on the work, Marianne Hirsch and Leo Spitzer describe it as follows:

> The depicted children are lined up in four rows facing forward and smiling; some are looking off to the side . . .
> In the installation, the picture is intact but blown up to huge proportions (Brodsky labels it a "gigantograph"). But each of the children's bodies is inscribed with a brief text written on the photo that connects the past to the present, some faces are circled and others are circled and crossed out. The text is simple, abbreviated: "Silvia is very tall as always. She is a physical therapist;"

Figure 2.1. *La Clase.* © Marcelo Brodsky, 1996.

"Carlos is a graphic designer;" "Claudio was killed fighting the military in December 1975."

In "Buena Memoria" the violent mark of erasure on the skin-like surface of the photographic print recalls the violence of selecting individuals out of the social body with the intention of annihilating them and their memory. The lines etched into the surface of the print transmit that violence, puncturing us as viewers. (Hirsch and Spitzer 2014: 270)

The second photograph we see in Visual Action is also a class picture of the Colegio Nacional de Buenos Aires. Instead of being a testimony of the past, this photo features the present. We see a class picture of 2014, in which young students of the Buenos Aires school are facing the camera holding up individual signs that together form the slogan "They took them alive, we want them alive/ Ayotzinapa," along with flags of Argentina and Mexico. The image serves as a bridge between past and present, as well as between the two countries. These students are aware of the fate of the disappeared students of the Colegio Nacional—the students recorded in the photo of 1967 were once sitting in that same classroom, playing in the same corridors—and it is precisely out of this memory of state terrorism, violence, and loss that they act in solidarity with the students suffering the same fate in the present—those of Ayotzinapa. Almost everyone looks solemn, serious, largely hopeless. Although appropriate for the occasion, this somber look contrasts with the expected cheerfulness typical of youth. In this regard, the prevailing atmosphere of the photo of *Buena Memoria* from 1967 diverges remarkably from that of 2014. The dissonance between the grief and sorrow of the facial expressions and the qualities of youth exposes the vulnerability of the group. They are young, they have a life to enjoy, they are innocent, but life reveals itself to be precarious, as it can be suddenly snatched away by the state. The viewer is confronted with the imminence of a violence that the students of the Colegio Nacional could, but fortunately did not, suffer. Moreover, what they testify to is the very absence of those lives that have been taken. In demanding the reappearance of the missing students from Ayotzinapa, they represent the image that is not included in the series, the photograph of the students alive. An impossible object—the disappeared picture, the picture of the disappeared—becomes the *punctum* of the project, an archival document of the erasure by violence. The exhibition thus conflates two temporalities: the meaning it aims to transmit is that what happened to the students of the Colegio Nacional de Buenos Aires in 1967 has happened again in Mexico, but with more cruelty. While in the initial photo two faces have been crossed out, in the missing picture we would see forty-three faces erased.

Figure 2.2. *Vivos.* © Marcelo Brodsky, Colegio Nacional de Bs. As., 2014.

Conclusion

The initiatives analyzed, though merely brief examples of the multiple ways in which global civil society became involved in the Ayotzinapa case, show the convergence of different strategies, as well as the common values underpinning the work of global justice. Did these initiatives work? Did they help to bring about a significant change? The answer depends on how we measure their impact. On the one hand, Ayotzinapa definitively opened up the debate on enforced disappearance in the country. Highlighting that Ayotzinapa was not an isolated case but an example of the complex situation of disappearances in the framework of the War on Drugs helped to bring visibility and meaning to the phenomenon. Groups of relatives of disappeared that existed from the period of the Dirty War and newly formed groups of relatives from the War on Drugs united in a new umbrella group called Movimiento por Nuestros Desaparecidos in order to struggle against disappearance in the political, social, and legislative dimensions. The Movimiento demanded a specific legal framework to address disappearances, and a new law was in fact approved in 2017. The Ley General en Materia de Desaparición Forzada de Personas, Desaparición Cometida por Particulares y del Sistema Nacional de Búsqueda de Personas adapts the international framework on enforced disappearance to the particularities of the Mexican context.

Even though some of these collectives and organizations existed before, Ayotzinapa helped them to articulate their demands in the framework of a unified a movement, which strengthened them. Many publications, documentaries, and films that discuss the history of disappearances tell the story of the current situation of violence in the country and recover a memory of human rights violations. From this perspective, the work of a transnational advocacy network that amplified the phenomenon not only made it visible and provided it with meaning but also helped to achieve concrete outcomes, such as the new law and measures to fight against enforced disappearance in the complex Mexican scenario.

Nevertheless, a more skeptical perspective is also possible. After all the activism that took—and still takes—place around Ayotzinapa, the case remains unsolved, and the whereabouts of the students have not been determined. Justice has not been achieved. At a general level, violence in Mexico has not decreased since 2014. The last years have registered the highest numbers of dead and disappeared people since 2006. For many activists who appeared hopeful about the possibility of change, Ayotzinapa meant a disillusion (Velez 2017).

Therefore, a categorical answer to the question "Does transnational civil society bring about change in struggling against human rights violations?" is not possible. If we measure the results in terms of radical change, the answer is probably no. But, if we consider, as Kurasawa or Sikkink suggest, that the results to be expected are always incomplete, contingent, and limited, and that the work of global justice has a Sisyphean character with no moment of transcendence, the answer changes to a more optimistic position. The Ayotzinapa case shows that even if partial or incomplete, the transnational work of memory has provided a frame and established new resources to continue the struggle.

Acknowledgments

This research has received funding from the European Research Council (ERC) under the European Union's Horizon 2020 research and innovation program ("Digital Memories," Grant agreement n° 677955).

Silvana Mandolessi is professor of cultural studies at KU Leuven. She is the author of *Digital Reason: A Guide to Meaning, Medium, Community in a Modern World* (with Jan Baetens and Ortwin de Graef) (2020) and coeditor of *El pasado inasequible: Desaparecidos, hijos y combatientes en el arte y la literatura del nuevo milenio* (2018), *Estudios sobre memoria: Perspectivas actuales y nuevos escenarios* (2015), and *Transnational Memory in the Hispanic World* (2014). She is currently director of the ERC project "We Are All Ayotzinapa: The Role of Digital Media in the Shaping of Transnational Memories on Disappearance."

References

Anaya Muñoz, Alejandro. 2013. "Non-state Actors as Violators in Mexico: A Hard Case for Global Human Rights Norms." In *The Politics of the Globalization of Law: Getting from Rights to Justice*, edited by Alison Brysk, 180–98. New York: Routledge.
Assmann, Aleida. 2014. "Transnational Memories." *European Review* 22 (4): 546–556.
Assmann, Aleida, and Sebastian Conrad, eds. 2010. *Memory in a Global Age: Discourses, Practices and Trajectories*. Basingstoke: Palgrave Macmillan.
Bleiker, Roland. 2004. *Popular Dissent, Human Agency and Global Politics*. Cambridge: Cambridge University Press.
Bond, Lucy, and Jessica Rapson, eds. 2014. *The Transcultural Turn: Interrogating Memory Between and Beyond Borders*. Berlin: De Gruyter.
Bond, Lucy, Stef Craps, and Peter Vermeulen, eds. 2017. *Memory Unbound: Tracing the Dynamics of Memory Studies*. New York: Berghahn Books.
Brodsky, Marcelo, ed. 2015. *Ayotzinapa: Acción Visual*. Santiago de Chile: Museo de la Memoria y los Derechos Humanos.

Chandler, David. 2004. *Constructing Global Civil Society: Morality and Power in International Relations*. Basingstoke: Palgrave Macmillan.
De Cesari, Chiara, and Ann Rigney, eds. 2014. *Transnational Memory: Circulation, Articulation, Scales*. Berlin: De Gruyter.
De Greiff, Pablo, and Ciaran Cronin, eds. 2002. *Global Justice and Transnational Politics: Essays on the Moral and Political Challenges of Globalization*. Cambridge, MA: MIT Press.
Dutrénit Bielous, Silvia, and Gonzalo Varela Petito. 2010. *Tramitando el pasado: Violaciones de los derechos humanos y agendas gubernamentales en casos latinoamericanos*. México: Flacso México.
Edwards, Michael, ed. 2011. *The Oxford Handbook of Civil Society*. Oxford: Oxford University Press.
Erll, Astrid. 2011. "Travelling Memory." *Parallax* 17(4): 4–18.
Erll, Astrid, and Ann Rigney. 2018. "Editorial." In "Cultural Memory Studies after the Transnational Turn," special issue, *Memory Studies* 11(3): 272–73.
Forensic Architecture. 2017. "Ayotzinapa: una cartografía de la violencia." Retrieved 17 March 2020 from http://www.plataforma-ayotzinapa.org/.
Garde-Hansen, Joanne, Andrew Hoskins, and Anna Reading, eds. 2009. *Save as . . . Digital Memories*. Basingstoke: Palgrave Macmillan.
Groes, Sebastian, ed. 2016. *Memory in the Twenty-First Century: New Critical Perspectives from the Arts, Humanities, and Sciences*. Basingstoke: Palgrave Macmillan.
Grupo Interdisciplinario de Expertos Independientes. 2015. *Informe Ayotzinapa: Investigación y primeras conclusiones de las desapariciones y homicidios de los normalistas de Ayotzinapa*. México: Grupo Interdisciplinario de Expertos Independientes.
———. 2016. *Informe Aytozinapa II: Avances y nuevas conclusiones sobre la investigación, búsqueda y atención a las víctimas*. México: Grupo Interdisciplinario de Expertos Independientes.
Hays, Sharon. 1994. "Structure and Agency and the Sticky Problem of Culture." *Sociological Theory* 12(1): 57–72.
Hirsch, Marianne, and Leo Spitzer. 2014. "School Photos and their Afterlives." In *Feeling Photography*, edited by Elspeth Brown and Thy Phu, 252–273. Durham: Duke University Press.
Hoskins, Andrew. 2018. "Memory of the Multitude: The End of Collective Memory." In *Digital Memory Studies: Media Pasts in Transition*, edited by Andrew Hoskins, 85–109. New York: Routledge. Kindle.
Human Rights Watch. 2015. "Mexico: Damning Report on Disappearances," September 6. Retrieved 16 March 2020 from https://www.hrw.org/news/2015/09/06/mexico-damning-report-disappearances.
Inglis, David. 2016. "Globalization and/of Memory: On the Complexification and Contestation of Memory Cultures and Practices." In *Routledge International Handbook of Memory Studies*, edited by Anna Lisa Tota and Trever Hagen, 143–57. London: Routledge.
Jelin, Elizabeth. 2017. *La lucha por el pasado: Cómo construimos la memoria social*. Buenos Aires: Siglo XXI.
Jordan, Lisa. 2011. "Global Civil Society." In *The Oxford Handbook of Civil Society*, edited by Michael Edwards, 93–105. Oxford: Oxford University Press.
Karl, Sylvia. 2014. "Missing in Mexico: Denied Victims, Neglected Stories." *Culture & History Digital Journal* 3(2): 1–17.
Keck, Margaret E., and Kathryn Sikkink. 1998. *Activists beyond Borders: Advocacy Networks in International Politics*. Ithaca, NY: Cornell University Press.
Keck, Margaret E., and Kathryn Sikkink. 2011. "Transnational Advocacy Networks in the Movement Society." In *Global Activism Reader*, edited by Luc Reydams, 24–34. New York: Continuum.

Kurasawa, Fuyuki. 2007. *The Work of Global Justice: Human Rights as Practices.* Cambridge: Cambridge University Press.

Neiger, Motti, Oren Meyers, and Eyal Zandberg, eds. 2011. *On Media Memory: Collective Memory in a New Media Age.* Basingstoke: Palgrave Macmillan.

Levy, Daniel, and Natan Sznaider. 2006. *The Holocaust and Memory in the Global Age.* Translated by Assenka Oksiloff. Philadelphia: Temple University Press.

Reading, Anna. 2011. "Memory and Digital Media: Six Dynamics of the Globital Memory Field." In *On Media Memory: Collective Memory in a New Media Age*, edited by Motti Neiger, Oren Meyers, and Eyal Zandberg, 241–252. Basingstoke: Palgrave Macmillan.

Rigney, Ann. 2016. "Cultural Memory Studies: Mediation, Narrative, and the Aesthetic." In *Routledge International Handbook of Memory Studies*, edited by Anna Lisa Tota and Trever Hagen, 65–76. London: Routledge.

Rothberg, Michael. 2009. *Multidirectional Memory: Remembering the Holocaust in the Age of Decolonization.* Stanford, CA: Stanford University Press.

Sierp, Aline, and Jenny Wüstenberg. 2015. "Linking the Local and the Transnational: Rethinking Memory Politics in Europe." *Journal of Contemporary European Studies* 23(3): 321–329.

Sikkink, Kathryn. 2017. *Evidence for Hope: Making Human Rights Work in the 21st Century.* Princeton: Princeton University Press.

Vélez, Alejandro. 2017. "México, entre ilusiones transicionales y violencias inasibles." In *La ilusión de la justicia transicional: Perspectivas críticas desde el sur global*, edited by Alejandro Castillejo Cuéllar, 431–453. Bogotá: Universidad de los Andes.

Chapter 3

ONLINE TRANSNATIONAL MEMORY ACTIVISM AND COMMEMORATION

The Case of the White Armband Day

Orli Fridman and Katarina Ristić

This chapter explores new forms of online commemorative practices and memory activism taking place on social media. More specifically, it analyzes online memory activism as manifested in the recurring online commemoration of the White Armband Day (Dan bijelih traka). We argue that the establishment of this online transnational memory network commemorating the atrocities committed in 1992 (during the war in Bosnia) in the town of Prijedor has managed to set 31 May as an important date for memory politics and memory activism in Bosnia-Herzegovina (henceforth "Bosnia") and the entire posåt-Yugoslav region. We analyze the ways in which the commemoration of the White Armband Day has emerged from a locally initiated protest against a ban on commemorating the twentieth anniversary of the events of 1992 into a reoccurring online transnational commemorative event, taking place annually on 31 May on social media, mainly Facebook, Twitter, and YouTube. Since its emergence, participants of this online commemoration have posted images of themselves wearing a white armband reminiscent of the order given in 1992 to non-Serbian communities in the town of Prijedor in Bosnia to mark their houses with white strips and put a white band on their left arms. We analyze this form of commemoration as an online transnational event that has great significance for memory politics beyond the local and national levels, as it has become significant for broader regional and transnational mnemonic practices, mobilizing thousands of people to participate and crossing borders, languages, and ethno-national belongings. We argue that the use of such online platforms for alternative commemorations, and the internationalization of the cause, have enabled the once-banned onsite commemorations to take place. It also has enabled and created the space for new alternative memory of the war that goes beyond the ethnicization of the victims (from here on de-ethnicized memory) to emerge and be more visible.

Our analysis addresses the following questions: Who was engaged in these online mnemonic practices, and what tactics did they employ? Who was the driving force behind the transnationalization of this mnemonic practice, and how did it occur? Do such transnational spaces for remembering silenced and denied atrocities and war crimes have the potential for the creation of new transnational mnemonic communities and novel mnemonic practices, significant for future politics of memory in the post-Yugoslav space? Can online memory activism enhance agency and enable additional venues for mnemonic practices? Finally, we highlight the need for further research focusing on online digital memory activism within the study of online activism.

In this chapter we approach these questions by focusing on (1) the actors who initiated and participated in the creation of this online transnational memory network, and their practices (digitally enabled connective actions, from forbidden onsite to online); (2) reactions to hegemonic memory politics of silence and denial (created by and resulting from the obstacles and opportunities provided by different political structures forbidding onsite commemorations) and the development of a de-ethnicized, bottom-up memory culture; and finally, (3) the outcomes of online memory activism (from online to onsite, from transnational to local).

We focus on the case study of the town of Prijedor in northwest Bosnia, which reflects the challenges of engaging in memory activism in a climate of silence and denial. As one Sarajevo-based scholar and activist put it, "The background of everything here [in Bosnia] is the war and the silence that followed . . . when you break the silence, you break the fear" (Ahmetašević 2015b). In what follows, we analyze the creation of the online commemorations of the White Armband Day and its link to the onsite commemorations, through the lenses of memory activism, as generating alternative knowledge in spaces otherwise dominated by silence and denial.

The Creation of the White Armband Day: A Short Overview

We situate the creation of the White Armband Day in a broader framework of analysis of the memory landscape and memory activism in postwar Bosnia.[1] This memory landscape, as Nicolas Moll (2013) has documented, can be approached within the framework of the political fragmentation and competition within the country, along ethno-national lines cemented by the Dayton Peace Agreement (DPA) that ended the war in 1995. The construction of three ethno-national identities (of the three constituent peoples, i.e., Bosniaks,[2] Serbs, and Croats) in Bosnia have been accompanied by strong memory politics and public commemorations (Moll 2013: 911). Often in Bosnia, the very same events are commemorated in various ways, given different or even contradictory interpretations, as no single community dominates the public memory landscape. Memory landscapes in Bosnia are therefore complex and fragmented but cannot and should not be reduced to those three ethno-national narratives alone.[3] Commemorative practices were developed within different political and administrative frameworks (Moll 2013: 912), especially as local communities commemorate past events and war crimes—a dynamic that makes the memory landscape even more fragmented and contested. Atrocities committed in the Prijedor area in 1992 during the war in Bosnia are well documented. As research shows, although war crime courts have compiled ample evidence about the ethnic cleansing of non-Serbs organized by Serbian forces in the municipality of Prijedor at the beginning of the 1992–95 war, the criminal events are still remembered in thoroughly different ways by the victims' and perpetrators' communities (Mihajlović Trbovc 2014: 25).

According to judgments of the International Criminal Tribunal for the Former Yugoslavia (ICTY) (including the trials of Tadić, Stakić, Sikirica et al.),[4] Serb forces captured Prijedor on 30 April 1992, facing no resistance (ICTY 1997: § 137). Bosnian Muslims in Prijedor were forced out of jobs, schools, and public institutions (ICTY 1997: § 150). After an unsuccessful attempt to regain control of the town of Prijedor on 30 May 1992[5] by a small group of poorly armed non-Serbs, non-Serbs in Prijedor were ordered to use sheets of white material to mark their homes and indicate that they surrendered (ICTY 1997: § 151). After the takeover of Prijedor and the outlying areas, the Serb forces confined thousands of Muslim and Croat civilians in the Omarska, Keraterm, and Trnopolje camps. During confinement, both male and female prisoners were subjected to severe mistreatment, which included beatings, sexual assaults, torture, and executions (ICTY 1997: § 154). By September 1992, all three camps were closed.[6] The overall death toll of non-Serbs in Prijedor is 3,173 people (Hodžić 2015). Despite clear documentation of torture, mass executions, and forced expulsion, none of the crimes committed in Prijedor qualified as genocide in any of the ICTY judgments.

The Dayton Agreement formed two political entities in postwar Bosnia: Republika Srpska (RS) and the Federation of Bosnia-Herzegovina. The town of Prijedor, with its postwar majority Serbian population, became part of Republika Srpska (RS).[7] Former residents began to come back to Prijedor in 1998, three years after the end of the war, but by 2007 less than a third had returned (Ahmetašević 2015a). Bosniak parties were elected in municipal bodies, while a number of mnemonic activities were tolerated. As the initiators of the White Armband Day told us, it was in 2003 when a plaque was erected in the Keraterm camp, while a number of Bosniak survivors publicly spoke about atrocities (interviews with the authors, 15 and 17 October 2017). In the following years, political animosity toward returnees' memory activism increased, while RS state officials blocked attempts to erect a monument in the former Omarska camp (Sivac-Bryant 2015; Brenner 2011). Occasional formal acknowledgment of the existence of the camps was combined with ongoing denial of the systematic persecutions and mass executions that took place in 1992 (Mihajlović Trbovc 2014: 32). Political changes after the 2006 general elections further blocked commemorative activities. This trend culminated in 2012 in the decision by local authorities not to allow any public gathering or commemorations in the town of Prijedor, including the commemoration of the twentieth anniversary of the events that took place in 1992 (interview with the authors, 17 October 2017). In this context, when the photo of Emir Hodžić, a Prijedor-born survivor and activist, standing alone in the Prijedor main square on May 2012, went viral on social media, it was integrated into the "Stop Genocide Denial" campaign, followed by the use of the hashtag #whitearmbandday.[8]

Online Memory Activism and Transnational Online Commemorations

Recently, scholars have analyzed the rise in use of social media as sites for expressing social dissent, mass mobilization, and uprisings. From North Africa and the Middle East, what was dubbed as the Arab Spring, to the Occupy movement, the rising role of social media has been extensively studied (Howard et al. 2011; Castells 2015). We here approach a narrower segment of online activism: online memory activism, which we analyze as a form of alternative commemoration. Mnemonic processes of remembering and forgetting of contested pasts, in the age of digital media (Garde-Hansen et al. 2009) and the connective turn (Hoskins 2018) are at the heart of our inquiry.

In conflicts over the narratives and representations of the past, memory activists are often "involved in the processes of symbolic transformation and elaboration of meanings of the past: human beings who 'labor' on and with memories of the past" (Jelin 2003: 5). As such, memory activists commemorate contested pasts, often crossing borders both in terms of their activism and in terms of their commemorative demands. Employed as a strategy of peace activism, memory activism is oriented toward the past as a knowledge-based effort for consciousness-raising and political change undertaken outside the channels of the state (Gutman 2017a: 15–16; 2017b). Globalization has enabled movement between different scales, from the local and national to the regional and global, signaling the multiscalarity of memory creation and frictions between meanings created at different scales (De Cesari and Rigney 2014: 5). These scales allow not only for different actors to engage in various mnemonic activities but also for other, non-ethnicized memories to be pursued, outside the channels of the state.

Recent research on new social movements and media trends has framed contemporary networks and transnational spaces as "sites where activists can model their values, ideals, and lifestyles, and live their personal and political commitments as an example for others to follow" (Lievrouw 2011: 156). Online memory activism, as analyzed here, indicates a process of uncovering contested memories in the aftermath of war and mass violence that are otherwise being denied and erased. While some claim that social media has led to an information overload, (Garde-Hansen et al. 2009: 5–7), the use of such platforms for alternative commemorations can help break the silence and counter the denial of past crimes.

As such, we understand the emergence of new transnational online memory activism as digitally mediated connective action (Bennett and Segerberg 2012), which is characterized as "personalized communication" enabled through "easily personalized ideas requiring little in the way of persuasion, reason or reframing to bridge difference with how others may feel about a common problem" (Bennett and Segerberg 2012: 744). As this chapter shows, acts of personal expression, such as the posting of individual or group pictures with a white armband, serve as a reenactment of past atrocities (Olesen 2018), personalizing and diffusing the message across the web. Furthermore, this type of online commemorative practice allows participants to highlight certain images that resonate with already existing cultural materials. Such networks do not require strong organizational control or a symbolic construction of a united "we," and yet they send a very clear message (Bennett and Segerberg 2012: 742–53). Importantly, media and information technologies not only provide channels for transmitting information but also constitute the practical field of action where movements themselves are created and contested (Lievrouw 2011).

Mobilization as a core concept across social movement theories, then, becomes crucial to our inquiry in social memory studies and, in particular, our analysis of online memory activism and online commemoration. How do people convert their collective concerns to collective actions? How does a concern related to denial of crimes and atrocities and banned commemorations translate into joint online transnational action? In her analysis of new forms of engagements with media, Lievrouw (2011: 2) highlights the opportunities for expression and interaction, especially among activists, artists, and other political and cultural groups around the world, who have found new media to be affordable, powerful tools for challenging mainstream or popular culture. Activists, including memory activists, can "aim to change public discourse and perceptions, and create the conditions for what they believe will be a better society" (Lievrouw 2011: 150).

This framework allows us to approach transnational online memory networks and online commemorative practices that take place outside the channels of the state by analyzing their potential to counter denial of past wrongs, to create transnational networks of solidarity, and to pursue particular mnemonic claims. In our discussion of the creation of the #whitearmbandday, we analyze the shift in commemorative actions from the local banned onsite to the transnational scale.

About the Research

Our data collection took place in 2017 in several stages. We first mapped the actors behind the #whitearmbandday and the participants in the annual online commemorative rituals. We then analyzed the postings and actions on social media (Facebook and Twitter), approaching them as sites of online commemoration. Lastly, we conducted interviews with organizers and participants and disseminated questionnaires among participants,[9] gathering novel data about the motivation to participate in online commemoration as well as information on new practices and tactics of online memory activism. This data also includes internal email exchanges prior to the launching of the campaign, shared with us by the organizers.

In our mapping of the agency behind the #whitearmbandday, we identified various groups of actors engaged in different kinds of actions, alliances, as well as divisions. We approached our data collection at the interview stage by identifying some of the main organizers of the online commemoration launched in 2012 and then conducted a snowball sampling of participants in the online commemorations from 2012 to the present for the questionnaires. We identified participants by setting the following categories: (1) individuals from Bosnia currently living in country; (2) members of the Bosnian diaspora (including but not limited to people originally from Prijedor); (3) individuals from other successor states of the former Yugoslavia; and finally, (4) individuals we defined as internationals, with no direct link by birth to the former Yugoslavia. In the interviews we conducted with the initiators of the Stop Genocide Denial website[10] and Facebook page,[11] as well as with the organizers of the Because It Concerns Me (Jer me se tiče)[12] initiative, we focused our attention on their initial aims and motivations, as well as on some of their early strategic decisions, from their decision to engage in online commemoration to the decision to internationalize the campaign through the promotion of transnational values.

In the analysis of the online commemorative practices on social media, we employed discourse analysis of both visual and textual modes. In the textual analysis we were primarily interested in discursive creation of a digital mnemonic community through online memory activism, exploring thematic areas, argumentation schemes, and means of realization (Wodak et al. 2009) used to fix the meaning of the #whitearmbandday in the online commemorative practices. As the main discursive mnemonic battle revolved around the ethnic identification of the victims, we were particularly interested in how different actors defined this group, as ethnically inclusive or exclusive, generalized or specific (Van Leeuwen 2008). In the analysis of the interviews and questionnaires, we were interested in how individual participants evaluated their own motivations and goals for participation, as well as in how they understood the type of memory produced through such practices. Finally, in the visual analysis, we focused on "identifying key themes in sources" (Rose 2001: 158) and basic visual grammar (Kress and van Leeuwen 2010) in order to categorize content of visual material.

Online Memory Activism and Commemoration: The Case of the #Whitearmbandday

In this section we focus on the emergence of the #whitearmbandday and its success in becoming a recognized and reoccurring online commemorative event. We address three elements of online commemoration: (1) actors and practices (from local/banned/onsite to transnational/online); (2) the creation of an online transnational mnemonic network that goes beyond politicization of victims' ethnicity, as a reaction to hegemonic ethno-national memory politics; and (3) the re-localization from online to onsite, from transnational to local.

Transnational Online Memory Activism: Actors and Practices

From "The Power of One" to the Creation of a Transnational Online Memory Network

"The power of one" was the slogan that was placed below the image of Emir Hodžić when it was first posted on the Stop Genocide Denial Facebook page on 23 May 2012 (figure 3.1). Soon after, the image, which featured Hodžić standing alone in silence with a white armband on his left arm and a white body bag in front of his legs in the Prijedor main square, went viral.

Figure 3.1. "The Power of One"—Emir Hodžić on the Prijedor main square, 23 May 2012. Source: Stop Genocide Denial Facebook group.

Four days after posting the photo on Facebook, Stop Genocide Denial called for further action: "If you are inspired by the act of Emir Hodžić, join the International day of the #whitearmbandday on May 31." Hodžić's photo in the square served as a blueprint for creative individualized online activism and commemoration, which we here address as memory activism, enabled by Web 2.0. The image itself has a profound aesthetic quality that conveys loneliness and the persistence of the individual in the midst of public apathy and disinterest. At the same time, due to its inter-iconic potential and based on a transnational memory of the yellow-star armband as a mnemonic symbol of suffering during the Holocaust, the photograph has a high resonance potential, easily recognizable as a case of discrimination and ultimate evil. The text announcing the commemoration in 2012 confirmed that the white armband was used to mark the "other" prior to extermination, establishing the iconicity of the images as an instance of traveling memory (Erll 2011): "This was the first time since 1939, when the Nazi decree required the Polish Jews to wear yellow armbands with the Star of David on their sleeves, that members of an ethnic or religious group were marked for extermination in such a manner" (Stop Genocide Denial website post, 11 May 2013). The global audience was asked to show support by mimicking the photo and reenacting the action. Within weeks, thousands of people from all over the world joined, sharing and posting their portraits with white armbands. A month later, the Stop Genocide Denial page had five thousand members, and their website counted thirty thousand visits from sixty-nine countries (Facebook page Stop Genocide Denial, 6 June 2013). In 2013 the number doubled, reaching ten thousand members.

From their inception, the Facebook page and the website Stop Genocide Denial served as the main online platforms for sharing content and mobilizing participants. The goal to address a global audience was clear: the initiative was dubbed International White Armband Day, and the website was available in several languages, including English, French, Arabic, and Spanish. During its first two years, the Stop Genocide Denial Facebook page regularly shared content about past genocides and atrocities from around the globe. For example, the photo of a person with a yellow armband in the Warsaw ghetto was shared, as well as a photo from Auschwitz, while followers were reminded of the International Holocaust Remembrance Day, the Rwanda genocide, the Armenian genocide, and a call to stop genocide denial from El Salvador, Guatemala, and Gaza to Burma and Syria. Such content helped make the campaign more meaningful to diverse groups at the global level.

We identify a variety of practices of online commemorative actions as related to the #whitearmbandday. Some participants chose to share posts by the organizers themselves, while others took their own picture and posted it, using the hashtag. Analysis of our 2017 survey data shows that most participants posted a personal photo with the white armband. Equally common was sharing or liking other people's content. The images shared included both individual and group photos, selfies, photos of children, flowers on the square, and buildings with white sheets placed in the windows, posted by citizens of Prijedor, Bosnia, or the region, members of the diaspora, local and international NGOs, as well as international human rights groups and institutions. Many of the posts were reenactments of the 1992 white armband order, usually in an everyday environment, taken in black and white, with a direct gaze at the camera or intentionally hiding the eyes, as if to indicate that the shame of the order is too much to bear. Such everyday reenactments have a significant potential to mobilize people, since they easily connect the viewer with the symbols of injustice (Olesen 2015). In addition to posting their own photos, some participants chose to share personal stories, family narratives, and memories related to Prijedor, what Bennett and Segerberg framed as an interactive process of personalization and sharing in the logic of connective action (2012: 746). This was the case with one participant who shared a selfie taken with her partner and also posted a text recounting what happened to her and to her family in 1992 (figure 3.2). In another post, she invited her MA program classmates to join her in a group picture with a white armband. Her request was followed by many questions and inquiries about the events that took place in Prijedor in 1992. While some people opted not to take part because of their lack of knowledge, as they explained, enough people

Stop Genocide Denial
Like This Page · June 1 2013

21 years ago Serb paramilitary forces occupied the city of Prijedor in Northwest Bosnia – my hometown. Non-Serbs were fired from their job posts and told not to report to work anymore. The paramilitary forces carried out arrests of all of Prijedor's intelligentsia. These arrests were colloquially referred to as 'missings'. Those 'missing' were executed in most absurd of places, including the building of Ministry of Interior and the Prijedor police station – which still stands today without a memorial.

Among the 'missing' was my father. He was arrested in an open market, in broad daylight, while everyone else went about their day. My father's colleagues, police officers, drove up next to us in a police car and my father was instructed to get inside the car voluntarily to avoid making a scene. He did, and I was left alone on the sidewalk, only 6 years old. As I stood there crying myself into an abyss someone allegedly recognized me and took me home to my mom. This I do not remember but I was later told. I never saw my father again and his remains were recovered only 14 years later in a ditch with 304 others. This took place in 21st century in Europe.

21 years ago on today's day, 31 May, all non-Serbs in Prijedor were instructed via radio to hang white bed sheets outside their windows and to wear white armbands for identification. No one was going to get

Figure 3.2. Facebook post, USA, 31 May 2013. Source: Stop Genocide Denial Facebook group.

participated to form a powerful group image (interview with the authors, 26 September 2017).

Another type of shared image we identify is the "posing image." Such images depict individuals with bright smiles and colorful clothes (in this case with a Bosnian flag and a Bosnian sports team uniform), hardly reminiscent of any atrocities, but rather showing defiance and celebrating life (figure 3.3). Various regional NGO groups, art collectives, and educational institutions also posted group photos with the white armband, emphasizing their solidarity with the victims of Prijedor and their action as against forgetting (figure 3.4).

Another group of posts featured the reenactment of imprisonment in camps, with shots of people standing behind barbed wire (figure 3.5),

Figure 3.3. Facebook post, Chicago, 2 June 2012. Source: Stop Genocide Denial Facebook group.

Figure 3.4. Facebook post featuring a Belgrade-based theater group, 23 May 2013. Source: Stop Genocide Denial Facebook group.

Figure 3.5. Facebook post, Germany, 31 May 2012. Source: Stop Genocide Denial Facebook group.

reminiscent not only of Holocaust images of inmates in Buchenwald and Auschwitz but also of the infamous Trnopolje camp images, published in 1992 on the *Time* magazine cover (Campbell 2002; Hirsch 2001). At the time, the image of Fikret Alić behind the barbed wire at the Trnopolje camp drew the attention of Western countries to the existence of "Bosnian Serb concentration camps at Omarska and Trnopolje" and led to a new policy of military engagement (Michalski and Gow 2007: 122). Images of emaciated bodies in front of barbed wire, like the armband itself, present powerful symbols of the unquestionable suffering of Jews during World War II. Online memory activists utilize this symbolic power as they combat silence and denial of atrocities in Prijedor.

Finally, there were artistic photos, with highly symbolic arrangements, such as the photo of a white piece of cloth placed on a broken tree branch (figure 3.6). The photo is divided horizontally: the lower part shows the tree image in black and white, while the upper part, in color, shows a man facing the light, which comes beside the colored green wood in front of him. Depicting simultaneously the remembrance of dark times and future light, the image is still hopeful and engaging. As the participant who posted that image wrote, "As I did a couple of years ago, I decided to shoot a photo for White Armband Day, May 31st." The message positions the #whitearmbandday as a *worldwide* reminder of genocide, in order to "let the victims in Prijedor and around the world know they are not alone" (figure 3.6).

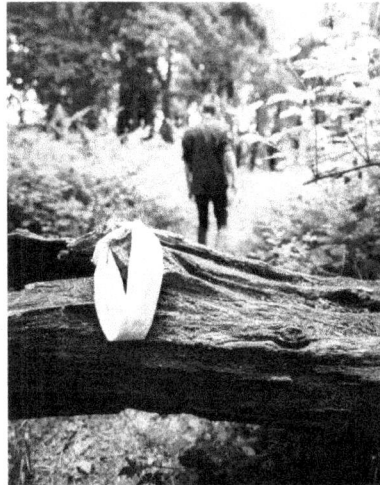

31. MAJ - SVJETSKI DAN BIJELIH TRAKA
Solidarnost sa žrtvama masovnih zločina počinjenih u Prijedoru i širom svijeta

MAY 31 - WORLDWIDE WHITE ARMBAND DAY
Let the victims in Prijedor and around the world know they are not alone

Figure 3.6. Twitter post, 31 May 2017. Source: @toallthings Twitter page.

Our survey data also confirms the continuing dedication of individuals and regional and international organizations (such as the Youth Initiative for Human Rights [YIHR] in Serbia, the Humanitarian Law Center [HLC], or international organizations such as the International Center for Transitional Justice [ICTJ] and ICTY) who have remained actively involved in the online commemorations throughout the years.

The importance of social media not only as a channel and a platform for activism but also as a source of knowledge and information was also confirmed. As one respondent from the Bosnian diaspora (born in Bihać) stated, her participation in the online commemorative platform was primarily motivated by a desire to learn more about the war: "A lot of what has happened in Prijedor, Kozarac and the area was new to me until I started following the #whitearmbandday. The #whitearmbandday on social media has definitely been very informative" (ENG questionnaire respondent #13, 27 August 2017). Accordingly, more than half of the survey participants affirmed the centrality of the online platform of memory in spreading information and knowledge about the case of Prijedor. As such, new social media not only provide channels for transmitting information but also constitute a practical field of action where movements are created, contested, and played out (Lievrouw 2011: 156). As the online and onsite commemorations gained more visibility after 2013, constant reports by traditional media (such as N1 and TV Sarajevo) ensured that the visibility of the commemorations went beyond engagement of the core group of initial organizers. In what follows, we analyze the actions of the initiators of the transnational online commemoration of the #whitearmbandday.

The Creation of an Online, Transnational Mnemonic Network

Although effective and engaging, "the power of one" can be a misleading title. Behind the individual revolt, there was a discussion among a number of activists about staging an action they had planned and responding to the local authorities' ban on the "Genocide in Prijedor—20 years" commemoration. Ideas had already begun circulating a number of weeks before Emir Hodžić appeared in the square and stood on his own.

In an internal email exchange between the organizers from early May 2012, the idea was shared to launch the #whitearmbandday campaign. As Refik Hodžić, a native of Prijedor then residing in New York City, and one of the main organizers wrote,

> Now we have a reason to take the anniversary to a global level. 20 years of crimes committed in Prijedor is certainly relevant for the world public . . . the most important thing now is to galvanize world/diaspora/Bosnia public, to support Committee and people on-site, who are heroically struggling to commemorate atrocities in Prijedor, and return the truth about what happened to the place where it happened and where it belongs. (email, 1 May 2012)

The second incentive for the international campaign came from the refusal of one of the largest steel companies in the world, ArcelorMittal, now the owner of the Omarska Mine—the site of the former Omarska concentration camp—to grant victims access to the premises of the former camp for commemoration purposes. A petition posted on Change.org was signed by twenty-five hundred supporters and received significant international media attention.[13] One of the reasons for the petition's relative success was that its posting coincided with the organization of the Olympic Games hosted in London that year, where the same ArcelorMittal group erected the *Arcelor-Mittal Orbit* sculpture and observation tower, intended as public art that would be part of the legacy of the Summer Olympics. The issue was picked up by scholars and activists who initiated the commemoration in London of a *Memorial in Exile*.[14]

These activities exemplify the "boomerang effect" strategy, where domestic actors "seek international allies to try to bring pressure on their states from outside" (Keck and Sikkink 1999: 93). Their efforts were facilitated by social media, partially due to their ability to offer a powerful and easily recognizable symbol of injustice, which in turn helped mobilize a large audience and expand the network. At the same time, the ability of the online platform to produce knowledge about the past and allow individuals to share their own experiences, and their claims about the past, further galvanized online participants.

The local authorities' ban on the commemoration also mobilized participants. This was especially evident among participants from the Bosnian diaspora and the region in their initial decision to join the online action in 2012. As one interviewee, who was a child when the war in Prijedor started and left Bosnia after the war, explained, "When it comes to memory about things I personally experienced, this is for me an uncompromising issue." Frustration that the 1992 atrocities are still silenced, denied, and not acknowledged provoked her to act: "I felt like I did not want to give them this easy victory in a way" (interview with the authors, 26 September 2017). For her, as for the organizers, asserting a truth that was denied openly was crucial. She also realized that her Facebook post held the potential to give agency to her position, and to people like her who left Bosnia during or after the war ended but never returned to claim their truth.

Against the Utilization and Politicization of Victims' Ethnic Belonging: Mnemonic Battles and Online Alternative Commemorations

In the attempt to break the division of ethnicized communities of memory in Bosnia, the organizers emphasized a non-ethnicized approach in their commemorative practices, combating "politicization of crimes, and politicization of 'our' and 'their' victims" (interview with the authors, 24 October 2017). Over time, as they nuanced their message and practices, the emphasis on trans-ethnic memory was crystallized. By 2013, instead of solely commemorating the Bosniak victims from Prijedor, a new, ethnically inclusive concept of victimhood emerged. As the organizers stated, "This year we want to remember the suffering of innocent children in the war, regardless of their nationality. We want to show that empathy can break ethnic barriers, and that at least when children are concerned, we can remember and empathize with victims, even when they do not belong to 'our side'" (Stop Genocide Denial, 11 May 2013). We understand this mnemonic choice as an important strategy in combating not only silence and denial but also ethno-nationalized politics and competition over victimization, common in the region, as well as in many other conflict-ridden societies worldwide.

In what followed that year, the main online commemorative activities were envisioned through the sharing of individually recorded videos, with statements proclaiming why the #whitearmbandday mattered, connecting individual participants with the personal story and biography of a child who was killed in Prijedor. As in 2012, the organizers offered the blueprint, and other activists and participants joined in by recording and sharing their videos. The organizers posted a promotional video titled "Remember the Killed Children," calling for the erection of a monument in Prijedor for the 103 children killed (Stop Genocide Denial, 22 May 2013). The video featured individuals who remembered victims with their names and their absence from social life in contemporary Prijedor. For example, Goran, an activist from Prijedor, made a powerful statement: "On the #whitearmbandday I want to remember Aida Bašić who was born in the same year as me. She was killed in Prijedor simply because she was 'the other'" ("Remember the Killed Children").

Fikret Bačić from Prijedor remembered his family, his mother Šehrija, his wife Minka, his son Nermin, and his daughter Nermina, who were all killed in 1992. He also remembered "Bajić Višnja who was 10 years old, from Visoko, and who was killed in 1992" (Stop Genocide Denial, 30 May 2013). Emphasizing the possibility to empathize with victims from the perpetrator's ethnic group, even by those who lost their loved ones, a powerful message was clearly articulated a year into the creation of this online commemorative platform. By choosing to remember the killed children from the "other" ethnic group, the organizers underscored the message against the politicization of victims' ethnicity, constructing an online commemorative platform as a shared site of remembrance. Such actions challenge existing hegemonic frameworks of memory politics not only in Bosnia (both in Republika Srpska and the Federation) but in the entire region. Such online memory activism reveals its potential for broader change in the creation of a post-Yugoslav region of memory, which places victims at the center of commemorative events and practices, regardless of their ethnic belonging.

One organizer stated clearly the trans-ethnic purpose of their memory activism: "Our fight is against discrimination, any sort of discrimination, regardless of nationality and ethnicity" (interview with the authors, 17 October 2017). For the organizers, the choice to turn to trans-ethnic commemoration was more than a campaign strategy: "It was a moral decision in how to respond to the trauma of war, a choice between becoming a victim or becoming a survivor" (interview with the authors, 24 October 2017). Since the war ended, state-sponsored commemorations in Bosnia were cast in ethnic terms in the service of identity-building, increasing the gap between ethno-nationalized communities of memory. Hence, the organizers reacted not only to the structural obstacles created by memory politics of silence and denial produced by Serbian politicians and institutions but also to pervasive Bosniak ethnic victimization, which dominates memory politics in the Federation.

The regional aspect of this form of online transnational memory activism in the post-Yugoslav space was evident in some of the videos taken by participants from the region. Activists from Serbia chose to personalize their messages by devoting their online participation to one victim, stating his/her name and dates of birth and death. "This person if he was alive today," as one participant from Belgrade stated, "would already be 21 years old. . . . He could have been a student at the faculty, or engage in sports or any other activities of people in their twenties. . . . It is important," she went on, "that we as people, should remember other people who were not given the right to grow up to become adults" (Stop Genocide Denial, 30 May 2013). For these regional activists, the #whitearmbandday platform serves a number of purposes. In their video messages they show solidarity, humanity, and empathy, and also emphasize the act of acknowledgment and responsibility. At the same time, they correspond to mnemonic dynamics in the region, as they play out in Serbia, where memory activists insist on discussing war crimes perpetrated, in this case in Bosnia, by Serbs. In that sense, the #whitearmbandday as an online digital mnemonic platform serves as a space that brings together regional alternative memories that are closely intertwined.

Finally, for some participants, the message goes beyond the local level. As one participant stated, "I wear the white armband not only for victims of genocide in Prijedor, but for nameless victims around the world who are subject to persecution, who are killed for nothing more than their race, ethnicity, religious beliefs, gender . . ." (participant Facebook post, 31 May 2013). This broadening of the message beyond ethnicity enables memory to serve as a reminder of any discrimination, moving away from its origin, which explains the threat such memory poses to national memory and identity-building.

For participants who identify solely as Bosniaks and insisted on commemorating only the Bosniak victims of the war, this threat was unacceptable. After 2015, there was an increase in the number of Bosniak diaspora Facebook pages dedicated to the exclusive commemoration of Bosniak victims. For example, the Anti-Dayton Group, a rightist Bosniak nationalist organization, seeks to remember "three centuries of genocide against Bosniaks in Sandžak and Bosnia" (Facebook post, 16 October 2017), calling on Bosniaks to "remember and never forgive." They also commemorate the #whitearmbandday both online and onsite. In 2017, they initiated a performance in Sarajevo, during which an installation symbolizing the Manjača camp was rebuilt in Baščaršija (the old town). In that performance, they reenacted a group of young men with white armbands who were taken to a camp by "Serbian soldiers" in uniform with rifles and guns. One of the Prijedor #whitearmbandday organizers referred to this performance as "a terrible, sick thing" in a complete disagreement with their initial intentions (interview with the authors, 24 October 2017). The performance reenacted fear and interethnic hatred, with no intention of constructing a more inclusive memory, that goes beyond the sole ethnic identity of the victims. The Anti-Dayton Group openly attacked the #whitearmbandday organizers for their trans-ethnic commemorations, irritated by their reconciliatory narrative and the call to commemorate all civilian victims in the war, regardless of their ethnicity.

Responding to growing political pressure from Bosniak parties in Sarajevo and attempts to instrumentalize the #whitearmbandday in Prijedor in 2017, Refik Hodžić, one of the core organizers of the #whitearmbandday, posted a comment on his Facebook page calling on citizens of Sarajevo to sign a petition in support of the erection of a monument for Serbian civilians killed in Kazani (Sarajevo) as a sign of support of Prijedor victims.[15] The call for Bosniaks to take part in commemoration of Serbian victims provoked harsh attacks, insults, and personal threats toward him and his family. The weekly *Stav* magazine published an article claiming that "the shameful act of Refik Hodžić insulted all victims in Prijedor, and all citizens of Sarajevo" (Hasić 2017). The Anti-Dayton Group reposted the article calling for physical violence against Hodžić, as "only an imbecile can write a comment like this" (Anti-Dayton Group, Facebook, 1 June 2017). Edin Ramulić, himself a survivor and activist from Prijedor, was also targeted as a traitor for "selling 'Bosniak suffering' to international donors for financial aid" (interview with the author, 17 October 2017).

Despite these internal mnemonic struggles, the core group of the organizers in Prijedor remained faithful to their decision to keep their on-site commemorations independent from any political instrumentalization by various NGO groups, political parties (nationalist as well as trans-nationalist), and international actors (foundations, organizations, etc.). The organizers' decision not to allow any politicians or political parties from Bosnia or any nationalist actors to take over their commemorative actions and message has also resonated with some participants of the online commemoration of the #whitearmbandday. As one participant originally from Zagreb stated, "The #whitearmbandday seems to me less politicized. . . . It is somehow less colored by ethnicity and manages to emphasize more the concept of citizenship" (BSH questionnaire respondent #12, 27 August 2017). She was not the only participant in our study to mention the difference between the annual commemoration of the Srebrenica genocide in Potočari and the online and onsite commemorations in Prijedor. On one hand, it seems to be a source of tension between victims themselves. As one Prijedor survivor, who organized an exhibition in St. Louis to raise awareness of the wartime crimes committed in Prijedor, explained,[16] some of the reactions he received from activists in memory of Srebrenica resembled a call "not to touch their genocide," reflecting competition over victimization (interview with the author, 22 October 2017). On the other hand, the tensions were used to highlight the support for the de-politicization of the #whitearmbandday. We argue that the online commemoration created the space for individuals to voice their own positions and articulate counterarguments to politics tainted by everyday nationalism in the entire region.

Outcomes: From the Transnationalization to the Localization of the #Whitearmbandday Memory Activism

One year only after the 2012 ban on the commemoration in Prijedor, following the successful mobilization and rise in the visibility of the online commemorative campaign, 31 May and the #whitearmbandday have gained an established place in Bosnia's memory politics and alternative calendar (Fridman 2015). The circulation from online to onsite commemoration is still ongoing. Given the limited scope of this text, we do not analyze here the onsite commemorations in depth but rather highlight the interconnectivity between the online transnational commemorations and the onsite local ones.

The first onsite commemoration in Prijedor was held on 31 May 2013 "for the victims' right to remembrance." Around four hundred activists from Banja Luka, Mostar, Prijedor, Zenica, Sarajevo, Tuzla, and other towns in Bosnia declared, "Enough segregation, enough discrimination of victims because of their ethnicity!" while 103 roses tagged with the names of the killed children were laid on the main square in Prijedor. The roses were meant not only as a commemoration for the victims but also as a demand for local authorities to allow the erection of a monument for the children killed in Prijedor.

As activities on the Stop Genocide Denial website decreased in 2014, the references to other mass atrocities worldwide waned, leaving posts about different commemorations in Prijedor as the predominant content. The Jer me se tiče initiative, which took on many social media activities in following years, clearly targeted a regional audience, providing posts exclusively in local languages and mainly promoting human rights activism in Bosnia. One of the organizers explained the shift from the global toward the local in the interview: "Our main target is Prijedor. Once we were able to work in Prijedor we were not that much interested in the global anymore" (interview with the authors, 15 October 2017). The importance of the onsite commemorations was recognized by online activists too. In one interview, a participant in the #whitearmbandday from the Bosnian diaspora expressed the wish for onsite commemorations to be broadcast live, in order to be inclusive of diaspora communities and other internationals.

Gradually, the demand to erect a monument for the children killed in Prijedor in 1992 has crystallized as the main goal of the onsite 31 May commemorations in Prijedor. In order to obtain wide support among their neighbors for the monument, the initiators in 2017 addressed primarily young people. As one interviewee noticed, "There are new generations now of young people who bear no responsibility for the war crimes committed. We wish not to generate more hate with our actions . . ." (interview with the authors, 17 October 2017). Youths were encouraged "not to take on your shoulders the baggage of crimes committed by older people, even if it was your parents or grandparents" (Jer me se tiče, 18 May 2017).

Moreover, in the 2017 announcement of the onsite commemoration, the organizers stated, "If you do not have job, or you work for miserable salary, if you do not have the same chance as children of politicians, you are already carrying an invisible band" (Jer me se tiče, 18 May 2017). From symbolizing ethnic discrimination in 2012, the white armband in 2017 came to raise awareness of class discrimination too, which is equally devastating for all ethnic groups in Prijedor and in Bosnia. The critique targeted political elites of both groups equally, while those commemorating the White Armband Day are regular citizens, regardless of their ethnicity. Although the organizers refrain from using the term "reconciliation," theirs is a message of peace and inclusion rather than one raising hatred and conflict.

In the transition from the global to the local, the development of the annual onsite commemorations has to some extent demobilized the original online activities. While many of the respondents of the questionnaire indicated the continuation of their participation from 2012 to the present (2017), participants in a number of interviews explained that once the onsite commemorations were established and permitted by local authorities, they no longer felt the need to take part in the online commemoration. As one interviewee from the Bosnian diaspora explained, once he saw the onsite protest in Prijedor, "The transition from that one picture of the guy standing depressively on his own in the middle of the town square changed dramatically over the last years, and so I felt it was not so necessary anymore" (interview with the author, 26 September 2017). Nevertheless, the majority of participants affirmed their willingness to continue and part take in the online commemorations.

Conclusions

The #whitearmbandday online commemoration emerged from the work of a core group of memory activists who used social media to mobilize a transnational memory network to combat denial of crimes committed in Prijedor in 1992. Their message was able to go beyond the local (Prijedor/Bosnia) and the regional (the post-Yugoslav space) thanks to their employment of the existing symbolic meaning of the armband in Holocaust memory, which offered an easily usable frame for reenactment and personalized content sharing. The mobilizing photography appealed to the wider audiences as an instance of traveling memory, attracting wide online participation. Already existing transitional justice networks consisting of local, regional, and international NGOs, legal and educational institutions, and human rights activists were quick to recognize and spread the message on social media. The 31 May commemoration of the White Armband Day was established as an important date in the alternative commemorative calendar. Both onsite and online memory activism were well planned, offering a blueprint for action for the followers. The success of the online commemoration in creating a free space for activism and in mobilizing a wider audience was then utilized to promote local memory activism and to effect social change in Prijedor.

The formation of an annual online commemoration as a transnational mnemonic network provided a significant impetus for the onsite commemorations. The return to the local and to the onsite has also marked a shift in the organizers' focus, toward promoting local remembrance rather than the continuation of their transnational activities, as a part of the fight against global injustice. Moreover, in the shift from online to onsite memory activism, they formulated a specific objective: calling for the erection of a monument for the killed children of Prijedor. Their turn toward the local was visible in their efforts to reach out to young neighbors in the Prijedor area as well as in their attempt to mobilize actors across diverse ethnic groups. Additionally, it also marked the placement of the mnemonic battles within other ongoing battles against socioeconomic injustice in Bosnia and corrupt political elites.

Both the online and the onsite have set 31 May and the White Armband Day as a unique commemorative event in Prijedor and in the broader regional commemorative landscape. This trans-ethnic memory was recognized and reinforced by regional and international participants, but it was also contested by some Bosniak groups, as it was perceived as a threat to national identity-building. Such struggles between ethnicized and de-ethnicized memory were visible in both the onsite and online commemorations. At the same time, the organizers managed to maintain their bottom-up approach and not let their cause and mnemonic actions fall into the trap of NGO-ization, becoming the aim in and of itself rather than the means for social change. Partially, this was due to the nature of the online framework and platform they managed to create for memory activism. As such, forced to act outside of the channels of the state, the online transnational network not only provided a space for commemoration and a tool for extensive mobilization, it also enabled the emergence of a specific type of memory that transcends ethnic boundaries.

Orli Fridman is an associate professor at the Belgrade-based Faculty of Media and Communications (FMK), Singidunum University, where she heads the Center for Comparative Conflict Studies (CFCCS). She is also the academic director of the School for International Training (SIT) study-abroad program in the Balkans. Her interdisciplinary research focuses on post-conflict trans-formation, memory politics, and memory activism. Her most recent publications include: "Peace Formation from Below: The 'mirëdita, dobar dan!' Festival as an Alternative to Everyday Nationalism" (*Nations and Nationalism*, 2020); "'Too Young to Remember, Determined Not to Forget': Memory Activists Engaging with Returning ICTY Convicts" (*International Criminal Justice Review*, 2018); "Protiv Nenormalnog: An Analysis of the #protivdik-tature Protests in the Context of Memory Politics of the 1990s in Serbia" (*Contemporary Southeastern Europe*, 2017); "Alternative Calendars and Memory Work in Serbia: Anti-War Activism after Milošević" (*Memory Studies*, 2015).

Katarina Ristić is a research associate at the Global and European Studies Institute, Leipzig University. Her research focuses on media representations and memory and their conjunction with war crime trials and transitional justice. After graduating from Belgrade University with a degree in philosophy, she obtained a PhD from the Faculty of History, Arts and Oriental Studies, at Leipzig University. Her first monograph, *Imaginary Trials—War Crime Trials and Memory in Former Yugoslavia* (Leipziger Universitätsverlag, 2014) deals with victims' narratives in trials and their media portrayal in Croatia, Bosnia, and Serbia. She was a research associate in International Security and Conflict Studies at the Helmut-Schmidt University/The University of the Federal Armed Forces in Hamburg and at Magdeburg University. Her recent publications include "The Media Negotiations of War Criminals and Their Memoirs: The Emergence of the 'ICTY Celebrity,'" (*International Criminal Justice Review*, 2018); and "Re-Enacting the Past in TV News on War Crime Trials: A Method for Analysis of Visual Narratives in Archival Footage," (*Media, War & Conflict*, 2019).

Notes

1. Beyond memory activism, which we focus on in this text, other vibrant forms of activism have been documented in recent years in Bosnia. See the analysis of social movements in Southeast Europe and civic engagement (Wimmen 2018) and the 2014 protests and Plenums (Arsenijević 2014; Lekić-Subašić 2019).
2. After the war, the term "Bosniak" for Bosnian Muslims became common, although many of our interlocutors refrain from identifying as Bosniaks, preferring instead Bosnians.
3. See, for example, Stef Jansen's analysis (2007) of the diversity of memory discourses among ordinary people in everyday life.
4. See the ICTY website: http://www.icty.org/en/outreach/documentaries/crimes-icty-prije dor (accessed on 7 April 2018).

5. For a detailed account of the events in mid- to late May in the greater area of Kozarac and in Prijedor, see ICTY 1997.
6. More than thirty thousand individuals went through the camps; some fifteen hundred died there (Hodžić 2015).
7. Before the outbreak of war in April 1992, Prijedor was a typical multiethnic Bosnian town. Like many other towns, its population of 112,543 citizens was a microcosm of the rest of the state. According to the 1991 census, the two largest ethnic groups were Muslims (49,351) and Serbs (47,582), living alongside Croats (6,316), Yugoslavs (6,459), and a smaller number of other ethnic groups (2,836) (Belloni 2005: 435).
8. The hashtag was used in both English and Bosnian/Croatian/Serbian (B/S/H) and read #whitearmbandday or #danbijelihtraka. Throughout the text, when referring to the day, we use the English version of the hashtag.
9. In total, we received questionnaire responses from seventy-six participants (thirty-nine responses to the questionnaire in Bosnian/Serbian/Croatian [BSH Questionnaire] from local and regional participants, and thirty-seven to the English questionnaire [ENG Questionnaire] mostly from internationals and individuals identifying as members of the Bosnian diaspora). Additionally, we conducted ten interviews mostly via Skype, given the spread of locations of the participants in the study.
10. While the website no longer exists, as the organizers terminated the maintenance of the website, we were able to retrieve some content, available at the Webarchive website: https://web.archive.org/web/20120829123545/http://stopgenocidedenial.org:80/ (accessed on October 17, 2017).
11. https://www.facebook.com/StopGenocideDenial/.
12. https://www.facebook.com/jermesetice/.
13. In May 2012, *The Independent* published an article on ArcelorMittal titled "Omarska: The Dark Side of the Olympics 'Orbit'"; in the following months, a number of articles appeared in regional and international media: see, for example, Balkan Transitional Justice, Refik Hodžić, "Shadow of London 'Orbit' in Bosnia: Mittal Suppresses Memories of Omarska," 20 April 2012; German TAZ, "Gedanken ist anderswo," 15 August 2012. E-Novine, "Dvadeset godina od genocida u Prijedoru," 31 May 2012; Dnevni avaz, "Poznati britanski novinar Ed Vulliamy: Milijarderu Mitalu kapital važniji od boli žrtava," 22 June 2012.
14. See Eyal Weizman's project, Forensic architecture: https://forensic-architecture.org/ programme/news/a-memorial-in-exile-in-londons-olympics-orbits-of-responsibility.
15. On the case of Kazani see Moll 2015.
16. The exhibition Prijedor Lives from Bosnian Genocide was first opened in 2007 at the Holocaust Museum in St. Louis with the support of the Jewish community and the Bosnia Memory project at Fontbonne University (https://www.fontbonne.edu/academics/ departments/english-and-communication-department/bosnia-memory-project/).

References

Ahmetašević, Nidžara. 2015a. "Bosnia's Unending War." *New Yorker*, 4 November.
———. 2015b. "Extended Interview with Nidžara Ahmetašević." ICTJ. Retrieved November 2017 from https://www.youtube.com/watch?v=WuKMFs9oyCg&list=PL5 AC587FC0368ED45&index=33&t=6s.
Arsenijević, Damir. 2014. "Protests and Plenum: The Struggle for the Commons." In *Unbribable Bosnia and Herzegovina: The Struggle for the Commons*, edited by Damir Arsenijević, 45–50. Baden-Baden: Nomos.
Belloni, Roberto. 2005. "Peacebuilding at the Local Level: Refugee Return to Prijedor." *International Peacekeeping* 12(3): 434–47.
Bennett, W. Lance, and Alexandra Segerberg. 2012. "The Logic of Connective Action: Digital Media and the Personalization of Contentious Politics." *Information, Communication & Society* 15(5): 739–68.
Brenner, Manuela. 2011. "The Struggle of Memory. Practices of the (Non-)Construction of a Memorial at Omarska." *Sudosteuropa-Zeitschrift Fur Gegenwartforschung* 59(3): 349–72.
Campbell, David. 2002. "Atrocity, Memory, Photography: Imaging the Concentration Camps of Bosnia—the Case of ITN versus Living Marxism, Part 1." *Journal of Human Rights* 1(1): 1–33.
Castells, Manuel. 2015. *Networks of Outrage and Hope: Social Movements in the Internet Age*. Cambridge: Polity Press.
De Cesari, Chiara, and Ann Rigney. 2014. "Introduction." In *Transnational Memory: Circulation, Articulation, Scales*, edited by Chiara de Cesari and Ann Rigney, 1–26. Berlin: De Gruyter.
Erll, Astrid. 2011. "Travelling Memory." *Parallax* 17(4): 4–18.
Fridman, Orli. 2015. "Alternative Calendars and Memory Work in Serbia: Anti-war Activism after Milošević." *Memory Studies* 8(2): 212–26.
Garde-Hansen, Joanne, Andrew Hoskins, and Anna Reading. 2009. "Introduction." In *Save as . . . Digital Memories*, edited by Joanne Garde-Hansen, Andrew Hoskins, and Anna Reading, 1–21. London: Palgrave Macmillan.
Gutman, Yifat. 2017a. *Memory Activism: Reimagining the Past for the Future in Israel-Palestine*. Nashville: Vanderbilt University Press.
———. 2017b. "Looking Backward to the Future: Counter-Memory as Oppositional Knowledge-Production in the Israeli–Palestinian Conflict." *Current Sociology* 65(1): 54–72.
Hasić, Nedim. 2017. "Refik Hodžić je sramnim ispadom žestoko uvrijedio sve prijedorske žrtve, ali i sve Sarajlije." *Stav*, 30 May. Retrieved 1 November 2017 from https://stav .ba/refik-hodzic-je-sramnim-ispadom-zestoko-uvrijedio-sve-prijedorske-zrtve-ali-i-sve-sa rajlije/.
Hirsch, Marianne. 2001. "Surviving Images: Holocaust Photographs and the Work of Postmemory." In *Visual Culture and the Holocaust*, edited by Barbie Zelizer, 215–46. London: Athlone Press.
Hodžić, Refik. 2015. "Flowers in the Square." International Center for Transitional Justice. Retrieved 1 November 2017 from https://www.ictj.org/sites/default/files/subsites/ flowers-square-prijedor/.
Hoskins, Andrew, ed. 2018. *Digital Memory Studies: Media Pasts in Transition*. New York: Routledge, Taylor & Francis Group.
Howard, Philip N., Aiden Duffy, Deen Freelon, Muzammil M. Hussain, Laia Jorba, Will Mari, and Marwa Mazaid. 2011. "Opening Closed Regimes: What Was the Role of Social Media during the Arab Spring?" Project on Information Technology and Political Islam.

ICTY (International Criminal Tribunal for the former Yugoslavia), 1997. *Prosecutor v. Duško Tadić a/k/a "Dule"*: Trial Judgement and Dissenting Opinion. The Hague.

Jelin, Elizabeth. 2003. *State Repression and the Labors of Memory*. Minneapolis: University of Minnesota Press.

Jansen, Stef. 2007. "Remembering with a Difference: Crashing Memories of Bosnian Conflict in Every Day Life." In *The New Bosnian Mosaic: Identities, Memories and Moral Claims in a Post-War Society*, edited by Xavier Bougarel, Elissa Helms, and Ger Duijzings, 193–210. New York: Routledge.

Keck, Margaret E., and Kathryn Sikkink. 1999. "Transnational Advocacy Networks in International and Regional Politics." *International Social Science Journal* 51(159): 89–101.

Kress, Gunther, and Theo van Leeuwen. 2010. *Reading Images: The Grammar of Visual Design*. New York: Routledge.

Lekić-Subašić, Željka. 2019. "Social Media and the 'Balkan' Spring." In *Social Movements in the Balkans: Rebellion and Protest from Maribor to Taksim*, edited by Florian Bieber and Dario Brentin, 96–112. New York: Routledge.

Lievrouw, Leah A. 2011. *Alternative and Activist New Media: Digital Media and Society Series*. Cambridge: Polity Press.

Michalski, Milena, and James Gow. 2007. *War, Image and Legitimacy: Viewing Contemporary Conflict*. New York: Routledge.

Mihajlović Trbovc, Jovana. 2014. "Memory after Ethnic Cleansing: Victims' and Perpetrators' Narratives in Prijedor1" *Journal of Ethnic Studies* 72: 25–41.

Moll, Nicolas. 2013. "Fragmented Memories in a Fragmented Country: Memory Competition and Political Identity-Building in Today's Bosnia and Herzegovina." *Nationalities Papers* 41(6): 910–35.

Moll, Nicolas. 2015. *"Sarajevska najpoznatija javna tajna": suočavanje sa Cacom, Kazanima i zločinima počinjenim nad Srbina u opkoljenom Sarajevu, od rata do 2015*. Sarajevo: Friedrich Ebert Stiftung.

Olesen, Thomas. 2015. *Global Injustice Symbols and Social Movements*. New York: Palgrave Macmillan.

———. 2018. "Memetic Protest and the Dramatic Diffusion of Alan Kurdi." *Media, Culture & Society* 40(5): 656–72.

Rose, Gillian. 2001. *Visual Methodologies: An Introduction to the Interpretation of Visual Materials*. London: Sage.

Sivac-Bryant, S. 2015. "The Omarska Memorial Project as an Example of How Transitional Justice Interventions Can Produce Hidden Harms." *International Journal of Transitional Justice* 9(1): 170–80.

Van Leeuwen, Theo. 2008. *Discourse and Practice: New Tools for Critical Discourse Analysis*. Oxford: Oxford University Press.

Wimmen, Heiko. 2019. "Divided They Stand: The Dilemma of Non-Formal Political Activism in a Divided Society." In *Social Movements in the Balkans: Rebellion and Protest from Maribor to Taksim*, edited by Florian Bieber and Dario Brentin, 9–29. New York: Routledge.

Wodak, Ruth, Rudolf de Cillia, Martin Reisigl, and Karin Liebhart. 2009. *The Discursive Construction of National Identity*. Edinburgh: Edinburgh University Press.

Chapter 4

MEMORY ACTIVISM ACROSS BORDERS

The Transformative Influence of the Argentinean-Franco
Court Case and Activist Protest Movements
on Spain's Recovery of Historical Memory

Andrea Hepworth

❧

Both Spain and Argentina have endured dictatorships in the twentieth century, but they have dealt with their traumatic historical legacy in very different ways. During the transition to democracy in Spain, the 1977 Amnesty Law was passed, which pardoned crimes committed during the thirty-six-year dictatorship in the name of national reconciliation. By granting impunity without first addressing the transgressions of the past, the law inhibited the formation of the discursive framework pivotal to the public vocalization of memories and overcoming of trauma. The law impedes the prosecution of human rights violations by Francoist officials in Spain to this day.

Conversely in Argentina, restorative justice mechanisms such as the National Commission on the Disappearance of Persons (CONADEP)—a truth commission—was established a year after the 1976–83 dictatorship ended, which enabled victims to air their grievances. The resulting *Nunca Más* (Never Again) report contained numbers and names of victims, as well as details of detention centers where individuals were murdered and tortured (Crenzel 2012: 85). By including the victims' names, age, gender, and profession in the testimonies, the report took a crucial step toward raising victims out of nameless anonymity and restoring their identity.[1] Even though the military approved an amnesty law before the transfer of power in 1983, the democratic government repealed the law in the same year, and the *Nunca Más* report was accepted as key evidence in the subsequent trial of the military juntas.[2] Subsequent amnesty laws were overturned in 2005. Instrumental in this, among other factors, was the continuous activism of the Mothers of the Plaza de Mayo and other associations.

This chapter mainly focuses on the bottom-up practices of transnational mnemonic space-making employed by three agent groups: the Argentinean Mothers of the Plaza de Mayo, the Spanish Association for the Recovery of Historical Memory (ARMH), and activist lawyers. This study argues that the transnational interconnection between Argentina and Spain regarding their respective traumatic pasts enables "memory entrepreneurs"[3] to establish a nonmaterial, multidimensional transnational space, in which memory is created and shaped. It will further be shown that the successful formation of this space—containing heterogenous mnemonic narratives—depends on "coordinating universalizing memory practices" (Trimçev 2017). The study identifies where "collective" (Snow 2001), "relational" (Edwards 2005), and "cultural" agencies (Taylor 2003; Sommer 2005) are at play and argues that mnemonic agency in its divergent forms is employed by memory activists who have transformed their grief about the disappearances into articulations of grievances and a claim for memory and justice. The analysis in this chapter further examines transnational links and diffusion of terms and practices, evident, for example, in the term *desaparecidos* (the disappeared), the application of the concept of universal jurisdiction in both countries, and the Argentinean Complaint, a court case initiated in 2010 by relatives of Spanish and Argentinean victims of Francoist crimes in Argentina. To pinpoint the scope and repercussions of the transnational dimensions of memory activism in Spain and Argentina, the chapter mobilizes scholarship on transnational social movements and investigates memory activists and the networks and processes that led to the diffusion of activism across borders. Finally, it examines the limitations of transnational memory in the confrontation of national traumatic pasts.

Transnational Diffusion of the Term *Desaparecidos*

A striking example for the diffusion of memory paradigms and terms across borders can be discerned in the use of the term *desaparecidos* in Spain. It is therefore necessary to first clarify what is meant by the term. International human rights laws define enforced disappearances as the arrest, detention, or abduction of persons "by officials of different branches or levels of Government, or by organized groups or private individuals acting on behalf of, or with the support, direct or indirect, consent or acquiescence of the

Government." These secret detentions are followed by official denial of the abductions and a refusal to acknowledge the "fate or whereabouts of the persons concerned," which in turn leave the detained without legal protection (United Nations 1992: par. 3) and families, friends and the public in complete uncertainty about their fate. The crime of enforced disappearances can be traced back to Hitler's 1941 so-called *Nacht und Nebel Erlass* (Night and Fog Decree) (Hall 1999: 221–22). Its purpose was to seize political activists and/or resistance fighters in Nazi-occupied territories and transport them secretly to Germany; hence they disappeared without a trace (United Nations 2002: 7).

In the late 1960s and early 1970s, enforced disappearances reemerged as systematic means of state repression in Latin America; first in Brazil, then in Guatemala. The term "enforced disappearances" itself is a translation of the Spanish *desaparición forzada* and was first used by Latin American non-governmental organizations (NGOs) (Council of Europe 2005: 142). The Inter-American Commission on Human Rights (IACHR) and the United Nations Commission on Human Rights (UNCHR) were the first international human rights entities to address enforced disappearances in Latin America. The IACHR, in which Argentinean human rights activists were especially involved, has played a pivotal role in Latin America (Sikkink 2008: 5). The first cases the IACHR responded to pertained to disappearances in Chile, but a decisive turning point in intergovernmental organizations' investigations into disappearances was marked by the IACHR's visit to Argentina in 1979, in which the methodical practice of enforced disappearances by consecutive military juntas was confirmed (United Nations 2002: 7). Testimony provided by Argentinean human rights activists formed a crucial part of the IACHR's subsequent report, and the formation of the United Nations Working Group on Enforced or Involuntary Disappearances (UNWGEID) in 1980 was aided by Argentinean activists and their supporters. The decision by these human rights movements to "go transnational" emerged from the inability to address human rights violations in their domestic settings. The UNWGEID, for instance, was formed as a direct result of the Argentinean government's blocking of demands for country-specific actions within the UNCHR (Sikkink 2008: 5).

To effect change in Argentina, activists needed to find an international platform on which to pursue their demands. Engaging in collective action increased the exposure of the human rights cause—it made the invisible *desaparecidos* visible again—but it also increased the activists' visibility, and hence vulnerability to repressive actions by the Argentinean government. The activists' strategy of mobilizing across borders can be described as a transnational mechanism defined as the "boomerang effect," in which domestic movements join forces with international organizations to coerce their governments to change domestic practices (Keck and Sikkink 1998: 36) and which, at the same time, affords the individuals some protection from the state through their connections to transnational advocacy networks.

Even though the term *desaparecidos* must itself be regarded as transnational—its historical roots extend across national boundaries—the term generally evokes the disappeared in Argentina. This corroborates the efficacy of Argentinean activist networks to increase public knowledge of atrocities in Argentina. The disappearance of persons is often described as *muerte argentina* (Argentinean death); thus the *desaparecidos* have become inextricably linked with Argentinean identity (Feinmann 1998: 107). In the prologue to *Nunca Más*—a term that itself connects the experience in Argentina with a previous genocide, the Holocaust—Ernesto Sábato further laments that it is a "sad privilege for Argentina" that the term is "frequently left in Spanish by the world's press" (1984).

The more recent use of the term to refer to the estimated one hundred thousand nameless dead in Spain's mass graves dating from the Franco dictatorship (1939–75), then, was a tactic of "symbolic politics." Symbolic politics focus public attention on the meaning of an issue by drawing on recognizable "symbols, actions or stories" that assist in mobilizing people to a cause (Keck and Sikkink 1998: 16), in this case the disinterment of the Spanish Civil War dead. Journalist Emilio Silva, the founder of the ARMH, and initiator of the first scientific exhumation of a Spanish mass grave in October 2000, referred to himself from the beginning as the grandson of a *desaparecido* (Silván 2015). Silva not only exerted individual agency but also engaged in acts of "collective agency," defined as the "action component of collective identity," which resides in a shared sense of community affixed to "shared attributes and experiences among those who comprise the collectivity" (Snow 2001: 2213). The appropriation of the term *desaparecidos* by ARMH memory activists, replacing the previously used terms *paseados* or *fusilados*[4] (Ferrándiz 2010: 171), sought to establish a transnational link between experiences under Latin American dictatorships—foremostly Argentina—and that under the Franco dictatorship. Notably, Silva and the ARMH interacted with, transformed, and recontextualized the memory narrative of the Argentinean *desaparecidos* to incorporate their own and thus attempted to create a larger community of those impacted by disappearances.

The figure of the *desaparecido* has taken center stage in public debates on historical memory in Spain, particularly with the first criminal investigation into Francoist crimes in 2008 by Judge Baltasar Garzón, who applied the legal category of "enforced disappearances" to the victims of these crimes (Ferrán 2013: 132). The appropriateness of the category for the Spanish case has, however, been critiqued, in particular—but not exclusively—its correct legal application. The Spanish High Court's chief prosecutor Javier

Zaragoza challenged Garzón's classification by arguing that the victims' executions were public knowledge at the time, thus these assassinations "ended the illicit situation of deprivation of liberty" and needed to be considered different crimes (quoted in Ferrándiz 2010: 167–68).[5] Historian Julián Casanova (2008) similarly argued the term should only apply to undocumented, clandestine deaths—which in Spain mainly occurred in the early stages of the Civil War—not to those that had been officially recorded.

The Argentinean media, which closely followed the developments of the historical memory movement in Spain, likewise stressed the uniqueness of the Argentinean case and highlighted the "otherness" of the Spanish *desaparecidos*, either referring to them as such, "*otros desaparecidos*," or putting the term into quotation marks (Elsemann 2011: 255–56). One of the main points of criticism is the phrase's direct transfer from Argentina to Spain without antecedents in Spain's history. However, cultural anthropologist Ferrándiz traces its first use in Spain back to the early years under Franco, when "*desaparecidos*" was introduced as an administrative and legal category referring to Civil War cases; he cautions, however, that the Spanish *fusilados* and Argentinean *desaparecidos* are not each other's exact equivalent (2010: 169–70).

The concept of "universalizing memory practices" by Trimçev proves particularly useful in the critical examination of the controversies associated with the application of the term *desaparecidos* to different contexts. Trimçev distinguishes between transnational memory practices that "establish equivalence among different interpretations of the past" and those that "coordinate between them" (2017: 631).[6] Stripping a mnemonic signifier—such as the term *desaparecidos*—off its contextualizing references, be they temporal, spatial, or both, increases its dissemination to other interpretations of the past. This view is supported by Mandolessi and Pérez, who propose that "transnational exchanges, crossroads, decontextualisations and recontextualisations . . . are characteristic of transnational memory" (2014: 603). Nonetheless, Trimçev suggests that mnemonic narratives first need to become reduced and abstracted to be linked to other memory scripts. Memory practices that establish equivalence put heterogeneous mnemonic signifiers on a level with each other (2017: 635). These attempts at equation are generally contested and create memory conflicts, as discussed above. During the process of contestation, a dominant pattern of interpretations is established. Notwithstanding, the first reduction of a universalized narrative is not necessarily recounted identically by all memory actors. It is, more precisely, a narrative that renders divergent variations visible to each other, due to them all adhering to the "same rhythm of narration." The initial reduction of the memory script forms the basis for its subsequent diffusion, which in turn expands its "mnemonically integrated space" (Trimçev 2017: 635–36).

In the context of the *desaparecidos*, this reduction can be illustrated through a distinction between the "archetypal disappeared," or "the Argentine standard," and their subsequent transformation into the less nuanced "transnational disappeared," spanning various countries and time periods. It is important to bear in mind that the superficial adaptation of the term to the different political, historical, and temporal contexts of Spain (and other countries), however, risks the depoliticization and homogenization of enforced disappearances (Gatti 2014: 155–63). Consequently, scholars such as Anstett, for example, are wary of the term's reduction and reject its equation. Characteristics inherent to the *desaparecidos* of the Southern Cone, that is, their kidnapping and assassination followed by the purposeful concealment of the bodies, she argues, are not always present in other cases. Therefore, such transfers to different contexts of human rights violations, such as in Spain, would negate the particularity and uniqueness of the survivors' and families' suffering and render the singularity of their experience invisible (Anstett 2017: 37, 40–41, 47).

However, Trimçev's model of coordinating universalizing memory practices addresses most of these concerns. An initial reduction of the memory narratives also occurs here, but the conflicting mnemonic scripts coexist with each other; memory entrepreneurs link "different layers of interpretation that all refer to their own time and context" (2017: 640). To coordinate these divergent memory scripts of the *desaparecidos*, then, the historical, social, legal, and symbolic differences of human rights violations and their particularities in Spain and Argentina need to be clearly established; it should then be possible to integrate them "into the same kind of transnational crime without confusing them" (Ferrándiz 2010: 175). Through the coordination of these heterogeneous memories, divergent layers of interpretation are linked, creating bridges between them, thereby expanding the transnational memory space (Trimçev 2017: 640). Correspondingly, Gatti suggests that the *desaparecidos* occupy their own space, "made of irrepresentability, of fractures, absences, exceptions, ineffability, and indefinability, of invisibility and destabilization" (2014: 167). Thus, absences, fractures, invisibility, and voids are transnational meanings ascribed to this mnemonic signifier after the initial reduction of the memory script. Its use is an essential instrument for the political claims of victims and their relatives; not only in Spain and Argentina but also in other areas.

Memory Activism in Argentina: The Mothers of the Plaza de Mayo

Rendering victims invisible, in addition to eradicating voices and physical bodies of political activists, dissidents, and those believed to be in opposition, was a main tactic of the Argentinean military dictatorship. To counteract the state's technique of disappearances as a means of limiting opposition, silent marches of mothers of *desaparecidos* began in April 1977 in front of the seat of the government on the Plaza de Mayo, the main square of Buenos Aires. By locating their protest in public space, the Mothers of the Plaza de Mayo defied the "unseeing" of the abductions and prevented them from disappearing from public memory. Their weekly, ritualistic demonstrations, circulating the square, drew much-needed public attention to their cause. The numbers of Mothers increased from just fourteen to hundreds over the years;[7] they claimed the "symbolically and politically charged urban space" of the square (Kovras 2017: 66) as a memory space. Staging these protests became a means of symbolic communication to catalyze and synthesize claims for truth and memory.

Early additions to these marches were small posters made from photographs of the disappeared; the Mothers would wear them on their bodies or hold them up while demonstrating. This evokes Connerton's observation that performative memory is bodily, that is, knowledge and images of the past are conveyed by ritual performances (1989: 59); the Mothers' silent processions hence connected the bodily experience to the memory of the missing, as well as constituting a performative strategy. From the protest actions of the Mothers emerged two powerful strategies: first, the visual politics of publicly displaying photographs of the vanished in a public setting, through which they became a "collective device" (Longoni 2010: 6). Second, the white headscarves the protesters wore became the most striking symbol representing the disappearances in Argentina and were "adopted around the world as an accoutrement of solidarity" (Feitlowitz 2011: 4). Both the photographs and the headscarves were transformed from items of the family realm to powerful, public symbols in the struggle of human rights movements.

From the beginning, the Mothers had aligned themselves with human rights associations operating in Argentina.[8] They also testified in the hearings held by the IACHR in 1979. The dangers these activist protesters faced are illustrated by the disappearances of some of the Mothers themselves. Despite this, the Mothers extended the scope of their actions to force the regime to disclose information on the *desaparecidos*, ranging from circulating petitions to approaching officials in other countries (Foss and Domenici 2001: 237). This involved collective as well as "relational agency," a concept developed by Edwards in the framework of cultural historical activity theory centering on individual minds and collective action. Relational agency affords an enhanced version of individual agency; it is the aptitude of individuals to identify another person as a "resource and . . . to elicit, recognise and negotiate the use of that resource in order to align oneself in joint action" (Edwards 2005: 170, 172). This type of agency is evident in the Mothers' fostering of collaborative personal relationships across networks and borders, such as exchanging information with political activists in exile (Guzmán Bouvard 2002: 83).

Owing to the links the Mothers established with transnational advocacy networks such as the IACHR, Amnesty International, and the UNCHR, the *desaparecidos* became the topic of transnational debate, resulting in changes to international policy on enforced disappearances. Hence, not only the establishment of the UNWGEID in 1980 must be attributed to the struggle of memory activists and relatives of the disappeared but also the Declaration on the Protection of All Persons from Enforced Disappearances in 1992 and the International Convention for the Protection of All Persons from Enforced Disappearances, which entered into force in 2010. Initial demands by the Mothers for truth on and memory of the missing later extended to a call for justice. Ultimately, the Mothers' actions contributed to the international discrediting of the military regime and were crucial to the creation of a legal framework now central to human rights debates and transitional justice matters. The Mothers had transformed from a group of concerned family members to influential political activists who brought the issue of Argentina's *desaparecidos* to public attention.

Strategies by ARMH Memory Entrepreneurs

Postconflict exhumations, one of the main endeavors of the ARMH in Spain, had been conducted in Argentina as early as 1984 (Lichtenfeld 2005: 2).[9] However, the motives for the exhumations were quite different in both countries. In Argentina, the disinterments were largely undertaken to collect forensic evidence for legal proceedings and were state initiated, whereas in Spain they were privately undertaken and served the purpose of breaking a political silence, as well as giving closure to relatives. Indeed, the disappearances affect different generations—in Argentina, the parents and grandparents are looking for their children and grandchildren; in Spain, the children and grandchildren are looking for their parents and grandparents. Moreover, the temporal distance between the disappearances and the exhumations is much larger in Spain; most mass graves date back to between 1936 and 1939, and only six thousand of the estimated one hundred thousand bodies have been exhumed since 2000 (Faber 2015).

Information and communication tools such as social media and the internet play an increasingly important role in lobbying practices (Feigenbaum and McCurdy 2015: 32). The ARMH not only records video testimony during the exhumations but also employs websites and social media to reach a wider audience. Faced with disinterest of the Spanish media to report on its first two exhumations in 2000 and 2001, the ARMH captivated interest for the topic inside Spain through transnationalization. The first exhumation was filmed by a German public television channel and screened in Germany on the twenty-fifth anniversary of Franco's death (Silva 2017: 323–24). More foreign press attended the second exhumation, and the third in 2002 was conducted with the help of volunteers from nine countries (Labanyi 2008, 151). Consequently, the transnational approach of the ARMH, not only in the pursuit of media coverage but also by incorporating volunteers and experts from other countries, did raise its profile, and their activity was henceforth also broadcast by Spanish television. The mediatization of the investigative exhumation process opened a new discursive space for the traumatic memories of the past in Spain and must be viewed as an action strategy of the historical memory movement. Images of the exhumed were displayed in newspapers, on television, and on social media, informing Spain's collective memory and resulting in grassroots organizations with similar aims to the ARMH springing up all over Spain.

Furthermore, the politics of visualization pursued by the Mothers of the Plaza de Mayo through public display of photographs of the missing has also been adopted with respect to the exhumations of mass graves in Spain, where the exhumed bones and skeletons are frequently combined with photographs of the victims before their assassination (Baer and Sznaider 2017: 80–83). The exhumations themselves have become the most recognized symbol of Spain's historical memory movement. Moreover, in a country where education was dominated by Francoism for decades, the ARMH focuses on an information-driven approach; exhumations and the processes that accompany them are viewed as educational tasks by the ARMH, a memory tool aimed at teaching the Spanish public about the past to redress more than seven decades of "official neglect, oblivion and denial" (ARMH 2015). Hence the ARMH and other similar organizations have stepped into a gap left by the state and taken over its responsibilities in terms of the physical recovery of bodies, as well as education.

Treating the mass graves as potential crime scenes and documenting the exhumations meticulously to enable the filing of legal reports with the local Guardia Civil police stations (Silva 2017: 327–28) serves as a catalyst to involve the criminal justice system. The ARMH has been an important player in transnational human rights activism. In 2002, for example, it lodged a complaint with the UNWGEID, which resulted in Spain's inclusion in a list of countries still needing to deal with forcible detentions and the subsequent disappearances of people (Cué 2002). Campaigning and advocacy actions—such as soliciting support from United Nations monitoring bodies—letter-writing campaigns, protests, demonstrations, and the media coverage often attracted by them are renowned action strategies to effect political change (Smith, Pagnucco, and Romeril 1994: 71) and were employed by both, the Mothers in Argentina and the ARMH in Spain.

Moreover, the ARMH's website serves as a media space for memory and a news hub for information not only on exhumations and Spain's memory movement but also on transitional justice in other countries, providing links to news and creating a digital transnational space. The website also provides access to the various human rights resolutions and reports the ARMH is involved in,[10] which increased the political leverage of the ARMH's cause and established its link to crimes against humanity as invoked by Judge Garzón in the Spanish context.

The Transnational Space of Universal Jurisdiction

A salient example of transborder links between Argentina and Spain are the legal investigations led by Judge Garzón into crimes committed during Argentina's military rule by applying the concept of universal jurisdiction. Following the 1985 trial of the juntas in Argentina, the passing of the amnesty laws Final Point (1986) and Due Obedience (1987) there made prosecutions of human rights abuses impossible. Subsequently, activist groups and legal advisors sought justice in Spain, whose legal system allowed the laying of charges by any private organization or citizen. The Spanish Union of Progressive Prosecutors in 1996 filed charges of torture, disappearances, genocide, and terrorism against several Argentinean military officers in the Audiencia Nacional, the Spanish High Court. Remarkably, the jurisdiction of the Audiencia Nacional not only covers Spain's entire territory but also international crimes coming under the competence of Spanish courts (Sugarman 2002: 108). The 1985 Judicial Powers Act further allowed for investigation and prosecution of human rights violations committed outside Spanish territory (Agencia Estatal 1985). The application of the principle of universal jurisdiction hence enabled the prosecution of human rights violations committed in Argentina despite amnesty laws prohibiting these in the country itself.[11]

Both the arrest of former Chilean dictator Pinochet in Britain in 1998 and the 2005 conviction of a former Argentinean officer in Spain for human rights abuses represent historic milestones. This "justice cascade" of transnational universal justice processes was driven by a small advocacy network of activist lawyers who "pioneered the strategies, developed the legal arguments . . . and persevered through years of legal challenges" (Lutz and Sikkink 2001: 1–2). These activist lawyers enabled transnational legal—but also mnemonic—action by being in a "unique position to bear witness, to dramatize, to nurture, and to universalize grievances"; they hence functioned as "political entrepreneurs" (Scheingold 1989: 87) as well as memory entrepreneurs. The court cases and the continuous activism of human rights movements played a role in the subsequent repeal of both amnesty laws in Argentina in 2003 (Lichtenfeld 2005: 9–10).

These transitional justice measures helped to further break the societal silence about the disappeared in Argentina, a process that arguably had begun in 1995 with the public acknowledgment by a former navy officer to the abduction, torture, and murder of *desaparecidos* in death flights, whose existence had been denied until then (Elsemann 2011: 116–18). The changes in the political context were accompanied by a generational change: descendants of survivors and *desaparecidos* began to become engaged in the memory struggles. This precipitated a veritable memory boom in Argentina about the recent past from the mid-1990s onward, resulting in cultural production such as literary, dramatic, and other cultural texts, as well as the springing up of a range of memory projects and commemorative practices.

New memory actors also appeared on the human rights scene, such as the new activist group Sons and Daughters for Identity and Justice against Forgetting and Silence (HIJOS), an organization founded by the children of the disappeared. The activist strategies used by HIJOS are those of a new generation further removed from fear by their temporal distance to the traumatic events; hence they are "more confrontational in their use of techniques and public space" (Taylor 2003: 182). HIJOS stage highly visible and vocal demonstrations known as *escraches* outside the homes of unpunished perpetrators to raise public awareness of their continued presence in Argentina; they also track down recent photographs of human rights violators and publicize them in the perpetrators' neighborhood to expose them. *Escraches*, proposes Taylor, combine the aesthetic with the political in a performative act (2003: 14). Following and extending Goffman's dramaturgical analysis approach (1959), she stresses the importance of performativity and, furthermore, suggests a link between human agency and symbolic forms. HIJOS exercises cultural agency, defined as a "range of social contributions through creative practices" (Sommer 2005: 1) to enact the collective trauma the families and friends of the *desaparecidos* have been scarred by; they demonstrate that its legacy is stretching into the present and confront society with it.

Similarly in Spain, the younger generations have confronted the past in a disparate manner to those who had lived through the Franco dictatorship and the transition. It was they who initiated the literal unearthing of bones and memories passed down to them through the fragmented memories of their elders to confront an "active or passive inheritance of the silence and pain of others" within themselves (Martín-Cabrera 2011: 132). Moreover, the successful application of the principle of universal jurisdiction in the Argentinean case sparked passionate discussions in Spain about Francoist crimes and the continued validity of the 1977 Amnesty Law. The rapidly growing number of organizations with a focus on the Francoist repression, together with the widely publicized exhumations of mass graves, amid other factors, saw the enactment of the so-called Historical Memory Law in 2007. For the first time, mass executions and other crimes committed during the Franco regime were officially condemned, and funding for the location, exhumation, and identification of those buried in mass graves was promised. The law was highly controversial and sparked numerous heated public debates, centered on, for example, the lack of state responsibility for the exhumations, as well as the ongoing application of Spain's amnesty law.

The transformation of this legacy of "commanded forgetting" in the form of political amnesty (Ricoeur 2004: 452) was attempted at least twice by activist jurist Garzón. In 2005, three years prior to his investigation into "enforced disappearances," the judge had campaigned for the establishment of a truth commission to investigate the disappeared under Franco, similar to Argentina's CONADEP. Both these attempts failed. Furthermore, charges were laid against Garzón, regarding not only his Francoist crimes case, which allegedly violated the amnesty law, but also a further three unrelated cases, and he was eventually disbarred in 2012. Even a complaint to the European Court of Human Rights (ECtHR) as an alternative route to justice was ineffective: the ECtHR came to a decision of inadmissibility in 2012 in a case of an enforced disappearance in 1936 due to the amount of time that had passed before filing a claim. The legacy of the Francoist repression that had "determined the victims' behavior, limiting their agency and ultimately their capacity of diligence," was not considered (Alija Fernández and Martin-Ortega 2017: 540). Hence the decades-long societal silence in Spain not only impedes the overcoming of national and individual trauma but also continues to have an impact on judicial outcomes.

After Garzón's indictment in 2010, thousands of demonstrators marched through Spain, some with photos of their disappeared relatives, demanding truth and justice. The demonstrations hence turned into a broader memorial act in honor of the victims of Francoism (Junquera 2010). Like the Mothers of the Plaza de Mayo in Buenos Aires, the historical memory movement in Spain now undertakes weekly demonstrations at Madrid's central square, the Puerta del Sol (Capdepón 2011: 89). Grandchildren of both the Spanish and the Argentinean *desaparecidos*, as well as—sporadically—the Argentinean Mothers and Grandmothers participate in these (Junquera 2010). The display of portraits of the disappeared, but also images of remains found during the exhumations of mass graves and video testimony of witnesses, now form part of "modes of visualizing traumatic memory" (Ferrándiz and Baer 2008, 2). This is evident in many countries with a history of genocide and enforced disappearances and clearly not limited to the cases of Spain or Argentina. Levy and Sznaider offer the explanation for such phenomena that in our age of globalization, "different national memories are subjected to a common patterning," although separate national memories continue to exist (2006: 6). The common denominator in forming this mnemonic space consists of the divergent traumatic memories and experiences of the families of the *desaparecidos*, linked through coordinating universalizing memory practices.

The Argentinean Complaint

The most salient manifestation of Francoist victims' agency is the initiation of and participation in the legal proceedings of the so-called Argentinean Complaint. It was filed in 2010 by victim groups and human rights organizations on charges of "genocide and/or crimes against humanity perpetrated in Spain by the Franco dictatorship, between July 17, 1936 and June 15, 1977," based on the principle of universal jurisdiction (Varela and Crespo 2017). For the first time, narratives of Francoist victims took center stage in a legal setting. Survivors and relatives hence could voice their traumatic memories that had been repressed for decades and denounce crimes committed during the dictatorship. The court case has been growing steadily, acquiring more than four hundred complaints and branching out in different areas of inquiry. The context of the litigation is entirely transnational, not only through its obvious connection between the two main countries involved but also through its extended network of exiles filing complaints at the consulates of various other countries (Montoto Ugarte 2017: 4). The complaint's inauguration utilized powerful symbolic language and made visible a palpable transnational link between memory activists: the litigation was promulgated on the anniversary of the Second Spanish Republic, 14 April, and in the presence of Spanish and Argentinean activist groups, among them the Mothers of the Plaza de Mayo (Druliolle 2015). It is therefore evident that different collective memories of disparate collectives of *desaparecidos* have become part of an activist political community through the acknowledgment of a variety of traumatic narratives.

Paradigms and vocabulary from Argentina's struggle for memory continue to impact Spain. They are utilized to articulate narratives and to inscribe the crimes committed under Francoism into the context of international human rights discourses. In the wake of the Argentinean court case, new memory actors have emerged in Spain; among these are various associations representing children of Republican sympathizers illegally appropriated by supporters of the Franco regime (Valente 2013). These memory entrepreneurs employ the tactic of symbolic politics by using the term *niños robados* (stolen children) for a crime that is closely associated with Argentina and has only recently been discovered in its magnitude in Spain, where the estimated cases now range from thirty thousand to three hundred thousand

(Badcock 2017).[12] These and other grassroots memory organizations, such as the ARMH, were instrumental in the 2013 creation of the Public Coordination Group in Support of the Argentinean Complaint (CEAQUA) in Spain (Coordinadora estatal 2013). CEAQUA further increased visibility of its cause by strategically seeking support from other transnational organizations, such as the European Parliament in 2015 (Elkin 2013).

The effects of memory activists such as the Mothers of the Plaza de Mayo on the development of Argentina's democracy are, moreover, invoked by Spanish human rights groups who link the lack of criminal persecution of crimes against humanity with Spain insufficiently living up to the principles of a democratic transition. Hence the goals of the historical memory movement have shifted: in the beginning, the exhumations by organizations such as the ARMH were aimed at breaking the silence; now there is the additional call to seek justice and accountability, very similar to Argentina's well-known quest for truth, memory, and justice.

Limitations of Transnational Memory

The opening of a mass grave in January 2016 ordered by Judge Servini, the judge in charge of the Argentinean Complaint, exemplified a pivotal moment for Spain's historical memory movement: it was the first court request for an exhumation agreed to by a Spanish court and a breakthrough after all prior requests for arrests and extraditions had been declined. After ascertaining that the first grave did not contain the remains of the plaintiff's relative, the opening of a second grave in June 2017 proved successful (Varela and Crespo 2017). However, despite the reburial of the remains attracting tremendous attention from international media, it was—eerily reminiscent of the early exhumations by the ARMH—not covered by Spanish media ("TVE" 2017). Equally, a law passed in 2014 to restrict universal jurisdiction in Spain, in order "to put a stop to politically troublesome claims," is disconcerting (Alija Fernández 2014: 717).[13] The judicial climate in Spain seems to have moved away from activist law. However, the struggle for the recovery of historical memory has been gaining traction in Spain, in particular on a local and regional level.

The 2015 elections broke the traditional two-party system in Spain, resulting in numerous municipal left-wing figures in power, keen to act more rigorously on the Historical Memory Law. Consequently, a Commission for Historical Memory was established in Madrid in 2016, which endeavors to create the first Memorial Museum in remembrance of the victims of Francoism located in Spain (Medina 2016). Furthermore, Francoist street names in various cities across the country, such as Madrid, Bilbao, Oviedo, and Cádiz, either have been or are in the process of being renamed (Yagüe 2017). In addition to these mnemonic activities, new regional judicial initiatives have also been established in the wake of the Argentinean Complaint, such as the Network of Cities for Justice and Memory—made up of nine cities so far—with the sole purpose of filing local lawsuits in Spain pertaining to Francoist crimes ("Asiron participa" 2018). However, the first two of these lawsuits in Vitoria and Pamplona have been dismissed by the courts, first, again, by invoking the 1977 Amnesty Law, and second, by questioning the right of regional authorities to function as public prosecutors (Elia 2017).

So which actors and transnational strategies have impacted the development of a transnational memory space decisively? And what can be concluded from this mixed bag of evidence as to the success of Spain's historical memory movement in particular and the limitations of transnational memory in general? The strategies of visibility and symbolic politics employed by activist groups in Spain and Argentina, such as the ARMH and the Mothers (and Grandmothers) of the Plaza de Mayo, have effected much change in both countries. The study has shown that various types of sometimes overlapping and intersecting human agency—such as individual, relational, cultural, and collective—exercised by these activists have assisted in shaping a transnational memory space for the *desaparecidos* and their relatives. An additional outcome is the establishment of a transnational legal space of human rights and universal jurisdiction by activist lawyers and human rights organizations, underpinned and motivated by transnational memory activists. In the intersections of both these transnational spaces—legal and mnemonic—things happen, progress is made, and the traumatic past can be confronted, resulting in fundamental change.

In conclusion, transnational memory activism does have the potential to disseminate global human rights politics. Visibility of these topics in the public arena is essential for their success, and memory activists are indispensable in garnering support; therefore, the Spanish media's silence on a milestone in the historical memory movement, such as the reburial of the first exhumed body by an international court order, is worrisome. Moreover, the failing of the legal cases brought forward by the Network of Cities for Justice and Memory in Spain show that this activist network is thwarted by structures of Spain's national judicial framework. The president of the Grandmothers of the Plaza de Mayo suggests that "the wound of injustice can only be closed with justice and memory" (Flotats 2012); hence, memory alone—local, national, or transnational—cannot heal injustices, cannot overcome the traumatic past, and has limitations. Memory can only plant seeds and keep mnemonic narratives of injustice alive and in the public arena; justice then needs to follow to transform the past. It is evident that to successfully confront the traumatic past, laws that inhibit justice need to be transformed long term.

Intersections between the transnational memory space and transnational legal space, however, are often shifting. In Argentina, the change of government from leftist to center-right has impacted both it and Spain: a request by Judge Servini to extradite Rodolfo Martín Villa—former minister of the interior under Franco—for crimes against humanity was overturned in August 2017 (Benevento 2017). A year earlier, in August 2016, the newly elected Argentinean president Mauricio Macri appeared to doubt the long-accepted number of thirty thousand Argentinean *desaparecidos*, which led to claims of a rise of "dictatorship denial" in Argentina (Goñi 2016). Thus, also in Argentina, commemorative vigilance is required to keep the discussions about responsibility for and memories of political injustices alive.

Andrea Hepworth is a lecturer in Spanish and Latin American studies at Victoria University of Wellington, which she joined in July 2015. Her research interests include the politics of memory in postdictatorship countries such as Spain, Germany, and those of Latin America's Southern Cone, in particular Argentina, as well as the legacies of authoritarian regimes, political violence, and state repression. Further research interests cover the intergenerational transmission of traumatic memories, memory activism, transnational networks, and human rights movements.

Notes

1. The report states the number of known victims as 8,960 but asserts that the list is not exhaustive (Comisión Nacional 1984). It is estimated that as many as 30,000 people were disappeared. The omission of names of perpetrators has been heavily criticized by organizations such as the Mothers of the Plaza de Mayo (Crenzel 2012: 139, 58).
2. For a concise analysis of transitional justice measures in Argentina, see Zalaquett 1995: 20–27.
3. Jelin defines memory entrepreneurs as those who "seek social recognition and political legitimacy" of their "interpretation or narrative of the past" and who are "promoting active and visible social and political attention on their enterprise" (2003: 33–34).
4. *Paseado* literally means "taken for a walk"; it implied being led away to be executed; *fusilado* translates to "shot."
5. All translations are the author's, unless otherwise stated.
6. Trimçev developed the concept for European memory, but it is also useful for other contexts.
7. The Grandmothers of the Plaza de Mayo, a distinct group established to locate the illegally appropriated babies of Argentina's last dictatorship, also joined the silent marches.
8. For more details, see Guzmán Bouvard 2002: 93–95.
9. Yet, much evidence was destroyed during these early exhumations, mostly due to inexperience.

10. For more details, see "Resoluciones e Informes" (ARMH 2016).
11. In July 1996, charges of genocide and terrorism were also filed against Pinochet and other members of the Chilean military.
12. The first "stolen children" trial in Spain only commenced in June 2018 in Madrid; the trial, however, concerns one private individual and does not investigate the former governments' involvement (Woods 2018).
13. The 2009 reform attempt had resulted in limited impact.

References

Agencia Estatal Boletín Oficial del Estado. 1985. "Ley Orgánica 6/1985, de 1 de julio, del Poder Judicial." Ministerio de la Presidencia, Relaciones con las Cortes e Igualdad. Retrieved 21 December 2018 from https://www.boe.es/diario_boe/txt.php?id=BOE-A-1985-12666.

Alija Fernández, Rosa Ana. 2014. "The 2014 Reform of Universal Jurisdiction in Spain: From All to Nothing." *Zeitschrift für internationale Strafrechtsdogmatik* 13: 717–27. Retrieved 20 November 2018 from http://zis-online.com/dat/artikel/2014_13_883.pdf.

Alija Fernández, Rosa Ana, and Olga Martin-Ortega. 2017. "Silence and the Right to Justice: Confronting Impunity in Spain." *International Journal of Human Rights* 21(5): 531–49.

Anstett, Élisabeth. 2017. "Comparación no es razón: A propósito de la exportación de las nociones de desaparición forzada y detenidos-desaparecidos." In *Desapariciones: Usos locales, circulaciones globales*, edited by Gabriel Gatti, 33–52. Bogota: Siglo del Hombre Editores.

"Asiron participa en Barcelona en las segundas jornadas de la Red de Ciudades por la Justicia y la Memoria." 2018. *Europapress*. Retrieved 23 January 2018 from http://www.europa press.es/navarra/noticia-asiron-participa-barcelona-ii-jornadas-red-ciudades-justicia-me moria-20180122154046.html.

Asociación para la recuperación de la memoria histórica (ARMH). 2016. "Resoluciones e Informes." Retrieved 27 April 2018 from http://memoriahistorica.org.es/resoluci ones-e-informes/.

———. 2015. "What Is the Association for the Recovery of Historical Memory (ARMH)?" Retrieved 28 May 2018 from http://memoriahistorica.org.es/who-are-we/.

Badcock, James. 2017. "Cómo una mujer en España que cree que fue una 'bebé robada' y buscó a su madre biológica terminó sentenciada a prisión." BBC News. Retrieved 30 June 2018 from https://www.bbc.com/mundo/noticias-internacional-40465823.

Baer, Alejandro, and Natan Sznaider. 2017. *Memory and Forgetting in the Post-Holocaust Era: The Ethics of Never Again.* New York: Routledge.

Benevento, Gina. 2017. "Will Spain's 'Disappeared' Find Justice in Argentina?" Al Jazeera. Retrieved 1 February 2018 from https://www.aljazeera.com/indepth/opinion/2017/08/ spain-disappeared-find-justice-argentina-170810110327087.html.

Capdepón, Ulrike. 2011. "The Influence of Human Rights Discourses and Practices from the Southern Cone on the Confrontation with the Franco Dictatorship in Spain." *Human Security Perspectives* 1: 84–90. Retrieved 4 February 2018 from http://www.etc-graz.at/ typo3/fileadmin/user_upload/ETC-Hauptseite/human_security/hs-perspectives/pdffiles/ issue1_2011/CAPDEPON_Artikel.pdf.

Casanova, Julián. 2008. "Desaparecidos." El País. Retrieved 17 March 2018 from https:// elpais.com/diario/2008/07/10/opinion/1215640805_850215.html.

Comisión Nacional sobre la Desaparición de Personas (CONADEP). 1984. *Nunca Más (Never Again)—Report of Conadep (National Commission on the Disappearance of Persons)—1984.* Part II: *The Victims.* Buenos Aires: CONADEP. Retrieved 12 January 2018 from http://www.desaparecidos.org/nuncamas/web/english/library/nevagain/nevagain_209.htm.

Connerton, Paul. 1989. *How Societies Remember.* Cambridge: Cambridge University Press,

Coordinadora estatal de apoyo a la Querella Argentina contra crímenes del franquismo (CEA-QUA). 2013. Retrieved 12 May 2017 from http://www.ceaqua.org/querella-argentina/.

Council of Europe, Parliamentary Assembly. 2005. *Documents: Working Papers, 2005 Ordinary Session (Fourth Part), 3–7 October 2005.* Vol. 7: *Documents 10671–10714.* Strasbourg: Council of Europe.

Crenzel, Emilio. 2012. *Memory of the Argentina Disappearances: The Political History of Nunca Más.* Translated by Laura Pérez Carrara. New York: Routledge.

Cué, Carlos E. 2002. "La ONU pide que se investigue dónde están enterrados republicanos fusilados tras la guerra." El País. Retrieved 20 December 2018 from https://elpais.com/diario/2002/11/16/espana/1037401213_850215.html.

Druliolle, Vincent. 2015. "Spain: Seeking Justice in Argentina." Fondation Hirondelle. Retrieved 21 May 2017 from https://www.justiceinfo.net/en/justiceinfo-comment-and-debate/opinion/430-argentina-the-right-to-intervene-in-spain.html.

Edwards, Anne. 2005. "Relational Agency: Learning to Be a Resourceful Practitioner." *International Journal of Educational Research* 43(3): 168–82.

Elia, N. 2017. "Los crímenes franquistas tampoco se juzgarán en Pamplona." El Diario. Retrieved 25 January 2018 from https://www.eldiario.es/norte/navarra/ultima_hora/crimenes-franquistas-juzgaran-Pamplona_0_703780470.html.

Elkin, Mike. 2013. "Franco's Forgotten Victims." *Newsweek.* Retrieved 4 May 2019 from https://www.newsweek.com/2013/12/13/francos-forgotten-victims-244898.html.

Elsemann, Nina. 2011. *Umkämpfte Erinnerungen: Die Bedeutung lateinamerikanischer Erfahrungen für die spanische Geschichtspolitik nach Franco.* New York: Campus.

Faber, Sebastiaan. 2015. "An Underground Landscape of Terror." The Volunteer: Abraham Lincoln Brigade Archives. Retrieved 15 August 2017 from http://www.albavolunteer.org/2015/06/an-underground-landscape-of-terror-anthropologist-francisco-ferrandiz-on-spains-civil-war-exhumations/.

Feigenbaum, Anna, and Patrick McCurdy. 2015. "Protest Camps as Media Stages: A Case Study of Activist Media Practices across Three British Social Movements." In *Beyond the Internet: Unplugging the Protest Movement Wave,* edited by Rita Figueiras and Paula do Espírito Santo, 31–52. New York: Routledge.

Feinmann, José Pablo. 1998. *La sangre derramada: Ensayo sobre la violencia política.* Buenos Aires: Ariel.

Feitlowitz, Marguerite. 2011. *A Lexicon of Terror: Argentina and the Legacies of Torture.* Oxford: Oxford University Press.

Ferrán, Ofelia. 2013. "Grievability and the Politics of Visibility: The Photography of Francesc Torres and the Mass Graves of the Spanish Civil War." In *Memory and Postwar Memorials: Confronting the Violence of the Past,* edited by Marc Silberman and Florence Vatan, 117–36. New York: Palgrave Macmillan.

Ferrándiz, Francisco. 2010. "De las fosas comunes a los derechos humanos: El descubrimiento de las desapariciones forzadas en la España contemporánea." *Revista de Antropología Social* 19: 161–89.

Ferrándiz, Francisco, and Alejandro Baer. 2008. "Digital Memory: The Visual Recording of Mass Grave Exhumations in Contemporary Spain." *Forum Qualitative Sozialforschung* 9(3): 1–23.

Flotats, Anna. 2012. "Sospecho de quien prefiere el olvido, detrás hay algo oscuro." Público. Retrieved 22 April 2017 from https://www.publico.es/espana/sospecho-prefiere-olvido-detras-hay.html.

Foss, Karen A., and Kathy L. Domenici. 2001. "Haunting Argentina: Synecdoche in the Protests of the Mothers of the Plaza de Mayo." *Quarterly Journal of Speech* 87(3): 237–58.

Gatti, Gabriel. 2014. *Surviving Forced Disappearance in Argentina and Uruguay: Identity and Meaning*. New York: Palgrave Macmillan.

Goffman, Erving. 1959. *The Presentation of Self in Everyday Life*. New York: Anchor.

Goñi, Uki. 2016. "Blaming the Victims: Dictatorship Denialism Is on the Rise in Argentina." *The Guardian*. Retrieved 2 March 2017 from https://www.theguardian.com/world/2016/aug/29/argentina-denial-dirty-war-genocide-mauricio-macri.

Guzmán Bouvard, Marguerite. 2002. *Revolutionizing Motherhood: The Mothers of the Plaza de Mayo*. Lanham, MD: Rowman and Littlefield.

Hall, Christopher K. 1999. "Enforced Disappearance of Persons." In *Commentary on the Rome Statute of the International Criminal Court*, edited by Otto Triffterer, 221–26. Baden-Baden: Nomos.

Jelin, Elizabeth. 2003. *State Repression and the Labors of Memory*. Minneapolis: University of Minnesota Press.

Junquera, Natalia. 2010. "Las marchas de apoyo a Garzón se convierten en un homenaje a las víctimas del franquismo." El País. Retrieved 30 November 2015 from https://elpais.com/elpais/2010/04/24/actualidad/1272097017_850215.html.

Keck, Margaret E., and Kathryn Sikkink. 1998. *Activists beyond Borders: Transnational Advocacy Networks in International Politics*. Ithaca, NY: Cornell University Press.

Kovras, Iosif. 2017. *Grassroots Activism and the Evolution of Transitional Justice: The Families of the Disappeared*. Cambridge: Cambridge University Press.

Labanyi, Jo. 2008. "Entrevista con Emilio Silva." *Journal of Spanish Cultural Studies* 9(2): 143–55.

Levy, Daniel, and Natan Sznaider. 2006. *The Holocaust and Memory in the Global Age*. Philadelphia: Temple University Press.

Lichtenfeld, Rebecca. 2005. "Accountability in Argentina: 20 Years Later, Transitional Justice Maintains Momentum." *International Centre for Transitional Justice: Case Study Series*: 1–9. Retrieved 22 February 2017 from https://www.ictj.org/sites/default/files/ICTJ-Argentina-Accountability-Case-2005-English.pdf.

Longoni, Ana. 2010. "Photographs and Silhouettes: Visual Politics in the Human Rights Movement of Argentina." *Afterall: A Journal of Art, Context and Enquiry* 25: 5–17.

Lutz, Ellen, and Kathryn Sikkink. 2001. "The Justice Cascade: The Evolution and Impact of Foreign Human Rights Trials in Latin America." *Chicago Journal of International Law* 2(1): 1–33.

Mandolessi, Silvana, and Mariana Eva Pérez. 2014. "The Disappeared as a Transnational Figure or How to Deal with the Vain Yesterday." *European Review* 22(4): 603–12.

Martín-Cabrera, Luis. 2011. *Radical Justice: Spain and the Southern Cone beyond Market and State*. Lanham, MD: Rowman and Littlefield.

Medina, Miguel Ángel. 2016. "El Comisionado de Memoria Histórica estudia proponer un museo del franquismo." El País. Retrieved 15 January 2018 from https://elpais.com/ccaa/2016/08/08/madrid/1470678101_823377.html.

Montoto Ugarte, Marina. 2017. "Las víctimas del franquismo en la 'Querella Argentina': Luchas por el reconocimiento y nuevas desigualdades." *International Journal on Collective Identity Research* 1: 1–25. Retrieved 4 February 2019 from http://www.ehu.eus/ojs/index.php/papelesCEIC/article/view/16919.

Ricoeur, Paul. 2004. *Memory, History, Forgetting.* Translated by Kathleen Blamey and David Pellauer. Chicago: University of Chicago Press.

Sábato, Ernesto. 1984. "Prologue." In *Nunca Más (Never Again)—Report of Conadep—1984.* Nuncamas.org. Retrieved 4 March 2018 from http://www.desaparecidos.org/nuncamas/web/english/library/nevagain/nevagain_002.htm.

Scheingold, Stuart. 1989. "Constitutional Rights and Social Change: Civil Rights in Perspective." In *Judging the Constitution: Critical Essays on Judicial Lawmaking,* edited by Michael McCann and Gerald Houseman, 73–91. Glenview, IL: Scott, Foresman and Company.

Sikkink, Kathryn. 2008. "From Pariah State to Global Protagonist: Argentina and the Struggle for International Human Rights." *Latin American Politics and Society* 50(1): 1–29.

Silva, Emilio. 2017. "Epilogue: Memory Walks, Justice Awakes." In *Legacies of Violence in Contemporary Spain: Exhuming the Past, Understanding the Present,* edited by Ofelia Ferrán and Lisa Hilbink, 319–33. New York: Routledge.

Silván, Vanesa. 2015. "El Bierzo recuerda a 'Los trece de Priaranza' en el 15 aniversario de su exhumación." *InfoBierzo.* Retrieved 1 May 2016 from https://www.infobierzo.com/el-bierzo-recuerda-esta-semana-a-los-trece-de-priaranza-con-motivo-del-15-aniversario-de-su-exhumacion/204701/.

Smith, Jackie, Ron Pagnucco, and Winnie Romeril. 1994. "Transnational Social Movement Organisations in the Global Political Arena." *Voluntas: International Journal of Voluntary and Nonprofit Organizations* 5(2): 121–54. Retrieved 26 February 2018 from https://link.springer.com/article/10.1007/BF02353983.

Snow, David. 2001. "Collective Identity and Expressive Forms." In *International Encyclopedia of the Social and Behavioral Sciences,* edited by Neil J. Smelser and Paul B. Baltes, 2212–19. Amsterdam: Elsevier.

Sommer, Doris. 2005. "Introduction: Wiggle Room." In *Cultural Agency in the Americas,* edited by Doris Sommer, 1–28. Durham, NC: Duke University Press.

Sugarman, David. 2002. "From Unimaginable to Possible: Spain, Pinochet and the Judicialization of Power." *Journal of Spanish Cultural Studies* 3(1): 107–24.

Taylor, Diana. 2003. *The Archive and the Repertoire: Performing Cultural Memory in the Americas.* Durham, NC: Duke University Press.

Trimçev, Rieke. 2017. "Two Models of Universalizing Memory Practices." *European Review of History* 24(4): 631–44.

"TVE no quiere saber nada de Timoteo Mendieta." 2017. El Plural. Retrieved 28 September 2017 from https://www.elplural.com/comunicacion/tve-no-quiere-saber-nada-de-timoteo-mendieta-todo-lo-que-suene-a-memoria-historica-lo-sepultan_109550102.

United Nations, Commission on Human Rights. 2002. *Civil and Political Rights, Including Questions of: Disappearances and Summary Executions.* Report, UN Economic and Social Council. Retrieved 15 May 2017 from http://www.un.org/ga/search/view_doc.asp?symbol=E/CN.4/2002/71.

United Nations, General Assembly. 1992. "Declaration on the Protection of All Persons from Enforced Disappearances, A/RES/47/133." United Nations. Retrieved 21 December 2019 from https://undocs.org/en/A/RES/47/133.

Valente, Marcela. 2013. "Denuncia de esquema franquista de robo de bebés cruza el océano." Inter Press Service. Retrieved 12 October 2017 from http://www.ipsnoticias.net/2013/09/denuncia-de-esquema-franquista-de-robo-de-bebes-cruza-el-oceano/.

Varela, Julia, and Hernan Crespo. 2017. "Digging up the Truth about Franco's Dictatorship in Spain." Telesur. Retrieved 15 March 2018 from https://www.telesurenglish.net/multimedia/Digging-Up-the-Truth-About-Francos-Dictatorship-in-Spain-20170724-0033.html.

Woods, Tom. 2018. "Former Doctor to Stand Trial Again in Spain's 'Stolen Babies' Scandal." EuroWeekly. Retrieved 5 September 2018 from https://www.euroweeklynews
.com/2018/09/04/former-doctor-to-stand-trial-again-in-stolen-babies-scandal/#
.XDvUTtJ7nIU.

Yagüe, Antonio M. 2017. "Los ayuntamientos españoles se lían con el cambio de nombre de sus calles." Crónica Global. Retrieved 30 September 2018 from https://cronicaglobal.ele
spanol.com/politica/ayuntamientos-nombres-calles_83717_102.html.

Zalaquett, José. 1995. "Confronting Human Rights Violations Committed by Former Governments: Principles Applicable and Political Constraints." In *Transitional Justice: How Emerging Democracies Reckon with Former Regimes*, edited by Neil J. Kritz, 1:3–31. Washington, DC: United States Institute of Peace.

Chapter 5

THE CREATION AND UTILIZATION OF OPPORTUNITY STRUCTURES FOR TRANSNATIONAL ACTIVISM ON WORLD WAR II SEXUAL SLAVERY IN ASIA

Mary M. McCarthy

The Issue

The "comfort women" were women and girls held in sexual servitude to the armed forces of Imperial Japan during the 1930s and 1940s. Scholars estimate the number of victims as up to two hundred thousand, approximately 80 percent of whom came from the Korean peninsula, which was a Japanese colony at the time. Although the existence of these women was generally known during and after World War II, historical justice for them did not begin to be pursued actively until the 1990s. This was due to a multitude of factors related to shame and the social silencing of women. This chapter focuses on the opportunity structures that opened up internationally and transnationally during the 1990s and after, allowing transnational agents to successfully pursue international recognition for these women and their plight.

Transnational agents had the power to create change due to the opportunity structures that developed organizationally and normatively as greater attention began to be paid to the plight of women and girls in conflict-ridden areas around the world. When these activists could not achieve their goals in interactions with their state governments, they pursued initiatives both below and above the level of the nation-state, through grassroots organization and appeals to the United Nations. Their strategic focus, as well as certain characteristics of the issue itself, led them to be able to take effective advantage of these new opportunity structures as well as create additional ones themselves. This chapter explores the actors, the structures, the processes, and the outcomes of this case of transnational memory activism. In so doing, it reveals how memory entrepreneurs can achieve their goal of creating a counternarrative to the state by simultaneously utilizing opportunity structures at the local (substate) and international levels and transforming into transnational actors.

Transnational Movements

Assmann and Conrad argue that "until recently, the dynamics of memory production unfolded primarily within the bounds of the nation-state; coming to terms with the past was largely a national project. Under the impact of global mobility and movements, this has changed fundamentally" (2010: 2). The comfort women issue exemplifies this evolution, as it reveals the importance of transnational civil society in memory politics, the networks it inspires, as well as how transnational civil society utilizes actors below the state, above the state, and of the state to achieve its goals. Keck and Sikkink (1998) explore the ways in which transnational networks develop and enact change, while He (2004) investigates the various ways in which these transnational actors interact with the state in order to achieve their goals. Transnational civil society has taken advantage of evolving norms and acted as norm entrepreneurs itself. Transnational actors have transformed state actor rhetoric and behavior in a number of issue areas, including disarmament and human rights (Price 2003). The comfort women must be added to this list.

Comfort women activists responded to domestic and international openings amid changing norms about women and state-citizen relations. Although some activity to increase awareness of the comfort women had existed prior to this time, it was limited by the lack of opportunities in the domestic landscape, in South Korea and elsewhere in Asia. Democratization and the dawn of women's rights activism, in the context of a global recognition of the responsibility of the state to ensure historical justice, changed this (McCarthy 2018). Comfort women activists promoted these new norms internationally by bringing issues of historical injustice into contemporary debates about women and violence and changing the rhetoric surrounding those historical issues. The comfort women movement is a case study of the efficacy of utilizing emerging norms to create change in collective memories. This requires awareness of newly opening opportunity structures and an alignment of agent characteristics with norm application to further expand opportunities.

Contribution

Although scholarship on the comfort women began to be produced as early as the first half of the 1990s in Japan and South Korea, the first academic publication in English was a 2001 edited volume (Stetz and Oh [2001] 2015). However, in the last ten years or so, political attention to the movement for historical justice for the women has led to a proliferation of scholarly research among historians, sociologists, anthropologists, gender studies scholars, and, most recently, political scientists. Although initial studies focused on unearthing the stories of the women and the nature of the comfort women system, through archival work and survivor interviews, scholarship on the politics of how these stories are becoming part of global memory has been lacking. The interdisciplinary fields of memory studies and international relations combine here to provide deep insights into this case and expand our understanding of how transnational memory spaces are connecting individuals all around the world, changing the way in which collective memories are created. In this chapter I use qualitative methods of interviews and site visits to explore the meaning of these spaces and how they came about, focusing on agents, structures, processes, and outcomes.

The Who: Transnational Agents

Memory entrepreneurs are the agents who pursue the creation of collective or public memory. Their characteristics are fundamental to understanding the opportunity structures that need to exist in order for them to achieve their goals. For example, the marginalized and disenfranchised have traditionally had little chance to promote their own historical narratives at a societal level. Until relatively recently, historical accounts have tended to exclude the varied roles of women, and the experiences or perspectives of women have been largely discounted (Tickner 2010).

Therefore, the characteristics of the transnational activists who have sought historical justice for the comfort women over the last thirty years are significant. First, they are mostly women. Soh ([2001] 2015) describes them as feminist humanitarians. For many this issue was not their first foray into activism. The early days of the movement in South Korea were linked to activism against sex tourism, particularly that of Japanese men who traveled to South Korea to engage in this pastime. In fact, the first documented mention of the comfort women at a formal venue was in 1988 at the Korean Church Women United's symposium on sex tourism (Soh [2001] 2015; Tsutsui 2006). The issue was raised by a female academic, Professor Chung-ok

Yun, of Ehwa University, a private women's university in Seoul founded by an American missionary of the Methodist Episcopal Church.

From the beginning, the movement for historical justice for the comfort women was entrenched in issues of women's rights, women's agency, and feminism. Mi-hyang Yoon (2017), representative of the Korean Council, discusses the rise of the comfort women issue into Koreans' social consciousness as part of the women's rights movement in South Korea and due to a "change in traditional perceptions of women." In fact, "the first people to find survivors [of the comfort women system] was a Korean feminist organization,"[1] according to Heather Evans, a Canadian associate campaigner for the Korean Council.[2] And the framework that transnational activists adopted to present this issue to the world was feminism.[3]

Arguably the most significant nongovernmental organization in this movement is the Korean Council for the Women Drafted for Sexual Slavery by Japan (generally known simply as the Korean Council). The Korean Council was created through the amalgamation of thirty-seven liberal and progressive women's organizations in South Korea with the goal of achieving historical justice for the comfort women from the government of Japan, in the form of official apology and reparations (Yoon 2017). The Korean Council also arranged for the first public appearance and statement by a former comfort woman, Hak-sun Kim, in 1991. This garnered international attention and completely transformed the movement, as Kim's statement encouraged other women from around Asia to come forward, inspired researchers to go into the archives in Japan, and put pressure on the governments of Japan and South Korea to respond.

The nature of the Korean Council as a feminist organization is fundamental to understanding the constraints and opportunities it faced, as well as the paths it took in activism. The Korean Council became a major force at the United Nations and other international organizations and venues in promoting its cause, in the name of women's rights as human rights. In 1992, five years after South Korea's transition to democracy, the Korean Council established the Wednesday Demonstration, the weekly protests in front of the embassy of Japan in Seoul, eventually becoming the world's longest-running protest on a single theme according to the Guinness World Records. In 2011, in commemoration of the one thousandth protest, the Korean Council erected a statue of a comfort woman at that spot.[4] These were women in a consolidating democracy practicing their liberal guarantees, even though they still faced considerable marginalization that led them to international venues.

Today the Korean Council runs the War and Women's Human Rights Museum in Seoul, which focuses on the history of the comfort women system but also includes a narrative of comfort women activism since the 1990s, and ends with an exhibit on wartime sexual violence around the world.[5] Their activism has led them to become transnational, even as their main concerns are closer to home. The Korean Council continues to engage in information gathering and dissemination, public education about the comfort women, and fundraising and other support for the surviving victims in their activism and in their daily lives ("Complaint" 1994). They maintain a home where two survivors are living out their final years.[6]

After the Korean Council, the next most significant nongovernmental organization on the issue of the comfort women is the House of Sharing in Gwangju, South Korea. The House of Sharing was established in 1992 through an initiative by Reverend Hyejin of the Korean Buddhist Commission on Human Rights, after it became known that some of the former comfort women were living in poverty. The number of residents has ranged from seven to seventeen over the years. In 1996, they expanded their practice to become a legally registered social welfare organization. Besides the residence for former comfort women, the House of Sharing has a Museum of Sexual Slavery by Japanese Military and an International Peace Human Rights Center. They are currently constructing a Commemoration Center, a Relics Center, and a Memorial Park as well. In 1999, the housing component transitioned from a for-rent residence to a free nursing home for all victims of Japanese sexual slavery (Ahn 2017).[7]

Few scholars have explored the religious aspect of comfort women activism.[8] A direct relationship does not exist as perceptions of religious morality have served as a constraint on the movement at times.[9] Yet a thread of Buddhist and Christian influences can be recognized across many of the actors that have been involved in the movement. Like feminism, Buddhist and Christian value systems are also transnational, and both create and exist within certain constraining and opportunity structures.

The House of Sharing supports and promotes the activism of their residents, as well as engaging in activism itself. It found Korean survivors of the comfort system living in China, helped them to repatriate to South Korea, and brought them to the House of Sharing. It also assists its residents in attending the Wednesday Demonstration. Probably the most significant activist activity of the House of Sharing today is education. They welcome visitors from all over the world to their museum. In recent years, many of the grandmas[10] are of an advanced age where they are unable to meet visitors, but the House of Sharing continues to facilitate individual meetings between grandmas and visitors when possible.[11] From 2013 through 2017, visitors included students from eleven separate Japanese universities and nine different Korean middle schools and high schools. Foreign dignitaries who have visited include former German chancellor Gerhard Schröder, former U.S. congressmembers Mike Honda, Lane Evans, and Eni Faleomavaega, and Swedish Riksdag members Susanne Eberstein, Eva Sonidsson, and Emil Kalistrom (Ahn 2017). They have also facilitated Skype conversations between the elderly residents and students abroad through Queensborough Community College's Asian Social Justice Program in New York.[12] In all these ways, they have promoted the transnationalism of the comfort women movement.

As this transnationalism suggests, not all the major actors in the movement are based in South Korea. In Japan, the premier NGO in this area is the Women's Active Museum on War and Peace in Tokyo. The museum was opened in 2005 by the core organizers of the Women's International War Crimes Tribunal on Japan's Military Sexual Slavery. The Women's Tribunal was held in 2000 by NGOs from around Asia, as a venue for achieving social justice for the comfort women. Sixty-four women from across the region testified in front of an audience of one thousand, representing countries from around the world (Nishino 2007). A panel of judges was gathered from Europe, South America, Africa, and Asia. One of the judges noted that this tribunal was "a striking example of the developing role of civil society as an international actor" (Chinkin 2001: 338). The museum was created to house the records from the Women's Tribunal and allow public access to permanent and revolving exhibits on the comfort women (Nishino 2007). It also plays a role in research and dissemination of information for national legislatures around the world seeking to pass a resolution on the comfort women or groups seeking to erect a memorial for the comfort women.

In 1992, the Taiwanese legislature enlisted the Taipei Women's Rescue Foundation (TWRF), which was founded in 1987 to provide help to women in the sex trade (TWRF n.d.), to identify former comfort women in Taiwan and act as an intermediary to provide living expenses to these women from the government (Ward 2018: 5).[13] The TWRF has since expanded its efforts to include legal and psychological support for former comfort women (TWRF n.d.). It has also engaged transnationally with other comfort women support organizations, such as the Korean Council and the Women's Active Museum on War and Peace (WAM). In 2008, the TWRF launched a virtual museum, called the Ama's Homepage—Taiwan's Virtual Museum on Sexual Slavery by Japanese Military. It provides a comprehensive overview of the Taiwanese and Japanese governments' responses to the comfort women issue, as well as the history of Imperial Japan's comfort women system and the stories of individual women who suffered from this system. It is available in Chinese and Japanese.[14]

The brick-and-mortar Ama Museum, dedicated to the comfort women, opened in 2016. It combines education and advocacy. For example, in July 2017, the museum launched an active campaign for Japanese government apology and reparations for the comfort women, asking museum visitors to pen letters to the Japanese government, which the museum subsequently sent to the Japan-Taiwan Exchange Association, the body that represents the Japanese government in Taiwan (Lai 2017). They also highlighted their transnational activities through a cooperative venture with the Anne Frank House in the Netherlands, which included displaying an exhibit on Anne Frank at the Ama Museum in 2018, called Anne X Ama—Girls under Fire in WWII.

Another important pocket of actors in this transnational movement is the Korean diaspora, particularly those who reside in the United States. In 2010 (the year of the last U.S. census), there were 1.7 million people of Korean ancestry living in the United States, making it the second largest group of Koreans living outside of the Korean peninsula. Ninety-five percent of this population constitute immigrants who arrived after 1965 and their children (Min 2013). In 2015, 62 percent were foreign born ("Koreans in the U.S. Fact Sheet" 2017). Economic, educational, and political opportunities in the United States that did not exist in South Korea prior to democratization were the major factors promoting this emigration (Min 2013). But they have maintained strong ties to their homeland and to their churches.

The first Korean Americans to pursue historical justice for the comfort women were Korean-born women. In 1992 Ms. Dongwoo Lee Hahm, of the World Bank, founded the Washington Coalition for Comfort Women Issues, Inc. (WCCW) with other Korean Americans of similar mind. They met at the United Methodist Church of Greater Washington and organized presentations and rallies that attracted media and political attention (Hahm 2017). One of the women she enlisted to join and become a member of the advisory board was Dr. Bonnie Oh, professor of Korean studies at Georgetown University. In 1996, Oh and Dr. Margaret Stetz organized the first academic conference on the comfort women in North America, which was cosponsored by Georgetown, the Korea Society, and the WCCW. This was amid significant pushback and warnings from the Japanese government, academic colleagues, and even members of the Korean American community (some of whom viewed the raising of these issues as unseemly).[15]

One of the WCCW's major goals was a U.S. congressional resolution calling on Japan to acknowledge and apologize for the use of comfort women. They achieved this goal in 2007 with House Resolution 121. Following this, resolutions were also passed by the European Parliament, the Netherlands, Canada, and Taiwan. Activists sought to put pressure on Japan from a variety of angles. This included national governments, international organizations, and global civil society. These legislative resolutions were a public declaration by states (or intergovernmental organizations) as allies of the transnational movement (McCarthy 2018).

In 2014, the WCCW successfully lobbied Fairfax County in Virginia to erect the Comfort Women Memorial Peace Garden on county grounds (making it the fifth comfort women memorial on public land in the United

States at that time). According to Grace Han Wolf, councilmember of the Herndon Town Council in Herndon, Virginia, and honorary co-chair of the Comfort Women Memorial Peace Garden Committee, the WCCW's "mission has changed. It used to be for official apology and official compensation [from the Japanese government]. H.Res.121 is as far as one can go with that in the U.S. The U.S. has no dog in this fight. Now the mission is outreach and awareness."[16] Besides supporting the erection of memorials, the WCCW collaborates with universities to offer college tours and lectures by the grandmas, as well as seminars, conferences, and exhibits. They are also engaged in a webinar project to collect and compile primary and secondary sources on the comfort women and the transnational movement to achieve historical justice for the women (Lee 2017).

The first comfort women memorial erected on public land was also in the United States, unveiled in Palisades Park, New Jersey, in 2010 in response to lobbying by Korean American Civic Empowerment (KACE), a civic organization aimed at voter registration, education, and mobilization. KACE had aided in the grassroots movement to support the passage of H.Res.121, at the request of the WCCW. After the passage, however, it seemed to KACE that momentum on the issue had stopped. Therefore, Mr. Chejin Park of KACE had the idea of erecting a memorial in the circle of freedom (with existing memorials to the Holocaust, the Armenian genocide, the Irish famine, and the Atlantic slave trade) outside the Bergen County courthouse.[17] Although it would take another three years for Bergen County to erect a comfort women memorial in that spot, they did identify a location in nearby Palisades Park, a town with a Korean American community that comprises 52 percent of the population, for that first memorial. Although the initial unveiling was relatively quiet, by 2012 this memorial had garnered international attention and inspired the erection of comfort women memorials throughout the United States (McCarthy and Hasunuma 2018).

Today we see memorials not only in the United States but also around the world. In 2011, as mentioned earlier, the Statue of Peace was erected in front of the Japanese embassy in Seoul, and later one was built in Busan. There is a comfort women memorial in Toronto in front of Korean-Canadian Hall; one in Sydney, in front of Korean-Australian Hall; and one in Wiesent, Germany.[18] These memorials are the result of grassroots, local movements, but the activists have been inspired by each other, have learned from each other, and have sought advice from each other, constituting transnational collaboration and cooperation.[19]

Although some of these activities may seem local or nation specific at first glance, they are the result of transnational activity. The transnational agents described above engage in activities around the world to share information and support each other. The Korean former comfort women who work with the Korean Council and the House of Sharing, and the activists who support them, have spent the last twenty years visiting legislative bodies that are considering resolutions, local governments that are debating or unveiling a memorial, and international bodies that are discussing historical justice. One example is Bok-dong Kim, a former comfort woman who spent the last decades of her life engaged in "tireless campaigning" to spread global awareness and to increase pressure on Japan to apologize (Choe 2019). Her death on 28 January 2019 was recorded in obituaries around the world, from the *New York Times* to the BBC to the *Straits Times* (Singapore), and South Korean president Jae-in Moon visited a mourning area in her honor at the hospital where she died.

These women (and men) who had little recourse in South Korea or Japan to enact policy change during and prior to the 1990s found opportunity structures internationally to pursue their cause. Through their efforts they inspired other women (and men) half a world away to undertake their own initiatives. With these endeavors, they challenged the state's monopoly on determining issues of memory by bringing these issues to international and local venues themselves, both above and below the level of the state. The United Nations, in particular, created agency for these less powerful actors. So did local governments around the world that were swayed by emotional stories and notions of justice delayed. Still, all of this could only occur once critical spaces opened for them to do so.

The Structure: The Opening of International and Transnational Opportunity Structures

As Soh describes, "In the context of the masculinist sexual cultures under the patriarchal states of Japan, Korea, and many other countries, it is not surprising that the official silence over the 'comfort women' issue had been maintained for more than four decades after the war ended in 1945" ([2001] 2015: 79). In fact, the 1944 Japanese Prisoner of War Interrogation Report No. 49 of the U.S. Office of War Information describes these women as camp followers, even while acknowledging that many were forced or manipulated into service. And, although the Temporary Court Martial Tribunal in Batavia, Indonesia (Dutch East Indies) included a death sentence for one and imprisonment for other Japanese officers found guilty of forced prostitution, among other crimes, the U.S. government and its allies chose not to include the comfort women in the International Military Tribunal for the Far East, the main Japanese war crimes trials held in Tokyo. Besides masculinist sexism, this decision may also reflect racism prevalent at the time, as the charges against the officers in Batavia were brought by Dutch women.[20]

During this period, other aspects of international law similarly did not give much agency to women as the targets of sexual violence during war. "The express articulation of sexual slavery as an international crime is relatively recent. What is also new is a greater awareness of sex crimes as crimes of violence and destruction rather than property crimes or offenses against the honor or dignity of the victim or her family" (Askin 2001: 7). The Geneva Conventions themselves followed this earlier pattern, as they discussed rape as against the honor and dignity of women rather than in terms of human rights (Soh [2001] 2015).

For decades, no government was interested in actively pursuing historical justice for the comfort women. The issue of comfort women was perceived to be more about male shame than about female human rights. It was something best hidden and not discussed. According to Hicks, "From the patriarchal point of view, it was seen almost as a kindness to the comfort women to pretend that this systematic brutalization had never taken place" (1994: supra note 20, pg. xxi).

At the same time, historical narrative creation was considered to be the purview of the state. Civil society actors in both Japan and South Korea were relatively weak. South Korea was ruled until the late 1980s by a military dictatorship: a government that never discussed the comfort women under the terms of the 1965 normalization of relations with Japan. Japan has maintained a strong state even under democracy (Horvat 2007). In order for survivors and activists to gain agency in bringing about historical justice for the comfort women, something had to change. Spaces for discourse needed to open first, and then avenues to project power.

In the 1980s and 1990s these critical openings for dialogue began to occur domestically in both South Korea and Japan. The late 1980s saw the democratization of South Korea and a civil society push for transitional justice for occurrences under both the authoritarian regime and Japanese colonization. The death of Japanese emperor Hirohito in 1989 with the upcoming fiftieth anniversary of the end of World War II in 1995 also spurred reflection within Japan. In addition, women's rights movements were developing in both countries.

After Hak-sun Kim came forward in 1991 as the first former comfort woman to speak publicly about her experience, she joined two other Korean women in suing the Japanese government in Tokyo district court for reparations. While the Japanese government denied state responsibility for the comfort women system, Japanese academic Yoshiaki Yoshimi uncovered government documents that provided evidence to dispute this claim. In 1993, Chief Cabinet Secretary Yohei Kono announced the findings of a Japanese government inquiry that included acknowledgment of state culpability (the so-called Kono Statement).

Still, these openings were limited and did not create significant opportunity structures for those seeking historical justice for these women. The
Japanese government continued to maintain that all wartime grievances had
been concluded with the San Francisco Peace Treaty and the 1965 agreement
between Japan and South Korea. Both the Kono Statement and other actions
taken by the Japanese government, such as the Asian Women's Fund, were
based on acknowledgment of moral responsibility and not legal responsibility.
Many activists rejected this as they sought the Japanese government to take
legal responsibility.

As Soh describes, "The efforts of women's leaders languished, however,
mired by the bureaucratic walls of evasion and the masculinist indifference
of the masses in both countries until 1992, when the activists appealed to
UNCHR" ([2001] 2015: 80). In order to create leverage on their governments, activists needed to find sources of external pressure. In fact, Dongwoo
Lee Hahm, of the U.S.-based WCCW, relates that the event that spurred
her activity on the comfort women was actually a discussion with Japanese
politician Takako Doi, former head of the Social Democratic Party and the
first female Speaker of the Lower House in Japan, who died in 2014. Hahm
details how Doi told her that without pressure from the United States, the
Japanese government would never act on the comfort women issue, and so
Hahm had to convince the U.S. government to pressure Japan (Hahm 2017).

The ability, as well as the idea, to go to the United Nations was the result of
normative and structural changes at the international level. The first was the
promotion of the idea of women's rights as human rights, and greater attention being paid to the specific vulnerabilities of women and girls in conflict
areas. Normative change empowered women with agency. It became easier
(although not easy) to come forward with stories of rape and sexual violence.
The Rome Statute of the International Criminal Court codified sexual slavery
into international law in 1998. And the end of the Cold War meant that
women's issues had been released from the constraints placed on their receiving broader attention by their being caught in the ideological war between
communism and capitalism (Harrington 2011). A precedent had also been
set in terms of the UN being able to produce Japanese governmental policy
change. Japanese activist Etsuro Totsuka had successfully brought Japan's
mental health policy to the UN when he could not bring about domestic
policy change from within (Totsuka 1998).

Women's groups from Japan and South Korea began to actively campaign
to have the issue of the comfort women heard by the UN Commission on
Human Rights (UNCHR) in the early 1990s. At first some members were
hesitant to consider a historical case. But, in February 1992, Totsuka, as
the East Asia representative of the International Education Development
(IED) NGO, was able to formally speak before the UNCHR about open-

ing an investigation into the comfort women. In May, representatives of the Korean Council joined the IED in presenting to the UNCHR Sub-Commission Working Group on Contemporary Forms of Slavery. The Working Group recommended that its Special Rapporteur pursue this investigation. And, in August, a former comfort woman told her story to the UNCHR Sub-Commission for the Prevention of Discrimination and the Protection of Minorities (Soh [2001] 2015; Hicks 1994). "The UNCHR series of formal hearings on the 'comfort women' issue . . . provided a major turning point in transforming the nature of the 'comfort women' debate, from a class action suit . . . to an international human rights issue supported by legal experts and feminist activists across nations" (Soh [2001] 2015: 69). The ability to have their argument heard at these important international venues was a huge success for the movement.

In addition, the strategy of the activists was not solely based on normative changes in the areas of women's rights and human rights. It was also based on international law that existed in the 1930s and 1940s. This afforded activists with another opportunity structure because it was an existing agreement under international law at the time of crimes perpetrated, namely the Forced Labor Convention, which Japan had ratified and which came into force in 1932, that they presented to these commissions and working groups, along with war crimes, as a basis for their appeal.

These early hearings at the UNCHR culminated in the inclusion of the comfort women in the 1996 Coomaraswamy report and the 1998 McDougall report. In 1994, the UNCHR adopted a resolution to appoint a Special Rapporteur on violence against women, including its causes and consequences (United Nations Human Rights n.d.). The first Special Rapporteur was Radhika Coomaraswamy, a lawyer and human rights advocate, who served in this role from 1994 to 2003. In 1996, she submitted a report based on her mission to Japan and South Korea to investigate the comfort women. She began her report with her assertion "that the practice of 'comfort women' should be considered a clear case of sexual slavery and a slavery-like practice in accordance with the approach adopted by relevant international human rights bodies and mechanisms," despite claims by the Japanese government that this is inaccurate. She concluded with a number of recommendations, including that the government of Japan pay compensation to the victims, punish the perpetrators, and educate the public about this historical injustice.

Prior to this, in 1993, the Sub-Commission on Prevention of Discrimination and Protection of Minorities, based on recommendations from its Working Group on Contemporary Forms of Slavery, appointed a Special Rapporteur on the issue of systematic rape, sexual slavery, and slavery-like practices in armed conflict. Gay McDougall served as the second Special Rapporteur, after Linda Chavez stepped down. McDougall writes in her final report, in 1998, that "one significant impetus for the Sub-Commission [on Prevention of Discrimination and Protection of Minorities]'s decision to commission this study was the increasing international recognition of the true scope and character of the harms perpetrated against the more than 200,000 women enslaved by the Japanese military in 'comfort stations' during the Second World War." After extensive exploration of international law and norms, she concludes that, in the case of the comfort women, "the Japanese Government remains liable for grave violations of human rights and humanitarian law, violations that amount in their totality to crimes against humanity."

Once these openings took place, activists could take advantage of existing structures, but they could also influence and change those structures. Although international norms became more receptive to the agency of women and the specific vulnerabilities that women and girls face in conflict, it took persuasion for these UN bodies to accept the investigation of a historical case. These reports now document both the atrocities and the international law and norms that govern their reception in the international system. This indicates the mutual constitution of agent and structure. The introduction of this issue at the United Nations led to changes in the way in which sexual slavery was discussed and moved the description of the comfort women issue as sexual slavery into the mainstream. The activists made the UN consider historical justice issues that some originally thought were not appropriate for modern tribunals. And these transnational activists convinced the Special Rapporteurs that their characterization of the comfort women as sex slaves was more accurate than the Japanese government's characterization.

The Process

Bringing the narrative of the comfort women to an international audience meant being able to tell a story that would make people care. The activists had to tell a story that came across as universal and human, not attached solely to a specific time and place. Sierp and Wüstenberg discuss "the construction of narratives that have the power to transcend national boundaries and the role of individual and institutional actors in driving those narratives to (un)successful representation" (2015: 324). Activists seeking historical justice for the comfort women have been extremely successful in this regard. As Heather Evans of the Korean Council argues, "Of all the human rights abuses [perpetrated in Asia during World War II] the comfort women has been the one able to mobilize the most support internationally. . . . It's the easiest for the international community to feel sympathy for."[21] She attributes this, at least in part, to "relatability." It had to be a story of people, not of governments. The frame of human rights and not Japan–South Korea relations was instrumental to its being embraced internationally.

The importance of this human component is why we have seen these elderly grandmas travel throughout the world over the last thirty years, to national and local legislatures considering resolutions on the comfort women, to UN bodies conducting formal hearings, and to the unveiling of memorials and statues recognizing the women. Phyllis Kim of the Korean American Forum of California argues that "the reason why [the comfort women issue] is so powerful is not only because of the merit of the case but also the activism of the grandmas is so moving." She relates the story of Grandma Lee coming from South Korea to a hearing of the San Francisco Board of Supervisors considering the erection of a comfort women memorial in that city:

> The hearing was held in a large room, but they could not accommodate every-body. There was spillover into several rooms, and they had to broadcast the hearing there. Deniers spoke with Grandma Lee there. They said something so outrageous as Grandma Lee is lying. She is sitting right there. So outrageous, so heartbreaking. Supervisor [Eric] Mar he almost cried, he did cry. Another member—David Campos—when it was his turn, he said he loves his friends in the Japanese American community and appreciates what people had to say, but he said, shame on you, shame on you, three times, to the deniers. The res-olution passed unanimously. That is the power of the grandmas.[22]

The proliferation of comfort women documentaries and feature films has also been an important tool, particularly as the grandmas themselves become increasingly elderly and unable to travel. The documentary *The Apology* rep-resents both the role of the grandmas in narrating their own stories and the role of documentary as a permanent transnational memory space, transcend-ing national borders and the earthly existence of the victims.

The Apology was written and directed by Canadian Tiffany Hsiung, and it follows the lives of three elderly former comfort women: Grandma Gil in South Korea, Grandma Cao in China, and Grandma Adela in the Philip-pines. Its awards or honors include best documentary at the Busan Interna-tional Film Festival (South Korea), audience award at the Cork International Film Festival (Ireland), official selection at the DocPoint Helsinki Film Fes-tival (Finland), and inclusion in the Human Rights Film Festival (United States). The comments on the distributor's website (http://icarusfilms.com/if-ap) all speak to the power of personal narrative. Frank Scheck of *The Holly-wood Reporter* writes, "They should sell Kleenex instead of popcorn at theaters showing Tiffany Hsiung's [*The Apology*]. This powerful documentary is alter-nately harrowing and uplifting, and always emotionally devastating." Yalda Hakim of BBC News states, "An incredibly moving, emotional film." The film is a product of transnational memory creation and promotes its continuation through the stories of the women themselves. It is the preservation of oral histories in a form that can easily cross borders.

Construction and Contestation of Memory

Still, we cannot assume that the narrative presented above is the only one. Since this issue was first brought forward publicly, a multitude of actors have sought to gain or maintain agency in constructing and controlling the narrative. The Japanese government has been the most prominent in this activity. They dispute the appropriateness of the term "sexual slaves" for the comfort women, and, at times, nationalist conservative elements of the government have refuted the notions that the government played any role in coercion—it was private contractors—or that the women were not acting voluntarily—they were well-paid prostitutes. Since the end of World War II, the Japanese government sought to maintain agency as a powerful state that could control public memory and memorialization. With the rise of the transnational comfort women movement, the Japanese government has shifted into an agent of counteractivism.

The reason that the Japanese government asserts so strongly its need to control the narrative may be best understood through Sierp and Wüstenberg's observation, in reference to Benedict Anderson (1983), that "memory is closely connected to collective identity formation and has been regarded as central to the formation of modern nation-states" (2015: 322). Japanese nationalist conservatives emphasize the importance of instilling pride in the nation's young people through education. They regard the comfort women narrative as promoted by documentaries like *The Apology*, or UN reports such as those by Coomaraswamy and McDougall, or the survivors' personal testimonies to hurt the international reputation of Japan and national pride. Therefore, the Japanese government has actively protested such activities.

Most recently, the Japanese government threatened to withdraw funding to UNESCO if they chose to include comfort women documents in their Memory of the World program. Japan is UNESCO's largest funder, and the organization arguably could not continue to function if Japan ended its support. UNESCO has chosen to delay any decision on inclusion of the comfort women documents submitted by Voices of the "Comfort Women," a group of activists from eight countries. In October 2017, after protests by Japan about the 2015 decision to include documents pertaining to the Nanjing Massacre, as well as consideration of the comfort women documents, UNESCO announced changes to its application process and declared that it would seek to avoid exacerbating political tensions in any future decisions about inclusion.[23]

As reflected by the difficult situation in which UNESCO found itself, "these supranational institutions dealing with memory politics are faced by a myriad of 'memory entrepreneurs,' ranging from representatives of member states governments to non-state actors, all vying for attention and influence" (Sierp and Wüstenberg 2015: 325). This is represented by the ongoing power struggle among the Japanese government and transnational actors—civil society actors in South Korea, the United States, and Japan—over the comfort women narrative and how the world will remember these women. As Sierp and Wüstenberg continue, with a nod to Wolfrum (1999), "Memory politics should therefore be considered a policy field in which different actors load history with their specific interests and meanings. As they compete for dominance, the invention of common memories can lead to the creation or affirmation of common values as a foundation for social or political communities" (2015: 325–26).

Creation and Maintenance of Transnational Memory Spaces

A number of activists, as well as the survivors themselves, are seeking to create and maintain transnational memory spaces where their common values take center stage. They seek not only to help the public remember the past but also to create specific collective memories through carefully considered depictions, images, and words.

As explored above, one way in which this has been accomplished is through films like *The Apology*. An earlier documentary that introduced many to the issue of the comfort women was Korean American filmmaker Dai Sil Kim-Gibson's *Silence Broken: Korean Comfort Women* (2000). Feature films and television dramas in South Korea have also included depictions of the comfort women. In terms of the creation of transnational memory space, most notable is *Spirit's Homecoming* (2016), a South Korean period drama about the lives of two young girls taken from their homes to sexually service Japanese soldiers in Manchuria. After opening at number one in the box office in South Korea, it was distributed worldwide and has been shown at universities and other venues in a variety of countries.

Another way to create transnational memory spaces is through the comfort women memorials and statues discussed above. Although private memorials have existed for decades, it has been memorials and statues erected on public land that have created transnational memory spaces. As of 2019, there were nine comfort women memorials on public land in the United States (in California, Georgia, New Jersey, New York, and Virginia). There are also two statues in very prominent locations in South Korea, causing diplomatic upheaval between South Korea and Japan. As mentioned earlier, one is in front of the

Japanese embassy in Seoul; the second is outside the Japanese consulate in Busan. The latter led Japan to temporarily withdraw its ambassador in 2017.

The Creation of Agency and Power

Through the processes described above, the former comfort women and the transnational activists who support them, have gained agency and power to enact change. They transformed the debate into one of sexual slavery, brought international pressure to bear on the Japanese government, and took control of the historical narrative in a number of ways. Heather Evans emphasizes how the issue "turned from shame and stigma to positive mobilization."[24] This was due to the successful strategies of the transnational actors and their ability to take advantage of opportunity structures that became available in the 1990s. As Evans continues, "These individuals [who are former comfort women] have gained stature from being able to claim a human rights framework."[25] The comfort women movement became one of international solidarity behind these women who suffered tragic lives. People connected emotionally to their personal stories and were led to associate these stories from seventy-five years ago with current atrocities.

Furthermore, what these women and their supporters could not achieve at the level of the nation-state or in interaction with the nation-state, they were able to achieve internationally and transnationally. This is not to suggest that transnational activists advocating for the comfort women have achieved all their goals. They have not. They still seek official apology and reparations from the Japanese government. They also seek an end to Japanese nationalist conservative questioning and undermining of the narrative of the comfort women that the activists seek to tell. And there are indications that the Japanese government maintains considerable power in setting the international agenda on these issues, as the UNESCO case suggests.

Still, the transnational comfort women movement has successfully created transnational memory spaces that will continue to exist through the coming generations. These are memorials, statues, UN reports, national legislative resolutions, documentaries, and feature films. Young people from around the world are more likely to learn about the comfort women today than ever before.

Conclusion

As the introduction to this volume mentions, agency is the power to create change. This chapter argues that change is brought about by an agent's refusal to stay within the bounds of the nation-state. Neither state-imposed collective memories nor country borders need contain memory entrepreneurs. Memory agents can create transnational memory spaces that impact global, national, and local collective memories. The condition for this is the opening of opportunity structures that align with the characteristics of the actors. Memory activists can also shape these emerging structures so that agents and structures are mutually constituted, as activists evolve to be successful within the new structures and structures are molded to support the goals of the memory agents.

The lesson of the comfort women movement is that domestic actors who seek to counter a state-imposed historical narrative (whether in their own country or another) can do so by breaking free of the constraints of the state or traditional hierarchies. In today's globalized world with evolving norms, new opportunity structures are emerging. Transnational civil society can utilize opportunity structures at the substate and global levels simultaneously and, thereby, initially bypass the state and later put pressure on the state to accept counternarratives. Creating transnational memory spaces further distances control of collective memory from the state, reinforcing agency of nonstate memory entrepreneurs.

Mary M. McCarthy is an associate professor of politics and international relations at Drake University. She specializes in Japan's domestic and foreign policies, with a current focus on the legacies of the Asia-Pacific War on Japan's foreign relations. She is editor of the *Routledge Handbook of Japanese Foreign Policy* (2018), and her most recent publications include "Coalition Building and Mobilization: Case Studies of the Comfort Women Memorials in the United States," with Linda C. Hasunuma (*Politics, Groups, and Identities Politics,* 2018). Dr. McCarthy received her BA in East Asian studies and her PhD in political science from Columbia University.

Notes

1. Interview with author, 7 July 2017.
2. "Associate campaigner" is how the Korean Council refers to someone authorized to speak on their behalf.
3. There is disagreement over whether the feminism promoted by these groups was more of a Western model (Evans, interview with author) or a transnational feminism that is coalitional, antinationalist, and antiexploitative (Thoma [2001] 2015). I argue that it constitutes a dialogue among various forms of feminism.

4. The erection of the statue resulted in a vociferous negative response from the Japanese government, which called the protests and the statue a form of harassment prohibited under diplomatic accords.
5. This is based on the author's visit in June 2018.
6. This was at the time of the author's visit in June 2018.
7. Ahn is the director of the House of Sharing.
8. Lim (2018) compares the women in their search for justice with Jesus's trials and tribulations on earth, caught between Roman and Jewish authorities.
9. Author's interview with Bonnie Oh, 18 July 2014.
10. Koreans commonly refer to the comfort women survivors as *halmonie*, which translates into English as "grandma." In Taiwan, they use the term *ama*, which is Taiwanese Hokkien for "grandmother."
11. They provided such an opportunity for this author in June 2018.
12. Dr. Jimin Kim, program director of the Asian Social Justice Program, Kupferberg Holocaust Center, Queensborough Community College, interview with author, 26 May 2015.
13. Dr. Chu Te-lan of the Academia Sinica in Taiwan, who conducted most of the interviews with Taiwanese former comfort women, concluded that approximately one thousand Taiwanese women were conscripted into sex service (Ward 2018: 1). The TWRF adopts the upper limit of two thousand.
14. As of January 2019, there was a tab for English, but it did not connect to any English page. Possibly that is under construction.
15. Bonnie Oh, interview with author, 18 July 2014.
16. Interview with author, 22 July 2014.
17. Chejin Park, interview with author, 21 April 2015.
18. This comes from a list composed by Dr. Naoko Kumagai of the International University of Japan and revised by the author.
19. Interviews with author.
20. This reflects the history of the evolution of international law covering sex trafficking, which was originally focused solely on the white slave trade.
21. Interview with author, 17 July 2017.
22. Interview with author, 8 August 2017.
23. For the Japanese government's perspective on this controversy of the Memory of the World program, see Matsui (2017).
24. Interview with author, 17 July 2017.
25. Ibid.

References

Ahn, Shin-kwon. 2017. "The Establishment of the Museum of Japanese Military Sexual Slavery and the House of Sharing." Presented at the Redress Movement for the Victims of Japanese Sexual Slavery: Looking Back at the 27-Year Movement Conference, Queens College, New York, 13–14 October.

Anderson, Benedict. 1983. *Imagined Communities: Reflections on the Origin and Spread of Nationalism*. New York: Verso.

Askin, Kelly D. 2001. "Comfort Women—Shifting Shame and Stigma from Victims to Victimizers." *International Criminal Law Review* 1: 5–32.

Assmann, Aleida. 2014. "Transnational Memories." *European Review* 22(4): 546–56.

Assmann, Aleida, and Sebastian Conrad. 2010. "Introduction." In *Memory in a Global Age: Discourses, Practices and Trajectories*, edited by Aleida Assmann and Sebastian Conrad, 1–16. Basingstoke: Palgrave Macmillan.

Chinkin, Christine M. 2001. "Women's International Tribunal on Japanese Military Sexual Slavery." *American Journal of International Law* 95(2): 335–41.

Choe, Sang-Hun. 2019. "Kim Bok-dong, Wartime Sex Slave Who Sought Reparations for Koreans, Dies at 92." *New York Times*, 29 January.

"Complaint." 1994. The Korean Council for Women Drafted for Sexual Slavery by Japan. Retrieved 15 March 2015 from http://www.vcn.bc.ca/alpha/learn/comp.htm.

Coomaraswamy, Radhika. 1996. *Report on the Mission to the Democratic People's Republic of Korea, the Republic of Korea and Japan on the Issue of Military Sexual Slavery in Wartime*. New York: UN Commission on Human Rights, Economic and Social Council.

Hahm, Dongwoo Lee. 2017. "Tracing the Twenty-Five Years of Comfort Women Movement in the U.S." Presented at the Redress Movement for the Victims of Japanese Sexual Slavery: Looking Back at the 27-Year Movement Conference, Queens College, New York, 13–14 October.

Harrington, Carol. 2011. "Resolution 1325 and Post–Cold War Feminist Politics." *International Feminist Journal of Politics* 13(4): 557–75.

Hasunuma, Linda C., and Mary M. McCarthy. 2019. "Creating a Collective Memory of the Comfort Women in the USA." *International Journal of Politics, Culture, and Society* 32(2): 145–62.

He, Baogang. 2004. "Transnational Civil Society and the National Identity Question in East Asia." *Global Governance* 10(2): 227–46.

Hicks, George. 1994. *The Comfort Women: Japan's Brutal Regime of Enforced Prostitution in the Second World War*. New York: W. W. Norton.

Horvat, Andrew. 2007. "A Strong State, Weak Civil Society, and Cold War Geopolitics: Why Japan Lags behind Europe in Confronting a Negative Past." In *Rethinking Historical Injustice and Reconciliation in Northeast Asia*, edited by Gi-Wook Shin, Soon-Won Park, and Daqing Yang, 216–34. London: Routledge.

Keck, Margaret E., and Kathryn Sikkink. 1998. *Activists beyond Borders: Advocacy Networks in International Politics*. Ithaca, NY: Cornell University Press.

Kim, Phyllis. 2017. "Walking with the Grandmas: Is There a Path to Winning?" Presented at the Redress Movement for the Victims of Japanese Sexual Slavery: Looking Back at the 27-Year Movement Conference, Queens College, New York, 13–14 October.

"Koreans in the U.S. Fact Sheet." 2017. Pew Research Center. Retrieved 20 March 2020 from https://www.pewsocialtrends.org/fact-sheet/asian-americans-koreans-in-the-u-s/.

Lai, Juvina. 2017. "Taiwan's Ama Museum Launches Campaign to Request Compensation for Families of 'Comfort Women.'" *Taiwan News*, 14 August. Retrieved 15 February 2019 from https://www.taiwannews.com.tw/en/news/3231738.

Lee, Jungsil. 2017. "Tracing the Twenty-Five Years of Comfort Women Movement in the U.S." Presented at the Redress Movement for the Victims of Japanese Sexual Slavery: Looking Back at the 27-Year Movement Conference, Queens College, New York, 13–14 October.

Lim, Sung Uk. 2018. "Bare Lives in the Shadow of Empires: Jesus, Comfort Women, and Theology of Resistance." *Theology Today* 75(2): 214–32.

Matsui, Nozomi. 2017. "Memory of the World to Change Rules after Asian Controversies." *Asahi Shimbun*, 19 October. Retrieved 15 February 2019 from http://www.asahi.com/ajw/articles/AJ201710190040.html.

McDougall, Gay. 1998. "Contemporary Forms of Slavery: Systematic Rape, Sexual Slavery and Slavery-Like Practices during Armed Conflict." New York: UN Commission on Human Rights, Economic and Social Council.

McCarthy, Mary M. 2018. "The Power and Limits of the Transnational 'Comfort Women' Movement." In *Handbook of Japanese Foreign Policy*, edited by Mary M. McCarthy, 364–78. London: Routledge.

McCarthy, Mary M., and Linda C. Hasunuma. 2018. "Coalition Building and Mobilization: Case Studies of the Comfort Women Memorials in the United States." *Politics, Groups, and Identities* 6(3): 411–34.

Min, Pyong Gap. 2013. "The Immigration of Koreans to the United States: A Review of Forty Five Year (1965–2009) Trends." In *Koreans in North America*, edited by Pyong Gap Min, 9–34. Lanham, MD: Lexington Books.

———. 2017. "A Critique of C. Sarah Soh's Rejection of the Japanese 'Comfort Women' System as Sexual Slavery." Presented at the Redress Movement for the Victims of Japanese Sexual Slavery: Looking Back at the 27-Year Movement Conference, Queens College, New York, 13–14 October.

Nishino, Rumiko. 2007. "Women's Active Museum on War and Peace and Its Role in Public Education." United States Institute of Peace. Retrieved 15 March 2015 from https://www.usip.org/sites/default/files/file/nishino.pdf.

Park, Yuha. 2014. *Teikoku no Ianfu*. Tokyo: Asahi Shimbun Shuppan.

Price, Richard. 2003. "Review: Transnational Civil Society and Advocacy in World Politics." *World Politics* 55(4): 579–606.

Sierp, Aline, and Jenny Wüstenberg. 2015. "Linking the Local and the Transnational: Rethinking Memory Politics in Europe." *Journal of Contemporary European Studies* 23(3): 321–29.

Soh, C. Sarah. (2001) 2015. "Prostitutes versus Sex Slaves: The Politics of Representing the 'Comfort Women.'" In *Legacies of the Comfort Women of World War II*, edited by Margaret Stetz and Bonnie B. C. Oh, 69–90. New York: Routledge.

Stetz, Margaret. 2017. "Making Girl Victims Visible: A Survey of Representations That Have Circulated in the West." Presented at the Redress Movement for the Victims of Japanese Sexual Slavery: Looking Back at the 27-Year Movement Conference, Queens College, New York, 13–14 October.

Stetz Margaret, and Bonnie B. C. Oh. (2001) 2015. *Legacies of the Comfort Women of World War II*. New York: Routledge.

Taipei Women's Rescue Foundation (TWRF). N.d. "About TWRF." Retrieved 20 June 2018 from https://www.twrf.org.tw/eng/p1-about.php.

Taiwan's Virtual Museum on Sexual Slavery by Japanese Military. N.d. Retrieved 20 June 2018 from http://www.womandpeace.org.tw.

Thoma, Pamela. (2001) 2015. "'Such an Unthinkable Thing': Asian American Transnational Feminism and the 'Comfort Women' of World War II." In *Legacies of the Comfort Women of World War II*, edited by Margaret Stetz and Bonnie B. C. Oh, 101–27. New York: Routledge.

Tickner, J. Ann. 2010. "You May Never Understand: Prospects for Feminist Futures in International Relations." *Australian Feminist Law Journal* 32(1): 9–20.

Totsuka, Etsuro. 1989. "The Changing Face of Mental Health Legislation in Japan." *International Commission of Jurists Review*, no. 42: 67–81.

Tsutsui, Kiyoteru. 2006. "Redressing Past Human Rights Violations: Global Dimensions of Contemporary Social Movements." *Social Forces* 85(1): 331–54.

United Nations Human Rights, Office of the High Commissioner. N.d. "Special Rapporteur on Violence against Women, Its Causes and Consequences." Retrieved 20 August 2018 from http://www.ohchr.org/EN/Issues/Women/SRWomen/Pages/SRWomenIndex.aspx.

Ward, Thomas J. 2018. "The Comfort Women Controversy: Lessons from Taiwan." *Asia Pacific Journal* 16(8): 1–14.

Yoon, Mi-hyang. 2017. "Unfinished Justice: The Restoration of Human Rights to the Victims of Japanese Military Sexual Slavery." Presented at the Redress Movement for the Victims of Japanese Sexual Slavery: Looking Back at the 27-Year Movement Conference, Queens College, New York, October, 13–14.

Chapter 6

THE POLITICAL AGENCY OF VICTIMS THROUGH TRANSNATIONAL PROCESSES OF FORENSIC ANTHROPOLOGY AND MEMORY CONSTRUCTION IN LATIN AMERICA

Devin Finn

Introduction: How Does Memory in Latin America Draw on Individual and Collective Experiences of Violence?

During the twentieth century, Latin American societies suffered the effects of oppressive governments, mass atrocities carried out by state and other armed actors, and violations of human rights. Decades of activism for justice and the restoration of individual rights have accompanied the search for human remains and evidence for prosecution. As a result of these activities and the places and events that have been memorialized as a result, can we speak of a transnational memory in Latin America—a legacy of shared experiences of violence, commemoration, and political struggles for justice for forced disappearance, atrocities, and corruption? What does a "transnational" or regionally shared and understood memory signify, and what are its political effects? These questions motivate an examination of existing collective action related to memories of violence and the connections among organizations that engage in claim-making to generate remembrance and political mobilization. Understanding the relationality of memory practices and actors reveals the existence of a Latin America memory culture by illuminating the shared politics of remembrance and mobilization for justice.

To pursue the question about whether the memory of forced disappearance illuminates the transnational texture of memory in Latin America, I focus in this chapter on forensic investigations as a locus for the creation of activism rooted in remembrance. Do the investigative activities undertaken by forensic anthropology organizations and relatives of disappeared victims help facilitate opportunities for creating memory by organizing and conducting searches for victims' remains? Do these memory activities engender activism, strategies, or shared purpose among victims and their relatives in different contexts of the region? I argue that memory emerges in specific ways through processes of forensic analysis and identification, and through interaction among family members and experts. Drawing on political memory-making through searches for human remains in postconflict Peru, I demonstrate that the existence of transnational memory depends on these actors' mutual engagement with structures that defy the production of memory, including political and economic forces, that frustrate the identification and delivery of the remains of the disappeared to their surviving relatives.

First, the chapter discusses existing theoretical arguments on how memory works within and transcends national borders. I introduce the argument, which emphasizes the intricate connections between justice and memory; the political agency that victims seize by participating in searches for the remains of loved ones; and how the trans-border discipline and practice of forensic anthropology (FA) both creates a space for social and political engagement by relatives and mediates their struggles through its elite connections and expertise.

Next, three empirical sections focus on, first, the historical development and methods of forensic anthropology organizations in their approach to scientific investigations of human remains and graves; second, how family members of victims participate in searches for bodies and make political demands; and third, how FA organizations communicate and collaborate among themselves to provide fora for memory-making. In the conclusion, I synthesize the argument and evidence and turn to a few implications of the study.

Forensic Anthropology and Transnational Memory Theory

Scholars have begun to stress the ability of memory to cross borders and circulate, shifting the empirical and theoretical focus from national "methodologies" and identities of memory-making to modes that try to capture "transnational" processes and sites. Transnational memory is jointly created or shaped by various actors at different putative sites or "places of memory," the contexts in which agents of memory interact, commemorate specific events, and seek political change. For a transnational memory to exist, it is not necessary that individuals' remembrances be of the same, or even comparable, events. Latin Americans' experiences of violence by state and non-state actors include systematized human rights abuses and violence against minority groups, repression of activists, and corrupt, negligent rule. While they take distinct forms shaped by context and history, these events have left behind memories that inspire political responses. One manifestation of memory-making in Latin American countries is elemental: processes of searching for bodies of disappeared citizens and the forensic investigations that identify and rebury them. Forced disappearance is defined as the arrest, detainment, or abduction against her will or deprivation of liberty of an individual by officials of different branches or levels of government, or by organized groups or private individuals acting on behalf of the government.[1] Disappearance is a "double crime": it is committed, first, against the abducted individual, and second, against the relatives and loved ones who do not know what happened to their family member.

In Peru, a newly created unit within the Ministry of Justice, the Directorate General of Searches for Disappeared Persons, or DGBPD for its acronym in Spanish, estimates that there are at least 20,329 disappeared persons in the country as a result of the country's civil war (1980–92).[2] Only 865 of these *desaparecidos* have been found and returned to their family members. In addition, according to the DGBPD, the whereabouts of 13,764 individuals reported disappeared have not been identified with certainty. The founding objective of the DGBPD's investigative work is of a humanitarian rather than a judicial or prosecutorial nature.

Forensic anthropology, which developed as a response to the phenomenon of widespread disappearances in Latin American countries, derives from the work of biological archaeologists and physical anthropologists and is defined as "the discipline that applies the scientific knowledge of physical anthropology and archaeology to the collection and analysis of legal evidence" (Burns 2007: 3). Forensic anthropologists recover, describe, and identify human skeletal remains. The development of forensic anthropology in Latin America has expanded since the 1980s, orienting family members of victims to a series of fundamental questions, beginning with: who was the missing person, and what happened the day that she disappeared? The facts that these initial questions produce are subject to the memory of those left behind—mothers, brothers, fathers, wives, sisters, children, classmates, friends. But these contestable facts are necessary for forensic experts and technicians to begin testing and digging in suspected gravesites. Family members' testimonies and remembrances, which may change with the passage of time, are essential to establishing a search for remains. The presence and participation of those anticipating finding their relatives is embedded into forensic anthropology.

The processes of investigation that forensic searches require invoke results that are less concrete than the bones they may uncover: descriptions of lives, events, and places that emerge in the context of these *búsquedas* (searches). The fora or spaces that forensic investigations generate bring distinct sets of victims, survivors, and relatives of victims together. They tell each other stories, sharing dates, details, and circumstances with one another, allowing their desires to find their loved ones' bodies to become linked and interdependent. Participants help create the space for remembering, which has specific objectives—gaining knowledge about the whereabouts of a loved one, locating a body or a grave, providing a proper burial (*entierro digno*), and, frequently but not always, seeking justice for crimes (Collins 2017). As contested political events in themselves, these processes may generate conflict among the family members and organizations who seek information and justice.[3]

A fundamental question emerges when we examine the nature of building memory across borders: is the existence of "national memory" in affected countries in the region necessary for the creation of memory that is transnational? I find that national processes of memory interact with transnational forms of remembrance and network construction in ways that allow for "recasting analytical frameworks" (Inglis 2015: 144) to encompass domestic and transnational phenomena ontologically together. The practices of a given community in Latin America—for example, the Nebaj people in rural Guatemala who suffered massacres during the civil war, or the families of justice system officials killed as a result of the M-19 rebels' siege of the Palacio de Justicia in Bogotá in 1985—generate their own distinct forms of memory-making and activism. But they comprise part of an aggregate response to impunity that emerges from the political activism embodied in sharing experiences of victimhood and searches. Crossing borders occurs in distinct ways, and not only across limits of nations and states; other kinds of "moving across" involve generational differences and boundaries that separate state from nonstate actors (Collins 2017: 1–3)—lines that are increasingly blurred.

Memory Within and Beyond Borders

Researchers have stressed the ability of memory to cross borders and circulate, moving the focus in the literature from national "methodologies" and identities of memory-making to modes that try to capture transnational processes and sites. With place as an anchoring force of memory, and more specifically national borders as limiting scope and process, the move toward trans-border processes is a potential theoretical advance (Wüstenberg, this volume). This study adopts the concept of memory construction as a product of intellectual and political negotiations between "social carriers of memory" (Müller 2002).

Transnational memory is jointly created or shaped by varied agents at different "levels," putative sites that stand in for the contexts in which agents of memory interact and seek political change. Drawing on the notion of memory as a shared construction that occurs at local, national, and global levels, this chapter demonstrates *how* family members of murdered and disappeared victims in Latin America produce memory through their participation in searches for the bodies of loved ones. How forensic anthropologists, and the methods, comparative knowledge, and scientific norms that they employ, interact with family members' mobilization and commemorations generates a space and various forms of political memory.

While the study of memory has been moving from a theoretical adherence to the nation as a primary driver of remembrance, researchers may not be able to elude fully the centrality of national dynamics even as conceptual contributions complicate the field. Some existing work highlights more rigid distinctions between national and transnational, but as they emerge in studies of memory and forensics processes in Latin America, the two "levels" shape and are shaped by one another. In these studies, while an elite-driven process of advocacy and justice-seeking dominates some spheres of memory-making like truth commissions and criminal prosecutions, transnational memory is not equivalent to "cosmopolitanism," as perhaps suggested in some studies of globalization and memory (Levy and Sznaider 2005).

The relationship between the national and transnational in Latin America is reflected in the relationship between justice and memory. If "justice and violence dwell in close proximity to one another" (Booth 2006), as the second half of the twentieth century and the last two decades have shown, activists orient memory-making toward political and social struggles against unjust oppressors and structures. The result is a "constant interaction between state and societal actors in the struggle for understanding and interpreting past violence and repression" (Jelin 2007: 138). As Cath Collins argues, "the interplay between institutional and informal actors and spaces now spins a web of multiple threads, vertical and horizontal" (2017: 14). This kind of advocacy and legal action emerged from individual agency and changing institutions, like the success of the right of individual petition introduced in the Inter-American Court on Human Rights. In an interaction between the national and transnational, relatives and victims engaged in searches for victims may connect directly to judges of the Inter-American Commission on Human Rights (IACHR). "Judges . . . become connected to individual claim makers—activists, relatives, and survivors—with or without the mediation of the lawyers or domestic justice system operators who are also part of this new, organic, and complex structure of accountability pathways" (Collins 2017: 14). Demands for truth and justice are, then, "from the very beginning, also demands for memory" (Jelin 2007: 140).

Grappling with political and social structures that resist and undermine the production of memory—including state institutions' lack of capacity or willingness to investigate crimes and treat victims as citizens—inspires a form of memory activism that takes place both within national borders and in and through sites that transcend these borders. The latter, obviously transnational sites include the Inter-American Court of Human Rights and other formal institutional settings, but also sites of communication and expression that we might consider purely "national." These include domestic trials of former military commanders and heads of state for war crimes, such as General Efraín Ríos Montt in Guatemala and former president Alberto Fujimori in Peru. These events constitute widely visible settings in which the gravity—of a potential legal precedent, an innovative use of evidence, the testimony of marginalized indigenous women about sexual violence—carries weight and interest for activists and family members in other contexts. This constitutive effect (Tannenwald 1999) is one form of national and transnational memory—and the normative demands that accompany memory—being created and interacting through domestic processes, in a version of what some scholars of norm development call "socialization." Some scholarship on post-atrocity and postwar Latin America assumes the existence of regional effects, including the effects of human rights trials on democracy, conflict, and violence in the region (Sikkink and Booth Walling 2007). The notion of a "justice cascade," the growing tendency for states to hold individuals accountable for past human rights violations, shows that, in contrast to claims made by democratic transition theorists like O'Donnell and Schmitter (1986) and Huntington (1993), efforts to seek justice for war crimes do not lead to greater numbers of human rights violations or diminish democratic processes.

I argue that whether a Latin American memory (*memoria transnacional*) exists depends not on a "unified memory regime" (Bernhard and Kubik 2014), or even on its elements coming together, but on parallel engagement with structures that defy the production of memory. These structural forces may include political and economic forces that, over time, frustrate and delay the delivery of relatives' remains and of justice to individuals.

Real differences divide and differentiate human rights and memory activists in different countries of the region, and these actors are bound by and are struggling against distinct political forces. The structural forces are rooted in and take shape because of historical processes specific to a national context. In some countries, continued denial by both members of society and state institutions such as the military and other elites may frustrate the efforts of lawyers, activists, and victims' relatives to pursue justice for crimes. The efforts of "memory entrepreneurs" (Jelin 2003), actors who link interpretations of the past with particular views of the future, lead to varied outcomes depending on the level of impunity, the integrity of institutions like courts and political parties, and the nature of attention to social processes like memory in education. In Peru, as one long-time activist and official in a forensic anthropology organization told me in 2017, "we have no national memory." Does the development of transnational memory require the existence of a national memory in societies in the region?

Activists, victims, and multiple generations of survivors in the region carry out memory activities that contribute to a perception that a *memoria transnacional* exists, uniting the efforts of disparate actors and building a network that facilitates remembrance and citizenship. In Los Angeles, California, and suburban Maryland, public notices advertise opportunities for residents to participate in a scientific process: if you are a Guatemalan immigrant and have missing relatives, you can provide a DNA swab ("just a saliva sample") and help find them (TechCampGuatemala, n.d.).

In another instance, a "Caravana de los 43" wended its way through the United States in 2015, beginning a couple months after the disappearance of forty-three students at Ayotzinapa Escuela Normal, a teaching college in Iguala, Mexico (Mandolessi, this volume). Family members of the missing students traveled across the border to generate awareness and narrate the highly publicized, developing investigation to make demands on policymakers and voters in their neighboring country. Caravana 43, the organization behind the caravan, emphasizes its identity as a movement speaking for Mexican citizens and with a cross-border message (Caravana 43, n.d.). For example, caravan members, some of whom are the parents of the missing students, draw attention to the adverse effects of "the Merida Plan" for Mexico[4] and ask for members of the U.S. Congress to change its gun policies and pressure the Mexican government on its own firearms laws.

A second suggestion of the operation of transnational memory also emerged from the Ayotzinapa disappearances. The prestigious Grupo Interdisciplinario de Expertos Independientes (GIEI, or Interdisciplinary Group of Independent Experts), was a team of jurists from Latin America and Spain, appointed by the Inter-American Commission of Human Rights (IACHR) to provide external investigative authority in the case, in which the Mexican government had been, at best, not forthcoming, and at worst, heavily implicated in organized crime and murder (Finn 2015). Based on its interviews with witnesses and officials and visits to the sites in Iguala, the GIEI, after six months of investigations, produced two reports on the events that occurred the night of the killings (Grupo Interdisciplinario de Expertos Independientes, n.d.). The five members of the GIEI, who include lawyers, judges, and a medical doctor, came from Colombia, Chile, Guatemala, and Spain. They made their reports public, presenting their "findings, advances, and recommendations to the Mexican authorities, the family members and victims, as well as the human rights community, media, and people who have followed this case closely" (ibid.).

At an early moment in the Ayotzinapa investigation, the Equipo Argentino de Antropología Forense (Argentine Forensic Anthropology Team, or EAAF) also contributed expertise and released a public statement on its own findings, adding to the speculation that the Mexican government's account of events was misleading. These layers of collaboration and engagement among regional experts who seek to construct scientific analyses of violent events blur the lines between national identity and transnational activism in pursuing justice. Indeed, forensic anthropologists interpret their own roles, particularly when states are potentially implicated in crimes and rights violations, as falling on a spectrum that captures scientific investigation and the defense of human rights.

Questions about Memory: Individual, National, and Transnational

Inherent in the notion of transnational memory in Latin America—and the collective efforts it inspires—is a shared, or mutually comprehended, sense of victimization and atrocity. Did individuals and organizations in the region suffer from the same kinds of atrocities and oppression? A few outstanding commonalities emerge as "regional" phenomena, like the military and intelligence collaboration Operation Condor; operations carried out by cadres trained at the School of the Americas; and a blanket policy, historically delimited, through which the U.S. government integrated combatting communism into its policies toward governments in the region, empowering strongmen who were countering militants domestically, which resulted in violent repression, torture, and death. But it is not necessary that individuals' remembrances be of the same or even comparable events. Experiences of state and nonstate violence, systematized repression of activists, and corrupt regimes have left behind memories that inspire political responses. Political agents, who include victims, their families, human rights organizations, artists, lawyers, and forensic investigators, interpret and articulate these political actions, which adopt distinct forms shaped by context and history.

Flowing from these mutually comprehensible efforts is the notion that justice and memory are inextricably connected. Given that criminal investigations and judicial processes legitimate and ratify a specific set of memories, told over and over by survivors and witnesses, accepted and agreed-upon stories and narratives of events dominate within and outside of these efforts. The expression and silences of these memories depend on who is present and on the political and social dynamics of remembrance, which are local, national, and international. When efforts to seek justice fail, are delayed, or are not pursued, memory serves to enshrine events, people, and—frequently—violent eras. This memorialization emerges in many forms, including through the elaboration of testimonies and truth-and-reconciliation reports.

Second, networks that have developed through shared training and investigative experiences link forensic anthropology organizations based in different parts of the region. A focus on these networks and how their members—individuals and organizations—draw on similar principles and activities to guide both their technical efforts and relations with family members of victims illustrates a shared orientation toward cultivating memory and human rights through scientific work. I show how these dynamics unfold in interactions between FA organizations and victims' family members. This is the third point made in the chapter: memory emerges in specific ways through processes of forensic analysis and identification and interaction among family members.

Notably, a tension exists between the transnational work carried out by activists—which frequently relies on connections to institutional bodies that transcend a given country's judicial institutions by appealing for regional normative and legal legitimacy—and the memory work that victims and family members do at gravesites and in their testimonies. As a result, we observe divergent tracks of elite and subaltern memory-making, which have different purposes. For family members of victims of forced disappearance and assassination, the objective of forensic investigations is receiving solace through knowledge and the tangible human remains they may find. For networked activists and jurists, some of whom have worked in multiple post-atrocity environments in the region and the world, their goals include the protection of victims' rights and justice for perpetrators. However, this relationship between elite activists and marginalized communities of survivors seeking answers is a productive tension: it leads to prosecutions of criminals in some cases and affirms the citizenship of victims as they seek knowledge and closure. The transnational nature of human rights activists' work is clearer; victims and their surviving family members are not typically in a position to create memories that cross borders through a process of interacting with other victims (Nelson 2015). Their efforts to create memory are, in fact, local and expressive, but no less consequential. Survivors' testimonies and struggles intersect with the efforts of other actors who work for the protection of human rights.

But survivors' memories inform processes of evidence collection, truthtelling, and artistic representation. They are often overlooked, however, and excluded from mainstream political discourse. Their memories—and the legitimacy of these remembrances—are frequently contested, derided, and disputed by powerful actors. To the extent that the construction of transnational memory spaces relies on consensus on memory within nations' borders, cross-border memory in Latin America is incomplete—and in tension with structures that prevent its consolidation as a genuinely transnational force. Still, memory engages with this structural tension through networks of diverse political actors, including forensic experts and family members, and as a result, it travels.

Memory-Making through Forensic Anthropology: Victims' Families and the Politics of Transnational Spaces

What Do Forensic Anthropology Organizations Do?

Over the last three decades, the groups in Latin America that practice forensic anthropology (FA) have developed and strengthened the connections in their work between human rights and the scientific diagnosis of remains. The balance between competing priorities, including ethical and political considerations (Rosenblatt 2015), shapes the mandates and activities of the organizations. FA groups carry out forensic procedures to identify skeletal remains, and they exploit their knowledge of archaeology to examine graves and establish a hypothesized series of events in a time line, an idea of what occurred to produce the human remains they find (Equipo Argentino de Antropología Forense, "About," n.d.). In addition to scientific procedures, essential to the process of developing this narrative are the stories, information, and remembrances of the family members of victims and witnesses to the crimes. Forensic experts and organizations work together in gravesites in different regions of the world, bringing a growing, comparative body of transnational knowledge and experience to bear on investigation and identification—a kind of memory of the bones they have unearthed and studied. The corpus of FA is inherently interdisciplinary, drawing on varied fields like forensic pathology, ballistics, and genetics.

The EAAF, which formed in 1984 to respond to the needs and struggles of victims' relatives, articulated an adaptive combination of mission and method from the beginning. In fact, the history of forensic anthropology in Latin America, which began in Argentina, reveals much about the transnational character of the discipline. There, mothers and grandmothers of disappeared individuals formed organizations during the military dictatorship (1976–83), Madres de la Plaza de Mayo and Abuelas de la Plaza de Mayo, to locate their missing loved ones (Rosenblatt 2015: 2–3; Hepworth, this volume). Estimates of victims of forced disappearance of the women's relatives reach ten to thirty thousand people, including the unborn children with whom some young women were pregnant when they were disappeared. In searches for evidence of their grandchildren's whereabouts, the *abuelas* developed extensive relationships with forensic experts, who later came to comprise the EAAF.

EAAF researchers describe the beginnings of their work in forensic anthropology as a response to "the material and immaterial consequences of the military regime" (Fondebrider and Scheinsohn 2015: 369).

Having become aware of the difficulties and technical limitations that Argentines were facing after the dictatorship ended, and at a moment when investigations of forced disappearance were a primary political focus of the day, the American Association for the Advancement of Science (AAAS) sent a delegation of forensic scientists to Argentina. This collaboration set the stage for attempting to recover the children and grandchildren the highly mobilized activists were seeking, using exhumation techniques that would prevent damage or destruction of evidence (Fondebrider and Scheinsohn 2015: 370).

The development of forensic anthropology as a discipline and set of practices occurred in direct response to violent events and impassioned desires to know the truth about the disappearance of missing Argentines. Later, some of the same forensic professionals searched for Latin American *desaparecidos* in multiple countries, including Brazil, Chile, Paraguay, Uruguay, Peru, Guatemala, El Salvador, Colombia, and Mexico. Clyde Snow, an American physical anthropologist who was a catalyst for training many young Argentine students, established a network of practitioners who learned the discipline together and developed its unique patterns of interaction with witnesses and relatives. By the late 1970s, the term "forensic anthropology" had begun to appear in the literature, identified by physical anthropologists as a field attuned to using forensics for skeletal identification and in turn building medicolegal expertise among practitioners. In a 1982 article, Snow wrote of the new and increasing role of scientific expertise in the courtroom, which generated opportunities for *forenses*[5] to provide authoritative information as testimony in criminal cases (Snow 1982).

How do *forenses* engage and resist political structures that are resistant to memory-making? Through their interactions with victims' relatives, FA organizations rely on spaces for relatives' concrete participation in processes of searching and for information about the victims and locations where violent events occurred. But FA groups' relationships with family members make them, in many contexts, a kind of civil society organization, an advocate, and a representative of marginalized communities. This level of activism varies widely depending on the regime, state institutions' capacity to conduct investigations, and the disposition of the FA organization. The Peruvian Forensic Anthropology team (EPAF, or Equipo Peruano de Antropología Forense) has worked closely with government ministries like the Public Ministry and the Ministry of Justice to identify and exhume bodies. However, EPAF has embraced its work as affiliated directly with the protection of human rights and advocacy for individuals and communities that suffered at the hands of state and nonstate actors. It is an independent, nongovernmental organization and a product of civil society (Tello 2002). EPAF staff members travel to remote towns and villages in regions heavily affected by the civil war's violence, and which suffered the most disappearances, to provide information about reparations and victimization but also about job training opportunities, implications of laws, and ways to access social services.[6]

A staff member told me that EPAF sees its role as bringing specific information to the communities, but also collecting it—facts, names, dates, events—to inform and verify processes of identification of remains and victims' registration that occur mostly in Lima. The staff member also mentioned that EPAF is "constructing a new relationship with the families, a relationship that the state never formed" (interview with activist, 2017). EPAF encounters issues in its unique role as independent interlocutor between citizens and the state, technical authority, and institutional partner of the state in some recovery efforts (Tello 2002). This role played by some FA organizations emerged from the experiences of violence that many communities in Latin America suffered. The family members' participation in the search, in the reckoning with reality, and in the mutual engagement with forensic and legal experts—sometimes representatives of the state and other times activists who fulfill a role that the state has not accepted—has generated a space for the creation of memory and, simultaneously, political agency. Victims and relatives make demands on the state in these spaces of recovery of remains; as they identify clothing fragments and belongings of their loved ones and retell painful experiences, they seek to protect their rights and invoke the right to know what happened.

The origins of forensic anthropology draw on these different, measured forms of engagement and resistance with authority, the law, and established norms. The EAAF traces its foundation and ability to investigate independently of state and academic constraints to the long-standing separation of archaeology from official institutions in the country. The distance was maintained and perpetuated by the suspicion and distrust held by the original students interested in investigations of mass graves, who associated forensic experts with police and judges allied to the military regime responsible for the disappearances (Fondebrider and Scheinsohn 2015: 374).

The newly adopted "humanitarian focus" of a new state institution in Peru, established twenty-five years after the end of the civil war, is a political achievement that catalyzes rather than resolves contestation over what the government's responsibilities are to victims' families. The General Directorate of Searches for Disappeared Persons institutionalizes the search for missing Peruvians in this unit (García 2017). Victor Quinteros, the former director of an effort within the unit to create a national registry of *desaparecidos* and manage forensic investigations, emphasizes that the state's approach has changed from treating the searches as a penal process aimed at finding perpetrators to a humanitarian effort, in which "the families decide and participate, for example, if there will or will not be an exhumation" (García 2017).

While many FA organizations in the region collaborate to various degrees with governments to conduct field investigations, the organizations' involvement and sustained interaction with the families of victims sets them on an autonomous path, through which their decisions and norms are defined more by their engagement with social and political dynamics than by the focus of the state. FA organizations make decisions about becoming involved in a case or context based on different criteria (interview with activist, 2017). But legal, normative, and bureaucratic procedures may frustrate their progress, forcing them to delay their own work in the process of complying with state procedures and time lines.

How Do Victims, Family Members, and Activists Participate in Searches for Bodies?[7]

In this section I describe memory-making in Peru, carried out for a range of purposes, activities that emerge from relationships between forensic anthropologists and victims' relatives and through the fora in which they interact. These interactions create a social and political space that empowers victims to seize political agency in fora—funeral processions and cemeteries, massacre sites, and courtrooms—where community members voice their political needs. The first step of any forensic study in the field is interviews with local individuals who have information on the geography and circumstances of violent events. Interviews with victims' family members and witnesses constitute the "verbal evidence" to which Burns refers in her "flowchart of a forensic investigation" (Burns 2007: 8). This phase is referred to as the preliminary investigation, and it produces verbal evidence: accounts of disappearances, killings, clothing, historical events that occurred before and following the events in question, and personal descriptions of disappeared or killed individuals. These interactions take place not only to create a climate of transparency and build trust with the families of the disappeared but also to generate information essential to the investigation (Fondebrider and Scheinsohn 2015: 374). Victims' testimonies are combined with other sources like information from truth commission reports, media accounts, and declassified military documents (Baraybar and Mora 2015: 464). Forensic anthropologists collect antemortem information on all potential victims during the preliminary investigation.

The recovery stage happens next, including the exhumation of remains, followed by the third phase, which is the analysis of the evidence. In Peru, after the examination of evidence, usually in a government morgue, EPAF submits a full report on the probable cause of deaths of the victims to the authority that requested the expertise. EPAF maintains direct communication with family members when its experts testify in court or inform legal cases and let them know the findings (Baraybar and Mora 2015: 464).

By sharing stories and showing photographs of their loved ones, victims take on agency and resist social and political structures that defy or delay discovering the knowledge about their loved ones' disappearances. By creating and multiplying memory in this way, and informing a technical investigation, victims demand visibility. Since the 1990s, civil society organizations, FA groups, and victims' associations have collaborated in the search for graves and supported the construction of memories of violence (de Waardt 2013). This process shapes the form and content of people's political claims. Through practices of remembering and searching, victims mobilize and seize political agency. They are joining a movement of families who demand that the state not only find the bodies and pursue justice but that their economic and social needs be addressed. The experience of violence affected how these family members see themselves as citizens, the state as both a violent and pacifying actor, and their rights in an unjust system.

In Hualla, a district in the department of Ayacucho that was deeply affected by both Shining Path insurgents' and security forces' actions during the conflict, family members of victims struggle for economic resources and infrastructure development. They also demand economic reparations, a promised component of an institutional transitional justice policy, to help them protect and feed their families and keep a roof over their heads. Despite their pessimism about how the state has responded to these needs over the last two decades, Huallinos continue to make demands on the central government within a framework of reparations. EPAF has helped to amplify their needs and these clamors for assistance, in a way that links wartime violence with the community's marginalization. On the community's annual "Day of Memory," 26 June 2013, residents proceeded after morning Mass to the cemetery,[8] where for a few hours during an assembly with the mayor, residents detailed the specific losses, damages, and debts they incurred as a result of a relative's death or destruction of property. Among other petitions, they requested state support for scholarships, a demand since before the war, and the construction of a new cemetery in Hualla. To *reclamar* (articulate a demand or complaint that requires a response) is an activity integral to Huallinos' struggle for state assistance and compensation and a form of participation in politics. Survivors' politics emerge in the physical and social spaces of mourning loved ones—it is one way of relating to and mediating the violence, individually and collectively.

Another political element of the process of family members generating memories that "travel" across borders is the notion that the identification of remains supports and insists on a culture of truth and transparency. The politics behind forensic investigations demand that norms change, that the exhumations form part of a struggle for concrete knowledge and acknowledgment—the *derecho de saber* (right to know)—of the family member is critical in FA organizations' relationships with survivors and associations of victims. This insistence on normative change occurs over a long period, but it generates mobilization for accountability for war crimes, drawing on a social contract between state and citizens. The degree to which citizenship is respected and extended to all citizens, particularly victims and their families, varies widely in different contexts. Finally, advocacy for accountability but also memory itself is a demand for a normative and political shift in many Latin American countries, which threatens the elites and long powerful actors who have incentives to conceal, or at least refuse to investigate, wartime wrongdoing.

After the dictatorship ended in Argentina, Raúl Alfonsín was elected in 1983 in part on a promise to search for and exhume the bodies of disappeared individuals, and this strategy supported the organizations' initial efforts to do so. But politicians frequently prefer the notion of "turning the page" on memories of violence and extrajudicial killings in favor of moving forward as a nation, as former Peruvian president Pedro Pablo Kuczynski did a year into his tenure (*La República* 2017). "We have no national memory," as the Peruvian activist observed. The history of the country's war is not taught properly in schools or explained to children, the activist argued, and state agents have mostly not been held responsible for crimes. Importantly, *how* to remember the past and twenty years of war is not discussed in Peru. The activist added that steps forward and backward in the development of a national memory depend on political leaders, but also on the kinds of information that ordinary people have access to and demand. While elected leaders engage in the politicization of memory and searches for bodies, victims' families also seek political strategies that counter forgetting and demand responses from perpetrators.

How Do FA Organizations Collaborate with One Another in Transnational Work?

As illustrated in this chapter, formal and informal connections among practitioners from numerous countries of the Americas sustained the development of a precarious field from its early days. As forensic anthropologists were increasingly called on to analyze mass graves in different contexts, the scope of their mission changed, for instance, dealing with different government-citizen relations and political conditions as they began working in the former Yugoslavia on mass graves in preparation for criminal cases in the International Criminal Tribunal for Yugoslavia (ICTY). Religious beliefs and traditions shaped their work in various contexts, particularly in Somaliland, where EPAF began working several years ago. Consistent in FA groups' practices were the inclusion and participation of victims' relatives in their investigations.

The Argentine FA team began undertaking projects, commissioned by governments and international organizations, to perform exhumations and analyses in environments where mass atrocities occurred. The EAAF has worked in forty-five countries and supports the improvement of national and international forensic protocols. The Latin American teams exchange members for cross-training and work together on international missions (Equipo Argentino de Antropología Forense, "About," n.d.). For instance, the EAAF investigated femicides in Ciudad Juárez, Mexico, a divisive process in which victims' families and representatives of state institutions clashed over responsibility and accountability (Rosenblatt 2015: 10). While many forensic anthropologists avoid direct engagement with local political dynamics, their presence and the nature of their operations bring to light dynamics of memory and often require political decisions that are contested by state and other actors.

In addition, FA organizations share methodologies across national borders. In carrying out the first scientific exhumation of remains dated to the armed conflict in Peru, EPAF employed techniques developed during the ICTY investigation. In Sillaccasa, Ayacucho, in January 2002, EPAF exhumed the remains of five peasants abducted and executed by the military during the conflict (Baraybar and Mora 2015: 463). In February 2003, forensic professionals in the region institutionalized their collaboration in the Asociación Latinoamericana de Antropología Forense (ALAF, or the Latin American Forensic Anthropology Association). Through ALAF, the *forenses* share practices, resulting in what one staff member called a regular *reencuentro* (reunion or renewed encounter). This collaboration among experts engenders discussion of techniques, like the use of DNA and the development of national genetics banks, to share specialized expertise. As one EPAF activist explained, a kind of "division of labor" exists among FA organizations when they enter into collaborations in external contexts, with each group focusing on different aspects of the process. For example, EPAF focused on antemortem documentation in Sri Lanka, while others handled archaeological and DNA analysis. This complementary approach catalyzes an acute cross-border exchange of method and process.

Conclusion

How do searches and struggles at gravesites generate opportunities for memory creation, and are these spaces transnational? Memory is dynamic and contested, as Steve Stern writes of "memory battles" in Latin America (2004).

Disputes over memory occur in transitions from authoritarianism to democracy and in periods, like the 1990s, when neoliberalism was taking hold of economic systems and becoming integrated in the region (Nelson 2011). By engaging and resisting structural dynamics—unjust use of state power, military abuses, discrimination, local and global economic forces—family members of victims pursue political strategies that allow them to claim rights and learn what happened to their disappeared relatives. Grappling with political and social structures that resist and undermine the production of memory, including state institutions' lack of capacity or willingness to investigate crimes, inspires a form of activism that takes place both within national borders and in and through sites that transcend these borders. These sites include regionally recognized symbols of commemoration and protest—like carrying placards with photos and names of missing relatives—and activist networks that draw on regional institutions to create legal precedents.

Victims' interests and voices are communicated and carried by multiple actors, including forensic anthropology organizations, which interact in a greater number of transnational spheres and convey to broad audiences the significance of norms like the right to know (International Committee of the Red Cross 2003). The urgency of the right to know stems from the prevalence of *desaparecidos* and constitutes a norm that victims' families and activists seek to establish as they pursue information about their relatives' whereabouts. Forensic investigations and the commemorations that sometimes accompany them generate a space for memory-making that derives meaning from violence because it allows citizens to make claims on the state. By providing witness testimony, sharing stories with fellow relatives of victims, and informing forensic investigations, family members invoke specific memories of violence. They take on a political role that challenges their own marginalization.

These practices suggest that, in some contexts, postconflict memory construction catalyzes processes related to state formation, specifically the extension of citizenship and norm construction. But nonstate actors—forensic experts, urban and rural survivors of violent conflict, and activists—carry out these political tasks. Family members of disappeared victims connect broken borders, physically, symbolically, and socially, through their participation in memory-making, committing to comprehending and changing the politics that made violence possible. The inscription on a memorial cross erected by activists of Asociación Nacional de Familiares de Secuestrados, Detenidos y Desaparecidos del Perú (ANFASEP, or the National Association of Relatives of the Kidnapped, Detained, and Disappeared in Peru) at a mass gravesite, La Hoyada, in Ayacucho, reads, "The truth breaks through. We remember because we want to build a more just country" ("La verdad se abre paso . . . recordamos porque queremos construir un país más justo," quoted in Rojas-Perez 2017: 233–34).[9] At gravesites that bear the physical weight and markings of violence after years and decades, memories of the lives and voices of lost individuals emerge, and the subsequent silences are deeply heard by their families. Here, they interact with the cross-border experiences of death and witness that *forenses* bring to the graves—all these, scars and symbols that go beyond the soil, the bones, and the borders.

Devin Finn is a lecturer in political science and public policy at the Universidad de los Andes in Bogotá, Colombia. Previously she was a research fellow at the Sié Chéou-Kang Center for International Security and Diplomacy at the Josef Korbel School of International Studies. Devin studies ordinary people's participation in violence and democratic politics in the context of civil wars and the political mobilization of memory and victimization, primarily in Latin America and South Asia. Devin has worked as a researcher at the United States Institute of Peace, the United Nations, and the Inter-American Dialogue.

Notes

1. This definition is adapted from the United Nations Declaration on the Protection of All Persons from Enforced Disappearance.
2. In June 2016 with the passage of Ley 30470, Peru created a new unit within the Ministry of Justice, *la Dirección General de Búsquedas de Personas Desaparecidas* (General Directorate of Searches for Disappeared Persons), authorized to centralize information on the whereabouts of the disappeared and provide this information and, when possible, their remains, to relatives. The revised estimates, which were announced on 23 April 2018, expanded the previous sum considerably from 15,731 *desaparecidos*, a figure that the state and civil society organizations had employed since 2003.
3. Collins emphasizes the contrasts in how different generations of victims view the purposes of searching for knowledge about disappeared family members, including her finding that some younger relatives in Chile are less interested in pursuing justice for perpetrators than older generations who were more immediately affected by disappearance.
4. The Merida Initiative facilitates government collaboration among the United States, Mexico, and Central America against organized crime and violence through anticorruption programs, police and judiciary sector training, and strengthening of community cohesion. "Office of Western Hemisphere Affairs Programs," retrieved 24 February 2017 from https://www.state.gov/j/inl/whp/.
5. *Los forenses* are the individuals who carry out forensic investigations and analyses.
6. These observations are informed by extensive field research conducted in Peru by the author, traveling with EPAF in Ayacucho, Peru, during 2013–15.
7. The empirical evidence in this section draws on the experiences of family members of victims and their communities in Ayacucho and Lima, Peru, based on interviews and ethnographic fieldwork.

8. This ritual is known as a "romería," a processional pilgrimage that commemorates the dead even before reaching the cemetery. Participants walk, carrying flowers, accompanied by musicians playing traditional songs in their midst. Since their remains have not yet been found, some disappeared individuals lack a gravestone, coffin, or patch of earth that families can visit after laying their loved one to rest. This yearning for closure takes many forms in different contexts.
9. Translation by Rojas-Perez.

References

Baraybar, José Pablo, and Franco Mora. 2015. "Forensic Archaeology in Peru: Between Science and Human Rights Activism." In *Forensic Archaeology: A Global Perspective*, edited by W. J. Mike Groen, Nicholas Márquez-Grant, and Robert C. Janaway, 463–69. West Sussex, UK: John Wiley and Sons.

Bernhard, Michael H., and Jan Kubik. 2014. *Twenty Years after Communism: The Politics of Memory and Commemoration*. Oxford: Oxford University Press.

Booth, W. James. 2006. "Preface." *Communities of Memory: On Witness, Identity, and Justice*. Ithaca, NY: Cornell University Press. Cited in Duncan Bell. 2009. "Introduction: Violence and Memory." *Millennium: Journal of International Studies* 38(2): 345–60.

Burns, Karen Ramey. 2007. *Forensic Anthropology Training Manual*. 2nd ed. Upper Saddle River, NJ: Pearson Prentice Hall.

Caravana 43. N.d. "Talking Points." Retrieved 24 February 2019 from http://www.caravana43.com/talking-points.html.

Collins, Cath. 2017. "The Politics of Justice 'From Below': Human Rights Defenders and Atrocity Crime Trials in Latin America." SSRC Working Paper, posted 28 September. http://dx.doi.org/10.2139/ssrn.3043703.

de Waardt, Mijke. 2013. "Are Peruvian Victims Being Mocked? Politicization of Victimhood and Victims' Motivations for Reparation." *Human Rights Quarterly* 35: 830–49.

Equipo Argentino de Antropología Forense (EAAF). N.d. "About." Retrieved 24 February 2019. http://eaaf.typepad.com/about_us/.

Finn, Devin. 2015. "Nonviolent Mobilization against State Impunity through Forensic Anthropology." Political Violence at a Glance (blog), 17 March. Retrieved 16 January 2018 from http://politicalviolenceataglance.org/2015/03/17/nonviolent-mobilization-against- state-impunity-through-forensic-anthropology/.

Fondebrider, Luis, and Vivian Scheinsohn. 2015. "Forensic Archaeology: The Argentinian Way." In *Forensic Archaeology: A Global Perspective*, edited by W. J. Mike Groen, Nicholas Márquez-Grant, and Robert C. Janaway, 369–79. West Sussex, UK: John Wiley and Sons.

Groen, W. J. Mike, Nicholas Márquez-Grant, and Robert C. Janaway, eds., *Forensic Archaeology: A Global Perspective*. West Sussex, UK: John Wiley and Sons, 2015.

Grupo Interdisciplinario de Expertos Independientes. N.d. "Informe Ayotzinapa, Investigación y primeras conclusiones de las desapariciones y homicidios de los normalistas de Ayotzinapa." Retrieved 24 February 2019 from https://www.casede.org/BibliotecaCasede/Informe_AyotziGIEI.pdf.

Huntington, Samuel P. 1993. *The Third Wave: Democratization in the Late Twentieth Century*. Norman: University of Oklahoma Press.

Inglis, David. 2015. "Globalization and/of Memory: On the Complexification and Contestation of Memory Cultures and Practices." In *Routledge International Handbook of Memory Studies*, edited by Anna Lisa Tota and Trever Hagen. Oxon: Taylor and Francis.

International Committee of the Red Cross. 2003. "The Missing and Their Families." 21 February. Retrieved 16 January 2019 from https://www.icrc.org/eng/resources/documents/report/5jahr8.htm.

Jelin, Elizabeth. 2003. *State Repression and the Labors of Memory*. Translated by Marcial Godoy-Anativia and Judy Rein. Minneapolis: University of Minnesota Press, 2003.

———. 2007. "Public Memorialization in Perspective: Truth, Justice, and Memory of Past Repression in the Southern Cone of South America." *International Journal of Transitional Justice* 1(1): 138–56.

"Kuczynski a Keiko: 'Tenemos que voltear la página.'" 2017. *La República*. 21 April. Retrieved 10 March 2018 from https://larepublica.pe/politica/1033839-kuczynski-a-keiko-tenemos-que-voltear-la-pagina.

Levy, Daniel, and Nathan Sznaider. 2005. *The Holocaust and Memory in a Global Age*. Translated by Assenka Oksiloff. Philadelphia, PA: Temple University Press.

Müller, Jan-Werner. 2002. "Introduction: The Power of Memory, the Memory of Power and the Power over Memory." In *Memory and Power in Post-war Europe: Studies in the Presence of the Past*, edited by Jan-Werner Müller, 1–36. Cambridge: Cambridge University Press.

Nelson, Alice A. 2011. "Conclusion: Marketing Discontent; The Political Economy of Memory in Latin America." In *Accounting for Violence: Marketing Memory in Latin America*, edited by Ksenija Bilbija and Leigh A. Payne, 339–64. Durham, NC: Duke University Press.

Nelson, Diane M. 2015. *Who Counts? The Mathematics of Death and Life after Genocide*. Durham, NC: Duke University Press.

O'Donnell, Guillermo, and Philippe C. Schmitter. 1986. *Transitions from Authoritarian Rule: Tentative Conclusions about Uncertain Democracies*. Baltimore, MD: Johns Hopkins University Press.

Quinteros, Victor. 2017. "Por fin se dará una respuesta a los familiares de los desaparecidos." Interview by Oscar García, Puntoedu, 12 October. Retrieved 20 June 2018 from https://puntoedu.pucp.edu.pe/entrevistas/por-fin-se-le-dara-una-respuesta-a-los-familiares-de-los-desaparecidos/.

Rojas-Perez, Isaias. 2017. *Mourning Remains: State Atrocity, Exhumations, and Governing the Disappeared in Peru's Postwar Andes*. Stanford, CA: Stanford University Press.

Rosenblatt, Adam. 2015. *Digging for the Disappeared: Forensic Science after Atrocity*. Stanford, CA: Stanford University Press.

Sikkink, Kathryn, and Carrie Booth Walling. 2007. "The Impact of Human Rights Trials in Latin America." *Journal of Peace Research* 44(4): 427–45.

Snow, Clyde C. 1982. "Forensic Anthropology." *Annual Review of Anthropology* 11: 97–131.

Stern, Steve J. 2004. *Remembering Pinochet's Chile: On the Eve of London 1998*. Durham, NC: Duke University Press.

Tannenwald, Nina. 1999. "The Nuclear Taboo: The United States and the Normative Basis of Nuclear Non-Use." *International Organization* 53 (3) (Summer): 433–68.

TechCampGuatemala. N.d. "Adn memoria histórica." LinkedIn SlideShare. Last modified 18 July 2012. https://es.slideshare.net/techcampguatemala/adn-memoria-historica.

Tello, Juan Carlos. 2002. Interview by Canal N. Audio. Accessed via Lugar de Memoria Centro de Documentación e Investigación, 7 December 2017.

United States Department of State. N.d. "Office of Western Hemisphere Affairs Programs (INL/WHP)." Retrieved 24 February 2019 from https://www.state.gov/j/inl/whp/.

Chapter 7

TRANSNATIONAL PLACE-MAKING AFTER POLITICAL VIOLENCE

Agencies and Practices of Site Memorialization
in the Latin American Southern Cone

Gruia Bădescu

As a "memory fever" (Jelin 2002) concerning the past military dictatorships emerged in societies in the Southern Cone (Cono Sur) of Latin America, the memorialization of sites related to political violence became an important battle. Important scholarly work has underlined the complex processes of memorialization in key sites of Chile, Argentina, and Uruguay, sometimes engaging in comparative work about Cono Sur countries or across continents (Birle and Schindel 2009; Hite 2012; Schindel and Colombo 2014; Sion 2014; Andermann 2015; Levey 2016). A number of authors have highlighted the transnational circulations of memorialization practices related to Holocaust sites in Europe, as well as globalized memorial architecture and museums in various Southern Cone contexts, with Buenos Aires a privileged place in research (Huyssen 2003; Sion 2014; Williams 2007). Nevertheless, the transnational circulations of site memorialization practices within the Cono Sur region itself have been discussed less often. This chapter examines the circulation of such practices, scrutinizing the emergence of a transnational space-making process in the region related to dealing with sites of memory, by analyzing how constellations of actors, functioning at a variety of scales, participate in the reconfiguration of sites. I discuss the practices of site memorialization that various actors put forward, the obstacles they face—related to existing structures and competing agencies—and the outcomes they produce. Moreover, I show that transnational circulations within the region not only form part of a global circuit but also link with memories and places beyond the usual suspects; I do this by tracing the intersections and frictions of a specific local context in the Cono Sur with memory threads from the former Yugoslavia.

A first endeavor of the chapter is to examine the outcomes of practices of site memorialization in the Latin American Southern Cone, most importantly the shaping of a transnational memory space of postdictatorship dealing with the past in Latin America. As such, I analyze general trends and patterns that suggest the circumscribing of this regional transnational space into a global memorial architecture regime. I utilize the example of Villa Grimaldi in Santiago de Chile, a pioneer in the memorialization of sites, to showcase how agency, mobilized by transnational links, put forward site memorialization as an important struggle and thus opened the road for the emergence of the transnational space-making process.

In a second part of the chapter, I discuss the memorialization of sites that are intrinsically related to transnational processes. I question the challenges and possibilities of different agencies to constitute what I call transnational memory place-making. I distinguish between transnational memory space-making, the framework of this volume, the process of linking places through practices of remembrance (i.e., in this chapter the transnational memory space of remembering military dictatorships in Latin America) and transnational memory place-making, which involves a process or an outcome with a transnational dimension. I employ two cases to develop this concept. First, Automotores Orletti in Buenos Aires was used as site of detention and torture as part of the transnational Plan Condor, which linked Southern Cone dictatorships in a network of detention and torture sites receiving political prisoners from the other countries involved (McSherry 1999). As such, the site faces the challenge of representing a transnational phenomenon in the deep urban fabric of the Argentine capital. The key question here is to what extent is the transnational space-making of Southern Cone dictatorship memorialization resulting in transnational place-making, the shaping of a site of memory that reflects its transnational nature. Second, the situation in Punta Arenas, a city in the far south of Chile, brings a different element of transnationalism to the foreground: diasporic communities. The discussion of the practices of site memorialization in the city highlights the interaction of a national story—the Pinochet dictatorship and repression—with local memories and transnational links, in this case to Croatia, where many of the inhabitants in Punta Arenas have their roots. The question here is to what extent site memorialization takes into consideration the "layering" of memories (Bernhard and Kubik 2014) and the transnational character of the local into memory place-making. As the chapter will show, this example also highlights the interactions, multidirectional memories and conflicts between very distinctive "memory regions" (Olick 2015). Consequently, the chapter showcases the emergence of a transnational space employing a regional model of site memorialization while interrogating the existence of transnational place-making that occurs in the process.

One key set of practices that this chapter addresses is the reconfiguration of sites through architectural-curatorial approaches. As such, it examines the role of architects, architectural design, and site curators within a constellation of memory actors. It scrutinizes the circulation of approaches on memorial architecture in the region. Analyzing how practices of memorial architecture circulate either through professional circuits (e.g., architects) or through alternative agencies and routes (e.g., activists), the chapter also interrogates the role of architecture in memorialization practices dominated by other agents and its possibilities for transnational place-making.

On Memory, Place, and Actors

Space can act as a mnemonic device, sustaining memories of political violence through a process of allegorization, relying on context as much as unconscious associations (Jameson 1997; Koepnick 2001). For Elizabeth Jelin (2003), through commemoration, space (abstract, impersonal) becomes place (meaningful and enduring), echoing phenomenological musings on space and place from geography (Tuan 1974).

The relationship between space, the built environment, and memory can be engineered by political power and institutions, which have a crucial role in reshaping the expressions of collective memories in the built environment by selecting which aspects are to be commemorated or ignored (Hoelscher and Alderman 2004; Lowenthal 2015). The analysis of local dynamics in spatial reshaping gives a more nuanced understanding of the spatialization of memory. At times, local agency shapes place and sites of memory at the local level in sharp contrast with national policy or top-down memory narratives (Fenster 2004). Furthermore, global circuits shape places of memory—actors dialogue with one another in the background of globalizing processes, while they insist on specificities of historical experience (Williams 2007; Andermann 2015). Consequently, looking at constellations of actors at different scales can account for understanding how ideas and approaches circulate, to what extent and in what ways actors are entangled, and, ultimately, how intertwined agencies shapes memory through place-making.

Memorializing Sites of Political Violence in the Southern Cone

A significant number of memorials, sites of memory, and museums related to the political violence of civic-military dictatorships have appeared in the last decades in the Southern Cone, connected in general with private initiatives, but also with government action in particular periods, including the first presidency of Michele Bachelet in Chile (2006–10) and especially under the Cristina Fernández de Kirchner administrations (2007–15) in Argentina. In Chile, memorials were built in most urban centers, and ex-detention centers like Villa Grimaldi or Londres 38 in Santiago were converted to sites of memory, while the government-sponsored Museum of Memory and Human Rights in Santiago became an international point of reference (Aguilera and Cáceres 2012; Andermann and Aguilera 2015; Collins, Hite, and Joignant 2013; Hite and Collins 2009). In Uruguay, only in the last ten years have national governments supported processes of memorialization, but local authorities have proven more accommodating to memorialization processes (Levey 2014; Levey 2016). In Argentina, Law 26 691 of July 2011 declared all sites used for political violence during the last civil-military dictatorship to be sites of memory, accounting for around six hundred sites spread across the country, including former detention centers Escuela Superior de Mecánica de la Armada (ESMA), Automotores Orletti, and El Olimpo in Buenos Aires and Pasaje Santa Catalina in Cordoba. Furthermore, Argentina has museums such as the Museo de la Memoria at Rosario (2010) and memorials found outside of sites used for political violence, such as the Parque de la Memoria in Buenos Aires (Andermann 2012; Memoria Abierta 2009).

While the speed and scope of the process of memorialization of sites in the three countries has been different, a number of common traits emerge. First, we see a change in the actors involved. During the 1990s, most initiatives were private, generally coming from victims' associations. From the 2000s, left-wing governments in the region became invested in shaping sites of memory. Second, there is a shift in the geography of commemoration: during the 1990s and much of the 2000s, the sites of memory that existed had a marginal role, either in a fringe location or peripheral to the rhythms of civic and political routines (Hite and Collins 2009); with the entrance of government actors into the memorialization process, the sites and memorials become more central and more prominent. These include flagship projects such as Santiago's Museo de la Memoria or ESMA in Buenos Aires, which, while marginal geographically, become invested symbolically and, in the case of ESMA, functionally, as Fernández de Kirchner's right-wing successor, president Mauricio Macri, decided to move the seat of the Argentine Ministry of Justice and Human Rights there. Third, the state interventions in urban space in the realm of memory contrast with the generic withdrawal of the state that is characteristic of the dominant neoliberal systems. Famously installed during the Pinochet regime in Chile, the socioeconomic framework remained unchallenged by subsequent democratic governments, including the left—a situation that also occurred in Argentina, particularly under Carlos Menem. As Jens Andermann (2015) writes, the "architectures of affect" of memorial projects are the only ones to challenge what Draper (2012) called the "architectonics of transitions" related to consumption, privatization and spatial exclusion. In cases like Uruguay, the main site of detention, Punta Carretas, is relegated exclusively to the latter category, as it was reconfigured into a shopping mall with no mention of its dictatorial past (Levey 2016). Fourth, there is a fault line in debates by victims' associations, human rights organizations, and memory activists on whether sites of political violence have to be preserved as such or even reconstructed—like in the case of Villa Grimaldi, demolished at the end of the dictatorship—in order to become sites of memory, or whether they should be converted into spaces of social and political action. The latter relates to human rights activism, but also to social concerns mirroring the worldview of the majority of the detained left-wing activists (Andermann 2012). Finally, processes of memorialization of sites in the Southern Cone can be seen as an interplay of local, national, regional, and international actors, which is an aspect I explore in this chapter.

The memorialization of sites of political violence usually includes a constellation of actors who are mobilized for different reasons and interact to advance various agendas within and against hierarchies of power. The first category of actors that I will examine in this study are the *afectados* (Gatti 2014), individuals, as well as groups, who were directly affected by political violence. They include not only former political prisoners and former exiles but also relatives of those killed and made to disappear (the "disappeared"). Some of them are mobilizing memory and justice agendas through associations of survivors or relatives. Second, there are human rights and memory activist groups that include members not directly connected to the victims and survivors of political violence. Third, state institutions, from local to regional to national level, have played a significant role in initiating, supporting, or, on the contrary, impeding the memorialization of sites. Fourth, land or building owners can play a role in favoring or blocking the memorialization of sites they own that were used for political violence during the dictatorship until organizations purchased the land or the state expropriated it. Fifth, heritage and built environment professionals, including site curators, architects, and artists, have played an important role in the transformation of the sites. Their agency is often mediated by other actors, such as groups and institutions that employ them, and it can be restrained by budget concerns. Nevertheless, the practices they put forward result in outcomes of a transnational memorialization regime, bridging regions, countries, and scales.

The agency of these actors to achieve palpable site memorialization outcomes is impeded by existing structures. The actors described above face constraints beyond their control. The left-right divide in Chile and the Kirchnerist/Peronist vs. anti-Kirchnerists in Argentina, as well as what party is in power at a particular time, can help or obstruct memorialization processes, as leftist governments have been more prone to support memory work. Furthermore, budgets and economic crisis, particularly in Argentina, have a limiting impact on the agency of actors. The (mis)matching of local and national party structures can also help or obstruct the process. The existence of particular legal and institutional frameworks, such as the above-mentioned law in Argentina or programs of Michele Bachelet's government to support memorials in Chile, boosted site memorialization. Finally, the layering (Bernhard and Kubik 2014: 28) of multiple memories has been a challenge or an opportunity for site memorialization actors, as we shall see in the following sections.

Transnational Circulations in the Memorialization of Sites in the Southern Cone

In the Southern Cone, memorial sites have usually engaged with a local spatial dimension, being focused on what happened on the site itself, with a few cases including a coverage of nationwide events. Most refer to the persons who were detained or disappeared at those particular sites or who belonged to related communities. In each country, a number of sites refer to the national dimension of political violence: the Museo de la Memoria, tucked away in Montevideo's periphery; ESMA in northern Buenos Aires; and the Museo de la Memoria y los Derechos Humanos, in a regenerating/gentrifying neighborhood of Santiago. The narratives of these latter sites are generally national, focused on the country's experience, and with little reference to the context of neighboring countries or of global issues, such as the Cold War. However, there is also a limited number of sites of memory and memorials that refer to transnational practices of repression or to victims of the entire region or Latin America at large. One of them is Automotores Orletti in Buenos Aires, a site where prisoners from the entire Southern Cone region were detained and tortured. The memorial Mujeres en la memoria in Santiago de Chile addressed the pan–Latin American assassinations of women during dictatorships (Hite and Menezo 2013: 28).

While the focus of sites is usually local, the practices of memorialization can be linked to a transnational dimension. The increased practice of memorialization of sites itself is part of a global, transnational phenomenon. According to Williams in his study on memorial museums, the rise of memorialization through sites of memory and museums is connected with decreasing conflict globally but also with transitions to democracy (2007: 164). Others link it to the transnational circulation of a politics and practices of regret related to the Holocaust (Olick 2007).

The link to the memorialization of the Holocaust in the attempts to make sense of sites of political violence in the Southern Cone appears in several accounts of interviewed practitioners. Bachelet's idea to create the Museo de la Memoria y los Derechos Humanos in Santiago is inspired by the memorialization of the Shoah.[1] Moreover, several early initiatives of site memorialization are linked by individual agents to the Holocaust, among others the first design project for Villa Grimaldi, Santiago,[2] as we shall see below; the design competition for the Pisagua camp in northern Chile[3]; as well as Argentine efforts to memorialize sites associated to the last dictatorship.[4]

With regard to the circulation of memorial aesthetics, there are several practices that reflect transnational orientations. According to architects interviewed in Chile and Argentina, memorial architecture design is influenced by international practice and a number of seminal works.[5] Maya Lin's Vietnam Memorial in Washington is credited with inspiring the Monumento a las Víctimas del Terrorismo de Estado in the Memory Park of Buenos Aires (Hite and Menezo 2013), while the monument of Patio 29 in Santiago's General Cemetery is inspired by Peter Eisenman's Memorial to the Murdered Jews of Europe in Berlin (Aguilera 2013). Michele Bachelet originally wanted the Museo de la Memoria to be made of transparent materials, to echo Norman Foster's approach on the Bundestag, with transparency as a proxy for democracy.[6]

While international precedents have played a role, the most important research insight from visiting dozens of sites in the Southern Cone and interviewing curators is the emergence of a dominant approach, which I call the "bare walls approach." Aiming to preserve an authentic place of memory, this practice consists of a minimal intervention just to prevent further deterioration (what in heritage practice is called "arrested decay"), leaving the buildings with exposed bare walls. This regional memorialization regime was mobilized by a number of actors, especially associations of relatives of survivors, who insisted that the bare materiality of sites has the capacity to convey to visitors the dimension of events and is therefore a form of proof. This was also supported by voices from the academic world who emphasized that keeping the walls in this state has a forensic dimension. The authenticity of materiality as witness becomes an important element in memory-making, akin to the preservation of concentration camps in Europe. Throughout the Southern Cone, the bare walls approach has been utilized for key sites in Buenos Aires and Londres 38 in Santiago to various neighborhood detention centers throughout the territory.

The preeminence of this approach is also related to the circulation of prac-tices in the region through the exchanges of site curators. In particular the existence of structures such as the Latin American network of Sites of Con-science (Red Latinoamericana de Sitios de Conciencia), active since 2005, supported the exchange of ideas and practices and was instrumental for the propagation of the site of memory with minimal intervention as a sort of regional model, resulting in a materialization of transnational space-making of dealing with dictatorships. While museum professionals from the Southern Cone participate at times in the conferences of the International Committee of Memorial Museums in Remembrance of the Victims of Public Crimes (ICMEMO), the Federation of International Human Rights Museums, and The International Coalition of *Sites of Conscience*, it is the regional meetings that seem to be more influential in the circulation of practice. These meetings are attended by more practitioners than the international ones, often because of the less prohibitive travel costs, but also due to the common linguistic heritage and a perception of a more shared historical context. The meetings constitute an arena where ideas and approaches circulate and where various constellations of projects, as well as entanglements of individual and institu-tional actors, are shaped.[7]

The scenarios that I examine below, however, differ from this regional model in a number of ways. By highlighting their difference, related to agency, outcome, but also their role in transnational space-making, I will sug-gest that transnational place-making can be a difficult challenge even within the remit of a rather coherent transnational space-making in the Cono Sur, where memorialization actors generally share a common ground and function within somewhat similar structural obstacles.

Parque por la Paz Villa Grimaldi: Agency Triggering Change

Villa Grimaldi in Santiago de Chile is the first site of political violence of twentieth-century dictatorship in the Americas to be opened as a site of mem-ory for the public (Hite and Collins 2009). It is an early example not only of site memorialization but also of local action linked transnationally with a repertoire of international references. Located at the foothills of the Andes in the sprawling Santiago municipality of Peñalolén, Villa Grimaldi might be geographically less prominent as the central Museo de la Memoria or deten-tion centers such as Londres 38, but it is a crucial site in both the history of dictatorship as well as in the history of memorialization in Chile.

A nineteenth-century rural estate, the Villa Grimaldi was used before 1973 as a meeting place for leftist intellectuals and artists. As it happened with several other meeting places of socialists and communists, it was expropriated and taken over by the National Intelligence Directorate (DINA) and converted into the clandestine detention and torture center Cuartel Terranova. Between 1973 and 1978, as many as 4,500 prisoners went through Villa Grimaldi, including at least 18 executed and 226 who were disappeared (Hite and Collins 2009). Expecting the end of the dictatorship, the military sold the villa to a developer, who demolished the buildings and applied for planning permission to build an apartment complex. Only the swimming pool, fragments of floor tiles, and trees remained. Former political prisoners, human rights organizations, and a local neighborhood group mobilized against the plan. After much lobbying, they convinced the government to expropriate the site in 1993 and open a competition for a memorialization design on the site. An existing design by landscape architect Ana Cristina Torrealba Medina was selected, and the Peace Park (Parque por la Paz) Villa Grimaldi opened in March 1997.

Villa Grimaldi's reconfiguration is indirectly linked through a series of encounters and entanglements to the memorialization of the Holocaust. In the conservative landscape of architectural education that she received, Ana Cristina Torrealba's project emerged thanks to a series of encounters that inspired and supported her field of action. As a university student at Universidad Catolica de Chile during the last decade of dictatorship, Torrealba was active on the human rights front, taking part in the Sebastián Acevedo Movement Against Torture, a Christian movement. For her diploma project, Torrealba, not finding her initial topic of social housing stimulating enough, was inspired by the conversation with a friend who mentioned how architects were involved in the landscape project for the Fossoli camp near Modena, Italy.[8] Encouraged by this precedent and, in a reluctant department, supported only by her thesis adviser, Torrealba set out to conceptualize a memorial landscaping of the Villa Grimaldi, which she heard about during her human rights activism. Seeing resistance from other members of the faculty, she removed any direct reference to the site and discussed instead a hypothetical site where she would work on an underground building project covered by a park of memory. Her advisor continuously advocated for her project, defended it, and displayed empathy—Torrealba mentions emotional support and crying together in relationship to the victims' stories.[9] While a number of scholars interpreted Torrealba's work as being directly influenced by her advisor's alleged experience in a Nazi concentration camp, the architect objected in her interview to this interpretation, underlining that she was not aware of such link.[10] Her advisor was important in an additional way: Torrealba's design was chosen for the site not only because she was known to the local activists after long consultations with them but also because her advisor advocated on her behalf with the mayor of Peñalolén.[11] Holocaust memorialization was therefore important in an indirect manner, as it triggered the mobilization of agents by providing a precedent.

While we have seen that Torrealba's work is indirectly linked to the memorialization of the Holocaust, its aesthetic repertoire is a local expression of design and memorialization. Torrealba's proposal emerged from a long process of documentation and discussion with victims of torture at the Villa Grimaldi, as well as continuous meetings of the organization of victims and the local neighborhood representatives. Drawn from the architect's own thought process on working with the site and the collected memories of the victims, as well as with an approach on symbols derived from New Age aesthetics, the park's design differs from contemporary sites of memory in Europe or subsequent memorialization projects in the Southern Cone. It includes the intersection of two visual axes, which should not be mistaken for a cross, the architect insists, as not all prisoners were Christian.[12] The entrance to the park is dozens of meters away from the old main entrance of the Villa, which was used in the Cuartel Terranova years when prisoners were brought in. That old entrance remains closed, seemingly for perpetuity. The design includes mosaics of recuperated tiles from the floor of the house, a fountain, a list of names, winding alleys. A rose garden is dedicated to women prisoners. The decorative elements of the site are attributed to Norma Rodriguez, recommended by the corporation itself. Nevertheless, Rodriguez's New Age–inspired design was at times controversial, especially her initiative to represent throughout the park figures from nature, including mules, condors, and pumas, in order to return the site to a primordial state. Victims protested that these animals were actually the names of DINA brigades, and the final design did not include them.[13]

An important element in this early memorialization process was the collaboration of victims' associations and human rights groups with the local municipality. As the site's curatorial team joined civil society networks and international memory site coalitions, its international profile became better known, and it became part of a transnational discussion on memorializing sites of political violence. Its administration has shifted between municipal and national agencies, and funding often came through project-based applications, including from the European Union, which financed its Oral Archive project. With the presidency of Michele Bachelet, herself detained at the Villa Grimaldi in 1974, the site gained both national relevance and visibility. Until then, it was visited more by international visitors than Chilean ones (Hite and Menezo 2013). The villa also became part of ritualistic visits by foreign dignitaries on official visits to Chile—a role more recently supplanted by the newly opened Museo de la Memoria.

The Parque por la Paz shows how the indirect trigger of memorialization of the Holocaust connected to a very local struggle and design expression. To a certain extent, the confluence of agencies could be described using Sharon Hays' concept of "structurally transformative agency" (1994): Villa Grimaldi showcases how agency, mobilized by transnational links, precedents, and personal experiences put forward site memorialization as an important struggle and thus opened the road for the emergence of the transnational space-making.

Automotores Orletti, Buenos Aires: Transnational Memory, Nationalized Practice

While Villa Grimaldi is a site of political violence of a national dimension that had transnational elements in its memorialization, Automotores Orletti is a site of memory related to a transnational political violence network. Deep in western Buenos Aires, in the neighborhood of Floresta, not far from the more visited and more famous clandestine detention center El Olimpo, Automotores Orletti brings forward a rather distinctive case of transnational entanglements: it was a site associated with the transnational Plan Condor, a place where countries in the region sent their own teams to torture and control detainees who were disappeared from their countries and sent to Argentina (Lessa 2015; McSherry 1999).

The Argentine State Information Service (Secretaría de Inteligencia del Estado, SIDE) rented the car repair workshop of Santiago Cortell, situated by the train tracks in Floresta, in May 1976. The two-floor building, with concrete floors stained by car oil, was called the Garden (El Jardin) by SIDE, but would remain described as Automotores Orletti—reportedly the peeling off of the letter "C" on the plaque with the owner's name would have led to this mistaken approximation. The practice of implantation in the middle of neighborhoods in seemingly inconspicuous locations was widespread in both Chile and Argentina. Here, SIDE organized a regional operational center, hosting the band of Aníbal Gordon and teams coming from a number of Plan Condor countries, who interrogated and tortured the captives, murdering many of them at the end. While Argentine prisoners were detained in the center, the majority of detainees were actually foreign citizens, from Chile, Paraguay, Brazil, Bolivia, and Uruguay, as well as Cuba. The center functioned only for half a year, as an unlikely escape by two prisoners, who went out through the garage door and took a passing train in front of the center, made SIDE fear the new threats to the security and anonymity of the site.[14]

Returned to use as a car workshop by the owner, who was perplexed by the sudden departure of the renter and the many bullet holes in the walls, the site entered neighborhood news in 2002 when it was denounced as a sweatshop, a place where Bolivian workers were kept captive and permitted only one hour per week to go outside (Draper 2012). In the meantime, it was also identified as a site of detention by victims' testimonies, using memory triggers such as the scent of car oil and the sound of trains. The bullets also helped identify the site. As in many other sites, materiality showed its use in forensics (Weizman 2010), triggering and later supporting both individual memories and collective ones. As such, Automotores Orletti became the subject of debates on memorialization between a number of actors, including *afectados*, memory activists, an initially reluctant state, and the owner himself. In contrast to other cases in the city, country, and region, victims' groups played less of a role, as most victims had been foreign and therefore less visible in the Argentine public sphere and memory landscape. Nevertheless, memory activists argued with the state for years until the government purchased the site from the private owner. In 2009, it became a site of memory, with an associated team, which has offered guided tours and supported the organization of theater and arts events, as well as workshops with schools in the neighborhood.

Perhaps because of its peripheral role in national debates, Automotores Orletti is rarely referenced in the literature on memory sites in Argentina.[15] It exhibits the same repertoire of practices as its somewhat earlier counterparts: a bare walls approach, housing a center of documentation with educational outreach. It did not play a particularly important role in the operations of the last military dictatorship in Argentina, but perhaps it is exactly why it is an important site, as it blurs the national frames of memory research.

While transnational par excellence, as a place of detention and torture in the 1970s and 1980s and one of sweatshop labor in the 1990s, linked with the wider Latin American region, its constitution as a site of memory has been, however, mostly a national affair. Part of the wave of declarations of sites of memory in Argentina under the Fernández administration, Orletti joined more celebrated sites of memory such as ESMA and Olimpo, the public profile of which was boosted by various political speeches and immortalization in films. It became a site of memory as part of a national move, and while there is frequent reference to its special character as a site of torture, and while events and visits take place, the Orletti team communicated that the approach to its memorialization is largely a local, Argentine initiative. From its entrance sign—in the typical white-on-blue panels that mark "spaces of memory" all over the city—to its homogenous aesthetic approach, it is very much typical for Argentine sites of memory.

The concept for the site and the overview of its curatorial management comes from one employee of the Buenos Aires municipality assigned to the site. The site concept was not the object of consultation with various stakeholders.[16] In this case, the role of architects was minimal. The only architectural intervention was the separation of a working space for the documentation center staff on the first floor, a distinction made in order to avoid using the office spaces employed by the Plan Condor teams.[17] The site does contain, however, objects that highlight the transnational nature of its past. Documents and objects stemming from Cuban and Uruguayan detainees, donated by relatives, occupy an important part of the small exhibition displayed on the ground floor.

The ongoing memorialization process functions at the local level, with transnational openings. While survivors and relatives from other countries are part of the Orletti memory working group, the meetings are local, taking place in Buenos Aires, and there is hardly any international participation. The events it organizes are largely connected to the local community, with occasional participation of local staff at events in Uruguay. Nevertheless, while Uruguayans made up most of the people detained there, a fact invoked frequently in the Uruguayan media, the input of associations and actors from Uruguay in the actual memorialization of site is limited. Regarding curators and staff, there is an increasing transnational cooperation, as the site team is involved in a series of collaborations, networks, and visits throughout the Southern Cone.

Despite the transnational nature of its history and memory, the memorialization of Automotores Orletti is circumscribed by a more national framework of practices, with an opening up through ongoing collaborations. As such, while it belongs to the transnational space-making of dealing with sites of political violence, it does not showcase a process nor a practice of transnational place-making.

Casa de los Derechos Humanos in Punta Arenas, Chile: Layering Transnational Memories

During the Bachelet and the Kirchner/Fernández de Kirchner presidencies, respectively, in Chile and Argentina, the state entered the memorialization of sites with great impetus. Local initiatives throughout the territory were boosted with new funds and new interest. New sites of memory, used to educate about the political violence of past dictatorships, usually illustrate a collaboration—not always linear or trouble-free—of victims' associations, local human rights groups, local authorities, and ministries such as the Ministry of Public Works in Santiago or the Ministry of Justice and Human Rights in Buenos Aires. Among the multitude of sites, the Casa de los Derechos Humanos in Punta Arenas, Chile, shows to a high degree the fissures between the members of the constellation of actors, the tensions between the competitive memory of sites, and the importance of local context in transnational linkages.

The House of Human Rights (Casa de los Derechos Humanos) started as the residence of architect Antonio Beaulier, built in the French neoclassicist style typical of Punta Arenas, the southernmost city of Chile, down by the Magellan straights, capital of Magallanes region. It became the headquarters of the Red Cross between 1950 and 1954, then a naval hospital, but from 1973 to 1975 it served as the torture center of the Military Intelligence Service (SIM). According to the report of the National Commission on Political Prison and Torture, it was the main center of torture and interrogation in the region of Magallanes. Ironically named "the palace of smile" (Palacio de la Sonrisa), the complex was used both for administrative tasks as well as a place of torture, interrogation, and confinement. Due to its central location on one of the main avenues of the city, it was recognized early on as a place of detention and torture by the inhabitants of the city and became part of the collective memory of the inhabitants of the region (Consejo de Monumentos Nacionales. Gobierno de Chile 2016). After the end of dictatorship, it was used as a meeting place for members of the socialist party. Upon the request of the local Union of Human Rights Groups in March 2013, the house was declared a historical monument in May 2016. Allegedly seeking a new project to boost his paltry record, the mayor of Punta Arenas at that time, Emilio Boccazzi, initiated a competition for the future of the site that was supposed to bring together the community in a participatory process.

There were two finalists in the competition. The first, supported by four of six groups of victims and relatives, used the site of memory approach present in the Cono Sur—no interventions, "bare walls," a focus on the testimony of materiality. On the first floor, it offered a space for the groups to organize meetings and events. The supporting associations invoked the example of ESMA in Buenos Aires as an example to follow.[18] This entry followed the style and approach that had become a regional staple following its popularity through dissemination, circulations, and entanglements in professional networks.

The second entry, nevertheless, departed from the dominant "bare walls" approach. According to its architect, Miguel Lawner, the place should not just engage with the memory of the site itself but also open up to reflect on the broader history of repression and violence in the region of Magallanes, in a Chilean, thus national, context. Lawner's proposal suggested adding an extra structure to the original two-story house to improve the visitor experience. The architectural renderings of the suggested exhibition reveal for the access space a museographic display of main violations of human rights that occurred in the region of Magallanes. The first panels present the extermination of the native groups of the area after the takeover by the Chilean state. A further panel describes the labor union's struggle of the early twentieth century and its oppression by the state. The following space is dedicated to state terrorism, focusing on violations of human rights by the Pinochet dictatorship, including those which took place in the house.

On the first floor, however, the majority of the space is dedicated to the concentration camp of Rio Chico, in the nearby Dawson Island (Isla Dawson). Isla Dawson is a high-profile Chilean story featuring the main figures of Allende's government, deported there after 15 September 1973. Architect Miguel Lawner himself, as director of the Corporation for Urban Improvement (Cormu) of the Allende government, spent two years as an inmate on the island. Located in the central Magellan Straits, one hundred kilometers away from Punta Arenas, Isla Dawson is part of the Tierra del Fuego archipelago, the South American frontier, commonly referred to as the southernmost point of the Americas, a cold, windswept place, as remote as possible from Santiago, the center of power. Isla Dawson has remained present in the Chilean memoryscape through several cultural productions of the recent decades. They have included popular prisoner autobiographies (Bitar 2011; Lawner 2003, 2004), external accounts (Esquivel 2013; Haltenhoff 2005), and films by the prolific Miguel Littin (Littin et al. 2009). In the book *La Isla Dawson: Testimonios de Oprobio y Dignidad*, Abel Esquivel (2013) calls Isla Dawson a concentration camp.[19] Lawner himself also calls it a concentration camp (Esquivel 2013). The name, used frequently in Argentina, echoes the one of Holocaust language and, as Robben (2012) comments, has been applied because of the transnational influence of the Holocaust. Isla Dawson is framed nationally as essentially a Chilean story, but it is transnationally relevant through its representation as a concentration camp and the trajectory of its prisoners and celebrated artifacts, including the drawings and sketches of Miguel Lawner of both Isla Dawson and Villa Grimaldi, done secretly, which ended up in the hands of the Romanian embassy and Romanian government (Lawner 2003).[20] The drawings have been used as sources of inspiration for both the reconstruction of the tower at the Villa Grimaldi as well as for the proposed spaces inside the Casa in Punta Arenas.

The last room in the winning design opens up a different transnational direction, with a multidirectional memory twist. The room is dedicated to the local prisoners on Isla Dawson and other sites in Magallanes. To pay homage to the local prisoners, a song is played in the room, "Tamo Daleko," described as "a traditional melody of Croatian origin" that, according to Lawner, local prisoners on Isla Dawson frequently sang. The lyrics are in Croatian, pointing out that an important migration to Punta Arenas took place in the nineteenth century from Dalmatia, especially from the island of Brač (Martinic Beros 1999). In Croatian, *Tamo daleko* means "there, far away," referring to the faraway Croatian homeland but also to how far from home Isla Dawson was for its prisoners.

This tribute to the Croatian presence and their memory makes, however, a factual error that is actually fundamental, which can then reverse and challenge the multidirectional aspect of memory in that room: "Tamo Daleko" is in fact a song that emerged in World War I on the Greek island of Corfu to express the longing of Serbian soldiers for their faraway landlocked villages. The last verse of the folk song includes the line "Long live Serbia," and thus "Tamo Daleko" became in the twentieth century one of the most well-known Serbian patriotic songs. Its meaning as a signifier for Serbianness was reflected by the outcry caused when the most popular Yugoslav rock group of the 1980s, Bijelo Dugme, played a song in 1988 in Croatia in which parts of "Tamo Daleko" were combined with the traditional Croatian anthem, "Lijepa Naša Domovina: (Our beautiful fatherland), leading to overt hostility at several concerts in Croatia. Frontman Goran Bregović stated that the booing of this song was an ultimate sign of Yugoslavia's impending collapse (Liotta 2001). By employing this song in the house of memory and human rights of Punta Arenas, the multidirectional memory inadvertently turns not only toward memories of migration and imprisonment under dictatorship but also, depending on the degree of familiarity of the observer, to war (the context of the song), nationalism, conflict, and disintegration.

The transnationalism of remembering Isla Dawson and the Croatian connection do not stop here. Far away, off the Croatian mainland, lies Goli Otok (Naked Island), an island very similar to Isla Dawson, barren, windswept in winter, and with a history as a detention camp for leftist political figures. Nevertheless, it was not a military dictatorship that deported left-wing politicians there but Marshall Josip Broz Tito himself. After the Tito-Stalin split of 1948, Tito sent to Goli Otok numerous communists whom he, or other League of Communists cadres, accused of being Stalinist. They were tortured, detained, and later freed under the condition not to talk about the island. For Yugoslavia's socialist past, largely regarded by historiography as the most open and liberal of all socialist regimes in Europe, an outlier from the Soviet bloc, Goli Otok is a place of memory that both left-wing and right-wing memory milieus tend to ignore. In Croatia, the left is adamant to discuss the memory of a lone outlier in a memory of emancipated, progressive politics that Yugoslavia came to symbolize in hindsight of the nationalist-colored dismantlement of the 1990s, topped with turbo-capitalism. The right wing, concentrated on building on the memory of the Homeland War of 1991–95 and on Croatian heroism for independence, is not interested in commemorating left-wing victims. Agents of memory such as the NGO Documenta work on bringing the memorialization of the island to the forefront of memory debates, and, as I point out elsewhere, the memorialization process in the Cono Sur is used as an important international precedent.[21]

Back in Punta Arenas, the wide scope of the Lawner proposal was met with apathy by many locals and with anger by four out of six of local victims' associations. The opponents of the project contended that it minimized the onsite experience of victims by widening its scope too much, preferring instead the first option dedicated to the events onsite.[22] Two groups supported the project, and the fact that Miguel Lawner was himself a survivor of political violence played a role in their defense of it.[23]

At the time of writing, Lawner's winning design is awaiting a permit from the National Committee for Monuments and the resolution of the contestation made by the four opposing associations. If Lawner's design is implemented, the house will mark a departure from the regional model of a "bare walls" site of memory, and it will open up to different periods of state violence and to different scales and geographies, including diasporas and life in exile.

Conclusion

We have seen that in the context of the postdictatorship Southern Cone, the (re)claiming and memorialization of sites associated with political violence has been a very local process, involving a constellation of actors at local and national levels. However, it has also related to a transnational circulation of professional practices and approaches as well as to the entanglement of actors beyond national borders. This chapter has discussed transnational regional entanglements of practices, including those in place-making and memory-making of multiple localities, actors, and scales. It has highlighted the emergence of a transnational space-making process involving practices of site memorialization. Parque por la Paz Villa Grimaldi in Santiago, Chile, provided an early example of local action with a repertoire of local and international references, showcasing how agency can spark change despite opposing structures. Automotores Orletti in Buenos Aires showed a case of transnational political violence that has remained memorialized in a more local and national set of practices, thus not meeting its potential for transnational place-making. Finally, the Casa de los Derechos Humanos in Punta Arenas, Chile, emerged as a contested, entangled site, where memory threads of the local, the national, and the international (including a Croatian link) intersect and challenge each other in their competition over filling the materiality of the site with a memorialization approach. The morphed and mutated ruptures of memory existing through diasporas bring an extra layer to transnational place-making.

The first key argument set forward refers to the Southern Cone: through site memorialization practices, multiple agents produced the outcome of a transnational regional space of site memorialization repertoires of past dictatorships, nested in a global memorial architecture regime. The second key argument is more general: transnational place-making can be a difficult challenge even within the framework of cohesive transnational space-making, as the Latin American Southern Cone experiences have highlighted.

The three cases underline the need for a periodization of transnationalism in memorialization in the Southern Cone. In the first decade after dictatorship, local action was to some extent inspired by the memorialization of the Holocaust—in prompting initiative rather than employing practices—and acted against the politics of amnesia and impunity at the government level. In a second period, after the 2000s, spurred by a shift in government support for memory action, a repertoire of aesthetics and practices developed at a regional level, ignited by professional interaction in regional networks. Using a victim-centered, localized approach is, however, challenged by different subsets of multidirectional memory, which include constellations not only of actors but sites as well, and which connect to larger transnational memorialization processes and practices of migration, conflict, and competitive memories. A dynamic of competing architects active at local, national, and international levels, political actors, local and national activists, and a transnational Croatian Chilean community transform the memorialization process of space into an arena of intersections and entanglements that span from the local to the national to across the Southern Cone in Latin America and overseas in Southeastern Europe through a multidirectional memory and a transnational memory-space.

Gruia Bădescu is an Alexander von Humboldt Research Fellow at the University of Konstanz. He holds a PhD from the Department of Architecture, University of Cambridge, and, before Konstanz, he was a Departmental Lecturer and research associate at the University of Oxford. His work examines the relationship between place and memory in postwar and postauthoritarian contexts. His research in Chile and Argentina was funded by a joint AHRC-Labex-Les Passés dans le Présent grant, part of the project "Criminalization of Dictatorial Pasts in Europe and Latin America in Global Perspective." His forthcoming monograph addresses architectural engagements with dealing with the past.

Notes

1. Interview, Ricardo Brodsky, former director of the *Museo de la Memoria y los Derechos Humanos*, 17 January 2017, Vicuña, Chile.
2. Interview arch., Ana Cristina Torrealba Medina, November 2009, DVD 1 from the Oral Archive, Villa Grimaldi.
3. Interview arch., Oscar Weber Caballero, Santiago, Chile, 3 January 2017.
4. Interview, Maria Jose Kahn (curator, ESMA), Buenos Aires, 6 February 2017.
5. Focus group with architects at Oficina Bravo in Santiago, January 2017; interview arch., Luis Ainstein, Buenos Aires, 6 February 2017; interview, Roberto Burgos Mann, Valdivia,

14 February 2017; interview arch., Christian Glavic, Santiago, 22 February 2017; personal communications arch., Carlo Meirovich, Santiago, 5 March; arch., Javier Vergara Petrescu, Santiago, 6 March 2017.

6. I owe this insight to Malena Bastias, PhD candidate on the Museo de la Memoria.
7. Interviews: Ricardo Brodsky (ex-director Museo de la Memoria y los derechos Humanos, Santiago), 12 July 2016, Milan, 17 January 2017, Vicuña, Chile; Roberto Fuertes (director, Parque por la Paz Villa Grimaldi, Santiago), 13 January 2017; Laura Diaz (coordinator, Museo de la Memoria, Montevideo), 1 February 2017; Maria Jose Kahn (curator, ESMA), Buenos Aires, 6 February 2017; Alejandra Naftal (director, ESMA), Buenos Aires, 7 February 2017.
8. Interview Torrealba, DVD 1.
9. Ibid.
10. Ibid., DVD 2.
11. Carolina Aguilera, personal communication.
12. Interview, Torrealba, DVD2.
13. Ibid.
14. Guided visit and interview, 9 February 2017.
15. See, for instance, collections like Memoria Abierta (2009); also Schindel et al. (2010), where it is barely mentioned as an example.
16. Interview, administrative staff, Automotores Orletti, 21 September 2018.
17. Ibid.
18. Interview arch., Pamela Beatriz Dominguez, Punta Arenas, 22 February 2017.
19. Official newspaper coverage in 1973 insisted that this is "no Siberia and no concentration camp. There is sufficient wood, food. . . . God willing, meditation and air of purity and holiness which flows through these regions could help them put in order their febrile minds" (Delia Silva Salas, "Isla Dawson, perla del estrecho," *El mercurio*, 5 October 1973).
20. According to Miguel Lawner, the drawings that he secretly made during his time at both Isla Dawson and Villa Grimaldi were handed through international dignitaries in packages to his wife, who gave them all for safekeeping to Sandra Dimitrescu, the wife of the ambassador of the Socialist Republic of Romania, reputedly the only socialist country that did not cut its connections to Chile after the coup (Lawner, 2003)
21. For more on the entanglements between memorialization in Chile and Croatia, see Bădescu (2019).
22. Interview, Ivan González, Group of Sons and Grandsons, September 2017.
23. This has similarities with the case of ESMA, the most important Argentine site of torture, but also in the memorialization of political violence. The main curator there, currently director of the site, Alejandra Naftal, was a former prisoner of the camp, which gives her legitimacy in the eyes of survivors associations to operate changes in the site (Naftal, personal communication, February 2017). ESMA thus constitutes a departure from the model of leaving bare walls with its concept and execution.

References

Aguilera, Carolina. 2013. "Santiago de Chile Visto a Través de Espejos Negros: La Memoria Pública Sobre La Violencia Política Del Periodo 1970–1991, En Una Ciudad Fragmentada." *Bifurcaciones: Revista de Estudios Culturales Urbanos* 14: 1–13.

Aguilera, Carolina, and Gonzalo Cáceres. 2012. "Signs of State Terrorism in Post-Authoritarian Santiago: Memories and Memorialization in Chile." *Dissidences* 4(8): 7.

Andermann, Jens. 2012. "Returning to the Site of Horror on the Reclaiming of Clandestine Concentration Camps in Argentina." *Theory, Culture & Society* 29(1): 76–98.

———. 2015. "Placing Latin American Memory: Sites and the Politics of Mourning." *Memory Studies* 8(1): 3–8.

Andermann, Jens, and Carolina Aguilera. 2015. "Memories and Silences of a Segregated City: Monuments and Political Violence in Santiago, Chile, 1970–1991." *Memory Studies* 8(1): 102–14.

Bădescu, Gruia. 2019. "Entangled Islands of Memory: Actors and Circulations of Site Memorialization Practice between the Latin American Southern Cone and Central and Eastern Europe." *Global Society* 33(3): 382–99.

Bernhard, Michael H., and Jan Kubik. 2014. *Twenty Years after Communism: The Politics of Memory and Commemoration*. Oxford: Oxford University Press.

Birle, Peter, Elke Gryglewski, and Estela Schindel. 2009. *Urbane Erinnerungskulturen Im Dialog: Berlin Und Buenos Aires*. Berlin: Metropol.

Bitar, Sergio. 2011. *Isla 10*. Santiago de Chile: Pehuén.

Bustamante Flores, Fernando Daniel, and Pamela Eugenia Vega Igor. 2013. *La Migración Croata En Punta Arenas: Un Siglo de Trayectoria Del Acontecer Social y Cultural*. Punta Arenas: Universidad de Magallanes.

Collins, Cath, Katherine Hite, and Alfredo Joignant. 2013. *The Politics of Memory in Chile: From Pinochet to Bachelet*. London: Lynne Rienner Publishers.

Consejo de Monumentos Nacionales. Gobierno de Chile. 2016. "Casa de Los Derechos Humanos de Puntas Arenas Es Monumento Nacional." 2 May. Retrieved 5 May 2018 from http://www.monumentos.cl/consejo/606/w3-article-58938.html.

Draper, Susana. 2012. *Afterlives of Confinement: Spatial Transitions in Postdictatorship Latin America*. Pittsburgh: University of Pittsburgh Press.

Esquivel, Abel. 2013. *La Isla Dawson: Testimonios de Oprobio y Dignidad* [*Dawson Island: Testimonies of Disgrace and Dignity*]. Santiago de Chile: Ediciones Copygraph.

Fenster, Tovi. 2004. "Belonging, Memory and the Politics of Planning in Israel." *Social & Cultural Geography* 5(3): 403–17.

Gatti, Gabriel. 2014. *Surviving Forced Disappearance in Argentina and Uruguay: Identity and Meaning*. London: Palgrave Macmillan.

Haltenhoff, William. 2005. *Dawson: sangre, penales y golpes*. Santiago de Chile: El Periodista.

Hays, Sharon. 1994. "Structure and Agency and the Sticky Problem of Culture." *Sociological Theory* 12(1): 57–72.

Hite, Katherine. 2012. *Politics and the Art of Commemoration: Memorials to Struggle in Latin America and Spain*. Abingdon: Routledge.

Hite, Katherine, and Cath Collins. 2009. "Memorial Fragments, Monumental Silences and Reawakenings in 21st-Century Chile." *Millennium-Journal of International Studies* 38(2): 379–400.

Hite, Katherine, and Jesús Cuéllar. Menezo. 2013. *Política y Arte de La Conmemoración: Memoriales En América Latina y España*. Talca: Mandrágora.

Hoelscher, Steven, and D. H. Alderman. 2004. "Memory and Place: Geographies of a Critical Relationship." *Social & Cultural Geography* 5(3): 347–55.

Huyssen, Andreas. 2003. *Present Pasts: Urban Palimpsests and the Politics of Memory.* Palo Alto, CA: Stanford University Press.

Jameson, Fredric. 1997. "Is Space Political?" In *Rethinking Architecture: A Reader in Cultural Theory,* edited by Neil Leach, 255–69. New York: Routledge.

Jelin, Elizabeth. 2002. *Los trabajos de la memoria.* Madrid: Siglo XXI de España.

———. 2003. *State Repression and the Labors of Memory.* Minneapolis: University of Minnesota Press.

Koepnick, Lutz. 2001. "Forget Berlin." *German Quarterly [H.W. Wilson—EDUC]* 74(4): 343.

Lawner, Miguel. 2003. *Isla Dawson, Ritoque, Tres Alamos: La vida a pesar de todo.* Santiago de Chile: LOM Ed.

———. 2004. *Retorno a Dawson.* Santiago de Chile: LOM Ediciones.

Lessa, Francesca. 2015. "Justice beyond Borders: The Operation Condor Trial and Accountability for Transnational Crimes in South America." *International Journal of Transitional Justice* 9(3): 494–506.

Levey Cara. 2014. "Of HIJOS and Niños: Revisiting Postmemory in Post-Dictatorship Uruguay." *History and Memory* 26(2): 5–39.

Levey, Cara. 2016. *Fragile Memory, Shifting Impunity: Commemoration and Contestation in Post-Dictatorship Argentina and Uruguay.* Frankfurt am Main: Peter Lang.

Liotta, Peter. 2001. *Dismembering the State: The Death of Yugoslavia and Why It Matters.* Lanham, MD: Lexington Books.

Littin, Miguel, et al. 2009. *Dawson Isla 10: Diario de un prisionero de guerra.* Santiago de Chile: Santiago Cinematográfica.

Lowenthal, David. 2015. *The Past Is a Foreign Country: Revisited.* Cambridge: Cambridge University Press.

Martinic Beros, Mateo. 1999. *La Inmigración Croata En Magallanes.* Punta Arenas: Hogar Croata.

McSherry, J. Patrice. 1999. "Operation Condor: Clandestine Inter-American System." *Social Justice* 26(4): 144–74.

Memoria Abierta. 2009. *Memorias en la ciudad: Señales del terrorismo de estado en Buenos Aires.* Buenos Aires: EUDEBA.

Olick, Jeffrey K. 2007. *The Politics of Regret: On Collective Memory and Historical Responsibility.* New York: Routledge.

———. 2015. "Foreword." In *Memory and Change in Europe: Eastern Perspectives,* vol. 16, edited by Małgorzata Pakier and Joanna Wawrzyniak, ix–xiii. New York: Berghahn Books.

Robben, Antonius. 2012. "From Dirty War to Genocide: Argentina's Resistance to National Reconciliation." *Memory Studies* 5(3): 305–15.

Schindel, Estela. 2010. "Lugares de Memoria En Buenos Aires." In *Memorias Urbanas En Dialogo: Berlin y Buenos Aires,* edited by Peter Birle, Vera Carnovale, Elke Gryglewski, and Estela Schindel, 83–99. Buenos Aires: Editorial Buenos Libros.

Schindel, Estela, and Pamela Colombo. 2014. *Space and the Memories of Violence: Landscapes of Erasure, Disappearance and Exception.* Basingstoke: Palgrave.

Sion, Brigitte. 2014. *Memorials in Berlin and Buenos Aires: Balancing Memory, Architecture, and Tourism.* Lanham, MD: Lexington Books.

Tuan, Yi-Fu. 1974. "Space and Place: Humanistic Perspective." *Progress in Geography: International Reviews of Current Research* 6: 211–52.

Weizman, Eyal. 2010. "Forensic Architecture." *Architectural Design* 80(5): 58–63.

Williams, Paul Harvey. 2007. *Memorial Museums: The Global Rush to Commemorate Atrocities.* Oxford: Berg.

Part III

Top-Down Agency

Chapter 8

MY GRIEF, OUR GRIEVANCE

Universal Human Rights and Memory Standardization
in Liberia's Truth Commission

Noga Glucksam

Universal human rights discourses are essential tools for spreading human-itarian values globally and holding abusive regimes accountable. Activists, governments, and international organizations widely accept the universal-ity of human rights and champion their protection and promotion across the world. The rights discourse is so influential that its ethical foundations have become close to a global truth, and its agenda an ultimate strategy for legitimating policy. Human rights also make a central pillar of transitional justice processes, perceived as an important objective and a condition for their success (Teitel 2000; Arthur 2009; Olsen and Reiter 2010; Sikkink 2011). However, this conception of human rights agendas often overlooks or even dismisses the possible problematic implications it might have for the population it seeks to protect. The universal rhetoric, critics argue, is easily manipulated, interventionist, favors elites, and limits the impact of grassroots activism and community stake-taking (Englund 2006; Mutua 2013; Robins 2012). Consequently, the standardizing quality of universal human rights norms is also at risk of undermining the agency of local affected communities who are subjected to these interventions.

This chapter aims to contribute to this debate by exploring the impact of the universal human rights discourse on memory agency in the context of truth and reconciliation commission. I argue that the dominance of universal-ethical discourses in these institutions leads to the re-articulation of memories of violence and atrocities to fit their set legal and normative categories. Consequently, private and community experiences become more meaningful for a transnational audience, serving a larger political purpose. This process, however, also disenfranchises the narrators, limiting their agency to articulate their truths and define their experiences independently and authentically. The repackaging of personal narrations of experiences in official reports is, in particular, an action of standardization, but it has been largely ignored so far. The impact of standardization on memory agency should receive more attention, especially because it stands in direct contradiction to the stated rationale of establishing a truth commission. Truth commissions are set up to give voice to the voiceless and expose the truth, even at the expense of achieving justice in its retributive sense. Numerous studies have demonstrated this quality, discussing its social and psychological merits as a viable trade-off for punitive measures (Hayner 2010; Rotberg and Thompson 2010).

Moreover, these are spaces of national memory, with particular resonance for case-specific experiences and cultures that may not be captured by the legal form of tribunals, for example. In practice, transnational normative actors and audiences give these spaces a multidimensional quality, where stories and narratives shift and adapt to fit familiar and impactful frames. I refer to this process as standardization. It is a process necessary to achieve traction in complex rhetorical spaces, by helping to reach larger audiences and affect outcomes by connecting specific circumstances to universally familiar normative frames. However, it also negatively affects the memory agency of the individuals and communities participating in the process by overwriting individual recollections with transnational narratives. Standardization is, paradoxically, both amplifying agency and limiting agency, making participation in such institutions both empowering and debilitating, and their outcomes are at once both amplifying voice and muting it.

The argument lends new insights into the study of memory structures and memory agency in a challenging transnational context. Following the premise of this volume, the concept of agency refers not just to the ability of actors to act but also to affect change (Wüstenberg, introduction to this volume). From a discursive point of view, this would mean influencing the overall collective narrative to reflect personal recollection and meaningful frames. Standardization of memory in the context of a truth and reconciliation commission, therefore, poses a significant challenge to memory agency. This chapter examines how the ethical legitimacy and dominance of universal human rights discourses acted as a standardization frame in the Liberian Truth and Reconciliation Commission (LTRC), which operated between 2007 and 2009. The LTRC served as the central transitional justice mechanism in the country after it experienced an oppressive military regime followed by fourteen years of civil war. The LTRC was celebrated for its broad participation and its extensive outreach program. It encouraged public debates on justice, account-ability, and forgiveness and confronted Liberians with their past, as well as lingering corruption and impunity in their political culture through a series of public hearings between January and April 2008. Its work was also steeped in controversies, predominantly due to the apparent use of the forum by elites and former warlords to cleanse their name. Other critiques included allega-tions of exaggerations and lies, of misconduct and commissioner infighting, and many other irregularities and scandals.

Moreover, the general public received the commission's final report with fierce criticism due to its extensive lists of names recommended for prosecu-tion or banning from holding political office, a list that many argued was a personal hit list of some of the commissioners for their political ambitions. Several published assessments of the LTRC discuss these implications (Liberia Media Center 2008). Absent from these reviews and studies, however, is an assessment of the impact of the LTRC process on its witnesses. This chapter offers a different critique of the LTRC, namely its limitation of memory agency of victim-witnesses. The study focuses on the public hearings phase of the commission. It examines how witnesses construct their memories and attempt to enact their agency and the consequential re-articulation of these narratives. The analysis further examines witnesses' engagement with com-missioners, who directed, highlighted and ignored certain aspects of the sto-ries, to fit a universal human rights discourse. Consequently, many of the testimonies were concluded with tension and dissonance, presenting multiple and incompatible versions and rationalizations to events. These hearings and the resulting controversial final report demonstrate the paradox as mentioned earlier of both amplifying and limiting memory agency.

This chapter draws on wider research on conceptual dissonances within the Liberia transitional justice process. Truth-telling was a major part of that process, in line with the international agenda of transitional justice, but also reflecting a desperate need of people across Liberia to voice their experiences and perceptions. However, and crucially, there never existed in Liberia a homogenous "peoples' voice" or even "victims' voice." Rather, it was char-acterized by multiple experiences, ideas, and interpretations. Though not unique in this condition, Liberia stands out for the overwhelming fragmenta-tion of its historical narratives, political perspectives, and collective memory narratives, including multiple contradiction and dissonances—cases where two contradicting meanings coexist without a clear resolution. Indeed, it is a common phrase in the country that in Liberia, the number of opinions is the number of people.

Researching cases of conceptual fragmentation and dissonance is, however, a considerable challenge in the social disciplines, where methods intend to overcome the occurrence of multiple and conflicting meanings by using clear variables and categories. A simple textual analysis of a chosen sample would not capture this complexity. For this reason, this research adopted a conceptual-historical and critical analysis approach to analyze a large dataset of public narratives and discourses. (For critical discourse analysis, see Pitkin 1972; Arribas-Ayllon and Walkerdine 2008; Wodak and Meyer 2009; Holzscheiter 2013. For conceptual history, see Skinner 1969; Bourdieu 1991; Olick and Robbins 1998; Mahoney 2000; Sewell 2005.) The dataset collects thousands of hours of transcribed, open-source, public hearings of the Liberia Truth and Reconciliation Commission, in addition to hundreds of opinion columns, interviews, and pamphlets published while the TRC was in operations. The study also utilizes a series of open-ended interviews conducted with peace-building and transitional justice activists and public officials in Monrovia in 2014. The analysis and discussion in this chapter draw from this larger qualitative study (Glucksam 2016). Due to space constraints, only a small sample of these discourses is reproduced here to demonstrate larger trends.

The chapter proceeds in three parts. It begins by developing the theoretical premise and argument about memory standardization, examining the nature of memory agency and considering its place in the global-ethical system of universal human rights. Next, it offers a systematic look at the process and dynamics of the LTRC's testimonies. It examines the relationship between witnesses and commissioners and the process of memory articulation and manipulation. Through this analysis, I identify two dominant dynamics of standardization: (1) framing individual hurt as part of a group atrocity, and (2) adopting a universal structure to explain the inexplicable. Both dynamics involve initially fragmented and dissonant narratives that consequently become standardized into pre-defined categories. Finally, the chapter draws broader conclusions about the complicated relationship between memory agency and memory standardization.

Memory Agency, Human Rights, and Standardization

What does it mean to have memory agency? The cognitive action of remembering is personal, and often intuitive and internal, to the extent that questions of agency seem almost irrelevant. In its social context, however, memorialization is recognized as narrative driven, suggesting that individual remembering is influenced, informed, and constructed by external frames. Memory agency, therefore, might present in the effect of contesting the socially accepted frame, but also in the act of conforming to enjoy the sense of power and acceptance and the related social meanings of the collective narrative. This insight poses a significant challenge for researchers, as it suggests that both conflicting outcomes may indicate the existence of memory agency, or provide evidence for its absence.

To resolve this issue, we can take some insight from neurological studies that define agency as "the awareness that one's own self is the agent or author of an action, a thought, or a feeling" (Vinogradov et al. 2006). In other words, agency is indicated by the sense of authorship and free voice. In social contexts, this includes an active recognition of agency by other members of the group. Recognition may present positively, by granting or affirming agency, as well as negatively, through practices such as denial and silencing. This aspect of agency is central for a multifaceted study of collective memory. Many explorations of agency in the context of memory studies focus on the contestation of official, usually national, narratives, by smaller communities of memory (Nora and Kritzman 1996; Lavrence 2005; Tabar 2007). These studies focus mostly on the historical-ethical implications of narrative contestations, usually limited by traditional national boundaries of analysis. Transnationality, on the other hand, invokes an investigation of the impact of local, national, and transnational agents and structures. It examines power relations in complicated sociopolitical settings that go beyond formal politics and requires a consideration of multiple power structures. Moreover, in many studies of normative contestation, power relations are analyzed as an independent variable, examining either relatively equal actors that compete in narrative-setting or distinctly unequal actors whose power differentials are apparent. Such analysis fails to address the dynamic and fluid nature of power relations, for example, in cases where empowering structures may become debilitating (see Dolan 2009; Kirby 2013). Therefore, the study of memory agency must look beyond formal structures and narratives and examine tacit sociopolitical complexes such as expression, recognition, acknowledgment and standardization.

Memory standardization, it emerges, both empowers and limits agency. It invites more participants to express their narratives and practice their agency, but within acceptable bounds of desired discourse that limit agency. Authoritative social or political agents are usually those responsible for orchestrating the standardization of memory narratives and for creating the hegemonic narratives, and the ones empowered by tapping into transnational discursive structures. Within these structures, most participants enhance the process of standardization through repetition and replication, thus demonstrating very limited memory agency, while more powerful agents can shape the standardized narrative or correct the discourse of participants to make them fit in the standardized frame. Paradoxically, the dynamic of standardization offers power and agency to participants who are willing to forgo their agency by accepting the standardized narratives. Similarly, insistence on individualist narratives that deviate from the standard may "reward" the rogue memory agent with excommunication from the mainstream narrative, along with the acknowledgment and belonging it produces.

Truth commissions are a unique site of transnational memory. Traditionally, truth commissions are national institutions, set up to uncover and narrate national histories and memories. However, they also contain many distinctively transnational traits. Although set up according to the unique needs and political constraints of their contexts, truth commissions around the world share the banner of the universal human rights and transitional justice movement (Hayner 2010: 25–26). This is evident in their setup, procedures, and most importantly, normative priorities, as well as in the practice of sending prospective commissioners and administrators for training in international organizations. The Liberian Truth Commission was established precisely in this way. It was suggested to belligerents during the peace negotiations of 2003 as a path to bypass war crimes prosecutions, directly referencing other examples, most notably that of South Africa. Its setup involved teams of consultants and trainers from African and Western NGOs, which utilized the structure and procedure of the international model and imported the corresponding norms of universal human rights.

The debate on the universality of human rights is too diverse and complex to summarize here sufficiently (see Brown 1997; Donnelly 2007; McGuinness 2011; Burke 2011; Chong 2014). Although different notions of human rights date back to diverse distant histories, modern structures of human rights are explicitly, perhaps even triumphantly, standardized (Evans 1996; Korey 2001). These norms are inspired mainly by the trauma caused by World War II and the authoritarian regimes associated with it, as well as by the liberal-universal zeitgeist that drove the establishment of many of the postwar institutions. These documents set forth a conception of universality, associated with the universal experience of humanity, while safeguarding the expression of cultural and political difference (Morsink 1999). Theoretically, their universal call should not come at the expense of a local agency. However, as the cold war ensued, global political and ethical divides became interchangeable and gradually even indistinguishable. Within just a few decades, the global agenda of human rights and its related international structure have become increasingly associated with Western hegemony and liberal identities of progressiveness and righteousness. As human rights institutionalized in international treaties, report mechanisms, and regional tribunals, the concept of universality became synonymous with uniformity. Proponents of this process often argue that only through global standardization can human rights fully achieve its goal of safeguarding a universal standard of humanity. In the post–Cold War era, human rights structures and discourse grew to inform more and more international policies, from development to peacebuilding, global justice to local reconciliation. The proceeding discussion traces the influences of multilevel agents on the set-up of the LTRC. It examines the impact of the universal normative structure on the memory agency of witnesses, with a particular focus on victims. The analysis confirms the theoretical hypothesis, providing evidence for a dual relationship between standardization and agency, and discusses the broader implications of this finding for the study of memory politics, transitional justice, and reconciliation.

Transnational Narratives and Memory Standardization

In his final public statement on the closing of the Liberia TRC, Chairman Jerome Verdier explained the TRC's mission "on behalf of the people . . . to explain how Liberia became what it is today," and presented the final report to "the people of Liberia, the Government of Liberia, the President of Liberia and the International Community who are moral guarantors of the Liberian peace process." What did he mean by "moral guarantors"? What role did the moral structures prompted by the many international actors play in the formatting of the commission and its conclusions? And how did that affect the ability of simple people to maintain their separate narratives of their experience of the country's turbulent past?

Over the course of fourteen years, the Liberian Civil War cost the lives of some quarter of a million people and led to the displacement of over a million. The war is infamous for its high toll on the civilian population, the widespread practice of ritual killing and cannibalism, and the mass recruitment of underage soldiers, as well as many other mass atrocities. In its aftermath, Liberian society was torn apart, its institutions corrupt and crumbling. In this context, postconflict reconstruction required engaging in multiple processes of reform and restructuring as well as social and political reflection and reckoning. For this reason, as well as due to the significant power warlords continued to hold in the country, a restorative justice approach was woven into the fragile peace agreement in the form of a truth and reconciliation commission, not only as a way to move the country forward to reconciliation but also to allow those in power to avoid severe accountability measures.

The Liberia TRC was established as a political compromise, meant to promote an end to the culture of impunity that overran Liberian politics and society for decades while also guaranteeing that no social, political, and legal consequences were placed on the country's rebels and politicians as they negotiated their share of power in the new interim government. In the face of ingrained practices of corrupt politics and dishonesty, the TRC sought to establish a "true truth," a factual history of violence in Liberia. However, no narrative is ever objective, and human rights and humanitarian agendas dominated the narrative that underpinned the TRC from its inception to the publication of its final report. The comprehensive peace agreement of 2003 that ended the Liberian Civil War had all parties committing to "promote democracy . . . on the basis of political pluralism and respect for fundamental human rights as embodied in the Universal Declaration on Human Rights, the African Charter on Human and People's Rights and other widely recognized international instruments on human rights . . . as well as promoting full respect for international humanitarian law and human rights." This task was given to a future truth and reconciliation commission that would "deal with the root causes of the crisis in Liberia . . . and to recommend measures to be taken for the rehabilitation of victims of human rights violations" (CPA 2003: Preamble, Article XIII).

Two years later, the TRC mandate was enacted, setting the investigation of gross human rights violations as the primary tool to promote national peace, security, unity, and reconciliation. The TRC Act outlines the objectives and purposes of the commission, listing the investigation of human rights violations first, and only later citing objectives such as "providing a forum" and an "opportunity for both victims and perpetrators of human rights violations to share their experiences" and "providing opportunities for [women, children and vulnerable groups] to relate their experiences" (TRC Act 2005: sec. 4). The commission was accompanied by an international technical advisory committee of three persons, representing ECOWAS and the UN high commissioner for human rights. The act continues to reiterate the mission of "helping restore the human dignity of victims . . . by providing an opportunity for victims, witnesses, and others to give an account of the violations and abuses suffered" (TRC Act 2005: sec. 26f).

After two more years of difficulties in setting up the TRC, nominating and dismissing commissioners due to a series of controversies and scandals, and struggling to secure the necessary funds, the commission finally set out in 2007 to begin its groundwork of collecting testimonies (Long 2008: 3). It collected twenty thousand testimonies from across all of Liberia's fifteen counties, several refugee camps in Guinea, and from diaspora communities in the United States. Six hundred of these witnesses were selected to feature in public testimonies, most of which were later transcribed and made available to the public on the commission's website. The two purposes of investigating human rights violations and providing a forum of free remembrance, which was intertwined in the TRC Act, continued to guide the TRC as a dual objective and did not raise any public or professional concern regarding a possible conflict between the two. However, when reviewing and analyzing the testimonies, especially those given by victims, a more tenuous relationship appears between the two objectives, revealing a tacit but formidable conflict of discursive and memory agency. A closer and systematic reading of the transcribed LTRC hearings illustrates the conflict between individual and standardized memory narratives and their consequences for a sense of memory agency.

First, it is necessary to differentiate between regular witness hearings, which invited to the stand both victims and perpetrators, and the thematic and institutional hearings, which featured political and cultural leaders, specialists, and academics. While the latter put the commissioners in the awkward position of defending their authority to established figures in the Liberian sociopolitical hierarchy, the former positioned them in a relatively comfortable position of notability, endowing them with a significant agency. The general structure of the testimonies was mostly uniform. Witnesses came up to the stand and first told their story freely, the way they wanted. The length of these testimonies varied significantly. A few of the more confident witnesses shared longer and more complex stories of their experiences of the war, including secondhand and hearsay statements. Most witnesses, however, demonstrated signs of intimidation and angst, only speaking for a few minutes and providing very little detail of their experiences, often struggling to find words. It was clear that their attempt to recount their experiences was made with great social but also personal difficulty.

The first testimony in the first public hearing in Monrovia exemplifies this conflict of agency. The witness, David Saweh, spoke in an associative manner, in what seemed like a highly emotional and unrehearsed recounting of the way he remembered events. The most dominant subject of the testimony was his sister, how close they were, how they went through everything together, how she tried to protect him when the National Patriotic Front of Liberia (NPFL, the main insurgency group that started the war) captured them, and finally her ultimate suffering as a victim of brutal gang rape and murder. His tone makes it clear that recounting was extremely difficult for him, not only because of his struggle to relive the trauma but also because of the identity of the man he identified as responsible for the attack. The commander of the group, known by the war name "Dearboy," became a famous musician after the war, and also a role model and a close friend to the president (Gberie 2008: 456). Identifying this perpetrator by name came at a tremendous social price. The testimony included many defensive remarks by the witness, such as "The TRC people came, I just gave them my records. I didn't explain anything, just for them to find the truth from me and I just repeat, but I just gave them my records." The witness reiterated the main point of his suffering, the main purpose of his remembering—his sister, and how her absence has left him alone in the world: "I never had nobody from 1990 up to this time." His last words to the commissioners were markedly defensive: "During the war we suffered, and everything that happened is what I am saying. There a lot of people who are aware of what happened to me" (Saweh testimony, 8 January 2008).

The defensive tone was subsequently repeated by many more witnesses, even when their testimony did not potentially implicate a high-profile figure. For example, when Dr. Jeremiah Walker, a former president of the Liberia Council of Churches, undoubtedly a position of authority among his community, came to recount his memories to the LTRC, he insisted several times, "I was here and all I was here. So just want to confirm that those things did happen in our country, that there was no need to act as though they did not happen" (Walker testimony, 8 January 2008). In his statement, the witness felt the need to defend his narrative, justify it, maybe even provide corroboration, as if just saying his truth was simply not convincing enough. There are many more examples of this defensive tone in other testimonies. In Saweh's final remarks to the commissioners, the first witness to appear in the Monrovia public hearing reiterated, "Everything that happened is what I am saying. Many people are aware of what had happened to me" (Saweh testimony, 8 January 2008). In another example, a woman from Nimba County told the story of her rape, concluding with the statement: "What happened to me and what I saw is what I have said; I cannot say anything else besides this" (Keiger testimony, 12 May 2008). A critical reading of these and other testimonies suggests that a power struggle was underpinning the process of remembrance in Liberia. However, because the TRC recorded similar dynamics in different and distant counties with diverse political terrains and ethnic groups, the simple political explanation of victims versus perpetrator offered by the traditional "peace versus justice" debate is rendered insufficient. The cause for this dynamic, I argue, is embedded in the normative and hierarchical structure of the commission.

This hierarchy is even more apparent in the second part of the testimonies when commissioners posed questions to the witnesses. Most of the questions sought factual information, asking for clarifications on names, dates, and places. Two other types of questions were more leading in nature. The first involved questions about behaviors and events that the witnesses did not initially mention but that commissioners believed to be a part of the story, and so they prompted the inclusion of these narratives through questioning. They asked, for example, if, in addition to the killing and abuse already described by the witnesses, any other killing took place, of how many people, if there was rape, looting, and so on. On some occasions, these questions enabled witnesses to expand their story, helped them add more content to their remembered experience, and, in that sense, supported their memory agency. On most occasions, however, witnesses offered confirmations for these expanded stories based on rumor, hearsay, or speculation. In some extreme cases, witnesses insisted on having no further knowledge, and seemed distressed at the apparent dissatisfaction of the commissioner (Zee testimony, 5 March 2008).

The second type of leading questions focused on causes and explanations for the event. Indeed, seeking the causes of the conflict and the atrocities it brought about was a central part of the commission's mandate. However, one must question the appropriateness of their execution of this mandate. On numerous occasions, the commissioners asked victims to explain why their family members were captured, tortured, and killed, or to provide reasons for why their villages were targeted. These sometimes took the form of an open question, but on many occasions they were leading and narrow. Most commonly, commissioners' asked witnesses to confirm the view that previous ethnic tensions were the trigger for violence, a narrative that was not always easily accepted. In fact, there were numerous occasions during hearings where witnesses tried to reject the "ethnic violence" framing of the conflict, insisting that in their village or community, ethnicity was never a significant cause of friction before the conflict (Larkor testimony, 16 May 2008; Togba testimony, 5 March 2008).

In contrast to the regular witness hearings, the thematic and institutional hearings, especially in Monrovia, featured high-profile figures, including well-known ex-commanders and influential political figures, many of whom were accompanied by entourages of supporters. These hearings often led to heated discussions and attempts by witnesses to undermine the credibility and authority of commissioners (Steinberg 2010). "The question of who is in control of the process at this point is difficult to say," a Liberian civil society and transitional justice activist wrote in 2008. "Alleged perpetrators are using TRC public hearings as a pedestal to vindicate themselves from abuses and violence committed against innocent civilians . . . with elaborate presentations; they grandstand and justify their actions as an inevitable outcome of a revolution" (Weah 2008). These dynamics suggest that a fierce power and agency struggle was the backdrop of the Liberia TRC. Other analyzes of the setup, operation, and conclusion of the commission actively support this assessment (Pajibo 2007; Gberie 2008; Steinberg 2010; Harris and Lappin 2010).

So far, the discussion has demonstrated how the hierarchical relationships between different groups of witnesses and the commissioners have affected the contestation of narratives in the Liberia TRC, adversely affecting victims' memory agency but also challenging the authority of commissioners when faced with more high-profile witnesses. The authoritative and standardized human rights discourse was invoked in various ways by the commissioners to reinforce their authority and to brush off claims of unfairness by anchoring the produced narrative along the lines of the agreed-upon meaning of justice. The following analysis demonstrates the impact of standardized memory narratives in two dominant frames: the tension between individual hurt and group victimization, and the rationalization for the remembered atrocities according to known causes of violence.

Individual Hurt and Group-Targeted Atrocities

Even from the initial review of transcribed LTRC testimonies, I found it striking how dominant the narrative of the witnesses' own victimhood was in this truth commission. Individual hurt is repeatedly the most important feature of the remembered experience and the primary reason for witnesses' decision to appear in front of the TRC. This, interestingly, is common to testimonies of both victims and former combatants. Even the highest-ranking commanders repeatedly emphasized their victimhood (Blayea testimony, 15 January 2008; Johnson testimony, 27 August 2008). Traumatizing experiences ranged from direct harm to attacks of family members, including both physical and psychological injuries. Common to most of these stories is the very personal and individual nature of the experience. Phrases such as "the war made me suffer," "I am suffering," "I have nobody to help me," or "I was treated badly" are particularly prevalent in the first part of testimonies. The narrative that emerges in each testimony is that of senseless violence, personally directed at the speaker due to unknown evil. In fact, reference to the devil was very common in the descriptions of atrocities (Ellis 2007: 278). Some witnesses recall experiences of being repeatedly raped, beaten, or burned. Others talk about their victimhood as related to the need to escape their homes into the bush, losing their business, having their children kidnapped, being left by their spouses, or even being disrespected as the primary cause of their despair. Most often, witness seemed not to know what caused the cruelty they suffered or who was ultimately responsible; their knowledge of their experience rarely expanded beyond the names of the people directly involved.

These recollections were notably altered as witnesses went through the questioning process. In many cases, commissioners, using leading questions, "suggested" to victims ways to contextualize their hurt within stories of mass atrocities, and to reframe their victimhood concerning known human rights violations. For example, when a woman told the story of her group rape with great pain, she repeated the phrase "I was not myself," stressing her fear, distress, and need for immediate assistance. Commissioner Pearl Brown Bull then answered her with narratives about mass rapes and universal experiences of women: "You have talked for plenty women," adding that her testimony will "go down in history." The witness was so lacking confidence in her testimony that she later sought reassurance from the commissioner, asking, "What I said about women, was it bad or good?" The next question kept challenging the woman's story of individual suffering with doubt: "Why you were raped amongst all the people?" She responded: "I do not want to lie" (Keigar testimony, 12 May 2008). The testimony of Samuel Karnley is one demonstrative example of this dynamic. Karnley's experience of the war included several attacks by different factions and resulted in the loss of his leg. After recounting his own experience, Karnley added that he also witnessed several gruesome killings. He was subsequently asked, "Do you know who headed the LPC at the time?" He answered, "I heard it George Boley who was heading it." After briefly discussing the issue of his lost leg, the commissioner asked the witness, "Did these groups have the same objectives?" Karnley responded, "No I do not think so, because if any of them had the same objective, I do not think they would have been attacking each other" (Karnley testimony, 22 January 2008). Once again, Karnley was asked a leading question that prompted him to offer general knowledge and conjecture rather than first-person recollection.

Similar dynamics were repeated in many more testimonies, indicating a trend where the initial testimony presented a narrative of personal and random harm, which the commissioners later attempted to reframe according to standardized categories: known mass atrocities, ethnic violence, specific known groups and persons. Witnesses, however, could rarely link their experience to a systematic pattern of violence, even though they showed considerable knowledge regarding what was happening in their regions and even further away. When they could make this connection, they shifted their manner of speaking to a more general tone, claiming additional knowledge through other people, switching to the third person plural, or becoming altogether very defensive. Thus, through the process of question and answer, narratives slowly transformed, until a standardized story emerged. In the previously quoted case, the painful story of being repeatedly raped by multiple strangers and the resulting psychological trauma and disassociation is molded into the narrative of systemic sexual violence fitting the "rape as a weapon of war" narratives that were heavily advertised in awareness campaigns of human rights activists (Kirby 2013). However, in such narratives, the personal experience of the specific women is overshadowed by the scope of the phenomenon, leading the woman to no longer speak of her own pain but rather to speak for many women.

Another indication of the individual understanding of hurt and trauma is reflected in the "final word" of hearings. At the end of their testimonies, when invited by the chairman to say their final word, almost all witnesses asked for a specific type of material and practical assistance. They commonly requested medical assistance, or for material assistance to build a house or send their children to school. A few examples clearly illustrate this trend: "I would want to say to anybody is that I am not too sure if that guy can replace my leg or anything can be done to him to replace my leg" (Karnley testimony, 22 January 2008); "I want to appeal to the government for good road and communications. There is no communication coverage there" (Vanday testimony, 15 April 2008); "The only thing I do not have strength and no food and only money can do everything" (Sackie testimony, 15 April 2008); "Please look at my condition, I want your [help] to please help me with money to do business to be able to help my mother" (Duo testimony, 16 May 2008).

Although it is important to mention that many witnesses also expressed the need for community reparation, the purpose of appearance for many of the witnesses was personal. Indeed, it arises from these texts that most of them were not aware of concepts of human rights, nor did they know how to articulate their memories in this sense even when they did. They predominantly sought personal help and agreed to talk to the commission in hopes of securing personal benefits. This critical observation was also raised by a statistical study conducted in parallel to the LTRC about popular attitudes about peace and justice in Liberia (Cibelli et al. 2009: 40). However, through the process of cross-examination, witnesses were directed to rearticulate their experiences to conform to a standardized narrative in line with the prestigious and influential universal human rights discourse, one that focuses on the systematic and widespread nature of violence rather than on its specific and nuanced impact on victims.

Universal Structure to Explain the Inexplicable

Another narrative some of the commissioners attempted to revise into standardized terms relates to ethnic violence and ethnic cleansing. In many testimonies, violence is described as senseless and lacking a clear cause. Witnesses often recall being surprised when exposed to violence, a response uncharacteristic to ethnic violence, which is often introduced by a period of ethnic tensions. In Grand Gedeh, for example, when rivalries between the Krahn and Gio tribes were politicized and militarized by local warlords, victims did not necessarily recall the violence as caused by an ethnic rivalry but rather by random cruelty and desire to assert power by local commanders. One woman, Amelia, recalled the senseless murder of her father, a pastor, along with her brother and uncle, in response to his daughters' attempt to escape to Ivory Coast. She was then asked by the chairman if the cause for the murder was ethnic affiliation. She was only able to answer using secondhand knowledge, as this was clearly not part of her own memory: "They say we were Krahn. . . . They say during the 1990 war they say the Krahn and Gio had problem but me I don't know since that time anytime war come, they can go for us" (Zee testimony, 5 March 2008). Other narratives of mass atrocities were interjected into this testimony. While the first part of the testimony was short and erratic, demonstrating a lack of clarity and a general sense of confusion and frustration about her situation, the questioning portion of the testimony was more structured, not focusing primarily on her own experiences but rather on her general knowledge of what was going on around her and in other places. In this manner, she was asked about her father's killer's affiliation, to which she answered, "We used to always see arm with him they say he was ATU (Anti-Terrorist Unit)." She was also asked about the community's experience with another fighting group, the LPC (Liberia Peace Commission). She answered, "I just heard about them I did not see them, I was in Ivory Coast." To questions about the kidnapping of girls, she responded similarly: "I was in Ivory Coast. . . . [They carried] about twenty girls." All these elements of the testimony were not, in fact, part of Amelia's own narrative of her experience and trauma, which is dominated by the murder of her father. However, through questioning, she delivered to the commissioners the desired narratives about ethnic violence, mass kidnapping, and rape. Gradually, this narrative became intertwined with her own recollections, and toward the end of the proceedings, she stated "I was small, but I can remember" with regard to some of these issues, which she did not associate with her story in her preliminary statements. Her memory was standardized. This exchange and the dynamics in many similar testimonies demonstrate the hierarchy between personal, erratic, and unorganized memories and the organized, predefined, and dramatic narrative of mass human rights violations. Numerous testimonies began with a witness recalling their experience of unprovoked, unexplained violence, seemingly out of the blue, and guided mostly by the viciousness and greed of the perpetrator. They were then led by commissioners who offered possible explanations, prompting witnesses to consider whether a personal experience of torture or rape was part of a mass atrocity pattern or suggesting antecedents in prior tribal relations (links that witnesses sometimes pushed back against).

These problematic dynamics of leading, doubting, and sometimes even bullying witnesses did not go unnoticed by the public. A few weeks into the hearings, the commission came under public scrutiny. As the testimonies began to mount, media columnists and radio commentators began to criticize the commissioners' conduct, their willingness to let perpetrators claim the stage to clear their names, and their problematic treatment of victims. In fact, on one occasion Chairman Verdier even scolded one of the commissioners while still in session for an offensive line of questioning toward a witness. The commission's chairman ultimately addressed this critique. In the first proceedings of one of the hearings in Grand Gedeh County, he acknowledged the controversy by saying, "We first admit that the commission is human-driven and there are times where emotions flare which may amount to misconduct, but that did not in any way affect our operations and the work of the commission." However, in the same remark, Verdier also reaffirmed the TRC's instrumental use of people's memories: "We asked [witnesses] to be relaxed to understand the value of their testimonies, we may not rebuild their houses we may not fix the roads, but they know they are contributing to a national duty for healing and reconciliation" (Verdier statement, 5 March 2008). This is a powerful and problematic statement by the chairman, substantially limiting the agency of witnesses in framing the purpose of their testimony and, as a byproduct, its key narratives as well.

Conclusion: Consequences of Memory Standardization in Liberia and Beyond

> I want to thank the TRC to give me the opportunity to say my story and secondly to the counsellors who encourage me to be able to tell my story. Thank you. (Mbamba testimony, 14 April 2008)

Truth commissions are complex institutions, attempting to achieve multiple ambitious goals in politically and socially volatile contexts. As such, they are almost inevitably bound to fall short of intentions and expectation. This critical analysis of the Liberia Truth Commission should not be read as undermining the commission's important service to the Liberian state and society. The sheer level of emotion directed toward the commission and the appreciation it received reflect the importance of this institution and the opportunities for open conversation and remembrance it created. However, the commission clearly struggled to establish its place within the political hierarchy of Liberia and to direct its potential for empowerment at those needing it the most. Through its tenure, the LTRC became a political actor, establishing a certain version of the truth based on its own narratives of continuity and disjuncture, right and wrong (Glucksam 2016: 92). The standardized discourse of universal human rights was consequently used at the commission as an expression of power, tethering it to the transnational political and ethical structure. Memories, consequently, were required by the commission to conform to these standard frames, at the expense of witnesses' agency.

The consequences of this process were seen throughout the commission's tenure but became even clearer in the aftermath of the publication of its final report. The report offered a detailed but inconsistent summary of the country's history and the unfolding of its civil war. These sections were criticized for their lack of corroboration and evidence and the many contradictions they contained. However, even more controversial were the copious recommendations, which included detailed lists of people to ban from political office, including the then-sitting president, or to prosecute for war crimes and crimes against humanity. These recommendations included no clear categories or methodology, leading to mounting speculation regarding the political and personal strings pulled to enter or escape the list (Grey-Johnson, interview May 2014). The clear disconnect between the personal nature of the testimonies and the removed, politicized, and instrumental usage of these stories in the final report generated a wave of controversy, criticism, and frustration in Liberia. Some, especially among civil society, supported the report and its recommendations and became outraged by the government's and the president's refusal to implement them completely and immediately. Others saw the controversy in the report itself, which many considered divisive, biased, and unnecessarily confrontational (De Ycaza 2013: 206). Ironically, almost everyone agreed that the report, in its current form and political reception, had very little chance of advancing the interests of reconciliation in the country. Indeed, surveys conducted in 2009, around the time the LTRC published its final report, found that 24 percent of the population felt that establishing the truth was not at all a priority and that it would be better to forget the violence, fearing that returning to it would bring up bad memories (Vinck et al. 2011: 69). The Liberia TRC report reaffirmed what many already felt, that engaging in the process itself was not part of the reconciliation process. The promise for emotional catharsis followed by genuine reconciliation had not been fulfilled, and many felt that the LTRC favored the perpetrators, offering them a way to whitewash their names instead of confronting them with the consequences of their actions, while depriving victims of their basic right to define their own memory and have their narrative acknowledged and respected.

This study offers important insights for the study of transnational memory agency beyond the case of Liberia. The notion of agency refers to the ability to act authentically, as well as to produce desired consequences. However, due to political, social, and psychological constraints, the two objectives may sometimes be mutually exclusive, or they may even contradict one another. Extreme violence, uncertainty, and insecurity, which go beyond the physical to threatening the very core of emotional and identity stability, make particularly challenging sociopolitical conditions in which the prospect of memory agency is itself in dissonance, where affected societies want at once to remember and to be acknowledged, and also to forget and to move on. Moreover, the juxtaposition of intimate hurt and mass atrocities creates cognitive and psychological barriers to agency due to the sheer inexplicability of experiences. In these cases, standardized discourses limit the ability to engage in authentic remembering but increase the possibility of identifying with collective narratives, tapping into the social and material resources they are connected to. This not only means that the subjects of memory might be in dissonance but that memory agency itself is also in dissonance, as this case demonstrates. This conclusion opens up the path to new and critical research on collective memory and memorialization, as well as on transitional justice and justice more broadly, from a perspective that accepts dissonance as a condition and embraces its unique impact rather than attempting to smooth it in organized models.

Noga Glucksam is an assistant professor in international relations and international law at Richmond the American International University in London. She received her PhD in 2017 from the School of Oriental and African Studies (SOAS) in London, where she studied conceptual dissonances in the transitional justice processes of Uganda and Liberia. Her research focuses on postconflict transitions, examining the political, sociological, international-legal, and security aspects of conflict resolution, peacebuilding, and transitional justice. Glucksam's work combines social-theoretical analysis and critical discourse analysis with a historical and comparative politics methodological approach. Her work has been presented in major international studies conferences and published in leading journals, such as *Civil Wars* and the *Cambridge Review of International Affairs*.

References

Arribas-Ayllon, Michael, and Valerie Walkerdine. 2008. "Foucauldian discourse analysis," in *The Sage Handbook of Qualitative Research in Psychology*, edited by Carla Willig and Wendy Stainton Rogers, 91–108. London: Sage.

Arthur, Paige. 2009. "How 'Transitions' Reshaped Human Rights: A Conceptual History of Transitional Justice." *Human Rights Quarterly* 31 (2): 321–67.

Bourdieu, Pierre. 1991. *Language and Symbolic Power*. Cambridge, MA: Harvard University Press.

Brown, Chris. 1997. "Universal Human Rights: A Critique." *International Journal of Human Rights* 1 (2): 41–65.

Burke, Roland. 2011. *Decolonization and the Evolution of International Human Rights*. Philadelphia: University of Pennsylvania Press.

Chong, Daniel P. L. 2014. *Debating Human Rights*. Boulder, CO: Lynne Rienner.

Cibelli, Kristen, Amelia Hoover, and Jule Kruger. 2009. *Descriptive Statistics from Statements to the Liberian Truth and Reconciliation Commission*. Benetech Human Rights Program.

De Ycaza, Carla. 2013. "A Search for Truth: A Critical Analysis of the Liberian Truth and Reconciliation Commission." *Human Rights Review* 14(3): 189–212.

Dolan, Chris. 2009. *Social Torture: The Case of Northern Uganda 1986–2006*. New York: Berghahn Books.

Donnelly, Jack. 2007. "The Relative Universality of Human Rights." *Human Rights Quarterly* 29(2): 281–306.

Ellis, Stephen. 2007. *The Mask of Anarchy: The Destruction of Liberia and the Religious Dimension of an African Civil War*. Revised ed. New York: NYU Press.

Englund, Harri. 2006. *Prisoners of Freedom: Human Rights and the African Poor.* Berkeley: University of California Press.

Gberie, Lansana. 2008. "Truth and Justice on Trial in Liberia." *African Affairs* 107(428): 455–65.

Glucksam, Noga. 2016. "Transitional Justice and Collective Identity: Contesting Concepts of Justice in Liberia and Uganda." PhD thesis, SOAS, University of London.

Haggard, Patrick, and Manos Tsakiris. 2009. "The Experience of Agency Feelings, Judgments, and Responsibility." *Current Directions in Psychological Studies* 18(4): 242–46.

Harris, David, and Richard Lappin. 2010. "The Liberian Truth and Reconciliation Commission: Reconciling or Re-dividing Liberia?" *Alternatives* 9(1): 181–91.

Hayner, Priscilla B. 2010. *Unspeakable Truths: Transitional Justice and the Challenge of Truth Commissions.* New York: Routledge.

Holzscheiter, Anna. 2013. "Between Communicative Interaction and Structures of Signification: Discourse Theory and Analysis in International Relations." *International Studies Perspectives* 15: 1–21.

Kirby, Paul. 2013. "How Is Rape a Weapon of War? Feminist International Relations, Modes of Critical Explanation and the Study of Wartime Sexual Violence." *European Journal of International Relations* 19(4): 797–821.

Lavrence, Christine. 2005. "'The Serbian Bastille': Memory, Agency, and Monumental Public Space in Belgrade." *Space and Culture* 8(1): 31–46.

Liberia Media Center. 2008. *Transitional Justice Reporting Audit: A Review of Media Coverage of the Transitional Justice Process in Liberia.* Monrovia.

Liberia. 2005. *An Act to Establish the Truth and Reconciliation Commission.* (TRC) of Liberia.

Long, William J. 2008. "Liberia's Truth and Reconciliation Commission: An Interim Assessment." *International Journal of Peace Studies* 13(2) (Autumn): 1–14.

Mahoney, James. 2000. "Path Dependence in Historical Sociology." *Theory and Society* 29(4) (August): 507–48.

McGuinness, Margaret E. 2011. "Peace v. Justice: The Universal Declaration of Human Rights and the Modern Origins of the Debate." *Diplomatic History* 35(5): 749–68.

Morsink, Johannes. *The Universal Declaration of Human Rights: Origins, Drafting, and Intent.* Philadelphia: University of Pennsylvania Press, 1999.

Mutua, Makau. 2013. *Human Rights: A Political and Cultural Critique.* Philadelphia: University of Pennsylvania Press.

Nora, Pierre, and Lawrence Kritzman, eds. 1996. *Realms of Memory: Rethinking the French Past.* New York: Columbia University Press.

Olick, Jeffrey K., and Joyce Robbins. 1998. "Social Memory Studies: From 'Collective Memory' to the Historical Sociology of Mnemonic Practices." *Annual Review of Sociology* 24(1): 105–40.

Olsen, Tricia D., and Andrew G. Reiter. 2010. *Transitional Justice in Balance: Comparing Processes, Weighing Efficacy.* Washington, DC: United States Institute of Peace.

Pajibo, Ezekiel. 2007. "Civil Society and Transitional Justice in Liberia: A Practitioner's Reflection from the Field." *International Journal of Transitional Justice* 1(2): 287–96.

Phillips, Anne. 2003. "Recognition and the Struggle for Political Voice." In *Contested Identities, Agency and Power*, edited by Barbara Hobson, 263–73. Cambridge: Cambridge University Press.

Pitkin, Hanna F. 1972. *Wittgenstein and Justice: On the Significance of Ludwig Wittgenstein for Social and Political Thought.* Berkeley: University of California Press.

Robins, Simon. 2012. "Transitional Justice as an Elite Discourse: Human Rights Practice Where the Global Meets the Local in Post-conflict Nepal." *Critical Asian Studies* 44(1): 3–30.

Rotberg, Robert I., and Dennis F. Thompson, eds. 2010. *Truth v. Justice: The Morality of Truth Commissions*. Princeton, NJ: Princeton University Press.

Sewell, William H. 2005. *Logics of History: Social Theory and Social Transformation*. Chicago: University of Chicago Press.

Sikkink, Kathryn. 2011. *The Justice Cascade: How Human Rights Prosecutions Are Changing World Politics*. New York: W. W. Norton.

Skinner, Quentin. 1969. "Meaning and Understanding in the History of Ideas." *History and Theory* 8(1): 3–53.

Steinberg, Jonny. 2010. "Briefing: Liberia's Experiment with Transitional Justice." *African Affairs* 109(434): 135–44.

Tabar, Linda. 2007. "Memory, Agency, Counter-narrative: Testimonies from Jenin Refugee Camp." *South-North Cultural and Media Studies* 21(1): 6–31.

Teitel, Ruti G. 2000. *Transitional Justice*. New York: Oxford University Press.

Truth and Reconciliation Commission of Liberia. "Public Hearings." Retrieved January 2014 from http://www.trcofliberia.org/hearings.html.

UN Security Council. 2003. *Peace Agreement between the Government of Liberia, the Liberians United for Reconciliation and Democracy, the Movement for Democracy in Liberia and the Political Parties*, 18 August, S/2003/850 (Comprehensive Peace Agreement). Retrieved 15 March 2017 from https://www.refworld.org/docid/5b3f3a107.html.

Vinck, Patric, Phuong N. Pham, and Tino Kreutzer. 2011. *Talking Peace: A Population-Based Survey on Attitudes about Security, Dispute Resolution, and Post-conflict Reconstruction in Liberia*. Berkeley: University of California Press.

Vinogradov, Sophia, Tracy L. Luks, Gregory V. Simpson, Brian J. Schulman, Shenly Glenn, and Amy E. Wong. 2006. "Brain Activation Patterns during Memory of Cognitive Agency." *Neuroimage* 31(2) (Spring): 896–905.

Weah, Aaron. 2008. "The TRC Struggles for Control . . . Unpacking the Conduct of the Institutional and Thematic Hearings." *The Perspective*, 7 October 2008. Retrieved 20 February 2019 from http://theliberianjournal.com/index.php?st=news&sbst=details&rid=539.

Wodak, Ruth, and Michael Meyer, eds. 2009. *Methods for Critical Discourse Analysis*. London: Sage.

Chapter 9

Transitional Justice in Public

Communicating Transnational Memories of Mass Violence

Courtney E. Cole

❧

In the aftermath of mass violence, societies and people face challenging and complex questions about how to deal with those who participated in and those who survived that violence, what to remember of that past, and how to create an account of the past around which a postconflict society can move forward. Further, because of the pervasive nature of genocide, civil war, and other forms of mass violence, people and societies who witnessed this violence—even remotely, from afar, or unwittingly—are also implicated in the memorializing of this mass violence, both as agents and audience members. One characteristic that unites transitional justice processes, including truth commissions, criminal trials, and even other practices like lustration, reparations, and reconciliation measures, is that they are public memory-making efforts. Transitional justice processes endeavor to provide a societal space—discursive, symbolic, material, and spatiotemporal—in which the horrors of the past can be discovered, discussed, and shared in order to illuminate, remember, and move forward from violence toward peace.

This research builds on previous work that argues for public hearings of truth commissions as a specific genre of public memory. This genre is characterized by the use of personal testimony at ritual performance events that engage audiences in their work (Cole 2018). In order to consider further the constitution and circulation of transnational memorializing of mass violence in transitional justice institutions, I consider the Truth and Reconciliation

Commission of Liberia, including its work outside of the country as part of its Diaspora Project. I also devote attention to the post–World War II war crime trials of Nazi leaders by Allied forces at Nürnberg and the criminal trials of civil war leaders at the Special Court for Sierra Leone in Freetown and the Hague, Netherlands. In addition, I draw on textual and document analysis of the truth commissions in Sierra Leone and Liberia, specifically the official reports authored by these commissions about their work.

Building on the understanding of truth commissions' work as fundamentally engaged in the creation of public memory, I extend this insight about the public memorializing function of truth commissions in two key ways. First, I move beyond truth commissions to include international criminal tribunals in arguing that transitional justice institutions more generally are engaged in official memorializing of mass violence. Second, I develop an understanding of transitional justice institutions as instruments of public memory by considering them as important agents in the creation and circulation of memory to transnational audiences.

In analyzing transitional justice processes through the perspective of transnational memory, I argue that they are distinguished by their engagement with vernacular memory. Transitional justice institutions transform some vernacular accounts of personal experiences of mass violence into official public memory, in the context of a globalized memory culture focused on human rights, the recitation of personal trauma, and mass violence. Transitional justice institutions create space and assert agency about the past through their fashioning and circulation of official accounts of past violence, creating and addressing transnational audiences in and through their work. In order to consider the role of transitional justice processes in the constitution and circulation of transnational memorializing of mass violence, I examine how diverse institutions of transitional justice in Liberia, Germany, and Sierra Leone have engaged in this public memory work within and across borders. In sum, in this chapter, I examine how transitional justice actors and institutions influence how the conflicts they address are remembered, both locally and transnationally.

Actors and Agency: Vernacular Memories of Victims and Leaders of Mass Violence

In this section, I focus on two particular actors who are essential to the process of, and who participate significantly in, transitional justice in postconflict contexts: victims of mass violence and leaders who perpetrated that violence. While there are many more actors who participate in transitional justice, the participation of victims and perpetrators is an essential aspect of these institutions and offers insight into particular aspects of transitional justice that distinguish it from other forms of public memory. In this section, then, I consider the distinction between vernacular and official memory through examination of how transitional justice institutions treat actors in these processes. This complicates the distinction between vernacular and official memory and provides further insight into it.

Public memory draws on both official and vernacular memory cultures, which create and support public commemoration of the past. Browne (1995), drawing on Bodnar (1992), explains that official memory culture is state-based in nature, communicated by, on behalf of, and in support of the state. Official cultures of memory focus on state unity and support existing political arrangements in that state. In contrast, Browne states that vernacular memory is individual- and community-based in nature, communicating ambivalence and social change in distinction to official memory. In this view, the tensions of public memory, then, are based at least partly on contestation between official and vernacular accounts of the past (Browne 1999; Cole 2010, 2018). However, in order to be seen as legitimate by their stakeholders, public memory processes need to incorporate local and personal experiences (Bodnar 1992). Wüstenberg complicates distinction, noting that "the state is encountered in many forms and in diverse spaces, including symbolic ones such as public memorials and museums" (2017: 27), which shows the interconnection between state and society in relation to official and vernacular memory.

This distinction between official and vernacular memory is further complicated in a number of ways by the context of the aftermath of mass violence. First, in the aftermath of mass violence, there is often no official culture upon which to create public memory. The postconflict dispensation is one that demands public memorializing precisely because societies lack shared narratives of the past. In addition, mass violence itself can be a function of the breakdown of official cultures of memory and/or conflict between competing vernacular cultures. The conflict creates and reflects divisions within and between official and vernacular cultures. Second, this binary is also complicated by recent scholarship on vernacular and grassroots memory. The theorizing of vernacular memory often emphasizes its organic, authentic nature, because it derives from individual experience, reflecting its basis in local life and community-based orientation (Marschall 2013; Bodnar 1992).

Further, even individual experiences and community-based memories are always constructed in relation to, and intertwined with, the official states and cultures in which these individuals and communities exist. Because communication from individuals and groups is always embedded within official cultures of memory, even in conflict and postconflict contexts, vernacular memorializing does not straightforwardly oppose or complement official regimes of memory. For example, soldier-produced videos from the United

States' war on terror reflect content that both affirms and resists dominant ideologies (Smith and McDonald 2011). This adds complexity to our understanding of vernacular discourse.

Truth commissions and international criminal tribunals, the transitional justice institutions that are the focus of this chapter, reflect the complex interrelationship between official and vernacular commemoration. They are state-oriented and transnational in nature. As such, they reflect states' post-conflict efforts to create a unified account of the past. However, the integration of vernacular memory is also an important hallmark of these institutions. Their importance and impact comes not only from being national and transnational institutions aimed at reckoning with the past; they are powerful precisely because they do so in and through the participation and stories of people's personal experiences of mass violence. In line with previous scholarship in public memory, the commemoration of these justice institutions is "a product of elite manipulation, symbolic interaction, and contested discourse" between vernacular and official accounts of the past (Bodnar 1992: 20). Thus, the terms and types of participation of actors in transitional justice processes is salient in theorizing the complex relationship between official and vernacular public memory.

To start, both truth commissions and international criminal trials are based on their engagement with and attention to vernacular memory. To do this, they call on two specific kinds of actors. Transitional justice institutions are built on the participation of both victims and perpetrators who give statements about their personal experiences of mass violence. They engage the public and legitimize their work through the collection of vernacular discourse. This firsthand testimony of those involved in mass violence—whether as victims or perpetrators—is integral to their organizational legitimacy. The participation of those most responsible for mass violence is crucial to ensure that transitional justice institutions create an account of the past that is seen as inclusive and thorough. Engaging victims of mass violence—whether those harmed and traumatized, or those who lost loved ones to the violence—is also an important aim of these processes. Including both victims and perpetrators as key actors, and empowering them as agents in processes of transitional justice, fulfills the state's goal of creating a shared, truthful narrative of the past in order to create a just, peaceful future (Lewis 2016).

In terms of survivors, the sheer number of victims is quite staggering in postconflict contexts that occasion transitional justice processes. The very scale of the suffering makes it nearly impossible for these institutions to be able to cope and respond. There are many more victims, and many more harms, than can ever be accommodated or addressed in temporary transitional justice institutions that aim to provide insight into and accountability for the past. Victims and survivors are seen as integral to transitional justice institutions, whose goal is in part to affirm and recognize their dignity. None-theless, not all can be afforded the same opportunity to participate as agents in their work. Victims who have been killed have no agency with which to testify. For those who survive, the demand to give statements outstrips the temporal, spatial, and material capacities of transitional justice institutions. Thus, only some victims and survivors are chosen, or have the capacity, to be actors in these processes.

In Sierra Leone, where most of the violence took place in rural communities far from Freetown and district towns, the reach of the truth commission was weak. In its final report, it acknowledged the incompleteness of its engagement:

> There were a number of constraints to organising hearings in the districts. Hearings could only take place at district headquarters despite the commission's desire to conduct hearings in as many communities as possible, in particular, in those communities that suffered greatly during the conflict. In many of the communities, the infrastructure that could support the hearings such as community halls or school buildings had been destroyed. (SLTRC 2004: vol. 1, p. 98)

Further, many of the witnesses lived more than eighty miles from district towns where regional hearings were held, making it difficult for them to travel to testify publicly (ibid.). There were many victims and survivors who wished to give statements, particularly in the rural areas, who the commission simply did not have the temporal, material, or personnel resources to accommodate (SLTRC 2004: vol. 1, chap. 5, p. 143). Similarly, in the Liberian Truth and Reconciliation Commission of Liberia Diaspora Project, survivors made up only a small percentage of those selected to give testimony in person to the commissioners (Cole 2018). Likewise, relatively few victims and survivors were chosen to be deposed as part of the criminal tribunals at Nürnberg, as testimony had to be considered relevant and reliable enough to meet the demands of international war crimes prosecution (Chakravarti 2008).

In contrast, the participation of individual perpetrators, particular leaders of mass violence, is exceedingly important in order for truth commissions and international criminal tribunals to be deemed successful. In the case of Nürnberg, the charging of the remaining living Nazi leaders was viewed as an important way to deal with Germany's World War II violence. Similarly, the participation of political and military leaders is often encouraged and negoti-ated by truth commissions. In the case of the Truth and Reconciliation Com-mission of Liberia Diaspora Project, Wilhemina Holder, one of the deposed elites who testified at the project's public hearings, thanked the nongovern-mental organization that organized them, saying, "Advocates for Human Rights because it was them that encouraged me to come and speak and people that supported me, Laura and Mark [advocates staff], they encouraged me to speak and I'm thankful for that" (Holder 2008: 5).

In Sierra Leone, perpetrators comprised only 10 percent of those who participated in that country's Truth and Reconciliation Commission. The simultaneous work of the Special Court for Sierra Leone likely had a deleterious effect on the willingness of perpetrators to participate in the truth commission process, because of fear that their testimony could be used against them in subsequent judicial proceedings. This meant that the commission had to work to encourage and elicit the testimony of perpetrators, making their participation valuable to its work, particularly when compared with survivors.

The symbolic importance of holding leaders accountable through public participation is an important aspect of transitional justice institutions. Thus, truth commissions and international criminal tribunals are especially invested in and attentive to the inclusion of those who did wrong, especially leaders, as actors in these processes. In creating shared accounts of the past, it is important that transitional justice institutions include attributions of responsibility for mass violence and other horrific crimes. This is often the rationale for encouraging the participation of and engaging publicly with those deemed responsible for violent atrocities—to name and shame them, and to assign them responsibility for their misdeeds. In contrast, there are far more victims and survivors, and the scale of the violence they represent is far more difficult for these institutions to address and integrate into their work. In examining the way that trials and truth commissions engage and endow participants as agents, the quality and quantity of participation varies greatly depending on one's location and role in the past conflict. It also highlights the organizing role of these processes in crafting and circulating particular stories of the past from these agents, which I discuss further in the next section.

Structures of Speech: Transitional Justice Processes as Institutional Arena

Public memory is about creating space, materially and discursively, in which to communicate publicly about the past. This is one of the functions of transitional justice processes, which are institutional arenas that focus particularly on public memory in relation to cultural traumas, as defined by Alexander et al. (2004). The spaces they make are always created and constrained by practices adopted by these institutions and the resulting discourses that emerge from them. Therefore, it is important to consider the types and allocation of space(s) constituted in and through transitional justice processes and the kind(s) of communication this creates and circulates about the past. The temporary organizing of postconflict transitional justice institutions does not attempt to create lasting structures for sociopolitical change in postconflict contexts, but it does construct temporary spaces that create and communicate new public discourses of the past. These discourses, in turn, are expected to become permanent records of a shared past on which postconflict societies can agree.

The commemoration that transitional justice institutions facilitate creates cultural space for official versions of the past (Browne 1995). Thus, transitional justice institutions construct and circulate official public memories of mass violence through their work. So, while they clear the space to communicate about the past publicly, they also control this space of public discourse about the past (Browne 1999). Thus, the role of transitional justice institutions is simultaneously to clear space for public remembrance and to influence the shape and substance of this official commemoration of the past. As discussed in the previous section, who participates in these processes and how they participate are important questions regarding the agency these institutions create for different actors. It is also essential to examine the structures of speech that transitional justice institutions enact and the resulting practices that result from these structures.

One particularly important aspect that distinguishes transitional justice institutions from other institutions and other genres of public memory is their forthright focus on addressing and adjudicating cultural traumas in the context of contested and painful pasts. Institutions of transitional justice address mass violence that has only just occurred, and they take place in the immediate postconflict dispensation. As institutions that forthrightly focus on issues of mass violence, authoritarianism, genocide, and civil war, the work of transitional justice is to acknowledge and reckon with cultural trauma in the recent past. They are institutional arenas that create spaces to tell stories of trauma, both the experience and the perpetration of it.

Transitional justice institutions construct and control the kinds of speech situations because of their institutional natures, and the rituals and practices they enact (these are discussed further in the next section). In their work on cultural trauma and collective memory, Alexander et al. identify six different institutional arenas within which a "new master narrative of social suffering" and trauma can be articulated and facilitated: (1) religious; (2) aesthetic; (3) legal; (4) scientific; (5) mass media; and (6) state bureaucracy (2004: 15). Although they do not focus on transitional justice institutions, such institutions call on aspects of these arenas while not fitting neatly into any one of them. I argue that transitional justice arenas enact and connect many aspects of these institutional arenas, with their focus on transnational public memory, forming a distinct seventh institutional arena.

The religious arena connects the articulation of cultural traumas by transitional justice institutions to questions of faith, evil, and redemption within a society and into its future. Aesthetic arenas use artistic genres and narratives to compel emotional understandings of traumatic experiences. The legal arena is the space where cultural trauma is used as evidence for the adjudication of wrongdoing and responsibility. Importantly, communication that occurs within legal institutions may not necessarily reflect perpetrators taking responsibility for their wrongdoing or audiences witnessing victims' suffering.

Scientific arenas focus on historical events through the use of accepted methodological and scholarly standards. This is how people understand and make claims about the past. Institutions of mass media are powerful tools for circulating or circumventing stories of cultural trauma. Mass media make some stories of trauma particularly prominent and enhance their persuasive power, while they can also restrict and neutralize the power of some stories through their elision or downplay within mediated arenas. State bureaucracy is relevant in situations where the government engages cultural traumas (Wüstenberg 2017). This can take the form of new laws, policies, reparations, and commissions of inquiry.

Transitional justice is mentioned by Alexander et al.: "In regard to binding definitions of war crimes and crimes against humanity, the 1946 Nuremberg Trials were critical . . . laying the basis for dozens of highly publicized lawsuits that in recent years have created significant dramaturgy and unleashed profound moral effects" (2004: 17). As part of the state bureaucracy arena, they use the South African Truth and Reconciliation Commission as an example, misrepresenting both the genesis and impact of its work. While the authors place these transitional justice institutions within these definitive categories, this oversimplifies and distorts the hybrid nature of these institutions in postconflict contexts.

Precisely because of the complicated work that transitional justice institutions are tasked with—dealing with both victims and perpetrators, as well as trying to create a coherent, shared account of the past—their hybrid structure reflects and integrates aspects of the institutional categories articulated by Alexander et al. (2004) while forming a distinct arena all its own. Transitional justice institutions often take on aspects of religious arenas by framing the public sharing of suffering and wrongdoing as redemptive acts that will pave the way for a new future, whether for the country transforming itself or for international human rights law that transcends particular contexts (AHR 2008). Transitional justice also calls on the aesthetic arena in the form of remembering cultural trauma through first-person testimony, particularly narratives of personal violence (Cole 2010).

In the scientific arena, transitional justice processes uncover past violence in creating an accurate historical record of the period. The public nature of transitional justice institutions (Cole 2018)—as well coverage of them by newspapers, radio, television, and online news outlets—shows how they function in the mass media realm. Finally, while transitional justice institutions work with the blessing (or sometimes mere tolerance) of the states in which they operate, they make pains to appear independent, both physically and symbolically, from these states. An important hallmark of their institutional identity is their nongovernmental and, as I argue in this chapter, often transnational constitution.

In drawing on aspects of these different institutional arenas, transitional justice institutions are tasked with the complex work of creating a fair, comprehensive historical account of cultural traumas in divided societies. However, as Alexander et al. point out, all institutional arenas "are mediated by the uneven distribution of material resources and the social network that provide differential [unequal] access to them" (2004: 21). Further, persistent social inequalities permeate and pervade these institutional arenas. For example, racial inequalities can make it harder for these participants to have their voices heard and their perspectives taken seriously (Mease and Terry 2012). Even supposedly open, transparent forums reflect and entrench inequalities along race, ethnicity, gender, religion, socioeconomic class, and other identity differences.

Thus, within the speaking situations offered by the institutional arena of transitional justice processes, differences in identity and therefore social location and power mean that people have unequal access to observe and participate in their work. So even as transitional justice institutions attempt to commemorate cultural traumas, they reflect inequities and competing societal priorities in the aftermath of mass violence. The structure of transitional justice processes—particularly their public hearings—is a particular type of institutional arena that transforms participants' vernacular testimony into the official memorializing of these transitional justice processes. The public work of official memory that these transitional justice institutions create, the new narratives of past conflict—both what happened and its meanings—occurs through their constitution as institutional arenas.

While Alexander et al. (2004) define six different institutional arenas, we can draw on these to identify transitional justice institutions as a distinct arena of its own. In doing so, we can envision an institution embodying multiple aspects to commemorate a conflicted, traumatic past. This better reflects the hybrid nature of transitional justice institutions, which exist between periods of conflict and peace, between state and society, and within other interstitial spaces of transition. Transitional justice institutions, particularly truth commissions and international criminal trials, adopt a number of common practices that serve as mechanisms to do this work of public memory, which I address in the next section.

Transnational Memorializing: Practices and Mechanisms of Transitional Justice

Based on their identity as institutional arenas in postconflict contexts, transitional justice processes function as mnemonic instruments, particularly in their public proceedings. Thus, it is important to consider how they recognize and remember the past, examining how memory is constructed in and through their work. In this section, then, I argue for the important role of transitional justice processes as events that create and constitute transnational memory of mass violence. In particular, transitional justice institutions do this through the staging of ritual performances, the use of personal testimony, and the engagement of an audience as three key attributes of their public hearings, which constitute a specific genre of public memory (Cole 2018). I build on this to argue that transitional justice institutions transform personal testimony in the service of cosmopolitan memorializing of a conflictual past through the specifically transnational witnessing.

The ritual aspects of trials and truth commissions stem in part from their structure as institutional arenas in postconflict contexts, as discussed in the previous section. Drawing on religious, aesthetic, legal, and mass media aspects of their work, these institutions stage ritual performance events. These events constitute the most public aspects of the work of these transitional justice processes, because they are open to public audiences to attend, often carried live on radio and television, and covered by mass media locally, nationally, and internationally. For truth commissions, the recent move to include public hearings as part of the process is an important aspect of ensuring that their work is viewed as accessible and transparent. International criminal tribunals exhibit many of the same characteristics in terms of engaging vernacular testimony about mass violence. Although much of the investigative, operational, and prosecutorial work of international criminal trials occurs behind closed doors, the actual trials occur in public, with participation of lawyers, judges, witnesses, and defendants.

Transitional justice institutions rely on legal ritual, particularly with its delineation of clear roles for different participants. For both of these types of transitional justice events, judges or commissioners set the tempo and tone of the event, inviting and shaping the participation of witnesses through their facilitation. The events occur in large courtrooms and auditoriums, venues at which the public can access their work and that put the trial and hearings literally on stage. Finally, the participants are invited to share their personal experiences of war or mass violence in these events, with the facilitation performed by lawyers, judges, and commissioners shaping this testimony.

These transitional justice processes often include specific practices that formalize their work and mark them as important rituals. For example, in the case of trials, lawyers and defendants rise when judges enter the courtroom. Participants are sworn to tell the truth before they give their testimony, and they must answer the questions of lawyers, rather than speaking freely. In the case of truth commissions, there is an official opening of the hearings, as well as introduction of participants. Many truth commissions, including in Sierra Leone and Liberia, require that participant testimony be given under oath. Following the personal statement of the participant, commissioners ask questions, to which the participant replies. All of these norms shape international criminal trials and truth commissions as ritual performance events.

The ritual performance events are an important way for these institutions to publicly highlight their inclusion and acknowledgment of vernacular memory. The legitimacy of transitional justice institutions' public memorializing comes from their reliance on vernacular memory, as discussed earlier. Thus, these institutions govern how people behave in relation to the past, as well as the space from which participants "can legitimately speak" (Mease and Terry 2012: 132). There are unwritten rules about how users negotiate and experience such spaces of commemoration, usually established by the physical layout (Gallagher 1999). These rules are governed by and implicit in the ritual itself, including who can talk, when, and about what (McComas et al. 2010). This is one of the most important ways transitional justice institutions determine who is allowed to speak about the past and in what ways (Cole 2018). While many people give personal statements to the truth commission and international criminal tribunals, only a select few are chosen to give their testimony publicly at the ritual performance events.

Another defining aspect of these processes is their construction of and orientation toward audiences. However, there has been little attention paid to the way that the official memory of transitional justice creates, reproduces, and transforms individual, vernacular memories of mass violence in the service of public memorializing of past conflict that is transnational in orientation. "Transnational" refers to the sharing and witnessing of memories of human suffering, without regard for the group identity of victims, constructing a community based on universal humanity and respect for global human rights (Törnquist-Plewa 2016: 145). Levy and Sznaider argue that the Holocaust was foundational for the creation of this orientation "outside the ethnic and national boundaries of the Jewish victims and German perpetrators" and remembered by those without direct experiences of it (2002: 88). Transnational memory, which is shaped and circulated by societal institutions, including transitional justice processes, is central to this global human rights culture.

There has been significant attention to transnational memory as an educational endeavor in relation to war and suffering (Graefenstein 2016; Törnquist-Plewa 2016). In a similar fashion, transitional justice enacts transnational memory as a public endeavor—that is, an attempt to create transnational audiences to witness and respond to mass violence. In particular, their public work allows for the experience and expression of regret, sorrow, and recognition through transnational witnessing of people's personal testimonies of a violent conflict. This is because truth commission public hearings and the proceedings of international criminal tribunals are produced particularly as ritual public events incorporating personal testimony for transnational consumption, as mnemonic processes moving within and across cultures (Kennedy and Nugent 2016). Understanding the relationship between transitional justice and transnational public memory highlights that, in the aftermath of genocide and other forms of mass violence, transitional justice efforts to reckon with these painful pasts across borders are an important aspect of remembering them.

Transnationalism engages the multiple scales and interweaving of the local, national, and global in contemporary life (Törnquist-Plewa 2016). A transnational approach to understanding the public proceedings of transitional justice institutions means paying attention to the diverse and divergent ways in which they engage audiences, both local and beyond. This concept helps to articulate an important third attribute of this genre of public memory—its engagement with audiences—through the perspective of transnational space-making. In particular, transitional justice processes function as institutions of public memory by creating and engaging transnational audiences in and through their work, through crafting and circulating official memories of mass violence with and beyond borders. They do this in two key ways—first, transitional justice institutions engage local populations in and through their work. Second, the communicative construction of memory by transitional justice institutions is founded upon communication technology and networks to transmit and circulate the personal testimony of participants far beyond the immediate audience.

First and foremost, transitional justice institutions orient themselves to the countries and communities in which they work. While there has been considerable criticism of transitional justice institutions for their failure to engage local communities more fully in their work, this is one of their goals, even if not completely realized. Transitional justice proceedings are held in public spaces located in the country, if not the district, town, or village, where mass violence took place. Because of this, local populations have access to attend, observe, and, to a limited degree, participate in this public work (Cole 2018; Gregor 2008). The local, in-person aspects of their work are important because a key practice of transitional justice is to function as a transparent, fair, and accessible process for all members of postconflict societies. The point of the public proceedings for these institutions is, at least in part, to perform their publicity: to enact and show that they are oriented toward the public. This is also part of the reason that they engage ordinary participants—victims, witnesses, and perpetrators—as agents in their work. This engagement demonstrates their accessibility and transparency in terms of the local context and population, as well as to show their willingness to work with those who were part of the conflict and its aftermath.

This leads to the second way in which transitional justice institutions create and constitute a transnational audience. These institutions are also created as events that will engage larger publics in their work. This means that they are purposefully constructed as ritual performances that allow for the public sharing and witnessing of firsthand testimony about the experience—of perpetrators, victims, and occasionally bystanders—of mass violence. In understanding these events communicatively, it is essential to consider how the construction of public memory is thoroughly mediated: "Technological changes in the means of communication are of central importance for the structuration of memory, time and culture" (Levy and Sznaider 2002: 91). This is particularly true in an era of digital and mobile media, which makes it easier than ever to share and move memories and personal testimony beyond individual experience and national boundaries.

In many ways, the Nürnberg trials were not only the founding example of transitional justice but also the first example of the transnational memorializing of transitional justice institutions in and through communication. The Allied trials of Nazi leaders were constructed transnationally from the very beginning. The lawyers and judges that staffed these legal proceedings were from Great Britain, France, Russia, and the United States, as well as Germany, which was the site of the prosecutions. Because the Nazi crimes were part of the world war in which Allied forces fought, there was considerable international interest in the postwar adjudication of German leaders. This meant that there was significant international media coverage of the trials (Delage 2014; Sharples 2013), which was an important aspect of the trials' construction of a transnational audience.

The transnational constitution of the Nürnberg tribunals in terms of lawyers, staff, and journalists is also an important aspect of the trials that gave rise to the use of technologies. The trials introduced simultaneous interpretation of the court's proceedings, which was an essential communication technology in terms of orienting its work toward and creating an audience across linguistic lines and state borders (Gaiba 1998). This allowed for the French, Russian, British, American, and German lawyers, defendants, court staff, and journalists covering the court to communicate synchronously, basically in real time. This meant that, for the first time in modern Western history, the postconflict adjudication of the past was able to be a(n imperfectly) transnational project. Reporters from the countries involved in the trials covered the proceedings for their home countries, which constructed the Nürnberg prosecution of Nazi leaders as an event with importance across national boundaries, particularly in the Allied nations. This, in turn, contributed to the development of a human rights culture that rejected genocide and other forms of mass violence as intolerable wherever they occurred and by whomever perpetrated them (Levy and Sznaider 2002).

More recent truth commissions also illustrate communication technology being used to create transnational witnessing of transitional justice processes. The increasing availability of satellite and streaming technologies means that transitional justice can move outside of the countries on which it is focused. The Special Court for Sierra Leone—which had to prosecute Charles Taylor in the Hague, Netherlands, in light of security concerns—streamed proceedings to the Special Court building in Freetown in order to allow Sierra Leoneans access to the prosecution of the court's most high-profile defendant. Further, prosecuting the country's most notorious war criminal in the Netherlands made the court's work accessible and relevant to journalists and audiences in Europe. This expanded the reach and impact of the Special Court's work well beyond the state of Sierra Leone.

Similarly, the work of the Truth and Reconciliation Commission of Liberia Diaspora Project, particularly the public hearings in Minneapolis–St. Paul, brought attention to the mass violence of the Liberian civil war—through the testimony of resettled Liberians—to the public in the United States. At the same time, the entirety of the public hearings in the United States were streamed online, available around the world. In both of these cases, the use of communication technology allowed transitional justice institutions to hold public proceedings outside their country of origin and still remain accessible in the home country, thus constructing transnational audiences for their work.

Transitional justice institutions use personal testimony in ritual public events. Through mediating and publicizing their work, they create a communicative space in which to remember mass violence by people directly involved. Most importantly in terms of a transnational memorializing, transitional justice processes commemorate these events locally and across borders through communication technology. Thus, transnational audiences who view themselves as interested or otherwise implicated through a global human rights culture are constructed by these institutions. They inculcate a public memory of mass violence that is built in and through communication, which is then circulated both locally and transnationally. The effects of these practices form the focus of the next section.

Outcomes

The effect of the public proceedings of transitional justice institutions have important impacts. First and foremost, they endow some people with the agency, through telling their stories, to become the public face(s) of past conflict. These narratives are widely circulated in public consciousness, particularly as coverage of the proceedings is available online and covered by mass media (Cole 2010). In the case of leaders and perpetrators, because so few of them choose to participate in the proceedings of transitional justice institutions, and because their participation is so integral to the success of these processes, they are therefore quantitatively and symbolically overrepresented in the public proceedings of truth commissions and international criminal tribunals. This also means that, as a result, the sheer number of victims of mass violence is not represented in and through the public proceedings of transitional justice. These proceedings thus distort the scale of violence, suffering, and injustice in their attempt to include perpetrators' voices and encourage the participation of leaders of mass violence.

In terms of the quality of testimony provided by participants, former perpetrators and leaders are often reticent to admit wrongdoing or to take responsibility for their actions in the public fora of transitional justice processes (Cole 2018). In international criminal tribunals, the structure of proceedings means that the defense must attempt to obfuscate and avoid responsibility. In the case of some victims, giving testimony and the public circulation of it afterward means their story is retold and framed in ways that do not resonate with the meaning of their own experiences (Cole 2010), and in other cases the testimony of the few victims endowed with the platform to speak publicly provides a limited and potentially distorted view of the past (Cole 2018).

From the perspective of transnational public memory, the impact of these public hearings can then be a quantitatively misleading and qualitatively distorted collection of testimony. The reversal of numbers of victims, perpetrators, and leaders in terms of those given a public platform to tell their story reinforces the power of perpetrators and leaders and gives them an outsized voice in terms of how past violence is remembered. For audiences who are far from the conflict, they may lack the experience or insight to know how representative the testimony of victim or perpetrator is.

Further, in terms of agents' stories, the public nature of these hearings means that the testimony of individual participants stands alone. It functions as an intact, extant story of personal experience of mass violence that is circulated both locally and transnationally. Because of its publicity, the public testimony of participants becomes the story of the past most recognized and remembered in the postconflict context. Because of the limited, temporary nature of truth commissions and trials as ritual public events, it is impossible for them to correct misleading or false statements made during the public hearings they facilitate, even though they do make efforts to ask critical questions of those who give dishonest or evasive testimony. While they do issue final reports and judgments, these voluminous documents are not as well circulated as public hearings, making them a meager corrective to misleading testimony or misinformation in personal testimony.

In terms of the structure of public memorializing, another important attribute of transitional justice institutions, and the speaking situations they facilitate, is that they are created specifically for the purposes of articulating experiences of suffering, violence, and—more broadly—cultural trauma. They are focused on testimony of wrongdoing and the perpetration of violence. Due to the specifics of their mandates, they are also required to engage those who perpetrated or experienced acts of cruelty, violence, and gross violation of human rights. As a result, the public proceedings of transitional justice institutions are particularly focused on specific types of violence. In the case of truth commissions, this often results in attention to bodily violence and, in the case of women, sexual violence (Ross 2008; Cole 2018).

In terms of practices, transitional justice institutions enact and construct both local and transnational audiences for their work. This practice draws attention to the difference between allowing access to the work of transitional justice institutions rather than working for substantive engagement from local audiences. In practice, simply locating the work of transitional justice institutions in or near the communities in which mass violence took place does not ensure that they are accessible to the populations they purport to serve. In fact, the actual construction of these hearings is such that the local population is often not a crucial or integral part of the proceedings.

For example, in the Nürnberg trials, Courtroom 600 was expanded in order to accommodate additional observers. However, the majority of those who observed the courtroom proceedings were international journalists covering the post–World War II legal process. This reinforces the view that the trials were an example of the Allies', and particularly the United States', desire to act as savior and witness in response to Nazi crimes (Levy and Sznaider 2002). For most ordinary Germans in Nürnberg, the business of simply getting on with life in the midst of the destruction and economic destitution of the postwar environment took far more precedence over following, never mind observing, the trial proceedings at the Palace of Justice (Gregor 2008). In Sierra Leone, its Special Court was lauded for being located in the country in which crimes took place, compared to the International Criminal Court for Rwanda, which was located in Arusha, Tanzania. However, the placement of the court in Freetown meant that it was inaccessible to most Sierra Leoneans, particularly those in rural areas who were most affected by civil war violence. The Diaspora Project of the Liberian Truth and Reconciliation Commission public hearings were held in the metropolitan area of Minneapolis–St. Paul, home to a large number of resettled Liberians in the United States. However, this siting ignored the much larger populations of displaced Liberians in the West African subregion. In addition, the streaming of these hearings meant they were only accessible to those with broadband internet access (Cole 2018).

All of these public hearings were symbolically rich in terms of their local orientation but materially limited in their engagement with their local audiences. In working to create both local and transnational audiences for their work, transitional justice institutions struggle to make themselves substantively accessible to the postconflict contexts they aim to serve. If proceedings are constructed in such a way that they are only somewhat or in principle accessible to the populations they aim to serve, important questions about their efficacy are thus highlighted. Further, as they aim to engage transnational audiences in their work, a dilemma is created about whom their work is addressed to. In the case of the public proceedings of transitional justice processes, the in-person audience may not be the primary or most important audience for these institutions. If we consider transitional justice institutions in transnational perspective, with their foundation in a globalized human rights culture, their orientation is likewise transnational in nature. However, this can come at the expense of substantive engagement with local audiences.

Conclusion: Transitional Justice as Transnational Memorializing

Engaging public commemoration of mass violence, the communicative work of transitional justice institutions is a particularly complicated, divisive, and contested process. In considering the actors, structure, practices, and outcomes of transitional justice processes, I extend in this chapter understanding of these institutions by highlighting the work they do in creating and circulating transnational memory of mass violence. In doing so, I draw attention to the communicative constitution of their work, particularly through the framework of this edited volume.

First, transitional justice institutions engage and endow particular people to speak and, as a result of their constitution as media events, circulate these stories prominently in postconflict dispensations. Thus, we can see that while these processes aim to engage key actors in adjudicating and remembering mass violence, it is important to examine who participates and in what way(s). This means paying attention to whom transitional justice institutions engage to give testimony in public, how their testimony is facilitated, and what the resulting picture that emerges from these public hearings looks like. While these processes explicitly rely on vernacular memory, not all vernacular memories are equally important or even included in transitional justice processes. The actors selected to give statements to the truth commissions or international criminal tribunals are chosen for their particular experiences and identities. This highlights the curatorial role of these institutions in the creation of an official culture of memory about past conflict. Further, the agency offered to participants as actors in transitional justice processes is only partial. Transitional justice institutions determine who is allowed to participate as an actor, and in what ways, in the official public memorializing facilitated by these processes.

This leads to the second point. As institutions, transitional justice processes rely on the participation of victims and perpetrators as key actors in uncovering and remembering the past. The work of official memory is to fix information from actors' diverse vernacular memories, along with investigatory and documentary evidence, into a coherent, official version of the past. Transitional justice processes are characterized by their hybrid constitution as distinct institutional arenas that draw upon arenas in law, religion, and media. Their temporary and transitional engagement with the past serves to adjudicate and remember mass violence by engaging the testimony of leaders and ordinary people. They are tasked with using this testimony, along with other forms of evidence, in order to create a common basis to understand the past and to move forward into a peaceful future. In order to accomplish this, transitional justice processes as institutional arenas rely on particular practices.

Thus, given their structure, transitional justice institutions feature some common practices that characterize their efforts at engaging participants in vernacular memory and transforming it into official memory, which can be used as the basis for a peaceful postconflict dispensation. Transitional justice institutions are ritual performance events that facilitate personal testimony about experiences of mass violence. They are also characterized by their simultaneous attention to and creation of both local and transnational audiences, through their use of communication technology.

Finally, the outcome of engaging actors in the institutional arena of transitional justice through ritual performance events that elicit testimony focused on vernacular memory of mass violence results in the circulation of particular stories both within and beyond the borders where mass violence occurred. The public testimony of those involved in mass violence, whether ordinary folks or leaders, is communicated in both public meetings and through streaming, video, and journalistic reporting about these meetings. Therefore, the public facilitation of personal testimony and its circulation makes an immediate impact and is often the most lasting legacy of transitional justice. Understanding the public hearings of transitional justice institutions as media events (Levy and Sznaider 2002)—in which live, concentrated local action is shared and transformed into a global event—means that we must attend to how distant others identify with and respond to the event and what the terms are of this dis/connection between the global and local.

In sum, the primary contribution of this chapter is an appreciation of the constrained agency that transitional justice institutions offer in creating and circulating transnational memory, as well as its powerful impact in terms of transforming vernacular memories of mass violence into official accounts that are communicated within and beyond borders of where this violence occurred. Transitional justice institutions offer some agency to participants in publicizing their personal testimony. While in principle they aim to encourage the broad participation of both ordinary people and leaders in the aftermath of mass violence, the quality and quantity of participation varies greatly depending on one's identity and experiences as well as the way in which the institution works to incorporate participation. Thus, while these processes offer temporary agency in terms of opportunities to speak, the ways in which transitional justice institutions engage with, circulate, and publicize people's stories constrains this agency significantly. Public hearings of transitional justice institutions expand the communicative capacity by transnationalizing audiences for their work. However, the work of balancing attention to and engagement with local and transitional audiences is challenging, particularly for temporary institutions. Often, communication with and to transnational audiences comes at the expense of local audiences.

This framework highlights the constrained agency that transitional justice processes offer participants, as well as the agentic differences, both in quality and quantity, offered to participants. In addition, this analysis highlights how these processes function as distinct institutional arenas in the post-conflict context, drawing on science, history, art, religion, law, etc. in order to constitute and anchor themselves in relation to important and accepted cultural symbols in their structures. Also, these institutions enact practices that create and constitute transnational audiences, and they also rely on communication technologies in order to accomplish this. Finally, the agency, practices, and structures of transitional justice institutions have immediate and long-term impact in how mass violence is remembered both locally and transitionally.

Courtney E. Cole (PhD, Ohio University) is assistant professor of communication at Regis College, near Boston. She is a qualitative scholar of transitional justice, peacebuilding, and organizational communication. In her work, she examines dynamics of peace and justice, post-conflict organizing, and the aftermath of mass violence through analysis of discourse, ethnographic observation, and interviewing. In investigating the organizing of transitional justice and peacebuilding processes, she calls upon theory in the areas of organizational studies, peace and conflict studies, and media and communication studies.

References

Advocates for Human Rights (AHR). 2009. *A House with Two Rooms: Final Report of the Truth and Reconciliation Commission of Liberia Diaspora Project*. St. Paul, MN: DRI Press.

Advocates for Human Rights (AHR). 2008. "Opening Ceremonies." Retrieved 10 January 2011 from http://www.theadvocatesforhumanrights.org/us_hearings_transcripts.

Alexander, Jeffrey C., Ron Eyerman, Bernard Giesen, Neil J. Smelser, and Piotr Sztompka. 2004. *Cultural Trauma and Collective Identity*. Berkeley: University of California Press.

Bodnar, John E. 1992. *Remaking America: Public Memory, Commemoration, and Patriotism in the Twentieth Century*. Princeton, NJ: Princeton University Press.

Browne, Stephen H. 1995. "Review Essay: Reading, Rhetoric, and the Texture of Public Memory." *Quarterly Journal of Speech* 81(2): 237–50.

———. 1999. "Remembering Crispus Attucks: Race, rhetoric, and the politics of commemoration." *Quarterly Journal of Speech* 85(2): 169–87.

Büttner, Sebastian M., and Anna Delius. 2015. "World Culture in European Memory Politics? New European Memory Agents between Epistemic Framing and Political Agenda Setting." *Journal of Contemporary European Studies* 23(3): 391–404.

Buttny, Richard. 2015. "Constesting Hydrofracking during an Inter-governmental Hearing: Accounting by Reworking or Challenging the Question. *Discourse & Communication* 9: 423–40.

Chakravarti, Sonali. 2008. "More than 'Cheap Sentimentality': Victim Testimony at Nuremberg, the Eichmann Trial, and Truth Commissions." *Constellations* 15(2): 223–35.

Cole, Courtney E. 2010. "Problematizing Therapeutic Assumptions about Narratives: A Case Study of Storytelling Events in a Post-conflict Context." *Health Communication* 25: 650–60.

———. 2018. "Commemorating Mass Violence: Truth Commission Hearings as a Genre of Public Memory." *Southern Communication Journal*: 1–18.

Delage, Christian. 2014. *Caught on Camera: Film in the Courtroom from the Nuremberg Trials to the Trials of the Khmer Rouge*. Philadelphia: University of Pennsylvania Press.

Erll, Astrid. 2011. "Travelling Memory." *Parallax* 17(4): 4–18.

Eyerman, Ron. 2001. *Cultural Trauma: Slavery and the Formation of African American Identity*. Cambridge: Cambridge University Press.

Gaiba, Francesca. 1998. *The Origins of Simultaneous Interpretation: The Nuremberg Trial*. Ottawa: University of Ottawa Press.

Gallagher, Victoria J. 1999. Memory and Reconciliation in the Birmingham Civil Rights Institute. *Rhetoric & Public Affairs* 2(2): 303–20.

Graefenstein, Sulamith. 2016. "After the Nation? Memory Work at Mauthausen Memorial in (Trans) National Perspective." *Australian Humanities Review* 59: 155–73.

Gregor, Neil. 2008. *Haunted City: Nuremberg and the Nazi Past*. New Haven, CT: Yale University Press.

Holder, Wilhemina. 2008. "Testimony of Wilhemina Holder." Retrieved 10 January 2011 from http://www.theadvocatesforhumanrights.org/us_hearings_transcripts.

Hoskins, Andrew. 2011. "Media, Memory, Metaphor: Remembering and the Connective Turn." *Parallax* 17(4): 19–31.

Kennedy, Rosanne, and Maria Nugent. 2016. "Scales of Memory: Reflections on an Emerging Concept." *Australian Humanities Review* 59: 61–76.

Laplante, Lisa. J. 2015. "The Role of the Media in Transitional Justice." In *Communication and Peace: Mapping an Emerging Field*, edited by Julia Hoffman and Virgil Hawkins, 265–76. New York: Routledge.

Levy, Daniel, and Natan Sznaider. 2002. "Memory Unbound: The Holocaust and the Formation of Cosmopolitan Memory." *European Journal of Social Theory* 5(1): 87–106.

Lewis, Alison. 2016. "Confessions and the Stasi Files in Post-Communist Germany: The Modest Scales of Memory and Justice in Traitor to the Fatherland." *Australian Humanities Review* 59: 209–22.

Marschall, Sabine. 2013. "Public Holidays as Lieux De Mémoire: Nation-Building and the Politics of Public Memory in South Africa." *Anthropology Southern Africa 36*(1-2): 11–21.

McComas, Katherine, John C. Besley, and Laura W. Black. 2010. "The Rituals of Public Meetings." *Public Administration Review* 70: 122–30.

Mease, Jennifer J., and David P. Terry. 2012. "[Organizational (Performance] of Race): The Co-Constitutive Performance of Race and School Board in Durham, NC." *Text and Performance Quarterly* 32(2): 121–40.

Murphy, Patrick D. 2015. "Voice, Visibility, and Recognition: Vertical and Horizontal Trajectories of Human Rights and Social Justice Media." *Popular Communication* 13(2): 101–4.

Olick, Jeffrey K. 2013. *The Politics of Regret: On Collective Memory and Historical Responsibility.* New York: Routledge.

Plessow, Oliver. 2015. "The Interplay of the European Commission, Researcher and Educator Networks and Transnational Agencies in the Promotion of a Pan-European Holocaust Memory." *Journal of Contemporary European Studies* 23(3): 378–90.

Radstone, Susannah. 2011. "What Place Is This? Transcultural Memory and the Locations of Memory Studies." *Parallax* 17(4): 109–23.

Rothberg, Michael, and Yasemin Yildiz. 2011. "Memory Citizenship: Migrant Archives of Holocaust Remembrance in Contemporary Germany." *Parallax* 17(4): 32–48.

Settele, Veronika. 2015. "Including Exclusion in European Memory? Politics of Remembrance at the House of European History." *Journal of Contemporary European Studies* 23(3): 405–16.

Sharples, Caroline. 2013. "Holocaust on Trial: Mass Observation and British Media Responses to the Nuremberg Tribunal, 1945–1946." In *Britain and the Holocaust: The Holocaust and Its Contexts*, edited by Caroline Sharples and Olaf Jensen, 31–50. London: Palgrave Macmillan.

Sierra Leone Truth and Reconciliation Commission (SLTRC). 2004. *Witness to Truth: Final Report of the Truth and Reconciliation Commission.* Graphic Packaging, Accra, Ghana. Available at sierraleonetrc.org/index.php/view-the-final-report/download-table-of-contents.

Smith, Christina M., and Kelly M. McDonald. 2011. "The Mundane to the Memorial: Circulating and Deliberating the War in Iraq through Vernacular Soldier-Produced Videos." *Critical Studies in Media Communication* 28(4): 292–313.

Törnquist-Plewa, Barbara. 2016. "Cosmopolitan Memory, European Memory and Local Memories in East Central Europe." *Australian Humanities Review* 59: 136–54.

Truth and Reconciliation of Liberia. 2009. *Consolidate Final Report.* Vol. 2. Monrovia/Ghana: Twidan Grafix.

Wüstenberg, Jenny. 2017. *Civil Society and Memory in Postwar Germany.* Cambridge: Cambridge University Press.

Chapter 10

TRANSNATIONAL MEMORY MOVEMENTS IN THE 9/11 MUSEUM

Amy Sodaro

In the preface to *Up From Zero*, his book about rebuilding Lower Manhattan following 9/11, journalist and architecture critic Paul Goldberger writes, "There is no instruction manual to tell a city what to do when its tallest buildings are suddenly gone, and there is a void in its heart. There is no road map to lead its officials and its citizens along the route of renewal, no guidebook to help them figure out whether renewal, in fact, is even what they want" (2004: xi). While perhaps this was the sentiment in the days, months, and even years following the attacks of 9/11, a visit today to the 9/11 Memorial and Museum[1] suggests that in fact those who created the memorial and museum did adhere to, if not a formal guidebook, a clear set of internationally agreed-upon best practices for memorializing political violence. The memorial and the museum are both exemplars of what the editors of this volume have termed "transnational memory spaces," familiar to anyone visiting Holocaust memorials or museums and memory sites dedicated to other forms of political violence. The memorial, called Reflecting Absence and featuring two gigantic reflecting pools in the footprints of the Twin Towers with water cascading from the sides into a void in the center, adheres to many of the tropes common in Holocaust and other commemoration (e.g., Young 1993; 2016). However, the creation of the 9/11 Museum, in particular, reflects today's transnational normative structures guiding public commemoration of political violence and serves as an exemplar of the global commemorative form of memorial museum.

As a memorial museum, the 9/11 Museum is intended to be not only a space of memory and history but also one of moral transformation and the promotion of democracy and nonviolence. In the words of its director, Alice Greenwald, the museum was designed to be "an agent of resolve, demanding that each of us, individually, nationally and globally, place a value on human life" (2016: 13). This broad mission appears to encapsulate what Levy and Sznaider (2006) have theorized as a cosmopolitan "memory imperative" and suggests an ethical power and duty ascribed to the museum's transnational forms of memory. The museum also reflects the ways that "carriers, media, contents, forms and practices of memory" travel the globe (Erll 2011: 11). Its lineage from Holocaust museums is evident, and it follows a set of "best practices" in the creation of memorial museums that have made their way around the globe, producing striking similarities between the 9/11 Museum and other memorial museums. At the same time, because of the nature of 9/11 as a terrorist attack—a catastrophic violence inflicted by "others" on "us"—and the complexity of creating a memorial museum on a site that is commercially, politically, and ethically so important and contested, the 9/11 Museum is in many ways a new kind of twenty-first-century memorial museum that I will argue is deeply problematic.

This chapter traces how the museum emerged from the "void in the heart" of New York City to become a twenty-first-century memorial museum. While a certain paralysis, as suggested by Goldberger, certainly shrouded the city in the weeks following 9/11, it was not long before earnest discussions began about what to do with this site. And while it may seem inevitable today that the site has developed into its current manifestation, with a massive memorial and museum anchoring the surrounding office, commercial, transportation, and public space, it was not necessarily inevitable in the beginning. Rather, the site and the museum in particular are the result of a deliberative process informed and shaped by many different actors, structures, and mechanisms. Wüstenberg writes that agency suggests "the power (either latent or exercised) to create change" (Wüstenberg, this volume), and in this chapter I examine the agency behind the creation of the 9/11 Memorial Museum; and yet in this case that agency works within existing normative structures vis-à-vis commemoration, making the 9/11 Museum an exemplar of the memorial museum form. However, despite the familiarity of the transnational memory forms deployed in the museum, an examination of the national and local context of its creation highlights the continued centrality of the nation in shaping memory. Though the museum's creators followed internationally agreed-upon best practices in a deliberate and careful process meant to avoid constructing a politicized, hegemonic memory and history of September 11, the interactions between the agents and structures in the process of creating the museum resulted in the opposite: a highly nationalistic and deeply political memorial museum that belies the potential of memory to promote cosmopolitan ethics.

Actors: Rebuilding Ground Zero

For many in the United States and around the world, the attacks of September 11, 2001 seemed to come out of nowhere, but as the smoke began to clear, the realization that things would never be the same began to settle over the New York City and the nation. As Lower Manhattan smoldered, the emphasis in the immediate aftermath was on rescue and—when rescue was no longer possible—recovery. But while many wanted to leave the entire site a memorial—a number of families, for example, felt that it was a burial ground that should not be built upon (Goldberger 2004; Young 2016)—many others began to almost immediately imagine how the site might be redeveloped and rebuilt. And so debates began, carefully and slowly, about what to do with this site that would honor the memory of the victims, rebuild Lower Manhattan, and symbolize the resilience of New York and the United States.[2]

The debates were slow and careful because the cast of characters was huge, diverse, and complex. The World Trade Center site was owned by the Port Authority, a government agency run by the states of New York and New Jersey, but leased just weeks before 9/11 to Larry Silverstein, a real estate developer. But clearly these two entities were not the only—or even the loudest and most influential—voices involved; there were also the families of those killed and the survivors. There were the thousands of people who lived or worked near Ground Zero, whose lives had been upended, as well as the many business owners in the area. And beyond those directly affected by the attacks, many New Yorkers, other Americans, and people around the world who had witnessed the attacks felt some kind of connection to the events and the place.

To attempt to give some order to the process, but also to keep it firmly within his control, the governor of New York, George Pataki, formed the Lower Manhattan Development Corporation (LMDC) to lead the rebuilding. At its helm was a group of corporate and civic leaders and 9/11 family members who launched an "unprecedented public outreach campaign," attempting to make the process of rebuilding open, inclusive, and democratic (LMDC and Port Authority 2003: 2). These public debates shaped a set of design parameters, which became the basis for the LMDC's Innovative Design Study, an open call for architects to redesign the site, which attracted over four hundred designs by architects around the world. From those designs, a panel of experts selected nine finalist teams, representing some of the world's top architects (LMDC and Port Authority 2003: 3).

Among the "starchitects" who presented designs for the master plan was Daniel Libeskind, a Polish American son of Holocaust survivors. He called his design Memory Foundations and stressed the importance of maintaining the footprints of the towers and preserving the slurry wall, which was constructed to hold back the waters of the Hudson River from the original towers, in a way that would allow visitors to "journey down into Ground Zero, onto bedrock foundation" (quoted in Goldberger 2004: 9). While the slurry wall and bedrock would anchor the site, he also designed a soaring, symbolic skyscraper that, at 1776 feet, in his words, "answered the call of the Statue of Liberty" (quoted in Goldberger 2004: 172). He linked his design to his own biography—the son of Holocaust survivors who arrived at thirteen years old with his family in the New York Harbor to begin a new life—drawing deeply on memory to sell his design. It worked; Goldberger writes that Libeskind "suggested that he knew far better than most architects how to communicate with a traumatized public" (2004: 9). An exhibition of the designs, public hearings, a mailing to the families of 9/11, and a broad solicitation of public comments (over thirteen thousand were received) found that the public liked many of Libeskind's design elements; so did Governor Pataki, who pressed the LMDC to select it (Young 2016).

Though control of the site's design would ultimately be wrested from him, the choice of Libeskind was one of the initial decisions that greatly shaped the ultimate redevelopment of the site and especially the museum. Despite Libeskind's role in the rebuilding of Ground Zero and his many other projects, he remains most famous for the Jewish Museum in Berlin. Though intended to be a museum celebrating Jewish history and heritage, not a Holocaust memorial, Libeskind's Jewish Museum is steeped in memory and meaning of the Holocaust. Some have wondered whether there is a type of "Jewish architecture," emblematized in the work of architects like Richard Meier, Peter Eisenman, Santiago Calatrava, James Ingo Freed, and Daniel Libeskind (Young 2016: 79–81). While it is not clear what this might mean, as James Young writes, "the forms of postwar architecture have surely been inflected by an entire generation's knowledge of the Holocaust," leaving Jewish architects in particular "strugg[ling] to find an architectural vernacular that might express such breaches in civilization without mending them" (2016: 81). Thus, although Libeskind's shimmering glass and steel skyscraper—the tallest building in the Western Hemisphere, dubbed the Freedom Tower by Pataki—is meant to be a symbol of rebirth and resilience, the Holocaust clearly influenced Libeskind's master plan and would continue to be a major source of inspiration for September 11 commemoration.

Although Libeskind infused his rhetoric and design with commemorative references, the master plan was never intended to be the memorial, and in April 2003 a design competition for the official memorial was called. A thirteen-person jury composed of public officials, civic and philanthropic leaders, 9/11 family members, artists, architects, and academics was established to oversee it. The inclusion of architect Maya Lin, who designed the Vietnam Veterans Memorial, and James E. Young, an academic who has authored some of the seminal texts on Holocaust and other memorialization, suggests the desire for the 9/11 memorial to adhere to an internationally agreed-upon commemorative ethos, reflecting yet another dimension of the actors and agency behind the memorial and museum. Lin's memorial, which was inspired by Holocaust commemoration, is generally considered to be a model for a new paradigm of self-reflexive and critical commemoration, and perhaps no one has articulated this more eloquently than Young, whose work has helped to crystallize this new ethos of memorialization. Unlike the open and inclusive process of selecting the site design, the public's involvement in the memorial selection was limited to a few public hearings (Wyatt 2003), reflecting a shift toward a top-down approach, where experts like Lin and Young were at the helm of the decision-making. Because of the prominence of the site and its redevelopment, those who held the ultimate power over the site's future—Pataki, Silverstein, and the Port Authority—turned over much of the agency, particularly when it came to the commemorative elements, to experts in urban design, civic renewal, architecture, and memorialization.

The jury received over five hundred official submissions from which they selected the design by Michael Arad and landscape architect Peter Walker called Reflecting Absence. Arad, who was born in Israel before settling in New York, proposed a plaza of trees, interrupted by two memorial voids, "open and visible reminders of absence" (Young 2016: 64). The selection of Libeskind's master plan punctuated by Arad's voids suggests what Young calls an "arc of memorial forms," reaching from World War II in Europe to today's New York City. While Young describes being flummoxed by a reporter asking him if Arad's design was not just another Holocaust memorial (2016: 2), it seems evident to students and scholars of memorialization that the 9/11 Memorial and Memorial Museum are clear descendants of Holocaust memorialization and firmly rooted in and reflective of today's transnational memory culture. The kind of "negative form" architecture focused on voids and absence that is the basis for Arad's design arguably began with Lin's memorial, and has become the key transnational architectural articulation of the Holocaust and subsequent memorial projects that look to Holocaust commemoration as a model.

With the master plan and memorial selected, attention turned to the underground space, which would house a museum. The memorial plaza had been conceived in much the same way as Berlin's Memorial to the Murdered Jews of Europe, with the memorial serving as a public site of mourning, reflection, and remembrance, anchored by an underground interpretive site.

In the case of the 9/11 memorial, the underground museum would be the "global focal point for telling the story of what happened on 9/11, what led up to it, and its aftermath" (Daniels 2016: 8). At the same time, it was meant to be a place where the individuals who were killed could be remembered and honored, together with those who survived and those who risked and lost their lives rescuing others. And it would serve as a place that could "inspire and change the way people see the world and the possibility of their own lives" (Greenwald 2016: 11). It was thus intended from the start to be a memorial museum—a space of history, memory, and moral education (Sodaro 2018).

To this end, two key individuals were brought on board to lead the project: Alice Greenwald and Clifford Chanin. Greenwald had a museums background; she served as director of the National Museum of Jewish History in Philadelphia and came to the 9/11 Museum project from five years at the U.S. Holocaust Memorial Museum (USHMM). Chanin had a slightly less direct route to the 9/11 Museum; after conducting undergraduate research on memories of Holocaust survivors and several years working in journalism and politics, he joined the Rockefeller Foundation, where he founded the Legacy Project, focused on establishing international networks of groups commemorating and coming to terms with past violence (Kenney 2015).

These two individuals were thus well versed—and in fact immersed—in today's transnational memory culture. They were deeply familiar with its commemorative forms and the ethical and practical expectations of commemorating political violence. And they were well aware of the difficult, emotionally charged, and contentious process that they were setting out upon. In order to navigate the potentially treacherous waters of commemorating an event as laden with meaning as 9/11, and with a nod to inclusivity but an emphasis on expertise, they began with a Conversation Series, which brought together memorial, museum, and trauma scholars with key stakeholders to discuss the potential and pitfalls of the project. Experts were called in to establish "guiding principles" for the development of the museum. For example Barbara Kirshenblatt-Gimblett, a museum scholar who has worked with the Jewish Museum in Berlin, the USHMM, and Warsaw's POLIN Museum of the History of Polish Jews, suggested that the 9/11 museum should create an experience in which visitors can "find themselves," to encourage "an emotional and intellectual alchemy . . . that encourages self-reflection, which in turn can lead to moral understanding" (Greenwald 2016: 14). And Edward T. Linenthal, an American historian best known for his books on the creation of the USHMM and Oklahoma City National Memorial and Museum, argued that the museum "should invite self-reflection and enable visitors to contemplate complexities without offering easy or reductive answers . . ." (*Museum Planning Conversation Series Report* 2008: 3).

Thus, through these early discussions, experts active in shaping and analyzing transnational memorialization practices laid the groundwork for a self-reflexive twenty-first-century memorial museum that anticipated not only the controversies such a museum would provoke but also the potential to offer a powerful and affective visitor experience that could encompass history, memory, and moral education.

At the same time that this elite group of memorialization experts served as key agents behind the design of the memorial and museum, there were also a number of associations and individual 9/11 family members with diverse agendas and opinions and a strong stake in the redevelopment of Ground Zero. Reflecting commemorative best practices of inclusivity, family members were incorporated into the process of rebuilding Lower Manhattan at all of the different stages; however, although they are often referred to in monolithic terms, 9/11 families are in no way a homogenous body with a shared agenda. Organizations proliferate with widely divergent political, moral, and commemorative agendas, such as the conservative 9/11 Families for a Safe and Strong America, led by the outspoken Debra Burlingame, versus the liberal 9/11 Families for Peaceful Tomorrows. And while some 9/11 family members and associations have been very publicly involved in the process of creating the memorial and museum, such as the group Take Back the Memorial, which successfully scuttled plans for an International Freedom Center on the WTC site, many others have felt sidelined and "steamrolled" by the process and outcomes (McCaffrey et al. 2018). Ultimately, although the Conversation Series was meant to be inclusive and open, 9/11 families are as divergent in their opinions as the rest of the public, and it was primarily memorial and museum experts who drove the creation of the museum.

While these stakeholders and experts were establishing the museum's guiding principles, two New York–based exhibition designers were selected to translate those principles into exhibits: Thinc Design, a firm led by Tom Hennes that, according to the website, works to "create experiences that provide springboards to action, that inspire dialogue, shift perception and invite participation," and Local Projects, an "experience design studio," headed by Jake Barton. Together, Barton's and Hennes's teams sought to capitalize on what was one of the most unique and challenging aspects of 9/11: how widely witnessed and mediated it had been, with as many as two billion people around the world witnessing the attacks. With this in mind, they settled on a core tenet of the museum's design: letting individuals tell the story of 9/11. Rather than "graft[ing] historical 'meaning' onto the events" (Greenwald 2016: 12), they wanted to create a museum that would provide a transformative individual encounter with 9/11. The museum creators sought to avoid the construction of a hegemonic, national narrative, instead looking to the fragmentation of individual memory and experience to create a diversity of stories and encounters. In this way, they were seemingly adhering to the best practices for memorial museums around which there has solidified some consensus, as well as accounting for the diversity in ideas about how 9/11 should ultimately be commemorated. But they were also adhering to many of the principles theorized in what has been termed the "third phase" of memory studies: the ways that memory moves across and beyond borders. Bond and Rapson write that "Memory . . . does not stay put but circulates, migrates, travels; it is more and more perceived as a process, as a work that is continually in progress, rather than as a reified object" (2016: 1). The creators of the 9/11 Museum sought to capture this restless movement of memory as a process by avoiding reifying, musealizing, and politicizing it. But as we shall see, by removing the historical and political context of the events, rather than remembering 9/11 apolitically, the museum is actually highly political.

Structures: The Memorial Museum as Commemorative Form

The years of deliberate and careful planning of the National September 11 Memorial Museum resulted in an ultramodern memorial museum. Memorial museums emerged in the second half of the twentieth century, initially in response to the challenges posed by Holocaust commemoration, and have since been constructed around the world by groups who have experienced political violence (Williams 2007; Sodaro 2018). Memorial museums focus on past atrocity in a way that goes beyond the work of museums or memorials alone. Like museums, they are houses of history that use narrative to explain and educate about the past; like memorials, they use memory to acknowledge the victims and attempt to repair and restore what was broken; and as hybrid memorial museums they use affect and experience to create an emotional response in visitors intended to morally transform them. To balance their efforts at history, memory, and moral transformation, they depart from the traditional work of museums as collectors and repositories that use material culture to educate; while many of them, like the 9/11 Museum, have large collections of artifacts, they focus primarily on ideas and narratives and use multimedia and experiential techniques to create affective and moving emotional experiences for visitors. The ultimate goal of memorial museums is to create a newly moral public that will work to prevent future violence, intolerance, and hatred (Sodaro 2018). They are thus not only a new form of museum-memorial hybrid but also a new normative structure for confrontation with and education about past violence that is increasingly popular within today's transnational memorial culture.

Memorial museums arise out of a broader interest in the past and its negative legacy. This emphasis on the negative past, variously referred to as a "politics of regret" (Olick 2007) or "reparations politics" (Torpey 2006), means that the political legitimacy of many collectives around the world today depends, at least in part, upon their willingness to attempt to come to terms with past violence and atrocity. Daniel Levy and Natan Sznaider (2006; 2010) argue that we can trace this phenomenon to the Holocaust. In an increasingly globalized world, they aver, the Holocaust has set a standard for dealing with past atrocities, creating a "memory imperative" that shapes how societies around the world remember, articulate, and come to terms with their own violent pasts vis-à-vis cosmopolitan ethics like human rights, democracy, and tolerance. Today there appears to be a global moral imperative that societies address past violence through the use of mechanisms like truth commissions, reparations, memorials, and memorial museums, which have proliferated globally, becoming normative structures shaping how groups around the world address past violence. This memory imperative, which in many ways is modeled on Germany's self-indicting reckoning with the Holocaust, entails an expectation that societies take responsibility for violence that they have perpetrated or are implicated in through the use of these kinds of structures and ethics; however, as the case of the 9/11 Museum demonstrates, it is much easier to adhere to this memory imperative and use its forms to commemorate violence perpetrated by others.

The global "memory imperative" has contributed to what has been described as "travelling memory" (Erll 2011), "transnational memory" (de Cesari and Rigney 2014), or "multidirectional memory" (Rothberg 2009), concepts that postulate that memory—its forms, contents, and modes—circulates over and beyond national borders, reflecting and producing a new form of global interconnectedness with great ethical potential. These "transnational [memory] processes can unsettle established memory regimes, especially nation state–sanctioned ones, and can involve the production of new forms of remembering, forgetting and nostalgia, as well as novel modes whereby different types of actors select what to remember . . . and thus the generation of new forms of solidarity and division as mediated through memory processes" (Inglis 2016: 145). Memorial museums are one such new form of memory that has traveled the globe, becoming a key form used to demonstrate the willingness of a collective to confront its negative past without constructing hegemonic national narratives, though the reality is often starkly different.[3] Memorial museums both remember and teach about the past, and work to use the lessons of the past to create a better present and future by inspiring moral transformation in their visitors.

The National September 11 Memorial Museum reflects this memory imperative and the traveling, multidirectional, and transnational forms that memory of the negative past takes in our globalized world. A team of experts with deep knowledge of Holocaust memorialization, memorial museums, and transnational memorial culture worked within the existing and expected normative social structures for remembering past violence, in this case creating an exemplary memorial museum. This interaction between agency and structure reminds us of what Wüstenberg describes as the "mutual constitution of the agency of *individuals, groups, and organizations* engaged in making, (re)producing, and dismantling narratives about the past and the *mnemonic regimes and structures* that both result from and shape these actions" (Wüstenberg, this volume, emphasis added). These agents who helped to shape the expectation within today's "mnemonic regime" that commemorative forms be imbued with cosmopolitan ethics turned to the very structure they had helped to create as the appropriate way to commemorate 9/11. However, the 9/11 Museum remembers a very particular kind of violence, different from other memorial museums—enacted on the United States by foreign actors, which, though lasting only moments, has had massive global consequences—and so its efforts to embody cosmopolitan ethics are very much compromised.

The Mechanisms and Practices of Memorial Museums

While the large reflecting pools of the memorial may astound with their sheer scale and the constant, deafening din of their waterfalls, Reflecting Absence does not offer any interpretation of 9/11. The 9/11 Museum, on the other hand, offers a complete 9/11 experience. Accessed through a sparkling steel and glass pavilion, designed by Snøhetta and tucked askew in a corner of the memorial plaza, the architecture of the pavilion is instantly recognizable to visitors of memorial and Holocaust museums and is strikingly similar to the Jewish Museum Berlin, the USHMM, the Museum of Memory and Human Rights in Santiago, Chile, and many others constructed in sleek and stark modernist memorial architecture. But it is inside that the memorial museum experience commences.

Libeskind's master plan highlighted the importance of descending to bedrock in order to truly experience the WTC site. The museum obliges with its exhibits located seven stories underground. To reach the bedrock, visitors journey from the light and airy pavilion into architect Davis Brody Bond's interior of smooth, dark wood and subdued lighting. A long ramp begins the journey, at the top of which is a massive photo of the twin towers on the morning of September 11, 2001, shortly before the terror of the day began. A huge map on the opposite wall shows the intended routes of the four flights that took off that morning, and their deadly detours. And all around are voices of individual witnesses with accents from around the globe recounting September 11. The overlapping voices and memories on the long ramp orient the visitor to the form of storytelling that is the foundation of the museum: the "collected" memories of individuals who in some way experienced 9/11.[4] The use of these individual memories, as we have seen, not only reflects an effort to avoid the historicization of 9/11 but also echoes a practice common in all memorial museums: the use of survivor testimony to create a more affective, authentic, and experiential connection to the past. However, unlike the Holocaust survivors who tell of the traumas they, as individuals, experienced decades before, these witnesses "experienced" 9/11 from all over the world, often mediated by television, internet, or radio, along with an estimated one-third of the world's population. This collected memory thus shapes the museum's narrative of 9/11 and distinguishes 9/11 as a particularly widely witnessed and mediated global event.

At the bottom of the ramp, the visitor can pause to take in the scale of the museum from a viewing platform that overlooks the slurry wall that Libeskind wanted to show, and that in the museum becomes the anchor of the soaring Foundation Hall. Scattered with massive artifacts, Foundation Hall reminds the visitor that she is in a museum, surrounded by artifacts that serve as evidence of the authenticity of the history being told, but on a scale that is truly staggering. And with each artifact—a badly damaged fire truck, the radio tower from atop the north tower—is an individual story meant to infuse mere objects—as twisted, burnt, and bent as they may be—with affect in order to illicit an emotional response. Punctuating the huge space are the two footprints that lie deep under the memorial pools and contain the two core exhibits of the museum: the historical exhibition and the memorial. True to its form, the 9/11 Memorial Museum combines memory with history in its effort to create an ethically transformative experience for visitors.

The historical exhibition is the interpretive heart of the museum and draws upon the now common experiential and affective exhibitionary practices used in memorial museums to provide visitors with not only a cognitive understanding of the past but also an emotionally charged, deeply affective *experience* of it. Called simply September 11, 2001, the historical exhibition is centered on a detailed timeline of the events of 9/11, which snakes its way through what are now, in striking contrast to the Foundation Hall, claustrophobic and cramped spaces. The timeline shows visitors what was happening—minute by minute—on the ground and in the sky with a focus on the 102 minutes from the first plane flying into the north tower to the towers' collapse. To fill in this otherwise potentially dry account of the day, the timeline is surrounded by a multimedia onslaught of images, videos, sounds, artifacts, and documents that vividly depict the events detailed on the timeline. Incredulous reporters try to make sense of the burning north tower as morning news shows play on endless loop; the second plane slams into the south tower again and again; screams, shouts, and sirens punctuate the commentary; and the banal belongings of the victims and survivors—dusty and damaged backpacks and briefcases, eyeglasses, and high heels—are displayed in glass cases as if they were works of art. And all of this is anchored by the relentless timeline.

This 9/11 timeline is strikingly similar to another 9/11 timeline, this one at the Museum of Memory and Human Rights (MMHR) in Chile, which opened in 2010 and is deeply influenced by Holocaust memorialization, reflecting the global reach of the memorial museum form (e.g., Sodaro 2018). In the MMHR, the timeline is much less detailed, but in a similar manner it recalls the events of September 11, 1973, when the Chilean army staged a coup against President Salvador Allende, installing Augusto Pinochet, who would terrorize the country for the next fifteen years. The Chilean timeline is also surrounded by images of destruction, with footage of the presidential palace being attacked by the state's own army. And like the U.S. 9/11 Museum, the timeline begins at the moment of the attack and gives no historical context to the violent event being depicted. Though there is no evidence that the museums were directly inspired by each other's depiction of their respective 9/11s, clearly they drew from the same exhibitionary practices that are increasingly transnationally used to tell the difficult past in memorial museums. Chronology and temporality are important in memorial museums because most tell of relatively long, drawn-out histories of oppression, violence, or genocide like the Holocaust or Rwandan genocide; in order to make their stories comprehensible, they work to tell a chronological story that starts at the beginning and explicates the events as they progress. The difference in the 9/11 Museum and the MMHR, of course, is that their 9/11s played out over relatively short periods of time. Thus, the museums apply the principles of historical storytelling used in other memorial museums to describe fleeting events; this constructs a narrative that is very much focused on time, but in an ahistorical way.

Despite this dehistoricization, as a history museum meant to serve as the "country's principal institution for examining the implications of the events of 9/11, documenting the impact of those events and exploring the continuing significance of September 11, 2001" (9/11 Memorial, "Museum"), the historical exhibition does offer a bit of historical contextualization of 9/11. Following the intense 102 minutes of the day are a few rooms focused on "Before" 9/11. A room depicting the Twin Towers in popular culture is followed by one describing the 1993 attack on the World Trade Center, underlining the symbolic significance of the towers to those who want to harm "us." Another room gives a perfunctory overview of the rise of al Qaeda, primarily in the form of a short film. This room gives way to two small rooms about the hijackers—how they conceived and carried out their plan. The inclusion of the perpetrators was highly contentious, with some families arguing that including them in the museum allows them a say in writing the history of 9/11 (Cohen 2012). Many memorial museums struggle with depictions of the perpetrators with the fear that their inclusion may degrade the memory of the victims; in the 9/11 Museum, this is particularly evident in the panel picturing and naming the hijackers, which is awkwardly hung at knee level.

Beyond these rooms are two rooms focused on "After" 9/11, with an emphasis on recovery, rebuilding, and the unity that emerged in the days and weeks after the attacks. A final room includes a set of ongoing questions raised by 9/11, like "How can America protect its citizens from terrorism?" "Who should be held accountable?" and "How should we remember?" In this room is the only mention of the wars in Iraq and Afghanistan, the U.S. government's use of torture and extraordinary rendition, controversial policies like the PATRIOT Act, the global rise of extremist terrorism, and other ongoing consequences of 9/11. Though exploring the causes and consequences of 9/11 is written into its mission as a memorial museum, this contextualization is given a fraction of the space that the experiential and affective depiction of attacks are afforded, making the historical exhibition strikingly ahistorical.

The other exhibit is the memorial, In Memoriam. Here, the influence of Holocaust-inspired transnational commemoration is perhaps even more evident. The footprint of this tower is lined with photographs of the victims, all the same size and scale. Victim photographs are, by now, a universal trope in memorial museums, meant to restore humanity and dignity to those who are being remembered. In his book *Memorial Museums*, Paul Williams (2007) traces the centrality of victim photographs in memorial museums to two very different cases: the small photographs of their missing children that the Madres de Plaza de Mayo would wear to their demonstrations against the military junta in Argentina and the now-iconic mugshots of those imprisoned, tortured, and murdered in S-21, the infamous Khmer Rouge Tuol Sleng detention center in Phnom Penh, Cambodia. Indeed, the Madres' and Tuol Sleng photographs remain powerful symbols of loss associated with political violence, serving as touchstones for the use of victim photographs in memorial museums around the globe, including the 9/11 Museum. But it was perhaps the USHMM's Tower of Faces, a three-story tower of photographs from a Lithuanian shtetl that was destroyed by the Nazis, that made victim photographs an essential exhibitionary component of memorial museums. The display of these images is meant to ensure that victims' lives are remembered, helping to form an emotional connection between visitors and victims. In the words of Marianne Hirsch, "[Photographs of the victims] bridge the gap between viewers who are personally connected to the event and those who are not" (1996: 668).

The 9/11 Museum's In Memoriam draws upon this transnational expectation that victims' photographs will be displayed as an integral part of preserving their memory. The effect is powerful; on one hand, the individuals are recalled in the exhibit as individuals—their unique personalities are meant to suggest themselves, though the photos are all uniform. At the same time, the sheer number of photographs, lining the massive footprint of the tower, overwhelms. The scale of destruction overtakes the individual loss, and the victims' faces tend to blur into one symbolic terror victim. To counter this, the museum has a darkened inner chamber where visitors can sit in silent contemplation as the names and brief biographical details of 9/11 victims are read out and projected onto the black walls. It is strikingly similar to the Room of Names in the information center at the Memorial to the Murdered Jews of Europe in Berlin, which is intended to "dissolve the incomprehensible abstract number of six million murdered Jews and to release the victims from their anonymity" (Stiftung Denkmal, "Room of Names"). This inner chamber also resembles the Area of Remembrance at Chile's MMHR, in which visitors can reflect upon a wall of photographs of the victims and, if so inclined, seek more information about them in the computer database. From the Holocaust in Europe to military dictatorship in Latin America to terrorism in the United States, forms of memory travel the globe, producing transnational tropes and languages of remembrance.

Put together, the raw experience of 9/11 depicted in the historical exhibition and the affective memory of the individuals lost in In Memoriam make for an extremely powerful museum experience. Visitors remember the lives of those who were killed and, in having their own encounter with 9/11 in an affective and experiential way, realize that it could have been them. The museum draws upon the many transnational practices common to memorial museums—the use of survivor testimony and victim photographs, chronological historical narratives, experiential and affective architecture, multimedia displays—to combine memory and history in a way meant to inspire moral transformation in visitors. However, because of the nature of 9/11 as a terror attack, the museum creators' decision to focus on individual experiences rather than historicization of 9/11, and the prominence of the event and site within the global geopolitical context, the museum constructs a highly divisive and political memory of 9/11 that is especially problematic in the current political environment.

Outcomes: The 9/11 Museum as a Transnational Memory Space

Wüstenberg describes transnational memory spaces "as instances or processes of remembrance that are anchored . . . in concrete locations . . . but that extend beyond national borders" (Wüstenberg, this volume). The 9/11 Museum is precisely this type of space in a number of different ways. On the one hand, the museum, while remembering the particular events that occurred in New York City, Arlington, Virginia, and Shanksville, Pennsylvania, reinforces throughout the exhibit the notion that 9/11 was a global event, and so memory of it spans the globe. The global nature of 9/11 becomes clear in the very beginning of the museum visit with the individuals from around the world recalling 9/11 as they witnessed it. Their words are projected onto columns to form the shapes of continents that converge to create a map of the world, just as the voices converge to create a shared, global memory of 9/11. Further on, in the historical exhibition, a display of newspaper front pages from around the world reaffirms that 9/11 did not just affect New York, Virginia, and Pennsylvania but also Tokyo, Baghdad, and Berlin. And of course, while many visitors to the museum are from the United States, many others among the museum's eleven million total visitors are international.

But the 9/11 Museum is a transnational space in more nuanced and important ways as well. As this chapter has documented, the museum was built deliberately and intentionally to be a memorial museum, a distinct cultural form that blends memory and history with a goal of moral education. Emerging from challenges to commemorating the Holocaust, the memorial museum has become a global commemorative form thought to be not only effective in coming to terms with past political violence but also often compulsory as an international symbol that the past has been thoroughly acknowledged and addressed vis-à-vis today's "politics of regret." Memorial museums, with their goals of promoting nonviolence, liberal democratic values, and the ethic of "never again" are an embodiment of Levy and Sznaider's "memory imperative" and are thus one of the expected structures used for the commemoration of violence in societies that wish to adhere to international political, social, and ethical norms associated with coming to terms with violence.

Indeed, the 9/11 Museum is deeply indebted to Holocaust memorialization, with a team of experts in the language and ethics of Holocaust commemoration behind its creation. Wüstenberg writes that transnational memory space "may evoke memories or experiences of transnational action or meaning, of transnational norms, of mobility and movement, of longing for places 'elsewhere' and more" (Wüstenberg, this volume). The 9/11 Museum evokes, at many turns, memory of the Holocaust and the kinds of international norms around human rights, liberal democracy, and "never again" represented in Holocaust commemoration. It is intended to evoke and teach precisely the cosmopolitan ethics that Levy and Sznaider argue shape memory of political violence today: the 9/11 Museum is meant to "inspire and change the way people see the world and the possibility of their own lives . . . demanding that each of us, individually, nationally, and globally, place a value on every human life" (Greenwald 2016: 13). While we can rightly critique the notion that memory holds this potential as overly utopian, the 9/11 Museum and other memorial museums around the world are built upon this premise.

And yet, the 9/11 Museum does not give any meaningful historical contextualization to the causes of 9/11 or its consequences, instead providing a deeply affective and emotional experience of the trauma of 102 minutes. The context for before and after 9/11 is alarmingly inadequate for a nuanced understanding of such a complex event, which ultimately compromises the mission of the museum to transform visitors. While the goal is for visitors to come away with the value of human life (re)affirmed, the ahistorical exhibit suggests that only some lives are valuable (for example, those of the victims of 9/11, as opposed to the tens of thousands of civilians killed during the wars in Iraq and Afghanistan) and that only one side has perpetrated evil acts (the hijackers and Al-Qaeda). Taking the trauma of 9/11 out of the context of why it happened and how the United States has responded tells a Manichean story of good (us/United States) versus evil (them/terrorists), producing a divisive and dangerous historical memory.

Rather than promoting moral transformation vis-à-vis cosmopolitan ethics, the museum seems to better reflect the retreat from globalization, cosmopolitanism, multiculturalism, and tolerance that we are experiencing in the United States and around the world in contemporary politics and public discourse. This move toward right-wing populism appears to be a parallel transnational process that sharply diverges from the cosmopolitan ethical potential that Levy, Sznaider, and others believe that memory potentially holds, reminding us of the more nefarious uses of memory. From Brexit in the United Kingdom to Donald Trump in the United States and the gains made by the far right in recent elections across Europe, anger and frustration with globalization and cosmopolitanism are stoking new political and social movements that seek a return to a past when the world was not so interconnected and ideas, people, and memories were not so transnational. While the agents and structures behind the creation of the 9/11 Museum were motivated and shaped by a completely different ethical premise than this right-wing populism, the ahistorical but highly emotional story and memory of 9/11 that it contains seems potentially ripe for manipulation by precisely these kinds of populist and divisive forces.

In attempting to avoid a hegemonic, national narrative of 9/11, the museum perhaps left too much space for individual interpretation without enough historical contextualization to encourage cognition and comprehension. Rather than historical understanding, the museum creates a vivid, moving, and frightening experience of 9/11, which ends in pain, confusion, and fear (with a side of redemption in the triumph of recovery and rebuilding), but no critical reflection. Although the museum appears to reflect the travelling, multidirectional and transnational nature of memory today, it is in fact a deeply nationalistic institution that tells a particular story of "us" being injured by "them." The only moral lesson of the museum seems to be that the United States will inevitably triumph because of its commitment to freedom, democracy, and human rights (directed solely toward those who are with "us"). Though the 9/11 Museum borrows a transnational commemorative structure meant to inspire critical reflection, in constructing its ahistorical and apolitical narrative, it gives the terrorists exactly what they wanted in many ways: the spectacular terror attack has been spectacularly immortalized. While the agency, actors, structures, mechanisms, and practices of the 9/11 Museum may reflect the transnational movements of memory, the outcome in the museum is a narrative of 9/11 that is entirely compatible with nationalist, nativist, and xenophobic rhetoric and politics.

Amy Sodaro is associate professor of sociology at the Borough of Manhattan Community College, City University of New York. Her research focuses on memorialization of atrocity in memorial museums. She is coeditor of *Memory and the Future: Transnational Politics, Ethics and Society* (2010) and *Museums and Sites of Persuasion: Politics, Memory and Human Rights* (2019). She is the author of *Exhibiting Atrocity: Memorial Museums and the Politics of Past Violence* (2018).

Notes

1. The legal name of the nonprofit that runs the memorial and museum is the National September 11 Memorial and Museum at the World Trade Center, and the memorial and museum were referred to as the National September 11 Memorial and Museum (with the museum called the National September 11 Memorial Museum); a recent, subtle rebranding has changed the name on the website and other public spaces to the 9/11 Memorial and Museum, and the museum is now called the 9/11 Memorial Museum. In this chapter I use the new name or the more colloquial 9/11 Museum.
2. It should be noted that a comprehensive analysis of the process of rebuilding Lower Manhattan is well beyond the scope of this chapter; the focus here is on the agents and structures that shaped the commemorative elements, in particular the memorial museum, within today's transnational memorialization culture.
3. In my research on memorial museums in the United States, Hungary, Chile, and Rwanda, I have found that, despite their efforts to be open, dialogic spaces for the difficult confrontation with past violence, they are highly political institutions (Sodaro 2018).
4. The distinction between "collected" and "collective" memory is one made by Jeffrey Olick (1999), who differentiates between the collected memories of individuals (a concept also developed by James Young [1993]) and collective memory that occurs sui generis within a group.

References

9/11 Memorial. "Museum." Retrieved 20 December 2019 from https://www.911memorial
.org/museum.
Bond, Lucy, and Jessica Rapson. 2014. *The Transcultural Turn: Interrogating Memory Between
and Beyond Borders*. Boston: De Gruyter.
Cohen, Patricia. 2012. "At Museum on 9/11, Talking through an Identity Crisis." *New York
Times*, 2 June. Retrieved 20 December 2019 from http://www.nytimes.com/2012/06/03/
arts/design/sept-11-memorial-museums-fraught-task-to-tell-the-truth.html.
Daniels, Joe. 2016. "Introduction." In *No Day Shall Erase You: The Story of 9/11 as Told at the
National September 11 Memorial Museum*, edited by Alice M. Greenwald, 8–10. New York:
SkiraRizzoli.
De Cesari, Chiara, and Ann Rigney. 2014. *Transnational Memory: Circulation, Articulation,
Scales*. Boston: De Gruyter.
Erll, Astrid. 2011. "Travelling Memory." *Parallax* 17(4): 4–18.
Goldberger, Paul. 2004. *Up from Zero: Politics, Architecture, and the Rebuilding of New York*.
New York: Random House.
Greenwald, Alice M. 2016. "Through the Lens of Memory: Creating the 9/11 Memorial
Museum." In *No Day Shall Erase You: The Story of 9/11 as Told at the National September 11
Memorial Museum*, edited by Alice M. Greenwald, 11–30. New York: SkiraRizzoli.
Hirsch, Marianne. 1996. "Past Lives: Postmemories in Exile." *Poetics Today* 17(4): 659–86.
Inglis, David. 2016. "Globalization and/of Memory." In *Routledge International Handbook
of Memory Studies*, edited by Anna Lisa Tota and Trever Hagen, 143–57. New York:
Routledge.
Kenney, Laurie. 2015. "The 9/11 Memory Keeper." *Wesleyan Magazine*. 7 December.
Retrieved 20 December 2019 from http://magazine.wesleyan.edu/2015/12/07/the-
911-memory-keeper/.
Levy, Daniel, and Natan Sznaider. 2006. *The Holocaust and Memory in the Global Age*. Phila-
delphia: Temple University Press.
———. 2010. *Human Rights and Memory*. University Park, PA: Pennsylvania State University
Press.
Lower Manhattan Development Corporation (LMDC) and the Port Authority of NY and NJ.
2003. *The Public Dialogue: Innovative Design Study*. Renew NYC. Retrieved 20 December
2019 from http://www.renewnyc.com/content/pdfs/public_dialogue_innovative_design
.pdf.
McCaffrey, Jim, et al. 2018. "Letter: 9/11 Memorial Was No Walk in the Park." *Charleston
Post and Courier*, 22 April. Retrieved 20 December 2019 from https://www.postandcourier
.com/opinion/letters_to_editor/letter-memorial-was-no-walk-in-the-park/article_99f31
e18-43dc-11e8-938d-4f5c9a91f471.html.
Museum Planning Conversation Series Report, 2006–2008. 2008. 9/11 Museum. Retrieved
2 August 2016 from https://www.911memorial.org/sites/all/files/Conversation %20
Series%202006%20-%202008_0.pdf.
Olick, Jeffrey K. 1999. "Collective Memory: The Two Cultures." *Sociological Theory* 17(3):
33–348.
———. 2007. *The Politics of Regret: On Collective Memory and Historical Responsibility*. New
York: Routledge.
Rothberg, Michael. 2009. *Multidirectional Memory: Remembering the Holocaust in the Age of
Decolonization*. Stanford, CA: Stanford University Press.
Sodaro, Amy. 2018. *Exhibiting Atrocity: Memorial Museums and the Politics of Past Violence*.
New Brunswick, NJ: Rutgers University Press.

Stiftung Denkmal. "Room of Names." Retrieved 20 December 2019 from https://www
.stiftung-denkmal.de/en/exhibitions/information-centre/room-of-names.html

Torpey, John. 2006. *Making Whole What Has Been Smashed: On Reparations Politics*. Cambridge, MA: Harvard University Press.

Williams, Paul. 2007. *Memorial Museums: The Global Rush to Commemorate Atrocities*. New
York: Berg.

Wyatt, Edward. 2003. "Panel, Not Public, Will Pick Final 9/11 Memorial Design." *New York
Times*, 9 April. Retrieved 20 December 2019 from https://www.nytimes.com/2003/04/09/
nyregion/panel-not-public-will-pick-final-9-11-memorial-design.html.

Young, James E. 1993. *The Texture of Memory: Holocaust Memorials and Meaning*. New Haven,
CT: Yale University Press.

———. 2016. *The Stages of Memory: Reflections on Memorial Art, Loss, and the Spaces Between*.
Boston: University of Massachusetts Press.

Part IV

HORIZONTAL AGENCY

Chapter 11

LINKS TO THE PAST, BRIDGES FOR THE PRESENT?

Recognition among Memory Organizations
in a European Network

Till Hilmar

❧❧❧

Civil society and governmental organizations are key actors in the process of memory formation (Wüstenberg 2017). They engage in education activities, provide access to archives and historical sites, and engage in research activities. They organize community activities and regularly attempt to bring different groups with varying perspectives on the past together. They constitute a bridge to journalism and the public sphere and often receive and channel public funds. Whether we understand the dynamics of memory as a field structured by actors' positions and practices (Steinmetz 2008) or as a public sphere constituted by carrier groups competing over sacred definitions of the past (Alexander 2004), both perspectives ask for a systematic inquiry into how memory organizations are aligned.

In this chapter, I explore the role of these organizations in the framework of a particular process of memory formation: the efforts of the European Union to create a common, shared frame of reference for remembering twentieth-century atrocities. The goal of a European cultural integration is decisively shaped by the multiplicities, alliances, and antagonisms between historical memories of the twentieth century in the West and East. While contemporary developments like immigration pose a serious challenge to the European project (Krastev 2017), historical memory is a space where normative, integrative forces can be found. The European Union's efforts to draft a common, European narrative of the recent past is characterized by a recurring tension, the antagonism between the memory of Nazism and the Holocaust and the memory of Communism.[1] This is just one among many struggles over the European past (see Sierp 2014), but it articulates itself repeatedly as a political tension in various venues, such as in the planning of the House of European History museum in Brussels (Hilmar 2016), in the European Parliament (Littoz-Monnet 2013; Mälksoo 2014; Kucia 2016), in the Council of Europe Parliamentary Assembly (Mälksoo 2014; Kübler 2012), in the European Commission's Active European Remembrance Program (Littoz-Monnet 2012), as well as in public debates over transitional justice and ongoing reinterpretations of the meaning of the 1989 revolutions in Eastern European societies (Mark 2010; Mark et al. 2015; Stan and Nedelsky 2015; Pakier and Wawrzyniak 2013).[2]

The legacy of twentieth-century authoritarian pasts surfaces on various levels of political and cultural life. While almost all of Europe has experienced Nazi or fascist rule, about a fifth of the current EU population lives in societies that have also experienced the rule of a Communist party. To be sure, there is a historical basis for the *transnationalization* of memories of war, mass violence, political repression, collaboration, or resistance. These phenomena affected most of the European continent in the twentieth century, though to very different degrees (see Snyder 2010). However, the political efforts of the European Union constitute a top-down approach aiming to connect, integrate, and de-antagonize the various parties concerned with these memories. Such an approach requires a larger vision and justification for integration beyond mere technical and economic arguments. While the way EU institutions negotiate these matters has been studied quite extensively, there is still a lack of evidence to evaluate how these tensions come to play at the level of civil society initiatives and organizations that are dedicated to preserving memory on the ground. The level of organizations seems particularly relevant from the perspective of a Brussels-based memory politics, since small and midsize organizations have a critical role in the coupling of local communities and transnational policies.

Against the background of the tension between the memories of Nazism and Communism, I address the following question in this chapter: How do memory organizations actively create a structure to make each other's voices and perspectives heard? To approach this issue, I first draw a network of relevant memory organizations in the field and discuss some descriptive findings from these measures. Among the actors in focus here are museums, memorial sites, NGOs, victims' associations, and governmental organizations. I propose a measure of *recognition* in a social network of these organizations. I pursue two empirical questions: Which other organizations do organizations nominate, i.e., refer to, on their website? And what patterns do single acts of nomination generate in terms of the larger network? I offer a qualitative basis for understanding digital links as a measure of recognition by incorporating into the analysis findings from a small survey designed and administered for this research and completed by memory organizations.

The chapter is primarily concerned with mapping a *structure* of memory actors. As highlighted in the introduction to this volume, this is a critical precondition for theorizing agency in memory. The structure that binds and separates European memory organizations is both a real and a normative space of transnational memory. I argue that it is a space created by actors on the basis of an economy of attention. A theoretical grid is needed to first identify a structure; in a second step, the analysis can work toward conceptualizing agency in its transformative and reproductive (Hays 1994) dimension. The structure revealed in this way is concerned with the distribution of recognition; it thus concerns a fundamental mechanism of social memory. In what follows, a discussion of the theoretically rich intersection of memory and network theory provides an angle that allows us to "see" the structure in question and reflect on the types of agency it confers.

In addition to this theoretical contribution, the chapter also provides an empirical snapshot that can be used to evaluate transnational policies of the European Union from *below*, by asking: To what extent do efforts to integrate and connect organizations across the European memory-scape actually work? Do they validate or challenge the European efforts to overcome antagonisms?

Social Memory Studies as the Study of Relationality

Social memory can be understood as "a set of representations of the past that are constructed by a given social group (be it a nation, a class, a family, a religious community, or other) through a process of invention, appropriation, and selection, and that have bearings on relationships of power within society" (Confino 2005: 48). Social memory is closely entangled with the concept of legitimacy, since giving account of where something comes from means equipping it, in both democratic and nondemocratic societies, with the authority of tradition. In postdictatorial democracies, the past might come to be remembered as a *negative template* for the present political system. While numerous studies in the field of social memory have demonstrated that memory has currency in the political domain, the focus on power should not lead scholars to conclude that memory can be reduced to politics. Most importantly, it is doubtful whether memory can actually be explained with the model of a rational, self-interested actor at its base (Bernhard and Kubik 2014). In such a model, actors are assumed to be primarily concerned with maximizing their power. The kind of power that guides action, in this case, rests with interpretations of the past that can be used to generate legitimacy for policies in the present. But agency in social memory is arguably more than a mere instrumental politics of the past.

Relational sociology offers a perspective to go beyond this narrow understanding of agency. There is a productive conceptual overlap between the study of social memory and relational sociology (as well as its application, social network analysis). The concept of social memory has been established around the observation that ideas and practices endure over generations and that individuals are born into existing meaningful cultural and social structures (Halbwachs 1992). Similarly, in relational sociology, the theoretical premise is that individual attributes should not be studied in isolation but as a function of a position in a network. This is commonly referred to with the concept of "embeddedness" (Granovetter 1985). Individual action follows the logics of positionality, a standpoint constrained and at the same time enabled by its environment (cf. Emirbayer and Goodwin 1994; Powell and Dépelteau 2013). Relations, instead of individual properties, are the fundamental unit of analysis in this perspective. Similarly, while social memory is first and foremost about the meaning of the past, it is also characterized by relational positions that emerge through approaches to meaning and that are in turn structured by content (see Mische 2011; Pachuki and Breiger 2010; Wüstenberg 2016). In Klaus Eder's view, "remembering is a construction that defines not only what is to be remembered but also who is part of the remembering community" (Eder 2006: 267). What the relation to the past looks like has implications for who one will consider part of one's "own" community. Mnemonic communities operate along and create group boundaries, and the logic of inside and outside positioning also reflects back on the meaning that memories and mnemonic practices might have. The decisive insight is that for network structures and mnemonic boundaries to emerge, the assumption of strategic, rational action on the part of the individual is not a prerequisite (cf. Emirbayer and Goodwin 1994: 1416f.). Instead, the individual is embedded in a net of relational forces, many of which are not predictable from a single point of view.

In democracies, social memory is crucially intertwined with the "politics of recognition" (Taylor 1994). This concept describes the tensions that emerge around notions of plurality sustained amid the perspectives of different ethnic groups and their political claims of membership (which are usually based on historical arguments, and the claim to recognize one's past and build an inclusive politics around it; see Eyerman et al. 2011). But the concept is useful beyond ethnic classifications of society. Recognition is a central symbolic resource in modern societies (Fraser and Honneth 2003). It originates in legal action but reaches far beyond the state in democratic societies. Recognition is a play of absence and presence: conferring it means signaling the power to potentially also withdraw it. This is the second decisive link between social memory and relational sociology, because social network scholarship is similarly concerned with the interplay of absence and presence. There, absence is always based on the *possibility of presence*, it is understood as missing ties, or "structural holes" (Burt 1992; Pachucki and Breiger 2010). Nonexisting ties still shape the emerging structure. If social memory is operationalized in terms of symbolic power relations, then the absence of particular memories, or acts of recognition of memories, requires us to analyze absence with respect to the possibility of presence, or the effect and significance of *missing links* within the framework of the observed network.

Finally, there are also theoretically informed reasons for studying memory organizations as the carrier groups in a relational field of memory. First, civil society is the domain where memory bonds are formed and transmitted (see Misztal 2003: 19–22; Wüstenberg 2017). Even if strong mnemonic attachments are generated on the semi-private level (Olick 1999), organizations provide the grounds and resources of their representation, and, therefore, their symbolic weight in the civil sphere. Second, organizations and their institutional frameworks sanction or suppress recognition, which ultimately decides whether certain interpretations of the past are considered important or not and/or ethical or not. In short, if we think of social memory as a constitutive cultural structure, then organizations are the agents through which individuals can make collective representations work in a meaningful and generalizable way. By linking the public and the private, they allow for memory to become truly processual and relational rather than just a property or preference of single actors.

European Memory: Divided Pasts?

The following brief discussion will provide two hypotheses on potential *recognition patterns* that can then be explored in the empirical part of this chapter.

The first dimension is derived from debates and divides between Eastern and Western European actors (Uhl 2016). A number of scholars suggest that the Holocaust has emerged as a negative "founding myth" (Assmann 2013: 27–29; Kroh 2008: 156–73) in Western European societies, but less so in Eastern European societies, where the experience of the rule of Communist parties and, specifically, political repression constitutes a key point of reference in public memory (Mälksoo 2014: 82-99). The contested meaning of the year 1945 can be regarded as an example of this dividing line (Sierp 2017; Troebst 2010: 56–63). In Western Europe, the year 1945 connotes the liberation from Nazism and, thus, a founding moment of contemporary democracy. In Eastern Europe however, 1945 is equally and at times predominantly remembered as the year of the beginning Soviet oppression, as well as a symbol of the West's reluctance to come to the aid of Eastern Europe in Stalin's grip. The transformations of 1989/91 have brought new struggles for recognition. Narratives of suffering are coupled with a new glory for national heroes (Zhurzhenko 2012), whose legacy had been systematically suppressed by the Soviet authorities. Some of these developments have alarmed Western European historians, politicians, and civil society alike. One fear concerns a tendency to relativize the crimes of the Holocaust by equalizing them with Soviet crimes in an effort to gain recognition for national (and/or group-specific) suffering during the Communist era (Leggewie 2008: 221f.) and the related failure to protect minority rights in the present. Eastern Europe has answered political and moral pressures with historical interpretations of the twentieth century as the epoch of "totalitarianism" as a way to incorporate the memory of both Communist and Nazi crimes. In countries such as Poland and the Czech Republic, the victims of Nazi aggression are remembered as one's fellow national compatriots (Stone 2012). The focus on the mass murder of Jews is perceived as too narrow a focus and as neglect toward one's national victims of both Nazism and Communism. In this view, what is sometimes disparagingly labeled as the politics of "self-shaming" (similar in structure to a globally articulated critique of a European "obsession" with the Holocaust) is seen as inimical to a process of national reconciliation after 1989. Western European governments and NGOs are understood to be strategically oblivious to and ignorant of these victims.

The second dimension concerns divides within Eastern European societies. There, the memory of the Holocaust is contested (Michlic 2006; Shore 2013), as is visible, for instance, in the public debates in Poland over Jan T. Gross's books *Neighbors* and *Fear*, works that raise unsettling questions about local traditions of anti-Semitism and challenge memory narratives aiming at national cohesion and purity (e.g., Törnquist-Plewa 2014). This contestation of national belonging also shapes the way the Communist regime is variously remembered. If antifascism was elevated to an official and somewhat empty state doctrine before 1989, it has, for some parts of the population in these societies today, been severely discredited. In several Eastern European countries (though also in the West), political movements have formed that venerate the tradition of fascist movements of the mid-twentieth century (such as the Croatian Ustahe or the Hungarian Arrow Cross movement). For others, antifascism has remained (or was reenacted) as the single most important historical narrative of the past decades (see Mark 2010: 33f.; Judt 2005: 824ff.; Stone 2014). Equally, the debate over the legal and symbolic meaning of victimhood and perpetratorship in different phases of Communist rule is far from resolved. At the level of transnational, European politics at least, various Eastern European actors have demonstrated their ability to form alliances on this question (Mälksoo 2014).³ Interpretations of the 1989 revolutions and the transformation time are also, if to a varying degree, a source of memory conflicts (see Bernhard and Kubik 2014; Mark et al. 2015). As part of a broader effort to regulate and provide access to Communist secret police, governments in most central Eastern European societies have established national memory institutes. In the long run, one important aim of these organizations is to alleviate the dividing lines that run through Eastern European societies when it comes to the evaluation of the legacies of the twentieth century. Keeping these multiple points of contentions in mind, it is possible—even if this is necessarily a partial view—to posit that a key tension exists between the memory of Nazism and that of Communism, as this issue often sits at the heart of mnemonic negotiations of national belonging, in these societies today. From this discussion, two hypotheses about the *structure of recognition* in a network of European memory organizations are derived:

1. First, a gap of recognition exists between Eastern and Western European organizations, funneled by diverging interpretations of the past.⁴ An absence of recognition between these two blocs will likely find expression in a cluster of Eastern opposed to a cluster of Western organizations.
2. Second, within the Eastern European memory landscape, there is likely an absence of connections (and therefore, a gap of recognition) between organizations working on Nazism and those working on Communism.

Data and Method

Data for this research was gathered in spring 2014 through the collection of links that memory organizations publish on their websites (for similar methods, see Adamic and Glance 2004; Scheitle 2005; Kurasawa 2014) and that connect them to other organizations.⁵ Organizations studied include museums, memorial sites, victims' associations, NGOs, and governmental bodies working on memory. The network was retrieved by a snowball sampling principle.⁶ Information on the links provided by 264 organizations from 28 countries was collected.

Two methodological issues arise: Would starting with a node inside the Communism cluster yield a different network pattern? And why did the analysis travel only four links from the initial node? With respect to the first, in the context of gathering data for a network, snowballing is not a unidirectional procedure. Nominations do not go one way—they can be reciprocated. This means that the timing (the question of when a node first appears) does not matter for its status in the network. If a single node is important in the network, it will still get a large number of nominations even if it only appears in the second or even third row. The second, methodologically more serious issue is when to *stop* gathering nodes, i.e., when to decide arbitrarily where the network ends. This research stopped after the fifth turn. While it is beyond the capacities of this research to document the entire network, there must be some justifying criteria for this decision. In the present case, it is the size of the Communism cluster documented. The number of nodes dealing exclusively with Communism is much smaller than the number of nodes dealing with Nazism, so that the analysis had arguably detected the "end" of the web link network of organizations in the Communism cluster. Either no new nodes appeared or else the new ones that appeared had only been nominated by a single organization, so they were increasingly marginal; or to put the matter less technically, the network *thinned out*. On this basis, the process of data gathering concluded at node 264.

Some organizations do not publish any links on their website, which constitutes missing data because the absence of links altogether does not have anything to say about a lack of recognition for other organizations. Some organizations differentiate between "partners" and "links" on their website. These links were counted as ties of the same quality.[7]

Web links are conceptualized as a broad measure of recognition. It is an empirical assumption that a website link indicates a way of support that one organization expresses for another. In order to gain empirical substantiation for this claim, a brief survey on the meaning and the use of website links was sent out to twenty organizations (considering variation in type of organizations, geographical locations, and topic). Nine answers were received. From these responses, distinct trends around the meaning and the use of website links from the perspective of organizations emerge. For many organizations, website links even signal cooperation; there is a general agreement that they are intended at least as a sign of support for the work of the organizations referenced. For some memory organizations, these links express an expectation of *mutual* support: organizations that are linked to by another organization are expected to reference back to the linking organization. Setting up or removing links must be understood as a type of agency exerted by organizations. Some organizations are committed to removing the link on the website to an organization that in any way violates their own historical or educational mission. Recognition is therefore a more conservative assumption than cooperation, and it captures the variation within uses and meanings of website links quite well. Website links are a way for organizations to decide with whom they would like to be associated with. On this basis, they can be used for a relational analysis.

With respect to the theoretical discussion above, recognition in this network is both an instrumental relationship and a type of cultural signification.

It refers to both recognition as conferring symbolic capital in the field, in the sense of valuing the work of organization or acknowledging that a single organization is an important actor in the field, and recognition as a category of social memory. In the latter sense, recognition is about taking claims of victimhood seriously, of not letting the specific memory of the past that is advocated by this organization be ignored or forgotten.

Findings: Network Characteristics

The network expresses relations at one point in time (spring 2014). Nodes are organizations. Ties are links from one organization to another. Ties can be unidirectional or mutual. For each node, in addition to all ties, four types of attributes were measured in order to compare them and to understand which of these properties might be consequential for the outcome variable recognition: *Geographic Location*—West or East (measured as the Cold War geopolitical territorial order); *Topic*—Nazism, Communism, or both pasts; *Type of Organization*—Memorial Site, Museum/Research Organization, NGO, Governmental Organization, Platform/Funding Organization; *Country of Origin*. The program Gephi was used for visualization and calculation of network measures.

The network is composed of 264 organizations from 28 countries.[8] Of these, in terms of location, 164 are "West," 100 are "East": there are more Western European organizations active in this network. In terms of topic, 182 work on "Nazism," 55 work on "Communism," and 27 work on "both pasts." More organizations in this network work on Nazism than on Communism or "both pasts."

The visualization consists of nodes (organizations) and ties (links between them). The graph was created in the program Gephi, using the Force Atlas and Force Atlas 2 layout algorithms. Figure 11.1 does *not* provide a geographical representation of the location of these organizations; instead, the location of a single node in the network is determined against the background of the general distribution of ties. Although figure 11.1 already provides an idea of subcommunities in the network, a given single distance or proximity between single nodes must be read and interpreted with caution. Questions must be directed toward the graph, as it does not serve as a neutral conveyer of information.

How well integrated is this network? The network's *average degree*, the number of ties that exist between the nodes on average, is 10.5. By network science standards (determined by what distinguishes observed network patterns from random network patterns), this is a fairly high number that demonstrates that the organizations captured form an actual network.

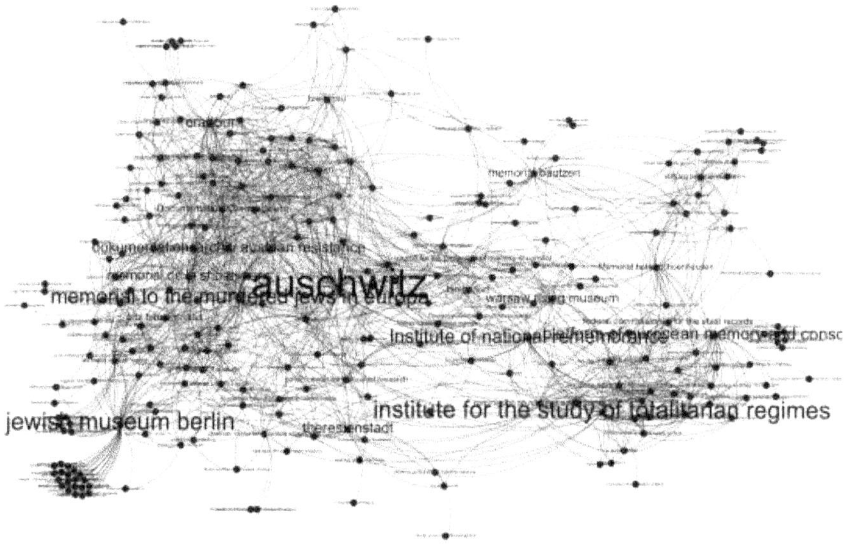

Figure 11.1. The network of memory organizations. Created by the author.

In turn, the *network density* (defined as the number of actual connections divided by the number of possible connections) is rather low. As density is "at the heart of community, social support and high visibility" (Kadushin 2012: 29), the overall network cohesiveness is also rather low.

Which organizations are most prominent in this network? Incoming degrees are the number of times an organization was nominated, i.e., linked

Table 11.1. Incoming degrees: the number of times a single organization was referenced on the website of another.

Name	Incoming Degrees
Yad Vashem	42
Auschwitz-Birkenau State Museum	37
Topography of Terror	33
Buchenwald Memorial	24
Memorial de la Shoah	24
Institute of National Remembrance	22
Ravensbrück Memorial	22
Mauthausen Memorial	21
Imperial War Museum	20
Institute for the Study of Totalitarian Regimes	20

to, by any other organization in the network (only single nominations are allowed). This measure is referred to as the "popularity" of a single node relative to all others in the network. Yad Vashem[9] and the State Museum Auschwitz-Birkenau rank highest in this score. Of the ten most popular institutions, three work on both Nazism and Communism: Buchenwald, the Polish Institute of National Remembrance, and the Czech Institute for the Study of Totalitarian Regimes. Surprisingly, the latter two are relatively young. Most of these have entered the field only in the course of the 2000s, but have achieved a remarkable presence.[10] As shown above, there are more organizations working on the topic of Nazism than on the topic of Communism. The high number of incoming degrees of Yad Vashem and the State Museum Auschwitz-Birkenau is still arguably an indication of the symbolic role of Holocaust memory in this field. While providing an interesting spotlight on power dynamics, this measure does not provide any information about the composition of the network.

Analysis of Network Structure: Topic as the Main Predictor of Recognition

The analysis of network structure aims to identify processes of clustering. Clustering refers to the existence of small subnetworks that are better connected among themselves than to the rest of the network. A high clustering coefficient means that some portions of the network are strongly connected but that the connection between these portions is rather weak. Identifying network clusters provides insights into the patterns of distance and proximity and can therefore be used to better understand the alignment of single nodes. The present network displays significant clusters, as evidenced by the relatively high clustering coefficient. What might drive the clustering? To unpack this question, the following strategy is pursued: First, single properties of organizations that were gathered along with nodes and ties (*topic, location, type of organization, country of origin*) are tested as potential drivers of clustering. Second, mutual ties of recognition are considered separately.

Among the properties of organizations gathered and compared, a single one stands out as the best predictor of network clustering: topic. Topic refers to the content that a single memory organization is working on and can take on three values: Nazism, Communism, or "both pasts" (figure 11.2). To the left, the network shows the cluster of organizations that work on Nazism (gray dots). It is only very loosely connected to the cluster to the right, which shows organizations that work on Communism (white dots). Organizations that work on "both pasts" (black dots) mediate between these two main clusters, but they also constitute a cluster on their own. In the present network,

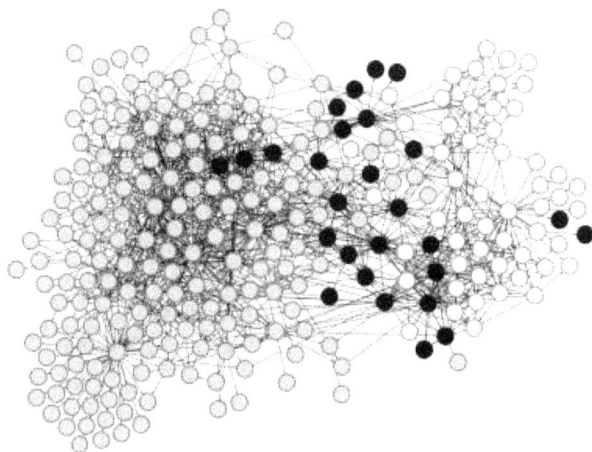

Figure 11.2. Topic as a predictor of recognition: Nazism (gray dots), Communism (white dots), and both (black dots) as the topic focus of a single memory organization. Created by the author.

topic turns out to be the major predictor of recognition. The network visualization underscores this point. The following graph displays only mutual ties to give an even more accurate picture of the clustered cooperation.

Some organizations that are linked on websites also link back to the same source. These cases constitute mutual ties. They provide an additional perspective on clustering, especially because, as is visible in figure 11.3, there is not a single mutual tie between an organization that works on Nazism and one that works on Communism. Within the only two mutually tied clusters, mutual ties are stronger between the Communism cluster and the "both pasts" cluster than they are between the Nazism cluster and the "both pasts" cluster. Some single-directional ties exist between organizations that work on Nazism and those that work on Communism; however, all but one of these run from topic Communism to topic Nazism (not shown).

The variable topic structures the network communities much better than does the property of being "East" and "West." In fact, the links cross through "East" or "West" along the topic property. Hypothesis 1, that the network will be split along a logic of "East" versus "West" position of memory organizations, can therefore be rejected. Equally, the variable type of organization (whether the organization is primarily a memorial site, a museum or research organization, an NGO, a governmental organization, or a platform/funding entity) as well as the variable national context do not predict the network structure as well as topic does.[11] The memory organization network displays a significant structuring along the topic variable. Substantively, in terms of

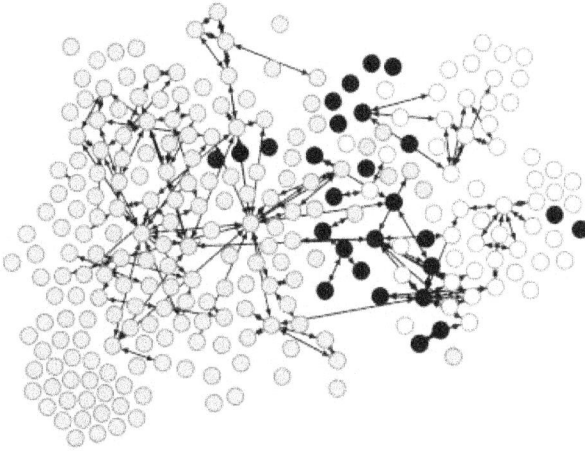

Figure 11.3. Mutual ties and clustering by topic: Nazism (gray dots), Communism (white dots), and both (black dots). Created by the author.

recognition, this means that there is a significant gap of recognition between the Nazism and the Communism clusters. To understand this gap better, the "both parts" cluster will be analyzed in the next section.

The second hypothesis held that Eastern European organizations are likely to be fragmented along the topic variable. This hypothesis is challenged by the data too. In fact, in the present material, Eastern European societies display tighter connections among organizations in their national context than most Western societies who tend to be more transnationally linked. The most fragmented case of a single national context (in terms of topic) is Germany: there, practically no connections exist between organizations working on Nazism and those working on Communism. One important caveat, however, is that there are generally fewer civil society organizations in Eastern Europe (see Howard 2003), and they tend to be more closely aligned with the state. In the present sample alone, the memory landscape in Eastern Europe features many more governmental organizations than does its Western counterpart.

Locating Mediating Roles in the Network

Applying another network measure, betweenness centrality (Marsden 2002), allows us to interpret the structural role of the mediating cluster ("both pasts") in the network. Betweenness centrality is a score that calculates how important a single node is in providing the shortest path to connect remote, not directly linked nodes. In other words, nodes that score highest on this measure potentially connect most distant areas of the network. The State Museum Auschwitz-Birkenau (POL), the Institute for the Study of Totalitarian Regimes (CZ), the Memorial to the Murdered Jews in Europe (GER), and the Institute for National Remembrance (POL) score high on betweenness centrality.

The mediating role that comes with a high score in betweenness centrality can be understood as a type of "brokerage" position held by a single organization. A brokerage position potentially controls the flow of information between nodes and can therefore have an important gatekeeping function; it "creates an indirect relationship where no direct relationship exists" (Fernandez and Gould 1989: 95). Brokerage is based on a tripartite pattern: "Any brokered exchange can be thought of as a relation involving three actors, two of whom are the actual parties to the transaction and one of whom is the intermediary or broker" (ibid.: 91). This is arguably a characterization that also fits the structure of the network uncovered here, with the mediating cluster of organizations focusing on "both pasts" playing the role of broker between the Nazism and Communism clusters. Brokerage can be regarded as a type of mnemonic agency as conceptualized in the introduction to this volume: a type of action that only is possible because of a given structure and that transcends the national container of memory in a particular way. Understanding brokerage as a type of transnational memory action also alerts us to the possibility that transnational connections do not per se create encompassing, or universal, bonds but instead can create new patterns of center and periphery (Shils 1975).

As this research is limited by a single point in time of data collection, the actual power of the mediating role or brokerage position of these organizations to enact change in the larger network cannot be explored in empirical depth here. However, there is a theoretically important observation to be gained from it. The type of agency that comes with potentially connecting two otherwise unconnected clusters in a network is a measure of power. Relationally speaking, the fact that organizations working on Nazism and Communism lock themselves in their respective cluster is what gives the brokering organizations in the "both pasts" cluster a potentially powerful agency in this network. From this, two implications can be drawn: First, the organizations with a brokerage role are likely to be agents of change. Such a power position is not gained out of strategic action; rather, it is because the two clusters are unconnected that the mediating cluster is maximally strengthened in this role. This is a relational process of role formation that can hardly be brought about by instrumental, rational action on the part of a single organization. Second, in this situation, it is an advantage for organizations that work on

Communism to *also* work on Nazism, as it gives them access to the larger network.

Bridges for the Present

In this chapter, network analysis and a small survey were used to create a measure of "recognition" among memory organizations in a European framework in twenty-eight countries. Two hypotheses about the field of European memory were discussed. The first suggests a divide between Eastern and Western European organizations. This hypothesis was rejected in terms of geographical location (there are numerous connections between Eastern and Western actors). The crucial predictor of recognition is the topic an organization is committed to. In 2014, when the data was collected, not a single mutual tie between the cluster commemorating the crimes of Nazism and that commemorating those of Communism could be found, yet the two clusters are *part of the same network* and therefore of a field of memory organizations that, voluntarily or not, exist vis-à-vis each other. Drawing on Klaus Eder's observation that "remembering is a construction that defines not only what is to be remembered but also who is part of the remembering community" (Eder 2006: 267), it can be asserted that *what memories you are committed to also gives you a structural position in a network*. Memory commitments determine who an organization is more likely to be associated with, which in turn also structures the larger dynamics of the field. The second hypothesis held that Eastern European societies are divided among themselves. Within the present empirical framework, they in fact tend to be more unified in terms of links between their memory organizations than most Western cases. Germany fits the model of a divided past most accurately in this network. This finding was formulated with some caveats: the measure of recognition used is much more apt to provide a sense of the global architecture of this network (and to show that it is indeed a network) than to explain specific divides within subcommunities.

Finally, with respect to the larger EU efforts to unite "both pasts," a mixed picture emerges. On the one hand, focusing exclusively on the divides in the European memory landscape fails to acknowledge the patterns of transnational cooperation and recognition that became evident in this analysis (and that are also indicated by transnational projects and cooperative efforts between organizations, as well as traveling exhibitions). The links between memory organizations in Europe are, to a great extent, already distinctly transnational. However, on the other hand, a structure of clustering driven by the content of memory can be discerned. These ties of recognition are arguably formed by cultural processes of interaction, encouraging us to further examine "how actors actively construct relations of solidarity or alliance through the communicative activation (or deactivation) of network ties" (Mische 2011: 88). The analysis has furthermore flagged the role of organizations that engage with "both pasts." Most of them emerged relatively recently, but they already hold a powerful structural position in the network of European memory organizations. For organizations that are concerned with Communism, incorporating Nazism as a *topic* is a success model, as it potentially gives them access to the larger network. This situation very much reflects Tony Judt's assertion that recognition of the Holocaust serves as an "entry ticket" into Western Europe (Judt 2005: 803). Of course, the question of whether these actors actively seek out this strategy or not remains to be explored. But if we accept the assumption that recognition among memory organizations is a measure for the emergence of a European field, then the role of organizations that work on "both pasts" is likely to gain further weight in the future.

Conclusion and Outlook

This chapter has called for the further study of the concept of recognition in memory fields both theoretically and empirically. It has identified brokerage as one type of mnemonic agency that is only conferred by structure. Brokerage creates new possibilities of cooperation. Dynamics in networks are created and sustained not merely by cooperation but also by acts of avoiding each other, as actors can choose to maintain, or increase, social distance. The present volume is committed to finding ways to study the construction and contestation of memory by a variety of actors. I suggest, in line with recent explorations in formal network analysis (Harrigan and Yap 2017), that one dimension of contestation can be further theorized in the power to avoid and ignore others. For the systematic study of social memory, scholars need to pay attention to the power of missing links and withdrawn recognition. Elaborating the concept of relational agency further can offer valuable contributions as we move forward to gain a broader and deeper understanding of both national and transnational processes of memory formation.

Till Hilmar received his PhD in sociology from Yale University and works as a postdoc at Bremen University's SOCIUM–Research Center on Inequality and Social Policy. His research interests include cultural and economic sociology, societal transformations post-1989, social memory, as well as social network analysis and network theory (including mixed methods). In his doctoral thesis, he examined popular experiences of the East German and the Czech transformations after the fall of the Wall in a comparative perspective.

Notes

1. I use the term "Communism" rather than "socialism" or "state socialism" solely for the purpose of clarity and brevity; therefore, I do not engage in the important debate about different historical phases of state socialism.

2. The Active European Remembrance Program (funding period from 2007 to 2013) and the subsequent Europe for Citizens—European Remembrance Program (2014–20), supervised by the Education, Audiovisual and Culture Executive Agency of the European Commission, comprise a particularly interesting framework, as these programs are accompanied by regular conferences bringing together small and midsize memory organizations from all over Europe. Beyond EU institutional venues, see Assmann 2013; Blaive et al. 2011; Mälksoo 2009.

3. Intervening in this debate, some Western European memory actors have underscored that Communism cannot be criminalized as such—since the majority of the population was involved in interchanging roles of perpetratorship and victimhood—and have asserted that the historical distinction between Stalinist mass terror and less extensive repression after 1953 has to be legally and morally upheld (cf. Hilmar 2016: 310, 319).

4. Given the data available, the hypothesis that the gaps of recognition are instead caused by a competition for resources cannot be tested here. This hypothesis merits further research, for instance, through a longitudinal analysis of the possible links between funding and cooperation patterns in EU-funded projects. I thank Aline Sierp and Jenny Wüstenberg for pointing this out.

5. Website links can usually be found in a section designated as "links" or "partners." At the time of data collection, about two-thirds of the organizations had these kinds of links up on their website. Organizations might also publish such links on social media, a source that this research has not considered because of asymmetries in use. Twitter networks, for instance, are an alternative measure, yet a significant number of smaller memory organizations, especially memorial sites, do not use Twitter. Measuring links between people who work in these organizations is another interesting alternative. But this would not so much serve as a measure of recognition than as one of power concentration (e.g., Farrell 2016).

6. Data collection initiated on the website of the organization State Museum Auschwitz-Birkenau. It documented the nominated nodes and, in a second tier, went to the websites of the nodes nominated by the first and documented the nodes there, repeating this four additional times (so that organizations that are four links away from the very first organization are still covered, but for the fifth round, only links to already-featured organizations were recorded).

7. Comprehensive lists of organizations were excluded from the measure: these lists, of which there are only a few cases, are intended as a service to the website visitor. The measure of recognition is lost because such a list does not capture the selection aspect or the working environment of an organization.

8. The following countries are represented by more than ten organizations in this sample: Germany (eighty-six), Poland (forty), France (twenty), Czech Republic (fifteen), Italy (fourteen), Austria (thirteen).

9. Yad Vashem is the only organization outside of Europe in this sample.

10. When the Polish Institute of National Remembrance was founded in 1998, it emerged out of the Chief Commission for the Prosecution of Crimes against the Polish Nation. The latter institution had been operating since the end of World War II, building over time an archival collection covering the Nazi period and later the Communist period. Thus, the outstanding tradition of this institution as a historical archive is arguably an

important factor contributing to its present "popularity." I thank an anonymous reviewer for pointing this out.

11. With respect to type of organization, an interesting descriptive finding is that there is a much larger number of memorial sites in the Nazism cluster than in the Communism cluster. Given the symbolic weight of memorial sites versus archives or other, more technically oriented organizations, this is arguably an important difference. This issue deserves to be explored further also with respect to the institutional consequences of memorializing certain types of violence.

References

Adamic, Lada A., and Natalie Glance. 2005. "The Political Blogosphere and the 2004 Us Election: Divided They Blog." Paper presented at the Proceedings of the 3rd International Workshop on Link Discovery.

Alexander, Jeffrey C. 2004. "Toward a Theory of Cultural Trauma." In *Cultural Trauma and Collective Identity*, edited by Jeffrey C. Alexander, Ronald Eyerman, Bernd Giesen, Neil Smelser, and Piotr Sztompka, 1–31. Berkeley: University of California Press.

Assmann, Aleida. 2013. "Europe's Divided Memory." In *Memory and Theory in Eastern Europe*, edited by Uilleam Blacker, Alexander Etkind, and Julie Fedor, 25–41. New York: Palgrave Macmillan.

Bernhard, Michael H., and Jan Kubik. 2014. *Twenty Years after Communism: The Politics of Memory and Commemoration*. New York: Oxford University Press.

Blaive, Muriel, Christian Gerbel, and Thomas Lindenberger. 2011. *Clashes in European Memory: The Case of Communist Repression and the Holocaust*. Innsbruck: Studienverlag.

Burt, Ronald S. 1992. *Structural Holes: The Social Structure of Competition*. Cambridge, MA: Harvard University Press.

Confino, Alon. 2005. "Remembering the Second World War, 1945–1965: Narratives of Victimhood and Genocide." *Cultural Analysis* 4: 46–75.

Eder, Klaus. 2006. "Europe's Borders: The Narrative Construction of the Boundaries of Europe." *European Journal of Social Theory* 9(2): 255–71.

Emirbayer, Mustafa, and Jeff Goodwin. 1994. "Network Analysis, Culture, and the Problem of Agency." *American Journal of Sociology* 99(6): 1411–54.

Eyerman, Ron, Jeffrey C. Alexander, and Elizabeth Butler Breese, eds. 2011. *Narrating Trauma: On the Impact of Collective Suffering*. Boulder: Paradigm Publishers.

Farrell, Justin. 2016. "Corporate Funding and Ideological Polarization about Climate Change." *Proceedings of the National Academy of Sciences* 113(1): 92–97.

Fraser, Nancy, and Axel Honneth. 2003. *Redistribution or Recognition? A Political-Philosophical Exchange*. London: Verso.

Gould, Roger V., and Roberto M. Fernandez. 1989. "Structures of Mediation: A Formal Approach to Brokerage in Transaction Networks." *Sociological Methodology* 19: 89–126.

Granovetter, Mark. 1985. "Economic Action and Social Structure: The Problem of Embeddedness." *American Journal of Sociology* 91(3): 481–510.

Halbwachs, Maurice. 1992. *On Collective Memory*. Edited by Lewis A. Coser. Chicago: University of Chicago Press.

Harrigan, N., and J. Yap. 2017. "Avoidance in Negative Ties: Inhibiting Closure, Reciprocity, and Homophily." *Social Networks* (48): 126–41.

Hays, Sharon. 1994. "Structure and Agency and the Sticky Problem of Culture." *Sociological Theory* 12 (1): 57–72.

Hilmar, Till. 2016. "Narrating Unity at the European Union's New History Museum: A Cultural-Process Approach to the Study of Collective Memory." *European Journal of Sociology/Archives Européennes de Sociologie* 57(2): 297–329.

Howard, Marc Morjé. 2003. *The Weakness of Civil Society in Post-Communist Europe*. Cambridge: Cambridge University Press.

Judt, Tony. 2005. *Postwar: A History of Europe since 1945*. New York: Penguin.

Kadushin, Charles. 2012. *Understanding Social Networks: Theories, Concepts, and Findings*. New York: Oxford University Press.

Krastev, Ivan. 2017. *After Europe*. Philadelphia: University of Pennsylvania Press.

Kroh, Jens. 2008. "Erinnerungskultureller Akteur und Geschichtspolitisches Netzwerk: Die Task Force for International Cooperation on Holocaust Education, Remembrance and Research." In *Universalisierung des Holocaust? Erinnerungskultur und Geschichtspolitik in internationaler Perspektive*, edited by Jan Moisel and Claudia Eckel, 157–73. Göttingen: Vandenhoeck & Ruprecht.

Kucia, Marek. 2016. "The Europeanization of Holocaust Memory and Eastern Europe." *East European Politics and Societies* 30(1): 97–119.

Kübler, Elisabeth. 2012. *Europäische Erinnerungspolitik: Der Europarat und die Erinnerung an den Holocaust*. Bielefeld: Transcript.

Kurasawa, Fuyuki. 2014. "The Long Shadow of History: The Paradoxes of Iconographic Reiteration in Anti-Slavery Advocacy." *American Journal of Cultural Sociology* 2(1): 3–32.

Leggewie, Claus, and Federike Heuer. 2008. "A Tour of the Battleground: The Seven Circles of Pan-European Memory." *Social Research: An International Quarterly* 75(1): 217–34.

Littoz-Monnet, Annabelle. 2012. "The EU Politics of Remembrance: Can Europeans Remember Together?" *West European Politics* 35(5): 1182–202.

———. 2013. "Explaining Policy Conflict across Institutional Venues: European Union-Level Struggles over the Memory of the Holocaust." *Journal of Common Market Studies* 51(3): 489–504.

Mälksoo, Maria. 2009. "The Memory Politics of Becoming European: The East European Subalterns and the Collective Memory of Europe." *European Journal of International Relations* 15(4): 653–80.

———. 2014. "Criminalizing Communism: Transnational Mnemopolitics in Europe." *International Political Sociology* 8(1): 82–99.

Mark, James. 2010. *The Unfinished Revolution: Making Sense of the Communist Past in Central-Eastern Europe*. New Haven, CT: Yale University Press.

Mark, James, Muriel Blaive, Adam Hudek, Anna Saunders, and Stanisław Tyszka. 2015. "1989 after 1989." In *Thinking through Transition*, edited by Michal Kopeček and Piotr Wciślik, 463–503. Budapest: Central European University Press.

Marsden, Peter V. 2002. "Egocentric and Sociocentric Measures of Network Centrality." *Social Networks* 24(4): 407–22.

Michlic, Beata J. 2006. *Poland's Threatening Other: The Image of the Jew from 1880 to the Present*. Lincoln: University of Nebraska Press.

Mische, Ann. 2011. "Relational Sociology, Culture and Agency." In *The SAGE Handbook of Social Network Analysis*, edited by John Scott and Peter J Carrington, 80–97. London: Sage Publications.

Misztal, Barbara. 2003. *Theories of Social Remembering*. Berkshire: Open University Press.

Olick, Jeffrey K. 1999. "Collective Memory: The Two Cultures." *Sociological Theory* 17(3): 333–48.

Pachucki, Mark A., and Ronald L. Breiger. 2010. "Cultural Holes: Beyond Relationality in Social Networks and Culture." *Annual Review of Sociology* 36: 205–24.

Pakier, Małgorzata, and Joanna Wawrzyniak. 2013. "Memory Studies in Eastern Europe: Key Issues and Future Perspectives." *Polish Sociological Review* 183(3): 257–79.

Powell, Christopher, and François Dépelteau. 2013. *Conceptualizing Relational Sociology: Ontological and Theoretical Issues.* New York: Palgrave Macmillan.

Scheitle, Christopher P. 2005. "The Social and Symbolic Boundaries of Congregations: An Analysis of Website Links." *Interdisciplinary Journal of Research on Religion* 1(1): 1–21.

Shils, Edward. 1975. *Center and Periphery: Essays in Macro-sociology.* Chicago: University of Chicago Press.

Shore, Marci. 2013. *The Taste of Ashes. The Afterlife of Totalitarianism in Eastern Europe.* New York: Broadway Books.

Sierp, Aline. 2014. *History, Memory, and Trans-European Identity: Unifying Divisions.* New York: Routledge.

———. 2017. "1939 Versus 1989—A Missed Opportunity to Create a European *Lieu De Mémoire?*" *East European Politics and Societies* 31(3): 439–455.

Snyder, Timothy. 2010. *Bloodlands: Europe between Hitler and Stalin.* New York: Basic Books.

Stan, Lavinia, and Nadya Nedelsky. 2015. *Post-Communist Transitional Justice: Lessons from Twenty-Five Years of Experience.* Cambridge: Cambridge University Press.

Steinmetz, George. 2008. "The Colonial State as a Social Field: Ethnographic Capital and Native Policy in the German Overseas Empire before 1914." *American Sociological Review* 73(4): 589–612.

Stone, Dan. 2012. "Memory Wars in the New Europe." In *The Oxford Handbook of Postwar European History*, edited by Dan Stone, 714–31. New York: Oxford University Press.

———. 2014. *Goodbye to All That? The Story of Europe since 1945.* Oxford: Oxford University Press.

Taylor, Charles. 1994. "The Politics of Recognition." In *Multiculturalism: Examining the Politics of Recognition*, edited by Amy Gutmann, 25–73. Princeton, NJ: Princeton University Press.

Troebst, Stefan. 2010. "Halecki Revisited: Europe's Conflicting Cultures of Remembrance." In *A European Memory? Contested Histories and Politics of Remembrance*, edited by Małgorzata Pakier and Bo Strath, 56–63. New York: Berghahn Books.

Törnquist-Plewa, Barbara. 2014. "Rhetoric and the Cultural Trauma: An Analysis of Jan T. Gross Book Fear; Anti-Semitism in Poland after Auschwitz." *Memory Studies* 7(2): 161–75.

Uhl, Heidemarie. 2016. "Universalisierung versus Relativierung: Holocaust versus Gulag; Das gespaltene europäische Gedächtnis zu Beginn des 21. Jahrhunderts." In *Gedächtnis im 21. Jahrhundert: Zur Neuverhandlung eines kulturwissenschaftlichen Leitbegriffs*, edited by Liljana Radonic and Heidemarie Uhl, 81–108. Bielefeld: Transcript.

Wüstenberg, Jenny. 2016. "Vernetztes Gedenken? Netzwerkmethoden und Transnationale Erinnerungsforschung." In *Jahrbuch für Politik und Geschichte: Geschichtspolitik und Erinnerungskulturen global (Band 6)*, edited by Harald Schmid and Claudia Fröhlich, 97–113. Stuttgart: Franz Steiner Verlag.

———. 2017. *Civil Society and Memory in Postwar Germany.* Cambridge: Cambridge University Press.

Zhurzhenko, Tatiana. 2012. "Heroes into Victims: The Second World War in Post-Soviet Memory Politics." *Eurozine.* Retrieved 10 May 2018 from https://www.eurozine.com/heroes-into-victims/.

Chapter 12

"Life Was a Precarious Dance"

Graphic Narration and the Construction of a Transcultural
Memory Space in the PositiveNegatives Project

Mihaela Precup and Dragoş Manea

❧

According to recent statistics published by the UN Refugee Agency
(UNHCR), as of June 2017 there are 65.6 million "forcibly displaced people
worldwide," of which 22.5 million are refugees and 10 million are stateless
people (2017b). Of these, 17 percent are hosted in Europe; 2,421 people
died in the first half of 2017 while trying to cross the Mediterranean, and
120,167 people managed to survive the dangerous journey by sea (2017a).[1]
Such precise figures—rather than broad references to the "refugee crisis"—are
also picked up by sympathetic segments of the mainstream media, as in a 17
August 2017 article in *The Guardian* titled "Spain Lacks Capacity to Handle
Migration Surge, Says UN Refugee Agency." However, few media outlets
focus on individual stories of displaced individuals, people who survived
human rights violations, or people who are negatively affected by conflict
and corruption in their countries. In the current international climate, few
European and U.S. publications name the victims and survivors of conflict
that arrive on their continents. The only persons identified by name, familial
background, and cultural background are usually victims of terror attacks
and the terrorists themselves.[2] Although commonly heard by rescue workers,
activists, and members or various humanitarian organizations, individual
stories of struggle and survival do not circulate widely.

In this context, the ongoing nonprofit project PositiveNegatives (figure 12.1), founded in 2012 and coordinated by British anthropologist and photojournalist Benjamin Dix, makes a conscious attempt to memorialize survivors of conflict and war, as well as facilitate transcultural dialogue through a growing repository of testimonies of resilience and survival. The core of PositiveNegatives is an expanding collection of personal narratives in comic book form (as well as some photography, motion comics, animation, and posters), hosted on the website www.positivenegatives.org, with the motto "True Stories. Drawn from Life." The stories featured in its expanding archive are free and easily downloadable, so that they may not only be read on a laptop, tablet, or smartphone but also distributed in printed form. However, the stories are not only disseminated through the project's website but also through wide-reaching publications such as *The Guardian* and *The Huffington Post*, as well as charitable and media organizations that often commission the works, and through educational institutions.

In this chapter, we are particularly interested in reading PositiveNegatives as a project whose agents participate in the creation of a common memory space, thus advancing transnational, transcultural remembrance in order to activate, mobilize, and regulate reader affect and action. We furthermore argue that PositiveNegatives' ability to signify and enable productive activist praxis stems partly from the fact that it fosters horizontal agency instead of relying on an evident hierarchy of power relations. This is also determined by the larger structure that governs the employment of graphic narration, photography, animation, and testimony at the level of transnational discourse and policy. As such, we situate our reading of PositiveNegatives within what Lucy Bond and Jessica Rapson have referred to as "the transcultural turn" in memory studies (Bond and Rapson 2014: 19)—the scholarly attempt at

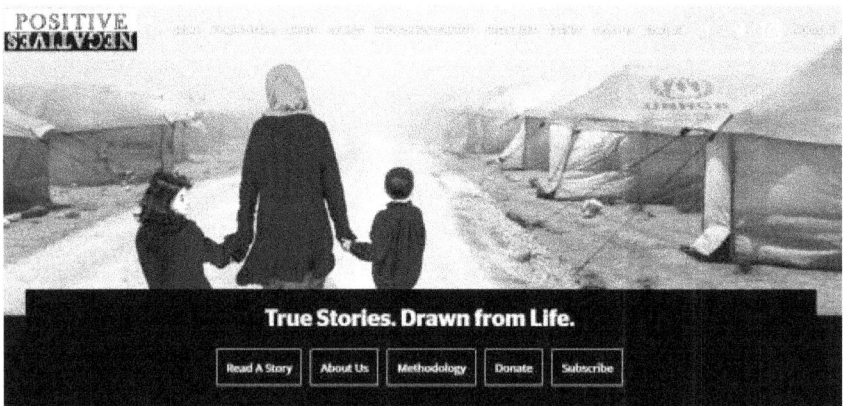

Figure 12.1. The home page of PositiveNegatives. Courtesy of PositiveNegatives Project.

mapping the transmission of memory sites, texts, and media in the age of globalization, within a framework that is particularly attuned to the way in which "commemorative tropes and techniques are transferred between events often distanced in time and/or space" (2014: 19). We are thus particularly interested in exploring graphic narration's ability to engender transnational affiliation and action, drawing on Ann Rigney's claim that literary works are capable of "arousing interest in the history of *other* groups and hence in creating new sorts of affiliations based on 'discontinuous' and cross-border memories" (2014: 389).

Collected by journalists, NGOs, and other campaigners, life narratives about human rights abuses not only provide evidence against perpetrators but also, as Kay Schaffer and Sidonie Smith note, "put a human face to suffering" (2014: 3). Schaffer and Smith thus draw attention to the importance of focusing on the "production, circulation, reception, and affective dimensions of storytelling" (2014: 7) in order to be able to answer questions about how these narratives can contribute to our understanding of the complex cultural, memorial, political, and affective dynamics of the representation of trauma and violence. In the West, this has been shaped by the vocabulary of psychoanalysis and structured around the demands for social justice from the civil rights movement onward, but also by the Holocaust (Schaffer and Smith 2014). Collective trauma—as well as individual trauma caused by ongoing traumatic situations like racism and other forms of discrimination—has been talked about in terms of either how it can and should be represented so that the horrors that caused it may never happen again or how the exemplary nature of the trauma itself defies representation (for an overview of the mimetic/antimimetic debate, as well as the main points of contention in trauma studies, see Rothberg 2000; Meek 2010; Craps 2013). More recently, memory studies scholars have drawn attention to the fact that Western patterns of interpretation and storytelling should not replace other local tropes of trauma-related testimony (Craps 2013) and that they should also not contribute to the consolidation of the current international hierarchy of suffering (Rothberg 2009). At the same time, the wide circulation of Western tropes of memory and trauma is responsible for the production of narratives that may inadvertently follow popular Western tropes of storytelling and healing such as that of the talking cure, which prioritizes event-based rather than ongoing trauma, thus pressuring certain non-Western subjects to produce public statements about personal trauma that may go against local cultural sensibilities (Craps 2013).

The comics medium has allowed for a number of productive approaches to the representation of the refugee experience. While we do not have the space here to put forward an exhaustive enumeration of the various projects and narratives that have attempted to illuminate the refugee experience, we would like to briefly mention some of the most representative works that have shaped the structure of norms and conventions that prefigures the production of a refugee narrative in the comics medium. Largely created by nonrefugee artists, the majority of these works are politically engaged and grounded in a logic of raising awareness of the hardships faced by refugees, both during travel and in the various camps, shelters, or detention centers in which they are placed upon their arrival in Europe or Australia (the two continents most often portrayed in refugee comics). Such works include Nick Olle and Sam Wallman's "At Work Inside Our Detention Centres: A Guard's Story" (*The Global Mail*, 2014), Tings Chak's "Undocumented—The Architecture of Migrant Detention" (*The Architecture Observer*, 2014), Reinhard Kleist's *Der Traum von Olympia: Die Geschichte von Samia Yusuf Omar* (Carlsen, 2015), Safdar Ahmed's "Villawood: Notes from an Immigration Detention Centre" and "Belonging: Post Villawood" (*The Shipping News*, 2015), Mike Loos's *Geschichten aus dem Grandhotel: Comic-Reportagen von Augsburger Design-Studierenden* (Wißner-Verlag, 2016), Carlos Spottorno and Guillermo Abril's *La Grieta* (Astiberri Ediciones, 2016), and Kate Evan's *Threads: From the Refugee Crisis* (Verso, 2017). Although these works do attempt to prioritize refugee voices by including elements of interview, biography, and autobiography, their ideal audience remains largely Western, and the narratives generally serve as a way of documenting refugee suffering in order to create or strengthen structures of empathy among Western readers.

There are, nevertheless, a number of narratives that are aimed at a refugee audience, such as A. David Lewis's *Haawiyat* project, a series of comic books for refugee children, drawing on Middle Eastern folklore. The International Medical Corps likewise published two comic books, illustrated by Diala Brisly, a Syrian cartoonist, and written by its staff: *Going Home Again* and *Home Is Where One Starts From* (2015). The two comics—which were distributed in refugee camps across the Middle East—are also largely geared to young audiences, as they document both the experiences of refugee children and offer important educational insights into the various problems that they might encounter.[3] Refugee artists have also contributed to the discussion, as is the case of Eaten Fish (Ali Dorani), an Iranian cartoonist who spent more than four years in an Australian-run immigration detention center on Manus Island before the International Cities of Refuge Network was able to find him sanctuary in Northern Europe, following a well-publicized "Save Eaten Fish" campaign. His work has been featured in *The Guardian*, the *Washington Post*, and by the ABC (Doherty 2017). Comics workshops have also been organized in Europe (by ComicInvasionBerlin and Ali Fitzgerald in Germany, World Comics Finland in Finland and Africa) and in Australia (by the Refugee Art Project) in order to help refugees tell their own stories in a medium that is not dependent on the mastery of the local language. These projects and narratives testify to the potential of graphic narration to illuminate the refugee experience and to engage with the larger world of politics in ways that may encourage or strengthen empathy among Western audiences, or that may help refugee readers better navigate their present predicaments.

This growing body of graphic testimonies indicates the formation of a wider framework for a transnational work of memory that actively attempts to encourage horizontal agency and enable a productive dynamic between local and global, as well as national and regional, factors. The PositiveNegatives collection of graphic narratives is part of this wider effort to record the refugee experience and contribute to the creation of a "transnational public sphere" (de Cesari and Rigney 2014: 12) by relying on the universal appeal of comics, the documentary strengths of photography, and the collaborative nature of oral testimony. Our chapter thus attempts to offer a theoretical and analytical framework that could easily be applied to other comics about the refugee experience. Here, we first examine the background of the growing archive of the PositiveNegatives project, and afterward we zero in on one specific graphic narrative—titled "Abike's Story"—for which we provide a close reading to answer questions raised by our theoretical positioning at the intersection of memory and trauma studies, photography theory, and comics studies.

We are also interested in understanding the "power dynamics and power struggles that are at the heart of the contemporary production of memory" (de Cesari and Rigney 2014: 11) as reflected in the visual-verbal testimonies of PositiveNegatives, which are both humanizing through the uniqueness of their protagonists and also predictable through the repetition of the same narrative elements that structure their respective ordeals. The sad predictability of the chronology of the life of these subjects—whom we encounter as they have either been granted asylum or are awaiting a decision after a long and traumatic journey—can, in fact, help structure the dialogue among these life stories: where some of the stories stop, others begin; where some of the narrators skip details or cut the story short, others provide more fully-fledged accounts. This is not to say that stories that arise from different cultural spaces can be equated or interchangeable, in spite of local specificities, but rather that the current international climate has produced strikingly similar routes of escape, whose contours are marked by the same networks of solidarity but also mechanisms of exploitation.

PositiveNegatives' Multiple Agents of Memory

The PositiveNegatives project contributes significantly to the production of a shared memory space that relies on collaboration and encourages a certain evenness of the cultural exchange and the creative process. There are two broad categories of memory agents that emerge from even a cursory reading of the PositiveNegatives website: on the one hand, there is the team behind the website itself and, on the other, the narrators of the stories published online. The team is led by Benjamin Dix, who has a doctorate in anthropology and has worked as a photojournalist and later for the United Nations in Sri Lanka; it comprises thirteen people, most of whom have previous experience working with refugees or people affected by conflict and human rights violations. They are responsible not only for the upkeep and constant growth of the website, through research and technical support, but also for many of the events that are created in order to disseminate the work as widely as possible. Since each story comprises two or three components ("comic," "animation," and "resources," but also, in some cases, "translation"), it is evident that the research goes not only into the creation of the comics (which seem to aim more at educating the public emotionally instead of being packed with information) but also in the construction and constant expansion of the "Resources" sections of the website.[4]

The team at PositiveNegatives is purposefully transparent about the manner in which they carry out the work that is behind the creation of comics based on extremely painful personal stories. The process is depicted on the website, under "Methodology," in both comic book form and in a recorded talk given by Dix at the Watson Institute (Dix 2017).[5] While the comic contains general information about funding,[6] it also touches on the main steps in the deeply collaborative process of recording and creation: connecting with the subject, often with help from a translator;[7] spending some time in the subject's community in order to become more familiar with everyday life and to take relevant photographs that can help the artist draw realistic images; and producing a draft of the script, if possible, while they are still in the presence of the subject so that they can change various details or inaccuracies. These are all pre-drawing stages of the production of the comic, after which an artist produces a first draft that is (if the situation permits it) shared with the subjects, so that other details may be revised.[8]

The artists who have worked on the PositiveNegatives stories so far are not generally from the same area and cultural space as the subjects, but Dix has mentioned that they are working toward changing that (Dix 2017). So far, they are Asia Alfasi, a Libyan-British artist; Gabi Froden, a Swedish illustrator; British artists Lindsay Pollock, Rob Davis, and Sophie Wolfson; Nigerian cartoonist Tayo Fatunla; and Syrian animator Wael Toubaji. There are a few other contributors, particularly in those situations where a story is also turned into a motion comic, in which case several people are involved in the production of the soundtrack (voiceover narration and music) as well as the animation. The twenty-seven comics published so far include fourteen stories on displacement from Somalia, four stories by Syrian refugees, a family's experience of the 2009 war in Sri Lanka, a story about drug addiction in Guinea-Bissau, one about disappearance in Columbia, another about being intersex in Uganda, one story on the hardships of the Roma community in Eastern Europe, as well as a story of displacement from Eritrea, human trafficking from Nigeria, the exploitation of an Ethiopian domestic worker in Saudi Arabia, and the story of a Yazidi mother who flees Iraq.[9]

According to the "Events" section of the website, ever since he founded PositiveNegatives in 2012, Dix has been tirelessly promoting and disseminating the work produced and published on the website through lectures at prominent universities around the world, but also at organizations that support human rights, such as Amnesty International, the United Nations, and Human Rights Watch. The PositiveNegatives team has also been involved in the organization of a number of workshops on drawing autobiographical comics for the Migrants Resource Centre (London). Some of the animations produced on the basis of the comics in the website's archive have been aired on TV stations such as BBC Africa and BBC World. Additionally, through Why Comics?, an educational charity launched by PositiveNegatives, the project has expanded to reach fourteen- to eighteen-year-old students and their teachers, who are educated about how to use comics in the classroom. According to the website, Why Comics? has so far been active in over five hundred schools in twenty-six countries.

The laudable transparency of the PositiveNegatives project offers readers some insight not only into how much the voices of the respondents are foregrounded and respected, but also the extent to which their stories are mediated. The decision to publish the process online unveils the complicated scaffolding behind the collaborative work of memory that relies on the selection, translation, editing, adaptation, and dissemination of stories that often contain such violent episodes that a separate kind of recalibration is necessary when they are transposed into the visual-verbal medium of comics.

Constructing a Transnational Memory Space through Graphic Narration

The narratives collected so far in the PositiveNegatives archive are visibly rooted in the specificities of the local cultures to which their subjects belong, but they also extend outside of national borders as they contribute to the creation of a wider mnemonic space. As these stories are told by non-Western actors that are usually unheard and invisible, and placed side by side on positivenegatives.org, they create a collective—but not amalgamated—plot of perpetration and survival, a network of the neglected whose life lines are now inevitably linked and whose testimonies, we argue, produce a space of memory where readers may be interpellated in order to both gauge the degree of their implicated subjectivity (Rothberg 2017) and understand how to become more involved in producing relevant social and political change. However, the creation of this compelling and constantly changing memory space is neither natural nor free; instead, it lays bare the interplay between agency and structure, as agents find themselves both empowered and constrained by certain structural patterns. Thus, the narratives and models of survival contained in these highly mediated stories are conditioned by a few factors: the organization that commissioned the work, the time frame imposed for the production, the fact that the final product needs to be relatively short and usable in classrooms, and the availability of translators who can work with the subject (but who can also later translate the work into other languages and, thus, help disseminate it). At the same time, the visuality of the testimonies is also predicated on the creators' and PositiveNegatives members' understanding of what the medium of comics can or cannot do for the telling of a certain story. The availability of a (largely photographic) visual archive that can help graphic artists illustrate the story is an evidently useful element, but it is important to also look closer at the way in which photography and drawing are employed as mnemonic and narrative strategies in these stories.

Even though the visual style differs depending on the artist, as well as other specific factors like the time frame and the requirements of the organization that commissioned the work, the transnational memory space created along the intersecting lines of the first twenty-seven stories published on the PositiveNegatives website is structured by a narrative blueprint that includes a few common elements. Thus, many stories initially construct a space of nostalgia, of life before conflict, usually described as a period of peace and hope, often in the presence of the whole family. This quickly comes into sharp contrast with a crescendo of suffering triggered by a violent deterioration of the general state of affairs in the narrators' countries, which negatively affects their condition, followed as it is by a period of hardships that produces displacement. The last part of the narrative structure—in the case of stories of displacement, as most of these are—is an uncertain arrival in a European country, where the denouement of the stories is left open unless the subjects are granted asylum or become reunited with their families. In either case, the policies of different countries are rarely discussed.

There are few or no details that might anchor the various stories in a specific political spectrum, as the narrators tend to find themselves at the mercy of overwhelming social and political forces whose clash they simply attempt to avoid. Only two stories show protagonists actively taking a political stance: "Hasko" and "Khalid," both featuring narrators who flee Syria after taking part in the protests against the Assad regime.[10] It is not clear whether this choice of narrator is deliberate or not, but at this point in the development of the PositiveNegatives archive, it works to build a collective portrait of its subjects as either apolitical or as people who are overrun by the force of such sweeping political events that they simply cannot struggle against them. In some contexts, opening up a conversation about political inaction would be superfluous and in fact insulting to the survivors, as in "Nadia's Story," where a Yazidi family from Iraq is threatened by ISIS and feels lucky to have been offered the chance to abandon their home instead of being murdered in it. At the same time, the overall absence of political detail is an articulation of the project's human rights activism, which, broadly speaking, focuses away from the political inclinations of vulnerable subjects and more on their quality as human beings worthy of protection (Beitz 2011).

However, the fact that sometimes a subject's misfortunes are summarily listed can distract attention from their gravity. The sheer accumulation of individual and collective traumas in one subject's life may, in fact, work against the effort of humanizing them, if the recollection of such moments is not staged through appropriate visual and verbal representation. For instance, in "Magool," a story from the *Meet the Somalis* series, the narrator, a Somali woman who lives in Sweden, goes from a happy life with her first husband and baby daughter to losing her husband, daughter, and parents in the war, within the space of only four panels. This condensation of major events from the subject's life is, on the one hand, understandable considering the fact that the story is only four pages long. At the same time, the main purpose of the *Meet the Somalis* project is not to dwell on the hardships the subjects endured in their home countries but to focus on "integration issues" of the Somali community in Europe and "to engage a wide, general audience" as part of the Open Society Foundations' research on this subject.[11] However, such narrative strategies that rely on a bare-bones enumeration of traumatic events risk obtaining a similar effect as that of media items that offer statistics instead of life stories.[12]

This is where graphic narration provides an important intervention in a narrative process that might otherwise run the risk of being reduced to a summary of misfortunes, by producing visual clues and representations of suffering and destruction. Here, again, some representational restraint can be observed for reasons of space, but also with the intention of preserving the dignity of the subjects and reaching a wide audience. As a consequence, PositiveNegatives artists provide representations of violence that are not extremely graphic. Even though most of the subjects have experienced conflict and war, and some have witnessed the death of family members and friends, it is rare that such events are depicted visually. Graphic scenes of violence are rare, like the beating to death of the narrator's friend by Assad's forces or his own torture ("Khalid") and the killing of two women by ISIS in Syria, their bloody corpses lying in the street ("Dana's Story"). Thus, the comics included in PositiveNegatives demonstrate that it is not always necessary to produce graphic visual representations of perpetration and that the medium of comics can enable the rendition of stories of horror by employing other narrative strategies.

Most of the stories rely on a popular understanding of trauma as an event whose sheer magnitude impairs or even destroys the subject's ability to accurately represent it. These are stories where death, destruction, and violence are recounted by appealing to the vocabulary of comics in order to point out the difficulty of the experience without actually showing it. For instance, in "Nadia's Story," the public burning alive of Yazidi girls in cages is not shown except as a reaction experienced by the narrator, whose terrified eyes mirror the flames. In "Musta," the narrator (who now lives in Leicester after leaving Somalia) does mention "the horrors" of war that he has witnessed in a panel that only depicts him, staring into space and pondering what he has seen. In "Anwar," the focus is once again not on the dead but rather on the suffering of the survivors as they bury the narrator's father in the desert during their arduous journey from Somalia to Kenya. Similarly, in "Faaid" the execution of the protagonist's father and two brothers at the hands of Al-Shabaab in Somalia is not depicted visually as such, and it initially even appears to have been cursorily visited only as a narrative exposition for the son's displacement. However, such summary depictions of human tragedy are firmly placed in the present through the vocabulary of comics, which allows the past and the present to inhabit the same space on the page (Chute 2010).

Thus, the few graphic depictions of traumatic events work not only to provide a sample of the horror that could easily have been depicted in all of the life stories included in the project; they also work to undermine the facile reading of the subjects' arrival in Europe as a happy ending. For instance, in "Khalid" the graphic representation of the traumatic past displaces the haven of the narrator's safe space, an asylum center in Norway where he is awaiting an official decision about his status. In the only full-color panel, we see Khalid walking through a Norwegian forest as he is suddenly interrupted by a post-traumatic memory. The scene of a friend's murder in Syria intrudes upon his present, and he watches it again, frozen, from a small distance. The visual vocabulary depicts haunting (produced by the narrator's PTSD) as presence, thus making visible the work of traumatic memory and offering readers more opportunity for experiencing empathy or at least a more complex understanding of the life stories of refugees, who do not simply sever all mnemonic ties to their past when they arrive in Europe. In fact, another visual hint that supports this interpretation is that narrators are often drawn with bent shoulders, carrying invisible burdens, either traumas or disappointment and exhaustion because of the constant pressure of explaining themselves to others. It is noticeable that there are few actual physical burdens in these stories about people who are forced to pack lightly, who have often either been left behind or simply lost their entire homes and family archives. Instead, they are burdened by the memory of their past traumas and the experience of living with the ongoing trauma of displacement and sometimes discrimination in their adoptive countries.

Another strategy of representing the precise moment of perpetration or loss is to rely more heavily on the scriptural part of graphic narration or on visual clues that make the scene understandable enough so that other—related—visual elements can be used without actually depicting violence. For instance, "Almaz" is the story of an Ethiopian migrant worker who is repeatedly raped, beaten, and finally thrown out of a window by an employer. The page that shows the unbearable routine of her constant exploitation and abuse resembles a calendar, everyday events placed side by side, being given equal attention and neatly separated as in a conventional time-keeping device that records the brutal chronology of perpetration during her time in Saudi Arabia (figure 12.2).

Three of the panels are black and puncture the narrative to provide a short verbal reading of the otherwise wordless unfolding of the events, in three minimalist captions that read like a poem: "For several weeks/Life settled/Into a horrible rhythm." On top of this grid of rhythmic suffering, structured

Figure 12.2. Calendar-like panels from "Almaz," showing the subject's repeated physical and sexual abuse at the hands of her masters. Courtesy of PositiveNegatives Project.

along the main moments of the day, two superposed central panels depicting the narrator and her mother suggest both disconnection and affection beyond absence. The thought bubbles above their heads, each containing one word, "Mother" and "Almaz," respectively, suggest not only that they are thinking of each other but also that they are unable to communicate with each other. Here, graphic representation manages to unfold a tightly packed story that speaks to a common predicament of displaced people who carry with them unseen burdens and are accompanied by thoughts, both comforting and painful, of lost friends and family whose protection and affection they can no longer directly experience.

The denouements of most of the PositiveNegatives stories of displacement specify whether the subject was granted asylum or not;[13] the fact that asylum is, sometimes, presented as the final step of an arduous journey may work to erase or diminish the respondents' subsequent struggle for integration and acceptance in a new community, which is often not recorded. This is precisely where the common space of these stories works against this type of reductionist interpretation of personal and collective trauma, as many of the stories (such as those in the *Meet the Somalis* cluster) pick up the narrative thread after asylum has been granted and show the ongoing suffering caused by exile, prejudice, and being separated from one's family. The mobile archive of PositiveNegatives leaves open gaps in some stories only to fill them in others, thus creating fragmented chronologies of suffering in some stories only to complete them in others; this ongoing process creates the expanding image and memory of a community of suffering.

"Abike's Story": Comics, Photography, and the Work of Memory

In a lecture given at the Watson Institute (Brown University), Dix explains why, even though he started out as a photographer, he turned to comics as the primary medium for PositiveNegatives; he also explains why he decided to incorporate photography in the work of memory performed through this project. Dix's opinions are important to look at in some detail not merely because they mirror many of the reasons comics are both lauded and disregarded, as well as some preconceived notions about the privileged position of photography in the work of memory, but also because they shape the stories included in PositiveNegatives. Some of the logic behind his preference for comics is related to the practical side of the project: interviewing people for a comic is much less intrusive than placing a camera in front of them. The medium also allows him to build a "participatory methodology" (Dix 2017): first he spends time with the respondent; then they share stories, write the script for the comic, and edit it together in order to pare down Dix's own personal interpretation and ensure geographical and cultural accuracy; finally, they go through the artwork. For reasons of safety, comics also proved to be an appropriate medium for telling stories about people without divulging their identities; at the same time, many respondents are excited about becoming comic book characters. Last, but not least, comics can rely on visual literacy for the telling of a story, even if readers do not speak the language in which the comic is written. Dix's high regard of comics is backed by theorists who often attempt to elevate the medium's reputation by emphasizing its special abilities and its unique contribution to storytelling (McCloud 1994; Gardner 2012; Chute 2010, 2016).

Dix also identifies certain representational challenges that comics and photography can or cannot meet, particularly in the work of memory. For instance, he correctly states that comics are able to represent processes that photography cannot, such as "people's memories," and thus "suddenly transcend time and space" (Dix 2017). Secondly, he points out that comics can also—more easily than photography and film—depict traumatic realities such as surviving torture. Still, photography remains an integral part of the process not only when it can ensure geographical accuracy but also because it can reinforce "to the audience that this wasn't a work of fiction, that this actually happened in a time and space" that "this is real" (Dix 2017). Dix's comment taps into the conversation on the narrative possibilities of photography, where scholars have been asking questions related to photography's privileged connection to the real (Barthes 1981), its limited storytelling abilities (Sontag 1977, 2003), its significant narrative potential (Butler 2009), as well as its ideological bias and the spectacle of atrocity it can create (Prosser 2012).

We consider some of these assumptions against a close reading of "Abike's Story," illustrated by Gaby Froden. This is the story of a Nigerian woman who is trafficked into the United Kingdom and manages to escape her captor after a year. She is then reunited with her children, from whom she had initially been separated by her husband's family. Dix claims that one of the main issues when working on this story was how to preserve the subject's dignity and avoid turning scenes of sexual abuse into pornography (Dix 2017). Secondly, it was important to provide the respondent with a safe environment and an interviewer with whom she could feel comfortable, and that is why he chose a female cartoonist and worked through Abike's female lawyers (Dix 2017).

The title page of the narrative uses both comics and photography in order to place Abike in a recognizable contemporary British cityscape (figure 12.3). It thus features a drawing of a disheveled Abike, dark circles around her eyes, superimposed against the background of a photograph of a street in London; she is glancing backward, terrified that someone might be following her, even though the street appears to be empty. The photograph of the empty street is an important choice because it anchors the story in the reality of the every-

Figure 12.3. The first panel of "Abike's Story," showing the title character fleeing her captors through the empty streets of London. Illustrated by Gabi Froden. Courtesy of the *Guardian*.

day life of a British city, where vulnerable individuals are often invisible. The image plainly states that no one helps her, even though there are probably people in the houses on the left-hand side, their daily routine untroubled by the stranger's flight for her life.

This story, on the other hand, also displays the ability of graphic narration to intervene in spaces that are inaccessible to photography. In doing so, "Abike's Story" provides important representations of "implicated subjects" (Rothberg 2017) instead of focusing solely on the perpetrators themselves. For instance, the two British prison guards who casually dismiss Abike's tears may not be perpetrators (figure 12.4), but they are bystanders, and the comic suggests that they are also to some degree responsible for her fate, through the routine indifference with which one labels and the other accepts that hers is "the usual sob story."

The frame of interpretation they provide mirrors the indifference of the people behind closed doors from the title page; this time, though, Abike's distress is evident to them; even though their backs are turned, they are already inured to this kind of trauma. Thus, Abike's testimony to the guards is an act of failed communication. This is also indicated by its framing, as Abike speaks from an opening in the prison door, a dark claustrophobic space that foreshadows many others that confine her throughout this comic. Her inability

Figure 12.4. The prison guards casually discuss Abike's situation as she is shown sobbing inside her cell. From "Abike's Story," illustrated by Gabi Froden. Courtesy of the *Guardian*.

to find a sympathetic audience continues to be emphasized through drawings that have us see her at the mercy of faceless adults, the story's arc suggesting that the odds were stacked against her from the beginning, her vulnerability enhanced by other individuals' indifference.

Here, comics as a form of storytelling makes the interpretation of the narrative evident without appealing to Abike's words, thus showing that there is not one single person who is solely responsible for her tragedy, but that there are various degrees of participation, from the people sitting in their homes, oblivious of the woman running for her life, to the prison guards and the perpetrators themselves. This is shown in the comic in the many instances where Abike finds herself mishandled by the disembodied arms of her captors and their clients. Gaby Froden's drawings manage to give readers access to the site of Abike's trauma (figure 12.5), and they also represent sexual violence in a manner that allows it not to be titillating.

Abike is not exposed more than is necessary to suggest that rape did occur; her face is covered, in shame, pain, and also as a futile a gesture of self-protection. The cross-hatchings on the walls of her room evoke the desperate scratches on prison walls, marking countless days of suffering, but also the difficulty of articulating or providing a visual representation for such traumatic moments. In one of the next panels, these cross-hatchings gel into representations of the heads of the perpetrators, not recognizable by any means,

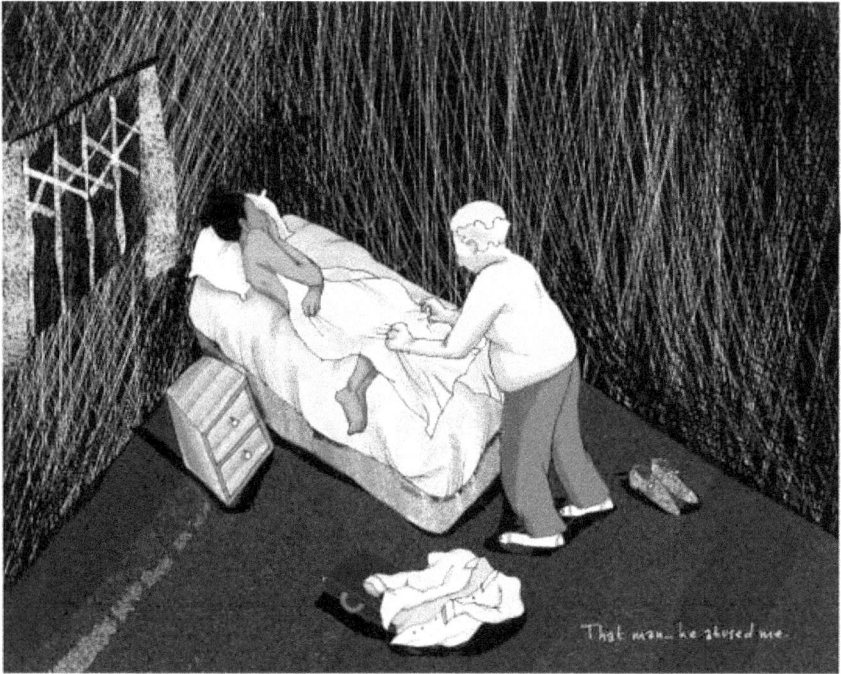

Figure 12.5. A panel depicting the first time Abike, a victim of human trafficking, is abused by one of her abductor's clients. From "Abike's Story," illustrated by Gabi Froden. Courtesy of the *Guardian*.

ordinary in their casual perpetration of such life-altering trauma, but also ordinary in that they will easily blend back into their daily lives as soon as the sexual assault has been completed.

The final panel returns to photography to situate the story in the everyday reality of British life (figure 12.6), while graphic narration is used to depict the psychological state of the narrator as well as to fixate her past trauma in the present. The scene is drawn against the background of a photograph of a neighborhood, apartment buildings once again on the right side; this time Abike is not running but standing still, her hair well-groomed, hands in pockets, smiling as she is watching her two children playing on the grass in front of the buildings. The text tells us that she has been granted asylum, that she has been reunited with her children, but the shadow drawn on the grass behind her shows an outline of her as the same disheveled woman who is held captive, lying on her side, arms drawn toward her head, a gesture of despair or futile attempt at self-protection. The text partly contradicts the story we have just read by claiming that "she doesn't talk about her past"; at the same time, although she is a survivor and has managed to go through a grueling two-year battle to regain access to her children, the representation of her past as

Figure 12.6. The last panel of "Abike's Story," showing the title character in the United Kingdom after she has been reunited with her children. From "Abike's Story," illustrated by Gabi Froden. Courtesy of the *Guardian*.

a shadow that "will haunt her forever" suggests that, in this case, the creators embrace a definition of trauma as a permanent wound, an interpretation that places Abike in the position of perpetual victim. At the same time, the fact that the narrative summarizes two years of hardships in one panel removes the emphasis from what must have been a very trying period in the subject's life and thus places insufficient stress on the role played by British bureaucracy in Abike's trauma. One could also argue though that the photographs included in "Abike's Story" are, in fact, superfluous, since the context of the production of the story—introduced to readers by the website, where they immediately find out they are true stories based on real personal experiences—already fulfills the function of connecting the narratives to the "real."[14] The employment of photography and comics in the story's conclusion confirms the representational premises of the entire PositiveNegatives project.

PositiveNegatives: Real-Life Outcomes and Transnational Remembrance

Even though it may be too early to determine PositiveNegatives' long-term effects in terms of the construction of a transnational memory space, the project has already started producing real-life changes and effects that are more readily quantifiable. For instance, "Abike's Story" became part of the Modern Slavery Act and was added to the set of documents that was submitted to the British Parliament. This produced, in Dix's words, a "humanized policy," not merely "legal, dry" statistics.[15] Similarly, "Fleeing into the Unknown" was added to an Overseas Development Institute policy report, "Journeys to Europe: The Role of Policy in Migrant Decision-Making." The *Why Comics?* charity generates direct feedback from students, teachers, and educational institutions, some of which is published online. Through media outlets that commission the work, as well as NGOs and other human rights organizations, the work is also disseminated to a category of the adult population, not all of which is perhaps already interested in or sympathetic to the situation of survivors of displacement and abuse.[16]

Together, when recorded, placed side by side, and disseminated, the voices of the displaced and persecuted form a transnational space of remembrance in constant flux, around similar experiences that occur in different cultural and political circumstances. In this space, individual experience is not canceled out for the purpose of providing a homogenizing collective narrative, even if perhaps more time could be devoted to cultural and political specificities in order to educate the public and to anchor stories more clearly. PositiveNegatives attempts to prioritize the agency of the respondents and to involve them as much as possible in every stage of the memory-making process, including the artwork. Thus, the project does provide a more concrete personal angle to the general conversation about human rights violations, displacement, and struggle under adverse social and political circumstances while also protecting the identity of the subjects who ask for their stories to remain anonymous. There is so far no evidence that the apparent standardization of the PositiveNegatives stories might stem from what Noga Glucksam identifies, in her contribution to this volume, as a power dynamic that disenfranchises the subjects and limits their freedom as storytellers.

However, PositiveNegatives—for reasons of space, certain requirements of the organizations that commissioned the work, and the attempt to keep the stories usable in the classroom—does not yet provide complex or even sufficient information about the cultural and political backgrounds of the respondents and the conflicts they have fled (these are instead often referred to as merely "the war" or "the fighting"). At the same time, this project has not yet opened up sufficient space for a conversation on issues such as the unreliability of memory and the impact of the ideology of the respondent on his reactions to both events in her home country and other cultural spaces. Another significant matter is the insufficient focus on providing more specific portraits of the perpetrators and the factors that contribute to the process of perpetration. Finally, since readers do not gain sufficient access to more information about norms of suffering and storytelling from the respondents' respective communities, it is difficult to gauge how these life stories are help-ing the respondents therapeutically. In the absence of these significant details, the PositiveNegatives archive runs the risk of producing, over time, a univer-salizing figure of the refugee, divorced from cultural and national specificities. Without a firmer anchoring of each story of migrancy in a real place, a con-crete home—instead of the more abstract, fluid, and dynamic digital space where these stories might converge and circulate—the PositiveNegatives proj-ect cannot pay enough attention to "the continuing significance of location, and, particularly, memories of 'home,' for the meaning-making and affective dimensions of life in the present" (Radstone 2011: 109). On the other hand, through its specific focus on points of contact, commonalities, but most of all physical, social, and cultural mobility, the PositiveNegatives archive remains a good case study that builds up the argument that "movement is what pro-duces memory and our anxieties about pinning it to place" (Creet 2011: 9).

Dix and his team's decision to include several visual media to tell these stories appears to stem from a desire for complete memory. As a consequence, these stories are haunted by a referential privileging of photography as a medium that connects the events represented to a lived reality. However, by appealing to the visual-verbal vocabulary of comics, the project successfully removes spectacle and titillation from the representation of violence and human suffering while at the same time offering access to sites of memory and trauma, since photography cannot be a belated witness to an event. Finally, PositiveNegatives can contribute to a wide audience's understanding of the process of perpetration as a complicated network that goes beyond the perpetrator-survivor binary and instead gesture at the audience's own poten-tial apathy and, thus, complicity through indifference and obliviousness to another person's suffering. This is significant particularly in the current inter-national climate, where Western tropes of memory still dominate the media, where stories of displacement, survival of conflict, and other human rights violations are almost exclusively portrayed through numbers and statistics, and where the need for transnational memory spaces is vitally related to the need for social and political changes that would protect the vulnerable and deflect intercultural tension.

Acknowledgments

Mihaela Precup's research for this chapter was supported by a grant of the Romanian National Authority for Scientific Research, UEFISCDI (grant no. 5/2018, PN-III-P1-1.1-TE-2016-0091, *Transcultural Networks in Narra-tives about the Holocaust in Eastern Europe*). Dragoș Manea's research for this chapter was supported by grant PN-III-P1-1.1-TE-2016-0697, no. 38/2018,

Witnessing Destruction: Remembering War and Conflict in American Auto/biographical and Documentary Narratives, offered by UEFISCDI.

Mihaela Precup is associate professor in the American Studies Program at the University of Bucharest, where she teaches American visual and popular culture, contemporary American literature, and comics studies. Her work explores the graphic representation of violence (particularly in the context of war and conflict), post-traumatic memory, autobiography, and subversive femininity. She has coedited three special issues of the *Journal of Graphic Novels and Comics* (on "War and Conflict" and "Sexual Violence"; with Rebecca Scherr). She is the author of *The Graphic Lives of Fathers: Memory, Representation, and Fatherhood in Autobiographical Comics* (Palgrave Macmillan, 2020).

Dragoș Manea is a lecturer at the University of Bucharest, where he teaches American literature, cultural memory studies, and film studies. His main research interests include the adaptation of history, cultural memory, and the relationship between ethics and fiction. Relevant publications include "Western Nightmares: *Manifest Destiny* and the Representation of Genocide in Weird Fiction" (*Studies in Comics*, 2017), and "Infantilizing the Refugee: On the Mobilization of Empathy in Kate Evans's *Threads from the Refugee Crisis*" (with Mihaela Precup, *a/b Auto/Biography Studies* 35, no. 2, Spring 2020). He is a recipient of the Sabin Award for Comics Scholarship (2017).

Notes

1. These figures were updated on 10 August 2017.
2. There is an important current debate around the issue of naming terrorists in the media. In the context of rising terror attacks, the old tactic of "naming and shaming" terrorists is currently backfiring as some take inspiration from journalism that identifies terrorists by name and background, thus unwittingly inspiring others to regard them as heroes (Kumar 2017: 15).
3. The two projects also, arguably, function as a kind of counternarrative to the message communicated by government-published comics in Europe and Australia. The medium of comics has been employed in both Germany and Russia in order to visually—and thus, presumably, more easily—explain local norms and customs, in a manner that has been read as condescending (Prospero 2017). The Australian Department of Customs and Border Control, on the other hand, published "Afghanistan Storyboard," a comic whose purpose was to discourage people from taking refuge in Australia (Nabizadeh 2016). The work, which has since been removed from the government website after criticism from human rights groups, features a protagonist who regrets his decision to leave war-torn

Afghanistan after he winds up in a refugee detention center with little hope of reaching Australia proper.

4. For instance, the three stories told by subjects who fled Syria, *A Perilous Journey*, is accompanied by fifteen resources that offer the reader information about various issues that are specifically related to the plight of the three storytellers. This section thus includes links to sources that provide details about the refugee crisis and EU immigration rules, as well as short films that show the Syrian perspective on the tragedy unfolding in their country.

5. The talk was given at the Watson Institute, Brown University, in the spring of 2017. The PositiveNegatives YouTube channel contains other recorded materials, such as Benjamin Dix's 2015 TED Talk.

6. The website of the project mentions that it is "funded by or in collaboration with" many charitable and academic organizations and media outlets such as *The Guardian*, the International Committee of the Red Cross (ICRC), The Overseas Development Institute (ODI), Norwegian People's Aid, *The Huffington Post*, Arts Council Lottery Fund, as well as other prestigious institutions.

7. In his Watson Institute lecture, Dix mentions that sometimes they also have conversations with their respondents in the presence of a psychologist or a lawyer, depending on the situation.

8. There are other references throughout the website to the methodology employed for the creation of these stories. At the end of the comic "Enrique's Shadow" there is even photographic evidence of Benjamin Dix talking to a woman who is presumably the sister of the eponymous character, who is one of the one hundred thousand disappeared from Colombia.

9. The PositiveNegatives archive is growing, but we limit our comments in this chapter to the twenty-seven comics that were published online until the end of 2017.

10. Khalid is imprisoned and still suffers from PTSD at the time of his conversation with Benjamin Dix.

11. Most of the comics included in the *Meet the Somalis* section do not linger on the life of the subjects before immigration but focus instead on how the narrators and their families have been integrated into the new European spaces they inhabit.

12. Additionally, readers never do find out why the narrator's second husband was prevented from joining her and their daughter in Sweden. This kind of truncated information that the audience receives is sometimes supplemented in the "resources" section.

13. Those narratives that remain open-ended are amended as soon as the PositiveNegatives team finds out if the person has been granted asylum.

14. There are other places in the PositiveNegatives archive where photographs do speak to the audience in a different register: when the interviewer is allowed to take photographic portraits of the subjects. They do not provide an augmented indexical function to the stories, but perhaps they shade some light on the process of representation and the transformative effect of drawing in comic book form.

15. The Modern Slavery Act is "the first piece of UK legislation focusing on the prevention and prosecution of modern slavery and the protection of victims," passed in 2015 in a context where, in the UK, "an estimated 13,000 people are working as slaves in agriculture, hospitality, fishing, private homes, brothels, nail bars and cannabis farms" (Kelly 2015).

16. At present there is little other quantifiable data, as Dix himself has observed. In his Watson Institute Lecture, Dix also admits that he cannot yet estimate the actual results of the project so far and that at least one more year would be necessary for assessments to come back and be quantified in some form.

References

Barthes, Roland. 1981. *Camera Lucida: Reflections on Photography*. Translated by Richard Howard. New York: Hill and Wang.

Beitz, Charles R. 2011. *The Idea of Human Rights*. New York: Oxford University Press.

Bond, Lucy, and Jessica Rapson, eds. 2014. *The Transcultural Turn: Interrogating Memory Between and Beyond Borders*. Berlin: De Gruyter.

Butler, Judith. 2009. *Frames of War: When Is Life Grievable?* New York: Verso.

Chute, Hillary. 2010. *Graphic Women: Life Narrative and Contemporary Comics*. New York: Columbia University Press.

———. 2016. *Disaster Drawn: Visual Witness, Comics, and Documentary Form*. Cambridge, MA: Harvard University Press.

Craps, Stef. 2013. *Postcolonial Witnessing: Trauma out of Bounds*. Basingstoke: Palgrave Macmillan.

Creet, Julia. 2011. "Introduction: The Migration of Memory and Memories of Migration." In *Memory and Migration: Multidisciplinary Approaches to Memory Studies*, edited by Julia Creet and Andreas Kitzmann, 3–28. Toronto: University of Toronto Press.

de Cesari, Chiara, and Ann Rigney. 2014. "Introduction." In *Transnational Memory: Circulation, Articulation, Scales*, edited by Chiara de Cesari and Ann Rigney, 1–25. Berlin: De Gruyter.

Dix, Benjamin. 2017. "Humanitarianism and Art: The Use of Comics and Animation in Human Rights Advocacy." Lecture, Watson Institute, Brown University, Providence, RI, 3 April.

Doherty, Ben. 2017. "Eaten Fish, Manus Island's Refugee Cartoonist, Given Sanctuary in Northern Europe." *The Guardian*. Retrieved 12 May 2018 from https://www.theguardian.com/australia-news/2017/dec/19/eaten-fish-manus-islands-refugee-cartoonist-moves-to-northern-europe.

Gardner, Jared. 2012. *Projections: Comics and the History of Twenty-First Century Storytelling*. Stanford, CA: Stanford University Press.

Kelly, Annie. 2015. "The UK's New Slavery Laws Explained: What Do They Mean for Business?" *The Guardian*. Retrieved 12 May 2018 from https://www.theguardian.com/sustainable-business/2015/dec/14/modern-slavery-act-explained-business-responsibilty-supply-chain.

Kumar, Akshaya. 2017. "When Exposing Abusers Is Not Enough." *Human Rights Watch Report 2017*, 15–26. Retrieved 19 August 2017 from https://www.hrw.org/sites/default/files/world_report_download/wr2017-web.pdf.

McCloud, Scott. 1994. *Understanding Comics: The Invisible Art*. New York: Harper Perennial.

Meek, Allen. 2010. *Trauma and Media: Theories, Histories, and Images*. New York: Routledge.

Nabizadeh, Golnar. 2016. "Comics Online: Detention and White Space in 'A Guard's Story.'" *Ariel* 47(1–2): 337–57.

PositiveNegatives. Retrieved 12 May 2018 from https://www.positivenegatives.org.

Prospero. 2017. "Graphic Novels and the Refugee Crisis." *The Economist*. Retrieved 12 May 2018 from https://www.economist.com/prospero/2017/02/23/graphic-novels-and-the-refugee-crisis.

Prosser, Jay. 2012. "Introduction." In *Picturing Atrocity: Photography in Crisis*, edited by Geffrey Batchen, Mick Gidley, Nancy K. Miller, and Jay Prosser, 7–14. London: Reaktion Books.

Radstone, Susannah. 2011. "What Place Is This? Transcultural Memory and the Locations of Memory Studies." *Parallax* 17(4): 109–23.

Rigney, Ann. 2014. "Ongoing: Changing Memory and the European Project." *Transnational Memory: Circulation, Articulation, Scales*, edited by Chiara de Cesari and Ann Rigney, 339–60. Berlin: De Gruyter.

Rothberg, Michael. 2000. *Traumatic Realism: The Demands of Holocaust Representation*. Minneapolis: University of Minnesota Press.

———. 2009. *Multidirectional Memory: Remembering the Holocaust in the Age of Decolonization*. Stanford, CA: Stanford University Press.

———. 2017. "Inheritance Trouble: Migration and Transcultural Holocaust Memory in Contemporary Germany." Keynote lecture at *Transcultural Memorial Forms*, Nordic Summer School, Tallinn, Estonia, 18 March.

Schaffer, Kay, and Sidonie Smith. 2014. *Human Rights and Narrated Lives: The Ethics of Recognition*. Basingstoke: Palgrave Macmillan.

Sontag, Susan. 1977. *On Photography*. New York: Picador.

———. 2003. *Regarding the Pain of Others*. New York: Farrar, Straus and Giroux.

UNHCR. 2017a. "Europe Situation." The UN Refugee Agency. Retrieved 12 May 2018 from http://www.unhcr.org/europe-emergency.html.

———. 2017b. "Figures at a Glance." The UN Refugee Agency. Retrieved 12 May 2018 from http://www.unhcr.org/figures-at-a-glance.html.

Chapter 13

A TRANSNATIONAL NATION

Roma National Identity in the Making

Balázs Majtényi and György Majtényi

❧

According to Pierre Nora, memory in contemporary society no longer exists in its real environment (*milieux de mémoires*), as it did in traditional societies, but instead it exists in places of memory (*lieux de mémoires*). Geographical locations, historical figures, events, texts, and concepts can constitute or mediate cultural memory, thus becoming places of memory. Such places of memory keep changing rather than being constant (1989). In this chapter, we search for the places of memory of the Roma nation's collective past, along with mnemonic practices linked to them, and examine their role in the Roma nation-building process. There are several important loci of Roma nation-building; in this chapter, we show how the Roma civil rights struggle has transcended the nation-state, how this struggle has evolved in the transnational sphere/space, and, relatedly, how the creation of shared transnational places of memory has helped to construct a Roma national identity beyond and alongside the earlier minority identity.

Various Roma organizations and politicians have long proclaimed their political goals of nation-building, with the hope that their recognition as a nation may lead to achieving rights, equality, and better advocacy. We refer to political movements fighting for these goals as "Roma nationalism" in general (Marushiakova and Popov 2001a; Binder 2008). According to László Fosztó (2002: 208), in the case of the Roma, nation-building essentially serves two interlinked goals: on the one hand, unification of Roma communities that have been isolated in the past, and on the other hand, defining common objectives for antidiscrimination policies fighting prejudice and exclusion. The evolving concept of Roma nationhood, therefore, builds on the model of majority nationalisms: common language, culture, history, and symbols (Acton 1974a: 233; Fosztó 2002: 208). The political approach of Roma elites and intellectuals has demonstrated that the imagined Roma nation is born from the interactions between Roma communities. In practice it manifests itself in organizations and interest groups established in the transnational sphere, while in theory it refers to the combination of goals and interests related to their struggle for political recognition. So far, this approach has been shaped by Roma and non-Roma politicians and intellectuals from different countries and transnational organizations (Gheorghe 2013: 41–99).

In our chapter, we analyze primarily the practices of mnemonic actors and agencies involved in the process of the making and reproduction of the shared Roma memory as part of their transnational nation-building. The question whether nation-building reaches the broader groups of the Romani people is beyond the scope of this study. Writing about the Roma as an "imagined community," Mátyás Binder defines the characteristics of the nation-building project in the following manner: "members of a heterogeneous category with different languages, identities and cultures integrating themselves due to external influence" (2010: 173).

Nation-building also appears in the form of struggles of memory politics, a process that involves Roma representatives shaping the Roma nation's places of memory, thus creating the community, and thereby proving the existence of the nation. These aspirations are described as "transnational nationalism" (Kastoryano 2006, 2007; Kapralski 2014), which represents a specific form of nation-building (Marushiakova and Popov 2005; Bernáth 2011; Kapralski 2014). Recently, Romani intellectuals and elites have defined the Roma also as a nation without a nation-state not independently from the "transnational space making" process. This process enables the Roma—as a diasporic population—to create or strengthen ties between the communities living in different nation-states. We describe this phenomenon using the term "transnational nationalism," illustrating also the internal contradictions of Roma nationalism (Acton 1974a: 233). For example, the political movement that seeks to unite the transnational minority communities builds on the model and symbolism of the nation-state and majority nationalisms—common language, culture, history, and national symbols. Thus, transnational Roma nationalism is a nationalist movement, which is in part independent of the nation-state framework. It renounces the objective to form a nation-state, which is the traditional form of the institutionalization of the nation, but it claims to secure rights for all Roma in the transnational sphere similarly to traditional nation-states. This strategy stems partly from the physical and symbolic distances between the different Roma groups, partly from the existence of the transnational institutional system, and partly from the interactions between them. In what follows, we describe the Roma nation-building process, using a bottom-up approach, discussing the events in a political-historical order, and analyzing how the different places of memory were founded. Naturally, it should be emphasized that this study, like other historical works, is retrospective (Lehners 2014: 34): it analyzes past events based on our contemporary knowledge and on recent identity politics struggles.

Furthermore, we examine the mnemonic actors, for example, NGOs, human rights activists, Roma politicians, and scholars, that have been and continue to be involved in the process of building a Roma transnational identity. Besides societal actors, we consider the role of formal institutions of power, i.e., mnemonic agencies, in transnational memory politics.[1] Our analysis follows a sequential order: (1) first, we look at Roma civil rights movements and organizations in given countries (within national borders); (2) next, we examine the history of evolving transnational Roma organizations serving nation-building purposes at the time that came about as a result of the cooperation between national organizations; (3) finally, characterizing the present perspective, we briefly show the role of international and supranational organizations in the formation of the transnational Roma nation. We pay special attention to the following elements of the process: (1) actors and agencies that determine transnational memory politics related to the Roma nation, (2) structures that enable and delimit their actions, (3) practices and mechanisms of remembrance, and (4) outcomes, i.e., the creation and functioning of transnational memory spaces.[2]

The Struggle of Roma Minority Institutions within National Borders

The first substantial Roma civil initiatives emerged within national borders, to the west of the Iron Curtain. We briefly analyze this history, focusing on the German and British civil rights movements, which were the most significant ones for the creation of the first transnational places of memory, i.e., the experience of a nomadic lifestyle in the United Kingdom and the Roma Holocaust in Germany. Furthermore, we consider the emergence of Roma nongovernmental organizations promoting the equality of rights as the beginning of the Roma civil rights movement. Thus, the roots of the current Roma civil rights movement date back to the 1950s, when the first relevant organizations appeared in Germany,[3] although its antecedents had been in East and Central Europe (ECE). For example, in 1901 Bulgarian Roma demanded equal political rights in their Vidin conference and submitted a petition to the National Assembly in 1905 (Binder 2008; Marushiakova and Popov 2001b: 374). Also, the first postwar Roma organizations were founded in East and Central Europe before the emergence of state socialist systems and their assimilation policies (Klímová-Alexander 2006: 605).

Besides the Afro-American civil rights movement in the United States, after 1989 it was only the German case that provided an applicable model for the Roma rights movement in ECE countries, greatly influencing the transnational nation-building process (Romsics 2018: 172). An important reason for the successes of the German civil rights movement was the well-designed network of legal institutions/agencies, because legal institutions determine institution-building and memory policy. In other words, the concept of human dignity in the German Constitution (Grundgesetz) was decisive, as well as the German state's consideration of international institutions and active participation in the building of new institutions of European and international law. In addition, rather than building a tragic historical narrative, unlike ECE countries, the German state eventually managed to successfully confront its historical sins. Finally, economic prosperity in Germany also provided a favorable environment for the Roma civil rights claims.

The earliest collective struggles of the Roma in Germany were related to the demands for justice and reparations for the genocide committed against them during World War II. To this end, in 1956 two Roma (Sinti) brothers and civil rights activists, Oskar and Vinzenz Rose founded the Association of Racially Persecuted People of Non-Jewish Belief (Verband rassisch Verfolgter nicht-jüdischen Glaubens) (Gilad 2002: 115). Their parents were killed in a Nazi extermination camp, and as survivors, they decided to fight for their own and their parents' justice. Besides historical justice, they also advocated for educational, labor, and residential integration. In 1971, Vinzenz Rose founded the Central Committee of Sinti in West Germany (Zentralkomitee der Sinti Westdeutschlands). In 1972, it was an important incident for the civil rights movement when in Heidelberg the police shot Anton Lehmann, a Roma, and in response Roma staged a demonstration evoking the Afro-American civil rights movement. In 1974, Vinzenz Rose erected a monument funded by private donations in Auschwitz-Birkenau to the Roma and Sinti victims (Reemtsma 1996: 136–38). The following words of the Roma civil rights leader Romani Rose, son of Oskar Rose, from a book on Sinti and Roma genocide assumed symbolic meaning within the civil rights fight of the Roma in Germany: "We are one nation" (dass wir ein Volk sind).[4] In 1979, Romani Rose was elected as head of the Central Council of German Sinti and Roma (Zentralrat Deutscher Sinti und Roma) in Heidelberg. Partly due to these efforts, in the 1970s the attention of German politics and public opinion was extended to the "non-Jewish" victims of the Holocaust and their compensation.

Besides the Central Council, West Germany too had various other organizations; differences between them often stemmed from their different policies toward Roma migrants and asylum seekers. In 1968, the International Commission for the Rights of the Roma (Internationale Zigeunerrechtskomission) was founded in Hamburg under the leadership of Rudolf Karway. It focused primarily on cases of Roma immigrants from East and Central Europe. In 1975, the Rom und Cinti Union was founded in Hamburg. The Polish civil rights activist Rudko Kawczynski played a significant role in the establishment and management of this organization, whose main aim was to improve the legal and social conditions for the protection of the Roma and Sinti cultural identities and help Roma migrants and refugees arriving in Germany (Bunescu 2014: 82). According to Kawczynski, Germany had a historical responsibility toward the noncitizen migrant and asylum-seeking Roma, not only toward Roma with citizenship. From the mid-1980s, the Rom Union and the Cologne Rom e.V. also struggled for similar goals.

In 1980, a group of Roma held a hunger strike at the Dachau Concentration Camp Memorial Site to demand justice and moral rehabilitation for their suffering during the Nazi era. Their spokesman was Romani Rose (Matras 2015: 254). The first major political achievement for the West German Roma movement came in 1982, when President of the Federal Republic of Germany (FRG) Karl Carstens and Chancellor Helmut Schmidt formally recognized the persecution of Roma during World War II as racial genocide (Wolfe 2014: 75, 90; Meyer 2013). In November 1985, the next chancellor Helmut Kohl supported this position in Parliament (Bundestag) (Reemtsma 1996: 139–40). In 1987, the Central Council of German Sinti and Roma established a Documentation and Cultural Center (Kultur- und Dokumentationszentrum), which was later supported by the government. With this, the collection of documents chronicling the German Roma collective culture and history was institutionally established (Reemtsma 1996: 142; von dem Knesebeck 2011). Since the 1980s, the German Roma victims of the Holocaust and their family members have been eligible for compensation.[5]

In May 1995, the Central Council achieved recognition for German Sinti and Roma (excluding Roma migrants) as a national minority, which allowed for a stark distinction between migrants and citizens.[6] This happened later than in some ECE countries, for instance in Hungary in 1993. The differentiation originated from the logic of European minority rights protection, which distinguishes between autochthonous national minorities and immigrant minorities. In 1997, German President Roman Herzog also confirmed that crimes committed against Roma during World War II are considered acts of racially motivated genocide, similar to the case of the Jews (Barany 2002:

266). As Romsics states, despite all the efforts listed above, the German state has shown only "limited solidarity" with noncitizen Roma (2018: 183).

The Roma Holocaust as a Place of Memory

Remembrance of the persecution and annihilation of Roma in Germany was an important building block for the birth of the Roma civil rights movement, and has since become a major element of the shared Roma national identity as a unifying negative historical reference point. After World War II, the tragedy of the Roma was hardly discussed in public. This may be due to the Nazi propaganda machine dealing with Roma less consistently than with Jews, annihilating them without registering their death, often as a result of pogroms. Another reason may be the multiple disadvantages and marginal societal status that Roma faced: they could not effectively represent their own interests, and consequently their fate has been less of a concern for the public in the past as well as today (Hancock 1995, 2013; Baumgartner 2013; Kapralski 2013: 230–32). For a long time, Roma did not receive reparations, similarly to the Jewish victims of deportations and their family members. This injustice was an important challenge for the civil rights struggle and for the self-organization of the Roma in Germany. In the 1990s, Roma researchers started writing about the collective history of trauma during the Roma Holocaust. To this end, a new term, the "Porajmos" (the Hungarian Lovara equivalent is "Pharrajimos"),[7] was introduced to signify the collective tragedy (similarly to the Jewish Shoah). Thereafter, Roma historians have carried out historical research entirely from the perspective of the Roma, marking the Porajmos as a common place of memory (Kenrick and Puxon 1972; Hancock 1987: 6–15).

In England, the Roma civil rights movement began evolving after the 1960s, led by Roma, as well as non-Roma politicians and intellectuals who sympathized with the Roma cause. The first political move in England is attributed to Norman Dodds, Labour MP, who represented the constituency of Dartford in the House of Commons from 1945 to 1965, where he regularly spoke up about the rights of Roma. Dodds and William Larmour established the so-called Gypsy Committee and, in 1947, drafted a nine-point charter for their fight for the equality of Roma. The next milestone of the Roma civil rights movement was the establishment of the Gypsy Council in 1966 with the cooperation of Grattan Puxon, a non-Roma journalist. Puxon then assumed the role of council secretary between 1966 and 1971, and Hughie Smith became president. The Council demanded, among other things, equal rights for Roma in education, labor, and housing, access to halting sites for traveler groups, and equal treatment. They also established the *Romani Drom* journal. Undoubtedly, British "black radicalism," with its goal to achieve equality between races, was a model that affected the Roma civil rights movement evolving in Great Britain in the 1960s.[8] This might have been the reason, apart from the societal exclusion of Roma, for categorizing their fight as an antiracist struggle, although some issues concerned all traveling communities in Great Britain and not only Roma (Mayal 2004: 206).

It was a significant achievement for the Roma civil rights movement when Parliament accepted the Caravan Sites Act in 1968, which mandated that councils should provide sufficient halting sites for traveler groups. Since the 1970s, several new Roma organizations have been formed in Britain (Taylor 2008: 187–217; Mayal 2004: 206).

Nomadic Lifestyle (Traveling) as a Place of Memory

For a long time, in Great Britain, as well as in other European countries, the stigmatization of Roma was based on their nomadic, nonsedentary lifestyle. Consequently, the struggles of the Roma civil rights movement in Great Britain largely dealt with this issue, as well as the social disadvantages stemming from it. According to these scientific arguments, Roma wandering between countries and later also within countries have been perennially persecuted due to the restricting state- and local-level regulations governing the lives of wandering groups, and the prohibition of their customs; yet, Roma have managed to preserve their freedom and independence from the laws and society of the non-Roma. Nevertheless, other authors emphasize that there has always been interaction between non-Roma and Roma, or groups considered to be Roma. Therefore, various texts and images depicting their wanderings have turned into an important place of memory, further advancing the Roma identity-building process. Many also connect the identity of the Roma, in general, to a common past and certain elements of tradition, i.e., to the practice of certain traditional Gypsy trades or the nomadic lifestyle. However, as is rather evident in modern times, old customs have lost much of their ability to provide solidarity. As Jean-Pierre Liégeois argued when examining the fate of Gypsy communities after the war, "It is at this point that tradition—having lost its dynamism—turns into ritual: it is transformed from a pillar of identity and lifestyle into a rigid identity in itself, a sort of last refuge" (Liégois 2007: 98).

Various Roma and pro-Roma organizations have been established in other Western, Southern, and Northern European countries since the 1960s, either pioneered by civil initiatives or supported by the state (Klímová-Alexander 2010: 108, 113; Mayal 2004: 204, 233, 235, 241).

In the formerly state socialist East and Central Europe, where the overwhelming majority of European Roma lived, the political system wished to assimilate the Roma partly through coercion, and partly through social measures, which occasionally led to short-lived improvements. In this region, eliminating the nomadic lifestyle was a common political pursuit, while in the West, states and intergovernmental organizations often recognized and protected nomadism as an essential component of Roma identity (Achim 2001: 217).

Meanwhile, within the socialist East and Central European state frameworks, there were some Roma organizations and state-sponsored events (Majtényi and Majtényi 2012: 59–106; Vermeersch 2006: 45–100; Barany 2002: 112–56; Majtényi and Majtényi 2016). In the 1970s and 1980s, numerous Roma organizations were established in the countries of the region, along with the emerging Roma grassroots organizations and civil rights movements (Matras 2015: 256; Trehan 2001: 135–36, 144–45). The Roma participated not only in civil society organizations but also in the political movements of the democratic opposition, for example in Charter 77 in Czechoslovakia, or the establishment of the Phralipe Independent Gypsy Association in 1989 in Hungary,[9] which called for an end to the party-state's Gypsy policy and for the true representation of the Gypsy community (Donert 2010; Blaha et al. 1995; Majtényi and Majtényi 2012: 99). In the same year, the Yugoslav Roma Association was established with a similar aim and to guarantee minority rights for the Roma (Barany 2002: 150).

Thus, in the initial phase of the Roma civil rights movement, it was still within the framework of the nation-state that the places of memory that advanced Roma identity were formed. This was the case for the Roma Holocaust in Germany and the nomadic lifestyle in Great Britain. These memory places, however, had the potential to unite other members of the community of remembrance, who were living beyond national borders; thus, they were growing into transnational places of memory. There was another notable change at the time: the newly established national organizations started to acknowledge the existing systems of Roma cultural traditions and customs, as well as languages and dialects spoken, which had earlier operated on a local level only as a way to recognize the minority group. Thus, they were also becoming shared places of memory and mnemonic practices. As a result, the process of network-building between these national organizations began, initially only within country borders.

From the 1950s onward, the first pro-Roma civil society actors, private individuals and mainly NGOs, initially operating within the framework of the nation-state but later extending beyond national borders, appeared. Due to their interconnection as shared places of memory, they formulated transnational memory politics and identity-building, which later became an essential foundation of Roma nationhood. However, at this state level, Roma politics was still characterized by the logic of the nation-state framework (e.g., restricting rights to citizens) and the narrow definition of Roma as a minority group fighting for their rights.

In the era of globalization, certain places of memory may generally become independent of specific geographic areas. Crossing the realm of localities, they may become transnational places of memory and part of the global discourse, overstepping the world of localities and the borders of nation-states. Places of memory generally intend to interpret the past in the present and often place local or national experiences in a transnational context.

Agents of Roma Transnational Identity-Building

In this section, we examine the role of the first Roma transnational organizations in constructing places of memory, including the shared language, traditions, and culture, which in turn became symbols of the Roma nation. Roma identity-building on a transnational level began in earnest during the early 1970s, though similar, albeit less consolidated, initiatives had existed before.[10] In the following, we focus on the activity of the World Romani Congresses, and particularly on the first Congress, as in our reading they had the most significant role in the process of creating transnational memory places.

The first powerful step toward establishing the Roma transnational movement was the foundation in 1960 of the Communauté Mondiale Gitane (CMG) (the Comité International Tsigane [CIT] after 1967) in France, which aimed to unite Roma communities worldwide. Initially, the agenda of the CIT contained the idea to create a Roma homeland. (It also included more specific tasks, such as the provision of reparations for Roma Holocaust victims and their families worldwide.) Evidently, the historical model for the imagined Roma state was Israel. For a long time, Roma leaders held the belief that, similarly to the persecuted Jewish people, they too would get a chance to establish their own state. After the 1970s, however, transnational forms of nation-building were dominant and largely replaced the nation-state model— a topic that is discussed in the subsequent section of this chapter.

In April 1971, the CIT, in collaboration with the British Gypsy Council, organized the first World Romani Congress in Orpington, near London, funded by the World Council of Churches and the government of India. According to different sources reporting the event, Roma organizations of eight or ten countries—among them also communist states—sent delegates, and there were surely observers from even more countries there.[11] It should be noted that representatives of the Yugoslav Roma played a prominent role at the Congress and later in the leadership of different world organizations (Barany 2002: 151). The Congress established five subcommittees, focusing on social, educational, language, and cultural issues, as well as crimes committed against Roma during World War II. Since the 1971 Congress, Roma organizations in various countries have established transnational agents of nation-building, i.e., the places of memory of Roma nationalism and the political language of this nationalism, linked to transnational memory places and practices. Thanks to these agents, they can speak to all Roma.

The Common Category of Roma as a Place of Memory

At the 1971 Congress, a common appellation for various groups—the Roma—was accepted instead of the many various forms, such as Sinti, Gypsy, or Gitane. Here, we can draw a parallel with the 1950s and 1960s Afro-American civil rights movement, where the category of "black" implied a common denomination that set the group aside from whites, symbolized pride and strength, and became a self-ascribed identity label. The Afro-American civil rights movements created a new self-identification using African American and Afro-American terms. Similarly, the constructed "Roma" category expressed a common (national) identity least associated with prejudice (Bernáth 2011: 59–60). The expression and adoption of Roma identity is connected to Roma political activism; i.e., they are results of a political movement (Vermeersch 2006: 13–15).

National Symbols as Places of Memory

During the Congress, the Roma accepted as a common anthem the Romani language song "Gelem, gelem," originally composed by Jarko Jovanovič in 1969 to the melody of an old Romani folk song and containing references to the scattering, to the persecution, and to the Porajmos. In Hungary, for example, a Hungarian-language song "Zöld az erdő" (The forest is green) is also used as a Roma anthem (which also has a Boyash language version) (Balogh 2011). Furthermore, in 1971, the "Opre Roma" slogan was adopted. The Congress approved a green and blue flag, which had previously been used at a 1933 conference organized by the General Association of the Gypsies of Romania. Since 1933 decorated with a chakra, i.e., a red wheel with sixteen spokes, it has become the international symbol of the Roma. The chakra at the center of the flag symbolizes India, the putative common homeland (Acton and Klimová 2001: 158–60). Furthermore, the Congress asserted the need for a standardized literary language, and the Lovara (Romani) language was temporarily adopted as the official shared language. Together with the shared language, the Romani alphabet was also codified as a first step toward a unified written language. Drawing on the model of Afro-American movements, delegates declared that the Roma are each other's "brothers" and members of the same nation. It was characteristic of the atmosphere of the Congress that, speaking as the leader of the British Gypsy Council, Grattan Puxon said the Roma were feeling part of a large nation rather than a separate minority. Later congresses created the common memorial days of the Roma (Mayal 2004: 205).

The Indian Homeland as a Place of Memory

The declaration of the common origin of all Roma and Roma communities has been of similar importance. At the end of the eighteenth century, non-Roma researchers had provided linguistic proof of the alleged common origin.[12] Following the linguistic arguments confirming the common Indian roots, later genetic research also demonstrated the connections between certain Roma groups. The Romani language spoken by various Roma groups was conclusively proven to have Northern Indian roots. (Nevertheless, some still question the common Roma origin, thus the ethnic-based kinship. Instead, they suggest the bond that ties these groups together is the marginal social status of nomadic groups.[13])

There are several Indian and Pakistani groups or castes who speak Northern Indian languages, Roma activists or researchers have identified as supposed kin. They include the Banjara people, who mainly reside in the Punjab state and whose representatives attended the second World Congress in Geneva,[14] and the Sapera people (also known as Kalbelia). When linguistic affinities had been established, institutional and personal relationships emerged between these groups (Ryder and Szilvasi 2017: 93) and the European Roma representatives, as well as between organizations (Bernáth 2011: 57–58). The pronounced celebration of Indian religions, traditions, and culture is visible among European Roma intellectuals. For example, Roma literature borrows not only Hindi themes but also Hindi words. At the same time, in India there is a recently developed tradition of cultivating kinship with Roma people as well. The government of Indira Gandhi already recognized the relationship with the Roma, and the support of the Roma as a kin-group has a tradition in India (Ryder and Szilvasi 2017: 93). Overall, the idea of India as the historical homeland related to Roma identity has become one of the most important places of memory for the transnational nation-building process (Bernáth 2011: 57–58).

History of Dispersion as a Place of Memory

Thus, Indian origin and historical homeland, along with the subsequent migration and scattering as shared experience, have grown into places of memory. Roma intellectuals have already written about the historical homeland and, based on the Jewish case, about the history of dispersion. After the first Congress, the Indian Institute of Romani Studies was opened in Chandigarh (Kenrick 2004: 90–91). The prime minister of the Punjab Province was invited to the next Congress held in Geneva in 1978 (Bernáth 2011: 57). Several Roma intellectuals in turn traveled to India to learn about the historical homeland, and later India became the theme in several literary and artistic works. In the life of Roma communities, as the role of traditions faded into obscurity, disappearing lifestyles and community cultures based on oral tradition have been taken over by commonly written history and the notion of a national past. Thomas Acton's 1974 article in the *New Society* characterizes the utter and unambiguous certainty that surrounded this "imagined" history concerning the common homeland of Roma; Acton claims that Roma "or more properly Rom, or Romanichals, are an Indian people who, leaving India in the tenth century, have slowly dispersed, like Jews, all over the world" (1974b: 563). The origin myth—which should be questioned as much as the unifying origin histories of any other people or nation—is accepted by various Roma communities themselves in different countries.[15] As a result, the need for history writers to form the conceptual Romani language of this history and the writing thereof has arisen.[16]

From then on, the Roma Holocaust, or Porajmos, as we have emphasized earlier, has also appeared as a crucial transnational reference point of shared Roma history. Based on the decision of the World Romani Congress, starting in 1972, the Roma victims, numbering over three thousand, exterminated by SS soldiers in the death camp of Auschwitz in the early morning of 3 August 1944 are to be commemorated. This day is the Roma Holocaust Memorial Day for all Roma victims of the World War II genocide.[17] Porajmos monuments erected in many countries are essential symbols of remembrance and reminders of the tragic events (Bernáth 2011: 58). In other words, not only origin stories but also the discussion about and working through collective traumas have a role in strengthening Roma national identity. It is largely Roma civil rights movements and Roma activists who have carried out the memory work by which the experiences and memories of individuals and the local community are preserved and repeatedly reformulated, and could be combined first at the nation-state level, then also at the transnational level. Meanwhile, the memory of the Roma Holocaust, as a result of these actors' identity politics struggles, has also become a cornerstone of the transnational Roma nation-building process.

Representatives of several international organizations, such as the United Nations, UNESCO, and the European Commission, attended the second Congress in Geneva in 1978. This Congress established a new permanent body, the Romano Ekhipe, better known as Comité International Rom (CIR), later International Romani Union (IRU), whose goal was to represent the interests of Roma in various international organizations. In 1993, the IRU received a consultative status at the UN Economic and Social Council (Acton and Klimová 2001). Later, other transnational organizations were established working along different strategies to improve the situation of the European Roma, e.g., the European Roma Information Office, the European Roma Rights Centre, the European Roma and Traveller Forum, and the European Roma Policy Coalition (McGarry 2011: 284). Remarkably, the dialogue between Roma representatives and international organizations clearly indicates that transnational Roma politics had overcome the challenges due to the lack of political acknowledgment of Roma, or failure to consider Roma as a nation because they have no homeland of their own. By affirming the presence of Roma in the national as well as transnational spheres, transnational memory politics, and the ensuing places of memory, played a significant role in these achievements.

In 1981, the third World Romani Congress was held in Göttingen, Germany. From then onward, the IRU took on the task of organizing all later congresses. The 1981 Congress was supported by the Gesellschaft für Bedrohte Völker, an NGO that campaigned against "all forms of genocide and ethnocide." The focus was once again on the Porajmos and restitution, with Simon Wiesenthal, one of the most authoritative fighters for Holocaust justice, among the speakers. During this event, there were suggestions regarding reparations for Porajmos, and the Indian origin was once again discussed (Acton and Klímová 2001: 160–61).

The fourth World Romani Congress was held in Serock, near Warsaw, in 1990, with a higher percentage of ECE representatives than before, and the majority of the presidency was elected from them (Fosztó 2003: 114). In advance of the Congress, a linguistics conference took place where standardization of the Romani language was discussed (Acton and Klímová 2001: 161–62). One of the most notable events at the fourth Congress was a concert of Roma music, as an independent national form of art symbolizing kinship and national unity. Moreover, the Congress adopted new resolutions about World War II reparations and announced the creation of a new Roma encyclopedia (Kenrick 2007: 294). Recalling the first World Romani Congress in 1971, they adopted 8 April as the National Day of the Roma, which the United Nations subsequently proclaimed as International Roma Day.[18]

The fifth World Romani Congress was held in July 2000 in Prague, Czech Republic.[19] Among the topics discussed were, once again, the need for further standardization of the Romani language, reparations for Roma victims of the Holocaust, and several issues concerning ECE Roma, such as the persecution of the Kosovar Roma or the migration of ECE Roma. A new IRU statute was enacted that declared the goal of recognizing Roma as one nation. The Parliament of the International Romani Union was set up with a permanent Roma representative and decision-making body to formulate the policy of the organization; a committee was also set up as the executive body (Acton and Klímová 2001: 168–200; Matras 2015: 262; Kenrick

2004: 293–95). The document entitled "Declaration of the Roma Nation," which begins with the phrase "We, the Roma nation," was drafted and distributed among the delegates of the Congress (Fosztó 2002: 222–224). The declaration describes the community as a nonstate nation, and, as such, the community formulates their demands (Goodwin 2004). The statement has an impact on documents later adopted by international organizations, such as the Council of Europe.

The sixth Congress was held in Lanciano, Italy, in 2004, and the seventh in 2007 in Zagreb, Croatia. Besides the nation-building project, these congresses decidedly focused on the marginal social status of Roma. In April 2013, during the eighth Congress in Sibiu, Romania, delegates accepted new measures to advance Roma nation-building (McGarry 2010: 143).

There were also new organizations emerging in opposition to the World Romani Congresses, refusing to acknowledge the IRU's authority (Kenrick 2007: 155–56).[20] For example, the second Roma World Congress—as an alternative international assembly of the Roma—was held in Lodz in May 2002; at this event, the organizers—primarily ECE Roma leaders and activists—considered the 1935 crowning of the Polish Roma king as the first World Congress and did not acknowledge the series of the above-mentioned World Romani Congresses organized by the CIT, later the IRU. At the Lodz Ghetto, participants held a commemoration ceremony to the memory of the Porajmos victims. The Congress set up three working groups responsible for discussing issues regarding the international representation of Roma, Holocaust reparations, and issues of Roma refugees and immigrants. At this conference, the Romany Council of Europe was established, and the idea of a European Roma Forum was suggested—an umbrella organization that would have included other Roma organizations. A peace song called "Is Love Enough?" suggested by the Macedonian (Kumanovo) Drom organization became the theme song of the Congress (Kenrick 2007: 155–56).

In sum, the main achievement of the second phase of the Roma civil rights movement is the establishment of the transnational places of memory for Roma national identity, with the help of Roma transnational organizations: these are the common Indian origin; the shared history of being scattered; national unity; such national symbols as the flag, anthem, and slogan; and the common language with its standardized alphabet, literary language, and shared symbols of Roma visual art. The process of creating and canonizing a shared transnational culture began with shared past traumas as historical reference points: namely, the experience of marginalization and exclusion, as well as Porajmos as a place of memory. Therefore, in the 1970s, in relation to the places of memory, the evolving transnational organizations developed appropriate practices and mechanisms for Roma actors to later become independent players in European transnational politics. With the removal of the myopic thinking bound by the concept of the nation-state, the barriers that had earlier prevented grassroots nation-building aspirations also disappeared.

We have to emphasize that after the fall of the Iron Curtain in 1989–90, Roma became the most populous minority first within the Council of Europe and later, after the accession of ECE countries in 2004 and 2007, in all of the European Union. International and supranational organizations as agencies began shaping and continue to shape the course of Roma politics primarily with nonbinding recommendations and policy suggestions. Official documents the organizations adopted, on the one hand, acknowledge the nation-building aspirations of the Roma civil rights movement and, on the other hand, adopt the traditional instruments of European minority protection to the Roma.[21] Transnational politics of memory and the ensuing places of memory played a significant role in these achievements by affirming the presence of Roma in the national as well as transnational spaces. However, primarily in ECE countries, but in other European countries as well, Roma continue to face multiple disadvantages compared to the majority population: they are often debilitated by residential and educational segregation. Moreover, Western European countries have had to confront similar social issues due to the migration of ECE Roma to their jurisdictions. The discourse developed at the European level directs attention to the experience of exclusion, constructs a shared identity, and puts forward several unresolved public policy issues, such as the socially disadvantaged situation of Roma or minority laws in general. The focus of such international and supranational organizations as the Council of Europe, the European Union, and the Organization for Security and Co-operation in Europe has gradually shifted from the process of transnational nation-building to the policies of integration and inclusion, considering the persistent exclusion of Roma in various countries partly due to the antidiscrimination focus of these organizations, and partly because of the ongoing exclusion of Roma. Importantly, Roma politics has assumed a European and transnational character due to the involvement of international organizations and espoused human rights and egalitarianism, as represented by human rights organizations as well as NGOs active in the national and transnational spheres.

Conclusions

In this chapter, we have analyzed the course of events that shaped Roma nation-building, a truly unique process: various players of nation-building and international organizations acted as mnemonic agencies of transnational space-making *outside* of the political framework of the nation-state, thus building practices with local- and state-level Roma communities, in turn elevating the incipient shared (national) identity to a transnational level. We have identified three important phases of this process. In the first phase, Roma activists and intellectuals, along with national NGOs—primarily through their interconnections and places of memory that gradually became collective—created the foundations for the expansion of transnational identity and memory politics, initially on the level of the nation-state, politically representing minorities only within their national borders. It was in this period that historical wandering and the nomadic lifestyle, as well as the experience of past persecution with its worst instance, the Porajmos, developed into the most significant places of memory. In the second phase, activists of the Roma nation-building project established a transnational organization, the World Congress. This way, collective decisions could be made regarding the transnational places of memory related to Roma national identity, and a shared culture could be established and institutionalized, including national symbols, national language, national culture, and national history. Finally, in the third phase, after Roma actors had entered the transnational sphere, truly powerful international and supranational organizations began shaping, and continue to shape, the course of Roma politics (i.e., Roma referring to the single, unified European minority), primarily with nonbinding recommendations and policy suggestions.

In terms of the *participating actors and agencies*, the three consecutive phases can be defined as follows: (1) unfolding of the civil rights movement within the nation-states; (2) founding of international and transnational nongovernmental organizations by actors of the civil rights movement; (3) recognizing the demands of these actors by transnational and international organizations, operating in the transnational sphere. There were several relevant *structures* influencing the behavior of actors that defined Roma politics at various times: (1) first they had to face political institutions within nation-states; (2) then, they formed a transnational network of alliances—partly informal and partly based on formal ties—between actors with institutions, which increasingly defined the context of their actions; and (3), they had to conform to the European institutional system and related international human rights regimes. In terms of *mechanism and practices of remembrance*, the process of Roma nation-building can be described as follows: (1) the first phase was concerned with establishing a shared identity and practices of remembrance for communities living within nation-states;(2) the second phase was about adoption of transnational symbols of national unity, or transnational nation-building; (3) the third phase involves cooperation between supranational and national organizations. Finally, considering places of memory and the *outcomes* of the three phases, the following steps should be highlighted: (1) first, identifying and creating places of memory that relate to the communities living in nation-states; (2) then, creating transnational place(s) of memory; (3) finally, international and supranational organizations recognizing the transnational (national) memory places of the Roma.

There are a few general remarks to be made about the current potential of Roma nation-building. While agents on the European level are capable of shaping the process of transnational nation-building, they cannot act effectively without the cooperation of nation-states. So far, efforts to meaningfully influence national policy-making in order to achieve more active political participation or expand Romani language education have largely been futile. Although the transnational nation-building process was unable to achieve substantial change in either the treatment of Roma by national institutions or in structural discrimination that Roma face, it has successfully created a language that can be employed to formulate demands, and has made the unity of Roma living in different countries an accepted idea. The concept of Roma unity or, in other words the transnational Roma nation, not only came into existence but due to the memory places established, has also become an almost indisputable reality in the transnational sphere, one that is acknowledged by actors and agencies in European politics.

Acknowledgments

We are very much thankful to Jekatyerina Dunajeva, Gergely Romsics, Marek Szilvasi, and Eszter Timár for valuable suggestions and ideas concening the manuscript.

Balázs Majtényi is the director of the Institute of Political and International Studies at ELTE Faculty of Social Sciences as well as Bolyai research fellow at the Hungarian Academy of Sciences. He holds a law degree (Eötvös Loránd University, 1999) and a history MA (Eötvös Loránd University, 2003). He completed his PhD at the same institution in political sciences (2006). His research interests include social history, nation-building, citizenship, and human rights, with a focus on issues of minority, migrant, and refugee protection, the Hungarian public law turn, and social history of the Hungarian Roma.

György Majtényi is a social historian and professor at Károly Eszterházy University. Between 2000 and 2011, he was department head of the National Archives of Hungary. He received his PhD in 2004 from the Eötvös Loránd

University with a thesis on social mobility in post-1945 Hungary and his habilitation in 2010. He completed several research projects in Austria, Germany, Hungary, Slovakia, and the United States thanks to various research grants. His recent research interests include Roma social history, the history of East-Central Europe in the twentieth century, intellectual history, and historiography.

Notes

1. See the definitions of actors and agencies in the introduction to this volume. For more, see Sierp and Wüstenberg 2015.
2. In this study, we consistently use the word "Roma," as it is the generally accepted term employed to define the national identity, while the wording of certain organizations may reflect other past or present self-definitions of Roma.
3. However, it is worth mentioning that comparable associations existed before as well, such as the British Gypsy Lore Society, which was established in 1888 (Mayal 2004: 152.)
4. He addressed his words yet to the Sintis, the German Roma (Rose 1980: 15). This could have referred to the famous two-hundred-year-old words of an author, under the pseudonym of Fürchtegott Leberecht Christlieb, who wrote on the German Jews: "Wir-Teutsche . . . wir ein Volk sind . . ." (Fürchtegott Leberecht Christlieb 1816: 50). See, for more, Rose 1995.
5. See, for more, "Aufruf des Zentralrat-Komitees der Sinti" (Deutschland, 1972); "Zentralrat-Komitee der Sinti an Bundeskanzler, Willy Brandt" (Deutschland, 1972); "Memorandum einer internationalen Delegation von Vertretern der *Romani-Union* und des *Verbands Deutscher Sinti*" (Deutschland, 1979); "Presseerklärung des Verbands Deutscher Sinti" (Deutschland, 1980); "Presseerklärung des Verbands Deutscher Sinti" (Deutschland, 1982); "Pressemitteilung der Bundesregierung" (Deutschland, 1982); "Zentralrat Deutscher Sinti und Roma an den Bundesminister der Finanzen," RomArchive, Civil Right Collection, Collection Jan Selling, retrieved 20 August 2019 from https://www .romarchive.eu/en/collection/i/?section=civil-rights;collection=collection-jan-selling& term=; "Zentralrat Deutscher Sinti und Roma an den Bundesminister der Finanzen" (Germany, 1982), Simon Wiesenthal Archive (SWA), U-Post 7/9/82, Matras 1998.
6. See, for more, "Central Council of German Sinti and Roma," Minority Council of the Four Autochthonous National Minorities of Germany, retrieved 30 November 2018 from http://www.minderheitensekretariat.de/en/minority-council/central-council-of-german-sinti-and-roma/.
7. Ian Hancock recommended the use of the term "Porrajmos" (1995). This is criticized in the following: Stewart 2004: 564. Other names or spellings are found in Auzias 1999; Bársony and Daróczi 2007.
8. See, for more, "Romani Guild Information: Brochure" (United Kingdom of Great Britain and Northern Ireland, 1972); "Towards Gypsy Power," Policy Documents from Association of Gypsy and Romani Organisations, National Gypsy Education Council and the Romani Institute (United Kingdom of Great Britain and Northern Ireland, 1977); "Association of Gypsy Organisations / National Gypsy Education Council Information Leaflet" (United Kingdom of Great Britain and Northern Ireland, 1978), RomArchive, Civil Right Collec-

tion, Collection Thomas Acton, Retrieved 20 August 2019 from https://www.romarchive
.eu/en/collection/i/?section=civil-rights&collection=collection-thomas-acton&term=.

9. Documents on the foundation of Phralipe, Open Society Archive (OSA) 356-2-3, Pál
   Schiffer Personal Papers, 4/10. Public Events Relating to Films: Public Activities.
10. There were several international meetings even before, such as the Cannstadt Conference
   in 1871 and the Sofia Congress in 1905 (primarily attended by Bulgarian Roma). In
   1934, the Romanian Gypsy Union organized the abovementioned Bucharest Conference.
   Similar events were held after World War II as well, for example the European Congress
   in Seville (Mayal 2004: 204).
11. Some reports indicate Roma delegates from only eight countries and observers from
   another four; other reports suggest delegates from ten countries in addition to observers
   from four. Several later sources describe even more participants. The congress has also
   been referred to in different ways. Here, we use the most prevalent name: World Romani
   Congress (Kenrick 1971: 107–108; Kenrick 2007: 189; Acton and Klímová 2001: 158;
   Marushiakova and Popov 2005; Bernáth 2011.)
12. Szilvási 2015: 4; Hancock 1992: 46–49; Hancock 2010: 47–53. Critical description of
   diaspora theory: Vermeersch 2006: 13–14.
13. See for the linguistic diversity and the multiple identities of Roma in East and Central
   Europe: Marushiakova and Popov 2015: 26–54.
14. World Banjara-Roma (Gypsies) Brotherhood Fostering and Cultural Research Founda-
   tion`s letter to Simon Wiesenthal (India, 1981), SWA, U-Post 3/9/81.
15. Ian Hancock (1998) generally emphasizes the significance of positive historical discourses
   that strengthened unity, for example that of discovering a common Indian origin.
16. For example, Hancock gave his book (2002) a Romani title, and he also named the
   periods and important events of Roma history in the Romani language in his chapter
   titles: "O Teljaripe: The move out of India," "O Aresipe: Arrival in Byzantium," or "O
   Baro Porrajmos: The Holocaust." Ian F. Hancock, *We Are the Romani People: Ame sam e
   Rromane džene.*
17. On the European legal recognition of Romani Holocaust, see European Parliament
   resolution on the situation of the Roma in the European Union (EU, 28 April 2005);
   European Parliament resolution of 25 October 2017 on fundamental rights aspects in
   Roma integration in the EU: fighting anti-Gypsyism (2017/2038 INI);
18. European Parliament resolution of 15 April 2015 on the occasion of International Roma
   Day—anti-Gypsyism in Europe and EU recognition of the memorial day of the Roma
   genocide during World War II (2015/2615 RSP).
19. See, for more, *A Report on the World Romani Congress Held in Prague* (United Kingdom
   of Great Britain and Northern Ireland, 2000), RomArchive, Civil Right Collection, Collection Thomas Acton, Retrieved 20 August 2019 from https://www.romarchive.eu/en/
   collection/i/?section=civil-rights&collection=collection-thomas-acton&term=; Thomas
   Acton and Ilona Klimová, 2001.
20. Several Roma organizations have questioned the legitimacy of Roma World Congresses
   or the organizations delegating candidates, for example, because party-state organizations
   from East and Central European countries could be delegated members too.
21. In this chapter we do not investigate the activity of the various international and transnational organizations in detail. See Majtényi and Majtényi 2017; Majtényi and Majtényi
   2018.

References

Achim, Viorel. 2001. *Cigányok a román történelemben* [Gypsies in the Romanian History]. Budapest: Osiris.

Acton, Thomas. 1974a. *Gypsy Politics and Social Change: The Development of Ethnic Ideology and Pressure Politics among British Gypsies from Victorian Reformism to Romany Nationalism.* London: Routledge.

———. 1974b. "True Gypsies: Myth and Reality." *New Society* (6 June): 563–65.

Acton, Thomas, and Ilona Klimová. 2001. "The International Romani Union: An East European Answer to West European Questions? Shift in the Focus of World Romani Congresses 1971–2000." In *Between Past and Future: The Roma of Central and Eastern Europe*, edited by Will Guy, 157–219. Hatfield: University of Hertfordshire Press.

Auzias, Claire. 1999. *Samudaripen: Le Génocide des Tsiganes.* Paris: L'Esprit Frappeur.

Balogh, Lídia. 2011. "Esztétikum közcélra: A szimbólumok, mítoszok, illetve allegóriák közösségi szerepéről, a roma nemzetépítesi törekvések példáján keresztül" [About the Role of Symbols, Myths, and Allegories through the Example of the Efforts of the Roma Nation-Building]. *Pro Minoritate* 3: 144–57.

Barany, Zoltan. 2002. *The East European Gypsies: Regime Change, Marginality, and Ethnopolitics.* New York: Cambridge University Press.

Bársony, János, and Ágnes Daróczi. 2007. *Pharrajimos: The Fate of the Roma during the Holocaust.* Budapest: CEU Press.

Baumgartner, Gerhard. 2013. *The Fate of the European Roma and Sinti during the Holocaust.* Wien/Paris. Retrieved 30 November 2018 from www.romasintigenocide.eu.

Bernáth, Gábor. 2011. "Transznacionális nemzetépítés kirekesztett kisebbségekből: tematizációk és többségi meghatározottság a nemzetközi roma mozgalomban" [Transnational Nation-Building from Marginalized Minorities: Agenda Settings and Majority Definiteness in the International Roma Movement]. In *Nemzetek Európában*, edited by Gergő Prazsák, 53–73. Budapest: ELTE TáTK Szociológia Doktori Iskola.

Binder, Mátyás. 2008. "A roma nemzetépítés—történeti és kulturális antropológiai keresztmetszetben" [Roma Nation Building in a Historical and Cultural Antropological Perspective]. *Eszmélet* 20(77): 130–60.

———. 2010. "Elképzelt kultúra: A roma/cigány kultúra egy lehetséges értelmezése és félreértelmezései" [Imagined Culture. A Possible Interpretation and Misinterpretations of the Roma/Gypsy Culture]. *Eszmélet* 22(86): 172–95.

Blaha, Márta, Gábor F. Havas, and Sándor Révész. 1995. "Nyerőviszonyok: Roma politikatörténet" [Winning Power Relations: Roma Political History]. *Beszélő* 15(5): 20–28.

Bunescu, Ioana. 2014. *Roma in Europe: The Politics of Collective Identity Formation.* New York: Routledge.

Donert, Celia. 2010. "Charta 77 and the Roma." In *Human Rights in the Twentieth Century*, edited by Stefan-Ludwig Hoffmann, 191–212. New York: Cambridge University Press.

Fosztó, László. 2002. "Van-e cigány nemzettudat?" [Is There a Gypsy National Identity?]. In *Társadalmi önismeret és nemzeti önazonosság Közép-Európában*, edited by Csilla Fedinec, 207–24. Budapest: Teleki László Alapítvány.

———. 2003. "Diaspora and Nationalism: An Anthropological Approach to the International Romani Movement." *Regio* 3(1): 102–20.

Fürchtegott, Leberecht Christlieb. 1816. "Warum versagt ihr den Juden das Bügerrecht?" *Nemezis* 8: 50.

Gheorghe, Nicolae. 2013. "Choices to Be Made and Prices to Be Paid: Potential Roles and Consequences in Roma Activism and Policy-Making." In *From Victimhood to Citizenship: The Path of Roma Integration; A Debate*. Edited by Will Guy, 41–99. Budapest: Kossuth.

Gilad, Margalit. 2002. "German Citizenship Policy and Sinti Identity Politics." In *Challenging Ethnic Citizenship: German and Israeli Perspectives on Immigration*, edited by Daniel Levy and Weiss Yffat, 107–20. New York: Berghahn Books.

Goodwin, Morag. 2004. "The Romani Claim to Non-Territorial Nation Status: Recognition from an International Legal Perspective." European Roma Rights Center. Retrieved 30 November 2018 from http://www.errc.org/roma-rights-journal/the-romani-claim-to-non-territorial-nation-status-recognition-from-an-international-legal-perspective.

Hancock, Ian F. 1987. "Gypsies, Jews and the Holocaust." *Shmate: A Journal of Progressive Jewish Thought* 17: 6–15.

———. 1992. "The Hungarian Student Vályi István and the Indian Connection of Romani." *Roma* 36: 46–49.

———. 1998. *The Indian Origin and Westward Migration of the Romani People*. Austin: University of Texas at Austin.

———. 2002. *We Are the Romani People: Ame sam e Rromane džene*. Hatfield: University of Hertfordshire Press.

———. 2010. *Danger! Educated Gypsy; Selected Essays*. Edited by Dileep Karanth. Hertfordshire: University of Hertfordshire Press, 2010.

———. 2013. "1938 and the Porrajmos: A Pivotal Year in Romani History." *Global Dialogue* 15(1): 107–17.

———. 1995. "Responses to the Porrajmos: The Romani Holocaust." In *Is the Holocaust Unique? Perspectives on Comparative Genocide*, edited by Alan S. Rosenbaum, 39–64. Boulder, CO: The Westview Press.

Kapralski, Slawomir. 2013. "The Aftermath of the Roma Genocide: From Implicit Memories to Commemoration." In *The Nazi Genocide of the Roma: Reassessment and Commemoration*, ed. Weiss-Wendt, Anton, 229–251. New York: Berghahn Books.

———. 2014. "Memory, Identity, and Roma Transnational Nationalism." In *Transnational Memory: Circulation, Articulation, Scales*, edited by Chiara De Cesari and Ann Rigney, 195–218. Boston: De Gruyter.

Kastoryano, Riva. 2006. "Vers un nationalisme transnational: Redéfinir la nation, le nationalisme et le territoire." *Revue française de science politique* 4(56): 533–53.

———. 2007. "Transnational Nationalism: Redefining Nation and Territory." In *Identities, Affiliations, and Allegiances*, ed. Seyla Benhabib, Ian Shapiro, and Danilo Petranovic, 159–80. Cambridge: Cambridge University Press.

Kenrick, Donald S. 1971. "The World Romani Congress." *Journal of the Gypsy Lore Society* 50(3–4): 101–108.

Kenrick, Donald. 2004. *Gypsies: From the Ganges to the Thames*. Hertfordshire: University of Hertfordshire Press.

———. 2007. *Historical Dictionary of the Gypies (Romanies)*. 2nd edition. Lanham, MD: The Scarecrow Press.

Kenrick, Donald, and Grattan Puxon. 1972. *The Destiny of Europe's Gypsies*. London: Chatto Heineman, Sussex University Press. (New edition: *Gypsies under the Swastika* [Hatfield: University of Hertfordshire Press, 2009].)

Klímová-Alexander, Ilona. 2006. "The Development and Institutionalization of Romani Representation and Administration. Part 3a: From National Organizations to International Umbrellas (1945–1970)—Romani Mobilization at the National Level." *Nationalities Papers* 34(5): 599–621.

———. 2010. "The Development and Institutionalization of Romani Representation and Administration. Part 3c: Religious, Governmental, and Non-governmental Institutions (1945–1970)." *Nationalities Papers* 38(1): 105–22.

Lehners, Jean-Paul. 2014. "Pleading for a New History of Human Rights." In *The Sage Handbook of Human Rights*, edited by Mark Gibney and Anna Mihr, 22–38. London: Sage.

Liégeois, Jean-Pierre. 2007. *Roma in Europe*. Strasbourg: Council of Europe.

Majtényi, Balázs, and György Majtényi. 2012. *Cigánykérdés Magyarországon, 1945–2010* [Gypsy Issue in Hungary, 1945–2010]. Budapest: Libri.

———. 2016. *A Contemporary History of Exclusion: The Roma Issue in Hungary from 1945 to 2015*. New York: CEU Press.

———. 2017. "Roma nemzetépítés és transznacionális emlékezethelyek" [Roma Nation Building and Transnational Memory Spaces]. *Regio: Kisebbség Kultúra Politika Társadalom*. 25(4): 5–56. DOI: 10.17355/rkkpt.v25i4.186.

———. 2018. "Roma Nation Building and International Organizations." Manuscript.

Marushiakova, Elena, and Vesselin Popov. 2001a. "Historical and Ethnographic Background. Gypsies, Roma, Sinti." In *Between Past and Future: The Roma of Central and Eastern Europe*, edited by Will Guy, 33–53. Hatfield: University of Hertfordshire Press.

———. 2001b. "Bulgaria: Ethnic Diversity—a Common Struggle for Equality." In *Between Past and Future: The Roma of Central and Eastern Europe*, edited by Will Guy, 370–88. Hatfield: University of Hertfordshire Press.

———. 2005. "The Roma—A Nation without a State? Historical Background and Contemporary Tendencies." In *Nationalisms across the Globe*, ed. Wojciech Burszta, Tomasz Kamusella, and Sebastian Wojciechowski, 433–55. Poznan: School of Humanities and Journalism.

———. 2015. "Identity and Language of the Roma (Gypsies) in Central and Eastern Europe." In *The Palgrave Handbook of Slavic Languages: Identities and Borders*, edited by Tomasz Kamusella, Motoki Nomachi, and Catherine Gibson, 26–54. London: Palgrave Macmillan.

Matras, Yaron. 1998. "The Development of the Romani Civil Rights Movement in Germany 1945–1996." In *Sinti and Roma in German-Speaking Society and Literature*, edited by Susan Tebbutt, 49–63. Providence, Rhode Island: Berghahn Books.

———. 2015. *The Romani Gypsies*. Cambridge, MA: Harvard University Press.

Mayal, David 2004. *Gypsy Identities 1500–2000: From Egypcyans and Moon-Men to the Ethnic Romany*. New York: Routledge.

McGarry, Aidan. 2010. *Who Speaks for Roma? Political Representation of a Transnational Minority*. New York: Continuum.

———. 2011. "The Roma Voice in the European Union: Between National Belonging and Transnational Identity." *Social Movement Studies* 10(3): 283–97.

Meyer, Gabi. 2013. "Offizielles Erinnern und die Situation der Sinti und Roma in Deutschland: der nationalsozialistische Völkermord in den parlamentarischen Debatten des Deutschen Bundestages." Dissertation, University of Konstanz, Germany. DOI: 10.1007/978-3-658-00230-5

Nora, Pierre. 1989. "Between Memory and History: Les Lieux de Mémoire." Special issue, "Memory and Counter-Memory," *Representations* 26 (Spring): 7–24.

Reemtsma, Katrin. 1996. *Sinti und Roma: Geschichte, Kultur, Gegenwart*. München: C. H. Beck.

Romsics, Gergely. 2018. "The Roma Holocaust and Memory Games (The Clash of Governmentalities and Roma Activism in an Imperfectly Europeanized Arena)." In *Roma Resistance during the Holocaust and in Its Aftermath: Collection of Working Papers*, edited by Evelin Verhás. Tom Lantos Institute. Retrieved 20 August 2018 from http://tomlantosinstitute.hu/wp-content/uploads/2018/05/RomaResistance_online.pdf.

Rose, Romani. 1980. "Vorwort an die Sinti." In *Sinti und Roma im ehemaligen Bergen-Belsen am 27. Oktober 1979: Erste Deutsche Gedenkkundgebung; "In Auschwitz vergast, bis heute verfolgt": Eine Dokumentation der Gesellschaft für Bedrohte Völker und des Verbands Deutscher Sinti*, 5–18. Göttingen: Gesellschaft für bedrohte Völker.

———, ed. 1995. *Der nationalsozialistische Völkermord and den Sinti und Roma*. Heidelberg: Dokumentations- und Kulturzentrum Dt. Sinti und Roma.

Ryder, Andrew, and Marek Szilvasi. 2017. "Marginality, Activism and Populism: The Roma and Postcolonial Indian Thinkers." *Indian Journal of Social Work* 78(1): 93–112.

Sierp, Aline, and Jenny Wüstenberg. 2015. "Linking the Local and the Transnational: Rethinking Memory Politics in Europe." *Journal of Contemporary European Studies* 23(3): 321–29.

Stewart, Michael. 2004. "Remembering without Commemoration: The Mnemonics and Politics of Holocaust Memories among European Roma." *Journal of the Royal Anthropological Institute* 10(3): 561–82

Szilvási, Marek. 2015. "Roma and the Contradictions of European Inclusion Policies: Citizens Associated with European societies." PhD thesis, University of Aberdeen. Retrieved 14 March 2020 from https://digitool.abdn.ac.uk/webclient/StreamGate?folder_id=0&dvs=1584196944318-409.

Taylor, Becky. 2008. *A Minority and the State: Travellers in Britain in the Twentieth Century*. New York: Manchester University Press.

Trehan, Nidhi. 2001. "In the Name of the Roma? The Role of Private Foundations and NGOs." In *Between Past and Future: The Roma of Central and Eastern Europe*, edited by Will Guy, 134–49. Hertfordshire: University of Hertfordshire Press.

Vermeersch, Peter. 2006. *The Romani Movement: Minority Politics and Ethnic Mobilization in Contemporary Central Europe*. New York: Berghahn Books.

von dem Knesebeck, Julia. 2011. *The Roma Struggle for Compensation in Post-War Germany*. Hatfield: University of Hertfordshire Press.

Wolfe, Stephanie. 2014. *The Politics of Reparations and Apologies*. New York: Springer.

Chapter 14

BORDER-CROSSING CULTURAL INITIATIVES OF MEMORY AND RECONCILIATION ACROSS THE COLOMBIA-PANAMA BORDER

Ricardo A. Velasco Trujillo

In this chapter I discuss three memory initiatives that developed in the border region between Panama and Colombia, with the aim of bringing to light how microscale flows of ideas, resources, processes of cultural activism, and the agency of actors from state institutions and civil society are able to produce transnational or border-crossing memory practices. These practices are entangled in the complex assemblage of initiatives that have emerged as a result of Colombia's national reconciliation process. I use the notion of *border crossing* in relation to the concept of "transnational memory," which, as de Cesari and Rigney (2014) have rightly observed, makes possible an analytical focus on the flow of memories and the material presence of borders. In their pioneer volume on the topic, the authors stress the urgency of identifying new sites for the study of collective remembrance beyond the nation-state. The border between Colombia and Panama in the Pacific coast region represents a key site for studying border-crossing memory practices due to the flow of forcibly displaced populations and an increasing interest in memories related to armed conflict in this remote region. In their entanglement with these complex historical and social processes, the practices that I describe in this chapter engage in what can be termed transnational memories in the making. I not only focus on the geopolitical border between the two countries as the primary object of transgression for memory flows, a border whose increasing militarization has responded in part to forced displacements and other dynamics of Colombia's internal armed conflict after the 1990s; I also consider technological access as border, as well as various symbolic borders being crossed in the initiatives discussed. These transgressions have resulted in the formation of transnational solidarities among social actors belonging to a wide range of sociocultural spheres, including forcibly displaced communities in rural areas at the limits of national sovereignty.

I situate the initiatives discussed in relation to the context of Colombia's current transitional justice conjuncture, bringing to light their relevance and potential for reconciliation among vulnerable displaced communities. This contextualization brings an understanding of some of the structural conditions in which the actors and initiatives described intervene. The focus, however, is on manifestations of agency in institutional and cultural processes that are actively shaping a postconflict imaginary beyond national borders. In a country in the process of coming to terms with more than sixty years of internal conflict, I argue that sustainable memory and reconciliation initiatives need to go beyond institutional models of memory construction and communication outreach strategies. The promotion of cultural processes from the grassroots level, and of the structures of support that enable them, must have a central role because these practices reproduce organically, fostering inclusion and participation in postconflict community-building, as well different manifestations of resilience and civic engagement around concrete community problems. This becomes increasingly relevant in areas with weak institutional presence—and particularly among forcibly displaced victims who have become stateless after forced migration—facing severe limitations in the access to information and resources for the support of this population. The contributions of transnational memory practices that emerge from the grassroots level have greater impact precisely in those spaces of neglect and marginalization. With this focus, I articulate my argument about the crucial importance of grassroots initiatives to counteract institutional centralization and what I term "structural amnesia," a term that helps illuminate the links between violence and state abandonment.

What actors, actions, and forms of agency are enabling border-crossing memory practices among displaced communities? How are these processes contributing to reconciliation efforts beyond national borders? To answer these questions, I first elaborate the historical and political context of the transitional justice process in Colombia to illuminate the relation I propose between border-crossing memories, reconciliation, and culture. I discuss some of the limitations of the institutional model, particularly with respect to the inclusion of communities that have migrated outside Colombia but are still entitled to their rights to truth, justice, and reparation. Second, I discuss civil society initiatives developed across the Colombia-Panama border, including my own critical-creative practice using audiovisual testimony for inclusive transnational memory construction. I focus on revealing new forms of memory practices by describing the communal interventions of a youth cultural collective with displaced populations in Jaqué, Panama. I discuss their approach to memory in articulation with social and environmental justice activism, and I reveal how their practices promote personal and collective projects of civic engagement and participation and a range of opportunities for their members and the communities with which they work. I refer to this form of collective action as "network agency," conceptualized as a network of border-crossing interactions through microscale flows of actors, resources, ideas, and memories involving different social groups. The dynamics of network agency reveal great potential for the strengthening of peace and reconciliation in rural areas at the margins of national sovereignty. They also reveal an understudied potential for activating practices of resilience and solidarity among communities that have been excluded from social and economic development in remote regions in Colombia and Panama.

Methodology

For this study, I rely on qualitative data from interviews conducted in 2016 with staff of Colombia's National Center of Historical Memory in the area of communication and public outreach. I also rely on testimonial documentation and archival research conducted in 2013 for the production of *After the Crossfire: Memories of Violence and Displacement*,[1] a film I produced in collaboration with a group of victims in Colombia's northern Pacific coast region. The discussion of the initiatives with displaced populations in Panama is based on ethnographic research conducted between 2016 and 2018. The empirical approach followed is intended to supersede what has been termed the "methodological nationalism" prevalent in memory studies (Erll 2011; De Cesari and Rigney 2014). Aligned with the third wave in the field and its attention to the complex mobile character of remembrance (Erll 2011), this approach allows me to focus on how processes and practices of memory circulate beyond the nation-state frame—even if produced and institutionalized within. The methodological design included an ethnographic engagement with practices and border-crossing mnemonic spaces produced through the agency of specific social actors. As a result, new articulations of memory practices emerging from tensions between the local, the national beyond state sovereignty, and the transnational are foregrounded. In what follows, I elaborate on the historical and political context that will situate my discussion of these practices.

Transitional Justice and the Emergence and Institutionalization of a Culture of Memory and Reconciliation in Colombia

The recent importance that memory has acquired in Colombia's public sphere can be located within a transnational context in which, by a particular conjunction of cultural, historical, and political factors, the victims of human rights violations and the problem of the reconstruction of the memory of atrocious events have become prominent moral concerns and state responsibilities. In countries that have undergone peace or democratization processes to overcome pasts marked by violence, systematic repression, and human rights violations, as is the case of Colombia, the preponderance and political relevance of memory is intrinsically linked to the institutionalization of transitional justice. Memory practices in Colombia emerge at the intersection of a transnational cultural and institutional entanglement, a space within a "global memory culture" (De Cesari and Rigney 2014; Assmann and Conrad 2010; Levi and Sznaider 2006) localized and propelled by transitional justice dynamics.

Transitional justice is defined as the set of judicial and extrajuridical institutional reforms initiated by a state to facilitate the transition from an authoritarian regime to a democracy, or from a belligerent condition to one of peace, through concrete political agreements (Rettberg 2005; Minow 2002). Even though there is no unique model to follow, the result of the agreements must incorporate measures for the prevention of impunity and guarantee the rights of the victims to *justice, truth, reparation*, and *guarantees of nonrepetition*, the so-called "Joinet Principles." Two elements are of fundamental importance within the operational dynamics of transitional justice with respect to these principles. First, the clarification of truth is not restricted to the juridical domain but conceived to encompass the search for a shared narrative about an abusive past (Maurino 2003). Second, the principle of reparation is not limited to material economic compensation and is understood as a broader category that includes different initiatives of symbolic character aimed to dignify the victims and to promote reconciliation.

In Colombia, it was only after the implementation of Law 975 "of Justice and Peace" in 2005 that the conditions for the emergence of public and official interest in the clarification of the events of the conflict were consolidated. After 2005, and during the subsequent stage of transitional justice that followed the implementation of Law 1448 "of Victims" in 2011, the consolidation of a memory of the conflict became a fundamental state responsibility. Classified as a mechanism of symbolic reparation, the preservation of the memory of atrocious events of violence was formulated by law as a duty of society and the state toward the victims for the reestablishment of their dignity and their rights. As such, the institutionalization of memory in Colombia is entangled in the transnational assemblage of discourses, trans-institutional and trans-governmental policies, practices, and modes of enunciation that define transitional justice according to the Joinet Principles model (Joinet 1997).

The normative framework that emerged as a state response to the atrocities of the armed conflict led to the creation of the National Commission for Reparation and Reconciliation (CNRR), and within it, the Sub-commission of Historical Memory (MH), founded in February 2007. In 2011, with Law 1448's mandate, the MH transitioned into the National Center of Historical Memory (CNMH). As one of its defining objectives and its ethical imperative, the CNMH proposes to "elaborate an inclusive and conciliatory narrative in tune with the voices of the victims" about the origins and evolution of the armed conflict in Colombia (Memoria Histórica 2008: 2). According to Gonzalo Sánchez, the CNMH's director from 2007 to 2018, the inclusion of victims' testimonies carries an ethical and political significance by being formulated as an act of symbolic reparation within the conceptual architecture of Laws 975 and 1448. According to Sánchez, the CNMH hopes that "the victims do not simply feel that truth is being told to them, but that they are actually part of its construction."[2]

The initiatives taken in order to achieve this ethical imperative include a range of cultural practices and activities of commemoration channeled through the annual celebration of "The Week for Memory." This space was designed to give visibility to the official reports presented in the form of editorial and audiovisual cultural products. With these vehicles of dissemination, the CNMH aims to make visible its case studies to a wide audience and construct a space for the dignification and recognition of the victims. In this respect, documentaries and other media products fulfill a crucial function. According to Natalia Rey, former communications coordinator, this is because the audiovisual language helps to emphasize the testimonial record and gives visibility to the victims, and because of the versatility of digital media formats as vehicles for the dissemination of the memories of the victims in the public sphere (personal communication, 2010). Exploiting this versatility became a central concern of the CNMH for reaching out to victims and actors across national borders. In what follows, I discuss the limitations of some of its digital communication initiatives to create an inclusive narrative of the conflict and promote reconciliation among rural communities in remote border regions, in a context defined by unequal access to these resources.

Current Transnational Initiatives of
the National Center for Historical Memory

The implementation of the Law 1448 in 2011 initiated a second stage in the transitional justice process with important institutional transformations, including the MH's transition into the CNMH. With a more robust institutional infrastructure and investments in the area of communications, the emphasis of the CNMH's public engagement campaigns has notoriously shifted from editorial production toward new communications strategies with the aim of bringing the results of the investigations to a wider audience and diverse sectors of the population, including diasporic victims. The production of official reports still is a fundamental aspect of the work of the center. However, since their circulation is limited mostly to academic and specialists' circles, audiovisual products and digital platforms for the dissemination of interactive content have come to the forefront of the CNMH's cultural production. In the words of Adriana Correa, coordinator of the CNMH's communications division,

> The reports about the cases are still central, but the issue is that those reports reach only a very limited audience. We asked ourselves: how do we translate a report into an audiovisual language or into infographics? Each of the reports has to have at least a communicative piece in a different format, for instance a digital edition. . . . Our goal is to bring the content of the report to an ever-larger audience[,] . . . and our website . . . is the launching platform for these new ideas and formats. (Personal interview, 2016)

With an inclusive objective, the statement reveals, significant efforts are being taken to diversify resources for dissemination and for making content accessible.[3] In the case of documentaries, YouTube is the main tool, while social media sites like Facebook and Twitter have become central for communication campaigns. These digital resources enable the possibility of reaching audiences beyond national borders as well as networks of human rights and nongovernmental organizations, memory initiatives, and transitional justice institutions worldwide.

The main initiative that developed with a transnational focus started in 2014, with the aim of including diasporic communities of victims in the process of memory construction and reconciliation. I refer to "Voces del Exilio" (Voices of Exile), a "virtual space" that makes visible personal and collective experiences of exile and return and brings together "the plurality of the memories of all victims of forced displacement beyond national borders" (Centro Nacional de Memoria Histórica 2018). The platform includes testimonies of victims, infographics, links, and resources with information on how the CNMH supports victims and their organizations living in exile.

It is also a space where victims can share information about their own initiatives. The resource is the first to include forcibly displaced and persecuted victims living outside the nation in the agenda of the center. Yet, despite its communicative functions, several problems limit its possibilities for outreach and inclusive transnational memory construction, three of which require particular attention.

First, the complex sociocultural geography of Colombia in the border areas, especially with Panama and Brazil, embeds communities in a situation of isolation. These are remote jungle regions historically marginalized by state institutions, with the highest indicators of poverty and unsatisfied basic needs and poor communications infrastructures. Rural communities in these areas lack proper internet connectivity or, in the majority of cases, even cultural venues where audiovisual materials can be presented or circulated. Internet connectivity is mostly achieved through cellular service, which varies significantly by age, income, and technological literacy. As internet access becomes central to active citizenship in today's social and political life (Brown et al. 2011), the severe gap in access to internet technologies can significantly impact the participation of rural border communities in the process of reconciliation and in the democratic transformations that the transitional justice framework has initiated. This is the case if the main approach to the inclusion of these communities relies on online dissemination and interaction platforms. In Jaqué, Panama, where the population of displaced victims from Colombia's Pacific coast region exceeds three hundred (according to officials of the Colombian consulate), there is only one public facility with five computers and internet access, mostly used by elementary and middle school children. All the victims I interviewed use internet services through cellular connection, which is often interrupted, and almost exclusively for personal communication through apps such as Whatsapp. All informants stated that they do not consult the CNMH's resources, and only a few have taken part in initiatives developed during visits by Colombian institutions of transitional justice. The unequal internet access in border regions and throughout rural Colombia constitutes one of the great challenges faced by these institutions in the implementation and development of their communication and outreach strategies, which is the foundation of their model for the inclusion of rural and diasporic communities in exile into the process of memory construction and reconciliation. It limits the possibilities for the flows of information and resources and their interplay with the institutions and agents that give meaning and enable transnational memory spaces.

Second, a large number of forcibly displaced victims who have crossed the national borders belong to ethnic minorities. Their cultural categories, dynamics, and habits, including uses of technology, greatly differ from those of majoritarian urban and particularly metropolitan groups, to which the commissioners and the CNMH staff belong. While the CNMH and other transitional institutions are driven by an inclusive ethos, their strategies and plans of action do not fully take into consideration the significant cultural gaps between urban groups and rural communities, especially in relation to information consumption and circulation. There are additional limitations of illiteracy among sectors of this population, as in the case of many elders of indigenous groups, which would require differential approaches designed specifically for the needs and limitations of this group. For indigenous communities, Spanish is a second language, and this makes access to the resources available for consultation even more difficult.

Exilio Colombiano, a recent report by the center on the effects of the conflict beyond national borders, states that the side of the history of exile that corresponds to Panama is "the least visible and understood of the memories of the Colombian armed conflict" (Memoria Histórica 2018: 151). The trajectories and experiences of thousands of Colombians who crossed the border along the Darien jungle, according to the report, still remain largely unknown. In the last section, I will discuss how the work of uncovering these experiences has started not through technological developments or communication strategies but through the agency of civil society actors involved in microscale cultural projects. Here it would suffice to suggest that digital transnational initiatives attempting the task of bringing to light the experiences and trajectories of displaced populations who cross the Panamanian border into exile are unlikely to prosper under the conditions discussed. This issue illuminates the complex dynamics between structural factors and the possibilities that these might enable or foreclose for the construction of networks of mnemonic practice or for the effective exertion of agency across these networks. In effect, transnationally focused digital initiatives developed by the CNMH have been more successful with victims that have migrated to urban centers in Ecuador, Venezuela, Spain, and other Latin American nations, where better connectivity as well as more dynamic interactions between mnemonic agents and institutions have yielded higher participation in memory construction. This is evident in the online platform "Voices of Exile," where most of the narratives and testimonies belong to these groups.

A last limitation of current official transnational memory is related to the centralization of institutional practices and resources. The CNMH's initiatives still remain structured around metropolitan approaches to culture, such as the annual celebration of the Week for Memory. The event showcases the cultural production of the center in prestigious cultural venues such as the Museum of the Bank of the Republic and the National Museum of Colombia, among others. Strategic alliances with these venues generate the institutionalization of the center's cultural products in what Pierre Bourdieu (1993) terms "a restricted field of cultural production." Bourdieu argues that within a field of cultural production, restricted cultural circuits have the property of attributing to the cultural products that circulate within the field the power and symbolic capital of those institutions that authorize and make them legitimate. But in contrast to the large-scale circuits of the cultural industries, the aim of which is the maximization of profit, institutions and actors within the field of restricted production "trade" mainly with symbolic values, such as prestige, authenticity, or legitimacy. By structuring their activities around this logic, the CNMH makes an "investment" by which their cultural products capitalize in power and symbolic values of official character. Individual victims and their organizations further contribute to this centralized valorization of cultural capital with the legitimacy that their presence bestows upon the events, if we consider the central importance that victims as social actors have within the transitional conjuncture.

The new communication and public outreach strategies aimed at disseminating the CNMH's work to national and transnational audiences follow a similar pattern. They are launched in the main cultural venues of the capitals of other Colombian departments or of the countries where displaced victims live. Because of unequal access to circuits of cultural production, those able to participate or benefit from these initiatives tend to be near main urban centers. While all efforts are concentrated in diversifying memory initiatives by using versatile formats, and in constructing a robust platform where these products can be viewed or consulted, less attention is being given to the assessment of the actual accessibility of digital resources for remote rural and border communities. The issue of how these resources are used and incorporated into actual practices of memory by actors within and across national borders also remains unattended. This becomes a crucial problem if we consider that transnational memory spaces, as Wüstenberg (this volume) rightfully contests, are enabled and made meaningful "through cross-border linkage and through the practices of transnational agents." In the context discussed, the design of the central initiatives and policies that structure and move official memory construction beyond national borders runs the risk of segregating some communities for participation in memory and reconciliation practices and of reproducing historical structural inequalities in the access to resources.

Victims and human rights activists react to these realities. For instance, at the end of 2016 it was announced that a report on the vast and understudied transnational problem of forced disappearances during Colombia's internal conflict was going to be publicly presented at the National Museum of Colombia. When the event was posted on the CNMH's Facebook page, a member of a victim's organization of Colombia's southeast region, near the border with Brazil, made a critical comment regarding the centralization problem that for him is characteristic of state institutions in general:

Too bad that for you the country is limited to Bogotá and Medellín. It will not do if you dress up as inclusive scholars, and at the end you reproduce and give strength to the centralist practices that have driven our country to be one that promotes exclusion toward the periphery. (Centro Nacional de Memoria Histórica 2016)

The commentary touches upon a sensibility that is deeply engrained in Colombian society, derived from the reality of the government's highly centralized structures, and one of the reasons why most of the benefits of economic and social development do not reach remote rural areas. The commentary does not do justice to the CNMH's efforts and its ethical imperative of inclusion, but it does point out the problem of an inclusive agenda that is difficult to achieve without close analysis of its condition of production, circulation, and reception in a centralized developing nation with most of its resources concentrated in the capital and a few other enclaves of economic development. After discussing the limitations and problems of this institutional model with respect to the challenge of a digital approach to transnational memory construction and the inclusion of border communities in the process, I will discuss two different approaches by civil society actors in the remote Colombia-Panama border.

Grassroots Civil Society Cultural Initiatives of Memory in the Border Region between Colombia and Panama

Audiovisual Testimony and Activist Research
in Memory Construction and Documentary Practice

On 12 December 1999, the Revolutionary Armed Forces of Colombia (FARC) attacked the remote coastal village of Juradó. A platoon of approximately five hundred men besieged the small town, assaulting naval and police bases. One noncombatant civilian and twenty-five members of the Colombian armed forces died in the attack. In addition, thirty-five marines were wounded, a group of seventy-five were taken as hostages, and a large part of the population was forced to leave the town, their homes, and all their possessions. On 14 December, after a forty-eight-hour delay, television news brought the case to light, a single incident among thousands in six decades of internal conflict.

Any news from this isolated village near the border with Panama was and still is rare. The northern Pacific coast region is an area of tropical rain forest with the highest indicators of poverty in the country. With a majoritarian Afro-Colombian and indigenous population, and peripheral to the imaginary of the nation, it is a region significantly abandoned by the institutions of the state and marginalized from the dynamics of social and economic development. Until the 1990s, the area had also remained largely isolated from the dynamics of the conflict. In fact, it was only during this period that cases of large-scale violence started to be reported.

Yet, only this event gained visibility at a national scale. From a military perspective, the attack could be interpreted as a strategy to gain control over what constitutes a key territory in the transnational arms and drug trade in an isolated jungle area where the presence of the state and the rule of law is weak. In effect, that was the narrative that prevailed once meteorological conditions allowed reporters to arrive in the field on 14 December. The preponderance of public narratives strongly emphasizing the military aspects of the event contributed to a process by which the dramatic effects of violence on the civilian population became invisible. This emphasis also contributed to downplaying the complex array of vectors that had configured the conditions for the emergence of war in the region. This regime of invisibility, which can be considered a common denominator in mainstream news coverage of the conflict throughout its recent history, became even more pronounced in cases affecting marginal rural communities inhabited by ethnic minorities. In effect, the only news that came after the initial reports on the attack were a few short newspaper articles documenting the closing of the police and military bases in Juradó. After this period, the case was forgotten.

With the aim of bringing this case to public light, in 2013 I started a collaboration with a group of victims for the production of the testimonial documentary *After the Crossfire: Memories of Violence and Displacement*. The country was in the middle of a "memory boom" at the time. Yet, the notion of memory didn't have any currency in this region, as it became evident in my initial interactions with collaborators and as I corroborated through archival research. As discussed above, the emergence of a preoccupation with memory had been introduced by the state through its classification as "symbolic reparation," and as part of the transitional justice mechanisms initiated in 2005. The CNMH played an initial key role in this process through the elaboration of reports about what they categorize as "emblematic cases" because of their capacity to illustrate differential dynamics of the conflict throughout its history. Particularly revealing was the fact that by 2013, only one investigation had been undertaken with respect to the conflict in the Pacific coast, a region that had suffered from an unprecedented escalation of violence and that represents a large portion of the national territory. A regime of invisibility was evident in how both the media and the state had almost completely ignored the dynamics of the conflict and its effects on communities in this border region. Several historical and social factors were at play, including geographical isolation, historical marginalization, and weak governance, as well as issues of racialization that are beyond the scope of this chapter to examine.

Nancy Wood has proposed that the circulation of the silenced voices of victims in public space demonstrates an institutional and political intentionality "on the part of a social group or artifact of power, in order to select or organize representations of the past" (Wood 1999: 2). For Wood, the silenced memory of a particular event begins to penetrate the public domain at the moment when this memory incorporates a social, political, or institutional intentionality, which promotes or authorizes its consolidation as "official memory." Following Wood's argument, I conceptualize the forgetting surrounding the dynamics of the conflict in the Pacific coast as a form of structural amnesia. In other words, the state had failed the people of the region in its memory duty, the same way it has historically failed in promoting institutions of social and economic development. There was no political or institutional intentionality to bring this case into public light, and the structural conditions made the possibility of oblivion a concrete reality. The very notion of memory was absent from public and civic discourse in the area.

During that period of the attack, a peace process between the government and FARC was in crisis. As the actors involved were trying to show their military capacities, violence escalated to unprecedented levels. The negotiations, which had started in May 1999, eventually broke off in February 2002. In this context, the media visibility of the attack on Juradó can be seen as serving an antisubversive propaganda purpose at a specific moment when the government wanted to make public FARC's contradictions regarding their intentions of peace and to use this as a leverage strategy at the negotiating table. This helps explain the emphasis given in the news to the military aspects of the event, but only partially the invisibility of the victims. While doing audiovisual archival research at one of Colombia's main private media networks, I corroborated how news coverage gave voice to officers and wounded soldiers; however, in contrast, the only members of the community interviewed were the priest and the mayor of the town, who gave brief statements mostly emphasizing the material damage. For the reporters at the time, the only people who had a voice were those invested with institutional authority.

In response to the invisibility and structural amnesia that had prevailed in the case, I follow a testimonial rather than a historical-archival approach in *After the Crossfire*. Its main communicative function is to make the victims visible as well as their experiences of war, without putting forward a totalizing truth claim. Yet the documentary process is about the social and collaborative interactions by which the victims actively exert their agency in the construction of a resilient memory that speaks not only about a violent past but also about present claims around the conditions and actors that made it possible. The documentary process also reveals the possibilities for disseminating memories beyond national borders. I followed the conceptualization of witnessing as a necessary condition of agency as proposed by Dominick LaCapra, who argues that witnessing can constitute a creative or transformative act by which a victim of trauma "may overcome being overwhelmed by numbness and passivity, reengage in social practice, and acquire a voice that may in certain conditions have practical [political, juridical or social] effects" (LaCapra 1998: 12). *After the Crossfire* creates these conditions in a context not constrained by the localized discursive frameworks of transitional justice. As in the case of the CNMH's work, these frameworks situate testimony among other nonjuridical mechanisms of reparation and reconciliation, therefore encoding the enunciation and inscription of the narrative within specific state rationalities, or what Allen Feldman (2004) calls normative and moralizing regimes of truth.

In the interviews I conducted during the production of the documentary, shifts in intonation and in the position of enunciation contradicted established conceptions of testimony. In contrast to the notion of a personal narrative enunciated in the first singular person (Beverley 1987; Yúdice 1996), the majority of the witnesses interviewed moved freely from the first singular to the first plural person, a shift emphasizing collective over individual agency. Through a constant shift from a narrative form of discourse in the past tense to an active present tense, they articulated their memories with claims about the abandonment of the state as the foundation for the emergence of armed groups in rural Colombia. They insisted to include specific statements regarding the emergence of paramilitarism and felt an urge to denounce the complicity of the state in this process, even though they were affected more directly by the actions perpetrated by FARC with the massive displacement that followed the 1999 attack. The medium of documentary was appropriated as a powerful tool to disseminate these claims.

The position taken by those giving testimonies carried significant risks, and for this reason I was asked to consent that the film could not be circulated through national TV. The fact that the documentary was being produced in a U.S. university became a motivation for wider dissemination in contexts that did not pose direct risks. It was through a dialogical approach and in response to these conditions that the documentary was developed with a transnational focus. The main avenues for dissemination discussed were international human rights film festivals and academic conferences, because of the receptivity of their audiences to the topic and the possibilities for debate these spaces can open. This process illuminates how the interactions between mnemonic agents and the particular investments with the possibilities of specific media can enable the conditions for the dissemination of memory narratives across national borders by nonstate actors. Through the documentary process, the notion of transnational memory was approached as an arena for symbolic struggles, a possibility that has been neglected in the absence of related initiatives within a regime of invisibility. Memory construction emerged as a dialogical encounter to engage with the past beyond the constraints of human rights and transitional justice discourses, making possible claims of justice with relevance in the present and concrete possibilities for transnational dissemination. This approach follows what Hale (2006) has termed "activist research," a method through which the researcher (1) affirms a political alignment with the struggles of the communities being studied, and (2) establishes a dialogue with these communities that informs and actively shapes each of the stages of research. Rather than the exclusive site of data collection, observation, and analysis, the field emerged as a space for the articulation of political praxis and, as such, a site where particular struggles, in this case memory struggles beyond national and discursive constraints, could be mobilized.

Individual agency, collaboration, and dialogical negotiation of objectives shaped the tone, structure, and communicative function of the documentary, which was planned to be disseminated transnationally through film cultural circuits and the traditional avenues for the circulation of knowledge within the university system. Between 2014, the year of its completion, and 2018, *After the Crossfire* has circulated in several international human rights film festivals and academic conferences. This reveals different possibilities for memory construction offered by the audiovisual medium as a platform for mediation of testimony and dissemination of cultural memory beyond national borders.

Border-Crossing Practices of Memory, Cultural Activism, and Community Engagement

In Colombia's current transitional conjuncture, the practices of memorialization and the cultural activism promoted by grassroots organizations reveal new articulations of agency for demanding and practicing inclusion and civic transformations in rural areas historically abandoned by the state institutions. Increasingly, these practices are also transgressing national borders and engaging with displaced populations living in exile.

This is the case of the practices of Hacia el Litoral, a collective and platform for creative praxis based in the city of Cali. Between January 2015 and July 2017, this collective developed a small program of artistic residencies and cultural exchanges between the northern Pacific coast region and the town of Jaqué, Panama. Jaqué is the first municipality across the Colombian border and a receptor of victims of the armed conflict who fled the escalation of violence in the region between the early 1990s and the late 2000s, particularly after the 1999 attack by FARC discussed above. The members of the collective, including its leader Yolanda Chois, are young graduates from art and communication programs at public state universities sharing an interest in social and environmental justice. A particular point of contact between their experiences has also been difficulties in finding stable jobs and sources of income in their early professional stage. However, their digital media literacies, and the wide range of opportunities taken up through their digital and cultural practices, have enabled them to connect transnationally with other cultural collectives interested in cultural activism and with a supporting network of grants provided by governmental and international nongovernmental organizations.

Livingston and Helsper (2007) discuss the digital divide in terms of a continuum in the quality of use of online resources, which maps the number and types of online opportunities taken up by users. These range from basic information seeking, through intermediate creative and entertainment uses, to more complex uses such as seeking financial support, networking, and showcasing creative work online. In the case of the members of Hacia el Litoral, their practices allow them to establish creative forms of collaboration among their peers and with other organizations with which they share interests across national borders. As observed by Ito et al., new digital media can enable "active participation of a distributed social network in the production and circulation of culture and knowledge" (2010: 19). This in turn allows for the distribution and maintenance of social capital within particular cultural and creative circuits, and the actual exertion of agency and citizenship through cultural practices, which in the case of Hacia el Litoral is shared and distributed with the local communities with which they work.

What started as a series of itinerant interventions of memory recovery in towns across Colombia's northern Pacific region, with actions that included mural painting, creative audiovisual documentation, and testimonial radio performances, converged in a process of community engagement in the village of Jaqué after the majority of the collective crossed the border between Panama and Colombia by boat in early 2015. There were already seeds of border-crossing environmental and cultural activism initiatives as well as an incipient infrastructure that made the site fertile for the project. In the early 2000s, a Colombian anthropologist and social activist fled the town of Juradó after the attack by FARC. In a few years after settling in Jaqué, she had promoted several initiatives that included the founding of a kindergarten she called "the little school for peace" (built with a grant by USAID), a program for the conservation of sea turtles, a yearly cultural and environmental event, and a program of volunteers for conservation efforts. This made possible both the material and cultural conditions for the program of residencies proposed by Hacia el Litoral.

A series of loose directives that grew out of improvisation and dialogue with members of the village were given to participants to dwell in the community for periods of four to twelve weeks, where they were to work around the theme of the social, economic, cultural, and environmental conflicts along the Colombia-Panama border and how these affect displaced populations. The topics proposed to stimulate creative actions included violence, the weak presence of institutions, and issues of food sovereignty, among other problems. The approach developed by the collective to these problems through cultural practices of memory focused on promotion of civic participation and activation of agency and resilience within the community. The central project developed with the participation of local residents of Jaqué and a group of displaced Colombian victims was titled "Jardines en Balsa" (gardens in canoes), founded by a small grant offered by a program of the office of United Nations in Panama.

The project tackled the loss of small-scale agricultural practices in the area, the lack of productive projects, and the severe problem of food autonomy and security faced by vulnerable families such as those belonging to displaced populations. In response to these issues, the project proposed to reactivate or bring back to life an ancestral family agricultural tradition among Afro-Colombian coastal communities to cultivate herbs, fruits, and vegetables in canoes no longer used or in small wooden structures that resemble canoes. For the cultural activists in residence, the conflicts at the border have contributed to the decline of this small-scale agricultural practice, with material effects in the daily lives of hundreds of families. Reactivating and fostering "Jardines en Balsa" promoted the notion of memory as the recovery of productive traditions, as a practice of resilience, and as a process of engagement with the past to face concrete problems in the present. This vision clearly deviated from that promoted by state institutions. Aware of the digital divide between their own urban context and the rural communities of this border region, they resorted to agency and focalized action by recovering a traditional practice in response to local needs and complex processes of displacement and deterritorialization.

By reactivating this specific form of cultural memory, "Jardines en Balsa" is bringing back to life an important tradition of local food autonomy and sovereignty and promoting resilience and the strengthening of social capital within a community in vulnerable conditions. Following Simich and Andermann (2014), I understand resilience not as the outcome of an inherent quality or capacity among individuals but rather as a dynamic process of social interactions among members of a community in response to external adverse circumstances. Memory as the process of recovery of a material practice of resilience, in the way proposed in this project, not only allows new opportunities for engagement with the past beyond national frameworks and discourses but also promotes a generative approach through the reorganization of social relationships and the production of new ties among social groups that are not founded exclusively on their belonging to a specific national territory. Yet the project promotes new forms of territorialization and engagement with practices of the land for those who have been dispossessed after forced migration. Through their cultural practices, the members of Hacia el Litoral are fostering links of solidarity and civic engagement among the local populations of Jaqué as well as promoting webs of support for the displaced Colombian community in this village. As a dynamic process of social interactions around local empowerment and peaceful coexistence, these practices reactivate autonomous processes and border-crossing mnemonic practices to counteract state abandonment and marginalization.

Other cultural practices that emerged out of this project included environment conservational efforts, such as the reforestation of the mangrove to prevent erosion, and communal interventions for plastic waste management. These efforts help in creating collective engagements that encourage the inclusion and assimilation of the displaced Colombian community within the local population, therefore fostering links of solidarity. The families of displaced victims find in these activities ways to contribute to the local community and environment, and to regain their social agency and adaptability in the process. Another memory initiative was developed with indigenous girls whose families have been forcefully displaced from river communities of the Darien Jungle, in the border region between Panama and Colombia. In a workshop, they were taught a series of narrative tools and then asked to create a story of how they remembered their communities, complementing these narratives with drawings and other graphic activities (see figure 14.1). The goal was to harness the potential of memory and narrative to strengthen ethnic identity among indigenous girls and promote a sense of pride in their cultural heritage and ways of living, a process of great importance in the context of vulnerability brought about by displacement and deterritorialization.

The cultural practices of memory promoted by Hacia el Litoral in their work with displaced communities are documented with video and used for different communication purposes. This documentation, made accessible through online social networks and other media ecologies, can allow other cultural activists to replicate similar initiatives or promote similar forms of cultural activism in other marginal communities in Colombia and neighboring countries. As Astrid Erll (2011) has pointed out, in a world of communication flows and population displacement, the global circulation of mnemonic media provides possibilities for the creation of new forms of solidarity. The work of Hacia el Litoral is promoted to other agents in their network, who in turn are able to exert their agency and contribute to the larger collaborative efforts of civic engagement and participation among displaced populations and communities of victims living in exile. The flow of information and cultural capital is not restricted by the structure of cultural production, as in the institutional logic discussed, but instead is shared and promoted across national borders and among participants in the network at large.

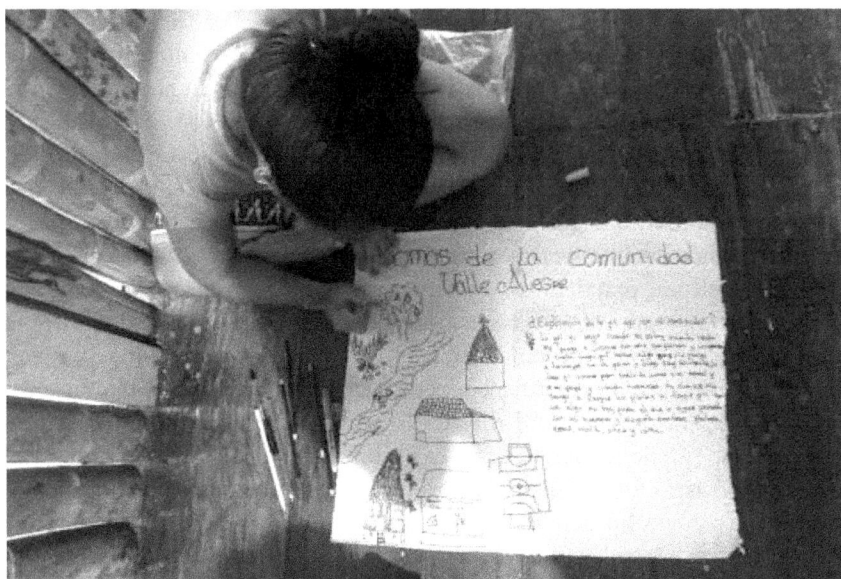

Figure 14.1. Narrative workshop with indigenous youth from families displaced by violence. Photo by the author.

This logic of cultural production and dissemination is the result of what I term "network agency." I use this concept to refer to the process by which individual or collective action and civic participation are exerted in coordination with a complex transnational flow of actors, information, resources, dispositions, and particular articulations of cultural and social capital. It is through the workings of network agency that the members of Hacia el Litoral leverage their media and cultural literacies to contribute to the creation of spaces of memory and reconciliation beyond national borders. Network agency allows the members of the collective to contribute to the promotion of inclusive practices of memory empowering displaced communities to confront and overcome some of their immediate problems. Their activism, cultural practices, and media literacies become platforms by which the communities they work with build or strengthen their social ties through what Robert Putman (2000) calls "bridging social capital." For Putman, this is a form of social capital that creates bridges across social cleavages, connecting people despite differences of class, ethnicity, race, or nationality. These cultural practices of Hacia el Litoral promote strong links of solidarity and resilience and motivate other youth creative groups to contribute to society with their social interventions in marginalized communities at a crucial historical and political conjuncture for Colombia and for displaced communities living in exile.

Conclusion

In this chapter, I have described the border-crossing memory practices promoted by state institutions and civil society actors working with forcefully displaced victims of the armed conflict across the Colombia-Panama border. The chapter provides an empirically grounded contribution to one of the central aims of the volume, that is to "identify ways of understanding the mutual constitution of the agency of individuals, groups, and organizations engaged in making, (re)producing, [or] dismantling narratives about the past" (Wüstenberg, this volume). The focus on transnational memory, as de Cesari and Rigney have argued, provides an analytical space to examine "the interplay between social formations and cultural practices, or between state operated institutions of memory and the flow of mediated narratives within and across state borders" (2014: 4). Following this approach, I have illuminated how institutions such as the CNMH develop initiatives to give visibility to the memory of the victims, as well as programs and platforms for the dissemination of resources and information about the process of national reconciliation beyond national borders. However, while this approach has brought the plight of the victims to the public sphere, creating awareness and a necessary cultural transformation of recognition and solidarity with the victims, centralized institutional dynamics limit the possibilities for fostering autonomous developments and civic participation among victims living in exile. This is particularly noticeable in rural border areas historically marginalized by the institutions of the state. When digital technologies are used with a transnational focus to reach diasporic communities in exile, they are incorporated into a dissemination logic that reproduces centralized policies that restrict and control the distribution of resources, and of cultural and social capital. Communication and dissemination strategies also fail to take into consideration the digital divide between urban and rural communities, which limit the possibilities for fostering inclusive transnational memory practices.

Activist research in testimonial documentary production is analyzed as a process of sharing agency in memory construction and as a form of participation in the shaping of counterhegemonic narratives of the past through a medium with significant potential for transnational dissemination. As I showed with the example of the documentary *After the Crossfire*, a collaborative approach to the stage of testimonial recollection can allow the strategic appropriation of the audiovisual medium by the victims both from their position as victims, which carries significant ethical implications, and from their position of historical marginality, which opens an important political potential. Beyond its concrete possibilities for memory construction and symbolic reparation, the act of testimony in the practice I describe emerges as an act of agency and resilience to denounce impunity, state abandonment, and what I have termed the "structural amnesia" surrounding cases of war in border areas at the margins of the nation.

Finally, the small-scale cultural initiatives implemented by the grassroots collective Hacia el Litoral have the potential to promote inclusive memory practices in which the experience of violence is re-signified while social ties are solidified through community-based interventions developed around concrete communal problems and necessities. Implemented in unstructured and contingent creative spaces, the practices designed around these local problems foster solidarity and promote resilience and effective civic engagement through a network of interactions that I term *network agency*. Cultural processes implemented through network agency developed in border-crossing environments through microscale flows of actors, information, resources, dispositions, and cultural and social capital. However, the practices of Hacia el Litoral are short termed and lack the infrastructures and resources needed for continuity. Yet, through the promotion of civic engagement, they offer important possibilities for inclusive memory construction and reconciliation beyond national borders. At a key historical conjuncture in Colombia, autonomous transnational memory agents can become key actors for the sustainability of inclusive memory and reconciliation practices that can reach beyond borders and engage with communities of victims forcibly displaced into exile.

Ricardo A. Velasco Trujillo, PhD, is a postdoctoral fellow of the Andrew W. Mellon Engaged Scholar Initiative in the College of Liberal Arts at the University of Texas at Austin. His research focuses on memory and cultural production in contexts of transitional justice, using ethnography, creative documentary practices, and digital humanities methods. His work explores the intersections between historical memory, human rights, cultural activism, and peace-building in Colombia. He is the author of the testimonial documentary *After the Crossfire: Memories of Violence and Displacement*, which premiered at the Bogotá International Human Rights Film Festival in 2016.

Notes

1. This documentary constituted my MA thesis in social documentation, completed in 2014, in the Department of Film and Digital Media at the University of California, Santa Cruz. It was produced with a grant from UC Berkeley's Human Rights Center, where I was involved as fellow from May to December 2013. More information on the documentary can be accessed at www.afterthecrossfire.com.

2. Public statement during the inauguration of the Second Week for Memory at the National Museum of Colombia in Bogotá, on 21 September 2009.
3. All content is accessible on the National Center for Historical Memory's official website, http://www.centrodememoriahistorica.gov.co.

References

Assmann, Aleida, and Sebastian Conrad, eds. 2010. *Memory in a Global Age: Discourses, Practices and Trajectories*. London: Palgrave Macmillan.

Beverley, John. 1987. "Anatomía del testimonio." *Revista de Crítica Literaria Latinoamericana* 13(25): 7–16.

Bourdieu, Pierre. 1993. "The Field of Cultural Production." In *The Field of Cultural Production: Essays on Art and Literature*, 29–73. New York: Columbia University Press.

Brown, Kate, Scott W. Campbell, and Richard Ling. 2011. "Mobile Phones Bridging the Digital Divide for Teens in the US?" *Future Internet* 3(2): 144–58.

Centro Nacional de Memoria Histórica. 2016. "Lanzamiento del Informe Hasta Encontrarlos. El Drama de la Desaparición Forzada en Colombia." Comment on Facebook post, 22 November 2016. Retrieved from https://www.facebook.com/CentroMemoriaH.

———. 2018. "Agenda Exilio." Voces del Exilio. Retrieved 25 January 2018 from http://centrodememoriahistorica.gov.co/vocesdelexilio/index.php/vinculos-de-interes/bibliografia.

de Cesari, Chiara, and Ann Rigney. 2014. "Introduction." In *Transnational Memory: Circulation, Articulation, Scales*, edited by Chiara de Cesari and Ann Rigney, 1–25. Berlin: De Gruyter.

Erll, Astrid. 2011. "Traveling Memory." *Parallax* 17(4): 4–18.

Feldman, Allen. 2004. "Memory Theatres, Virtual Witnessing, and the Trauma Aesthetic." *Biography* 27(1), 163–202.

Hale, Charles. 2006. "Activist Research v. Cultural Critique: Indigenous Land Rights and the Contradictions of Politically Engaged Anthropology." *Cultural Anthropology* 21(1): 96–120.

Ito, M., et al. 2010. *Hanging Out, Messing Around and Geeking Out: Kids Living and Learning with New Media*. Boston: MIT Press.

Joinet, Louis. 1997. "Informe final del Relator Especial sobre la impunidad y conjunto de principios para la protección y la promoción de los derechos humanos mediante la lucha contra la impunidad." ONU, Comisión de Derechos Humanos. Subcomisión de Prevención de Discriminaciones y Protección de las Minorías Doc. E/CN.4/Sub.2/1997/20/Rev.1, anexo II.

LaCapra, Dominick. 1998. *History and Memory after Auschwitz*. Ithaca, NY: Cornell University Press.

Levi, Daniel, and Natan Sznaider. 2006. *The Holocaust and Memory in the Global Age*. Philadelphia: Temple University Press.

Livingstone, Sonia, and Ellen Helsper. 2007. "Gradations in Digital Inclusion: Children, Young People and the Digital Divide." *New Media & Society* 9(4): 671–96.

Maurino, Mauricio. 2003. "A la búsqueda de un pasado en la democracia Argentina." *Revista del Instituto de Estudios Comparados en Ciencias Penales y Sociales*. Córdoba, Argentina, octubre.

Memoria Histórica. 2018. *Exilio Colombiano: Huellas del Conflicto Armado Más Allá de las Fronteras*. Bogotá: CNMH.

————. 2008. *Narrativas y voces del conflicto: Programa de investigación*. Bogotá: Comisión Nacional de Reparación y Reconciliación.

Minow, Martha. 2002. *Breaking the Cycles of Hatred: Memory, Law and Repair*. Princeton, NJ: Princeton University Press.

Putman, Robert. 2000. *Bowling Alone: The Collapse and Revival of American Community*. New York: Simon and Schuster.

Rettbergh, Angelika. 2005. "Reflexiones introductorias sobre la relación entre construcción de paz y justicia transicional." In *Entre el perdón y el paredón: preguntas y dilemas de la justicia transicional*, edited by Angelika Rettbergh, 1–15. Bogotá: Ediciones Uniandes.

Scott, James, and Thomas Johnson. 2005. "Bowling Alone but Online Together: Social Capital in E-communities." *Community Development* 36(1): 9–27.

Simich, Laura, and Lisa Andermann, eds. 2014. *Refuge and Resilience: Promoting Resilience and Mental Health among Resettled Refugees and Forced Migrants*. New York: Springer.

Wood, Nancy. 1999. *Vectors of Memory: Legacies of Trauma in Postwar Europe*. Oxford: Berg.

Yúdice, George. 1996. "Testimonio and postmodernism." In *The Real Thing: Testimonial Discourse and Latin America*, edited by George Gubelberger, 42–57. Durham, NC: Duke University Press.

Part V

OUTLOOK

CONCLUSIONS

Agency in Transnational Memory Politics— Guidelines for Inquiry

Aline Sierp

Memory matters politically, socially, legally, and culturally. Despite their broad agreement on this statement, scholars continue to lament that we know very little about how this importance is manifested. This book tries to fill this evident lacuna in existing scholarship by investigating agency in transnational memory politics.

Agency is not a binary or typological in quality but needs to be analyzed as a multidimensional field that includes elements of self-interpretation, social meaning-making, and multilevel processes of interaction with social and political structures of competing narratives. Agency is about power. It implies the possibility and the potential (either latent or exercised) to create or prevent change. This does not mean, however, that it can be reduced to politics. Agency in social memory is more than a strategic politics of the past with rational, self-interested actors at its base. It is not linear, and it is not the property of a single actor, but rather it results from a combination of elements that interact in complex and recursive ways. As Zoltan Dujisin writes, transnational memory politics are best understood as networks drawing mnemonic resources from across disparate fields. It is thus not enough to look at actors and their agency in a vacuum; rather, we need to focus on the question of how change is brought about through the interplay of national, regional, international, and global dynamics, the agents that drive them, and how this impacts the sociopolitical outcomes of memory politics.

What emerges from all contributions to this volume is the recognition that collective memory is a process that is shaped by (1) *agents* that engage in transnational memory politics, (2) *structures* that enable and delimit transnational mnemonic action, and (3) *practices and mechanisms* of change that are employed by memory actors. It is the dynamic interaction between those three elements that creates new transnational memory spaces that touch existing borders and that can be highly significant in terms of the political stakes of the memory action at hand. In the following, I will investigate all four elements in turn on the basis of the fifteen chapters that constitute this book. Together with our division into top-down, bottom-up, and horizontal practices of mnemonic space-making, these chapters form a matrix structure that can provide an overall guideline for the investigation of agency in transnational memory politics.

Agents

The analysis of agents in this book is not predicated on a fundamental ontological position on agency. To understand agency, one needs to investigate actors' biographies, their fields of action, their social capital, and their alliances. Agents distinguish themselves by differential access to resources, media usage, institutional clout, and reputational power. State actors and entrepreneurs naturally have a lot more access to those elements than marginalized minority communities. This difference becomes particularly evident in the contributions of the second part of the book dealing with top-down approaches. Noga Glucksam, Courtney E. Cole, and Amy Sodaro describe how the power differential between actors can lead to a dynamic of imposition of particular mnemonic norms or resources.

However, it is not only differences between actors that shape transnational memory spaces but also their constellations. Memory agents are entangled in mnemonic coalitions that cannot be easily or arbitrarily changed. The ability to alter the composition depends on the fields they inhabit and the habitus they embody. This in turn influences the directionality of action. Because these tend to be uneven, there is not an equal exchange between actors located at different scales but rather one that is characterized by distinct power differentials. This means at the same time that the unequal starting point faced by actors without access to funding, media outlets, and institutional support can be balanced by their often considerable social capital and alliances. As Till Hilmar demonstrates in his chapter, especially small and mid-size organizations have a critical role in the coupling of local communities and transnational politics. Nonstate organizations are the agents through which individuals can make collective representations work. They create the connections needed to make memory processual and relational rather than individual, the property or preference of a single actor. In his case, organizations working on both Nazism and Communism allow them to assume a mediating position. This brokerage role gives them a potentially powerful agency in the network, making them more likely to be agents of change.

The impact and effectiveness of an actor in shaping memory spaces is thus relative and depends on many factors. When analyzing memory politics, one should not jump to quick conclusions based on the position of the various agents. Instead, looking at the constellation of actors at different scales can account for a better understanding of how ideas and approaches circulate. What emerges from many contributions in this book is that particularly agents that are conventionally thought of as "powerless" have been highly effective in tapping into transnational narratives and networks to push for changes in local or national memory politics. Transnational civil society often utilizes actors below the state, above the state, and of the state to achieve its goals. Devin Finn describes in her chapter how the interactions between agents located at different scales and in possession of very different power resources create social and political space that permits victims to seize political agency in previously state-dominated areas (i.e., funeral processions, massacre sites, and courtrooms). Family members of victims of state violence pursue strategies that allow them to grapple with social and political structures that resist and undermine the production of memory. How important transnational civil society and the networks it inspires can be for the empowerment of seemingly weaker individual agents is also revealed by the analysis of the PositiveNegatives project by Dragoș Manea and Mihaela Precup. In the case described, it is the transmission of the testimonies of refugees into graphic narration and the act of making them accessible online and through educational material that gives individuals a voice and makes their past visible to a wider public.

Mobilization in this context seems to be one of the core concepts running through all chapters. Keck and Sikkink's (1998) "boomerang effect," describing the transnational mechanism in which domestic movements join forces with international ones, is particularly present in chapters dealing with bottom-up approaches. The result is twofold: on the one hand this allows actors to pressure national governments to change domestic practices, and on the other it affords the individuals some protection from the state through their connection to transnational advocacy networks. In many cases described in this volume, mnemonic actors were able to achieve internationally and transnationally what they were not able to achieve at the level of the nation-state or in interaction with the nation-state. While in some countries (i.e., those described by Andrea Hepworth and Mary M. McCarthy) this is a result of the impossibility or inadequacy of (safely) remembering locally or nationally, it is needless to say that memory internationalization strategies can potentially have the power to imperil the nation-state's monopoly on memory-making, especially if actors are first sidestepping the state only to force it later to react to the developments that unfolded.

At times, this can result in harsh reactions by institutions and state-like organizations, which try to preserve dominant discursive structures and impose a standardized narrative that fits a prescribed political, social, or legal agenda. Personal memories can get reframed under the influence of a universalizing discourse leading to a rearticulation of memories at the expense of individual voice and agency. Authoritative agents backed by institutions are powerful memory-makers who can seriously limit the agency individual, local, or nonstate actors have when forced to act within such structures. The extent to which national and supranational institutions try to impose a dominant discursive structure so that they do not lose the prerogative over memory politics becomes evident in the second part of the book dealing with top-down agency. It also brings me to the second element shaping collective memory and influencing agency: structures.

Structures

Structures can enable and delimit transnational mnemonic action. Memory officials, activists, entrepreneurs, and others are usually very aware of this and interact with the position of their interlocutors in mind while respecting prevailing cultural norms and historical contexts. This means that in order to understand the character and influence of agency in memory, it is necessary to examine its relationship to a variety of structures. These can be narrative "blueprints," media systems, normative regimes, universalizing discourses, and standards of the global memorialization sectors, broader political opportunity structures, and internationally agreed best practices. Whether a transnational memory exists depends not on a unified memory regime but rather on the mutual engagement with structures that defy or permit the production of memory. The varied outcomes depend on, for example, the level of impunity, the integrity of institutions (courts and political parties), and the nature of attention to social processes (i.e., education). Actors seeking to influence any form of memory must take into account existing "cultural maps," bear in mind normative expectations, and directly address existing institutions (at multiple scales) if they want to be successful.

On the surface it might look as if structures are directly related to questions of power. However, as several contributors to this volume have shown, there is a risk of analyzing power relations exclusively as an independent variable, influencing either relatively equal or distinctly unequal actors. As Noga Glucksam rightly notices in her chapter, such analysis fails to problematize the dynamic and fluid nature of power relations. In some cases, empowering structures may become debilitating and vice versa. Any form of memory standardization is a good example of this. Moving within existing normative structures can both empower and limit agency. It can increase the narrative space but limits the bounds within which the expression of agency can take place. This means that any analysis must look beyond formal structures and narratives and equally examine tacit sociopolitical complexes. Among them are questions of expression, recognition, and acknowledgment. Mary M. McCarthy demonstrates how spaces for discourse needed to be created first before survivors and activists were able to gain the necessary agency that allowed them to bring about historical justice for the comfort women. Equally, Courtney E. Cole examines the structures of speech enacted by participants of transitional justice processes.

Despite the seemingly similar structural conditions, both come to different conclusions illustrating the tension between actors, structures, and outcomes. McCarthy shows how under certain circumstances, the engagement of discursive structures can bring about recognition and acknowledgment. Both concern a fundamental mechanism of social memory since they confer symbolic capital. In the case of the comfort women, it was the increasing international recognition of the harms perpetrated against the victims that activists could use to take advantage of existing structures, but they could also influence and change those structures, indicating the mutual constitution of agent and structure. In Courtney E. Cole's case, structures of speech and opportunities to speak intersected with a global memory culture that hampered the victims' right to expression. Particular actors tend to have limited agency when having to operate within universal moral structures. Cole notes how vernacular memory in postconflict transitional justice processes in post–World War II Germany, Liberia, and Sierra Leone transformed into official memory within the narrow boundaries of a universal narrative focused on human rights, personal trauma, and mass violence. The long-term impact can be standardization and marginalization of narrative diversity. The challenges connected to this can appear even in places that are considered rather cohesive in terms of type of actors and structural obstacles as in the Latin American Southern Cone vividly described in Gruia Bădescu's chapter.

The tension between structure and agency is in many cases productive of new memory spaces that result from dynamic practices. Memory engages with this structural tension through actors, and as a result it can cross boundaries. Under certain circumstances, however, the opposite can be true, as is demonstrated in Amy Sodaro's contribution. In the case of the 9/11 Museum in New York, it was the interaction between agents and structures in the process of creating the museum that resulted in a highly nationalistic and deeply political memory place belying the original intention of the curators to create an open cosmopolitan memorial space. This brings me to the next point: the importance of the various practices and mechanisms of change that are employed by different types of agents.

Practices and Mechanisms

Practices and mechanisms used by memory agents vary as much as do their bearers. They can include traditional memory work (archiving, collecting testimony, exhibition-making, performing rituals of mourning/remembering, etc.), alliance-building, and solidarity or publicity campaigns and persuasion. What mechanisms agents choose depends on their status and their position within the mnemonic network. In many cases, practices are geared toward an attempt at creating community. Through the adoption of transnational symbols of national unity or transnational nation-building, a shared identity and practices of remembrance for societies are established. Balázs Majtényi and György Majtényi demonstrate in their chapter how this process can take place outside of the political framework of the nation-state while adopting the very same mechanisms of identity-building usually reserved for the state level. The staging of public events of a ritualistic nature can then in turn facilitate the diffusion of personal testimony, creating in that way transnational audiences. By focusing on and prioritizing the agency of individuals, a sort of "network agency"—as Ricardo A. Velasco Trujillo calls it in his chapter—can be created, which entails a border crossing process with microscale flows of actors, resources, ideas, and memories involving different social groups and sectors of civil society.

Incidents of network agency are particularly pronounced in regions where the state has failed the people in supporting them in their memory duty. In those cases, practices of memorialization can emerge as fields of contestation in the context of demanding inclusion in postconflict societies. Individual and collective action and participation is exercised in coordination with a complex form of agency. Implemented in unstructured and creative spaces, it fosters solidarity and promotes participation and effective engagement. Memory in this context can turn into a material practice of resilience. Through the articulation of cultural and social capital, this allows agents to denounce state abandonment, impunity, and structural amnesia. Connecting otherwise unconnected agents and networks, exchanging information, and producing oppositional knowledge are a form of power exertion. This process is a double act of recognition, one with respect to the present and the other with respect to the past. Recognizing the other agents within the mnemonic network also means recognizing their version of the past. This can balance the otherwise unbalanced relationship between different memory agents and their networks.

The following table lists the types of agents, structures, and practices analyzed in the fifteen chapters in this book. It provides a quick overview for scholars studying agency.

Table 15.1. Agents, structures, and practices.

Agents participating in and driving transnational memory processes	• Entrepreneurs (narrow definition: economic actors, such as heritage tourism providers) • Epistemic communities/memory professionals (memorial officials, museum actors, academics) • State actors (non)elected officials, bureaucrats at all levels of the state) • Memorials, museums, academic institutions as collective actors • Memory activists (narrow definition: nonprofit advocates) • Collective state actors such as parliaments, institutions • Social movement or civil society organizations • Supranational institutional actors • For-profit companies • Families/individuals • Diasporas/migrants • Writers/artists
Structures shaping memory agency and that are shaped by agents in transnational memory processes	• Discrimination and marginalization (gender, class, location, ethnic) • Normative structures (human rights, women's rights) • Recognition and acknowledgment • Transitional justice discourses • Political and party systems • Impunity and corruption • Institutional frameworks • Discursive structures • Digital mobilization • Transnational links • National laws • Best practices • Funding
Practices occurring and composing transnational memory processes	• Memory work (archiving, collecting testimony, exhibition-making, rituals of mourning/remembering, etc.) • Identity-qualifying, temporal cuing, multiple targeting • Frame bridging, amplification, extension, innovation • Building alliances and solidarity (boomerang effect) • Diffusion of mnemonic techniques or policy options • Producing oppositional knowledge • Semiotic and institutional practices • Layering of mnemonic narratives • Scale or boundary-making • Building virtual memory • Exchanging information • Publicity campaigns • Persuasion

Collective memory is a process that is shaped by (1) *agents* participating in and driving transnational memory processes, (2) *structures* shaped by agents and that are shaping memory agency, and (3) *practices and mechanisms* that are occurring and composing those processes. The dynamic interaction between those three elements creates a distinct outcome: new transnational memory spaces.

Transnational Memory Spaces

Transnational memory spaces are not necessarily geographical places in the strict sense of the term but rather instances or processes of remembrance that can be anchored in concrete locations but can equally exist in an imaginary rather than material sense. What communes them is the fact that they extend beyond national borders. Gruia Bădescu, for instance, distinguishes clearly between transnational space-making that links places through processes of remembrance and transnational place-making that entails the mobilization of sites that specifically engage transnationalism through its development or its outcome. Memory elements of the local, the national, and the international intersect and challenge each other in their competition over taking a specific memorialization approach. In this process, the local often turns into the global whenever a transnational space emerges that employs a regional model of site memorialization.

At the same time, globally recognized memory elements like the Holocaust, for example, can act as triggers for agents. The agency of actors in this case is mobilized by transnational links, precedents, and personal experiences, and thus opens the road for the emergence of transnational space-making (as described in the case of Villa Grimaldi in Argentina for example). For a transnational memory to develop, it is not necessary that individuals' remembrances be of the same or even comparable events. On the contrary, transnational spaces link up multiple, often imaginary, places through which memories of transnational events, norms, or mobility are evoked. As a result, not only are new memory spaces created, but actors involved in the creation of such spaces can also receive legitimization. This dynamic is particularly pronounced when a transnational interconnection is formed that enables memory entrepreneurs to form a multidimensional transnational space containing heterogeneous mnemonic narratives within which memory is created and shaped. Through the coordination of those different memory narratives, divergent layers of interpretation are combined, creating bridges between them and thereby expanding the existing transnational memory space.

At the same time, stripping a mnemonic signifier of its contextualizing temporal or social references can increase its distribution and application to other interpretations of the past, which in turn increases the available memory space. How this works in practice is shown in Andrea Hepworth's chapter on how the application of the term *desaparecidos* has sparked controversies on the one hand but also created new mnemonic spaces that allowed the connection between divergent traumatic memories and experiences through coordinated universalizing memory practices. It created both a human memory space for relatives and a legal space of human rights and universal jurisdiction. At its intersection, the traumatic past received a wholly new form. In the case of McCarthy, it is the documentary *The Apology* that produces an autobiographical memory space, allowing the grandmas to narrate their own story, and a permanent documentary space that transcends national borders and disconnects the universal story from the earthly existence of the individual victims.

The extent to which the transnational work of memory can provide a frame and establish new resources to continue the struggle for recognition of certain memory narratives by connecting the local with the global is demonstrated in Silvana Mandolessi's contribution. In the case of the Ayotzinapa, it was the work of a transnational advocacy network that not only made the phenomenon of disappearances and human rights violations visible and provided it with meaning but also helped to achieve concrete outcomes on the local level. Also in the case of the White Armand Day, aptly analyzed by Orli Fridman and Katarina Ristić, it is the internationalization of the cause on the one hand and the use of alternative unconventional platforms for protest and knowledge exchange on the other that has paved the way to new, previously banned actions. The creation of new spaces thus allows actors to link individuals around the world and to cross boundaries—both in terms of their activism and in terms of their commemorative demands. The importance of technological innovations causing or paving the creation of transnational memory spaces should not be underestimated in this context.

The effort to raise consciousness and produce political change often takes place outside the state channels. This either transforms or safeguards existing spaces or opens up new ones, allowing agents and practices to not only make transnational remembrance happen but also reproduce or transform the multilevel structures that confine and enable them. In Fridman and Ristić's case for example, it was the use of different platforms for the purpose of alternative commemorations instead of onsite actions prohibited by the government that led to the breakthrough of social masks of silence and denial. At the same time, technological innovation brought together regional alternative memories and placed victims in the center of commemoration regardless of their belonging. It was thus able to contribute to the avoidance of ethnic divisions, ethnicization of victims, and exclusive claims of victimhood.

Memory matters politically, socially, legally, and culturally. In order to demonstrate how this importance manifests itself, this book presents a coherent picture of how transnational commemoration operates in practice. In doing so, it focuses not just on theory but on concrete questions of agency in transnational memorialization, which have thus far been neglected in existing scholarship. All contributions to this book demonstrate that transnational memory spaces are the result of deliberative processes that are informed and shaped by many different actors that need to take into account diverse structures that can enable and delimit transnational mnemonic action. The guidelines of inquiry outlined above aim at providing a baseline for future research by scholars interested in transnational relations, remembrance, transitional justice, and agency, as well as specific regional and institutional contexts. Especially the refined definition of "transnational memory" as practices or narratives of remembrance that extend across or beyond borders, which are shaped by agents located at various levels of analysis or are produced in global or supranational forums on the one hand and the description of concrete outcomes in the form of "transnational spaces of memory" on the other, will guide further research. We hope it will turn the present volume into an anchor text in this emerging field for years to come.

Aline Sierp is Associate Professor in European History & Memory Studies at Maastricht University (NL). Her research interests cover contested histories, memory politics, questions of identity, and European integration. Aline is the co-founder and past Co-President of the Memory Studies Association and the Council of European Studies' Research Network on Transnational Memory and Identity in Europe. For more details, see https://www.maastrichtuniversity.nl/sierp.

INDEX